The Dictator'

A Practical Manual
for the Aspiring Tyrant

by Randall Wood and Carmine DeLuca
First edition: June 2012

The Dictator's Handbook: A Practical Manual for the Aspiring Tyrant
by Randall Wood and Carmine DeLuca ©2012

ISBN 978-0615652429 (Gull Pond Books)

Contents

Forward

> Democracy is the theory that the common
> people know what they want and deserve to get
> it good and hard.

> H.L. Mencken

YOU would like to be a dictator. And why shouldn't you? Play your cards right and it's the best job on earth. Think about it: is anything lovelier than unbridled power, limitless economic opportunity, and the pleasure of crushing those who oppose you? Does the morning air not smell sweeter knowing your enemies are humbled, crippled, or dead, and the wealth of your nation lies at your personal disposal? And is there any goal more satisfying than being indispensably at the nexus of your country's government, economy, and society, controlling, choosing, and taking your cut? And are you a family-minded sort? Then you'll want to ensure your son or daughter steps in to follow in your footsteps as you age, to protect the family fortune and continue your legacy. And finally, let's be honest: doesn't it feel good to be revered as a demi-god? Of course it does!

Don't be foolish: it's not going to be easy. You will have enemies on all sides, difficult choices to make, and the whole world watching your every move. But you've also got lots of impressive examples to follow. You've been watching those who preceded you, and thought to yourself: surely, they're using a practical manual, a playbook, a map to the top! A manual indeed exists, and you're holding it in your hands. Read on, young dictator, and if you learn well you too will taste ultimate power.[1] Soon you will be able to add your own chapter to the Dictator's Handbook: The beauty of autocracy is the myriad nuances, personal variations, and cultural backdrops that facilitate creativity and interpretation. Your own country's culture, economy, and socio-political context will provide you with boundless opportunities for experimentation: Stand on the shoulders of the giants who preceded you, and when it comes time to pass on some of that wealth, remember these humble authors![2]

---

[1]For the rest of you, this book will also serve as a partial catalog of some of the barbaric, shameless, self-serving, and opportunistic practices of the world's leaders. Too many students and practitioners of political science, development, and economics graduate with knowledge of best practices, and are flabbergasted by how few of those theories are actually employed. The world's tyrants understand "best practice" but are operating out of a rule book of their own: *this* is that book.

[2]When we say, "remember these authors," we mean, "share some of the loot," not "throw us into some bottomless pit."

Dedication and Thanks

This book is dedicated to our own little dictators: Valentina, Diego, Giovanni, and Alessio. May you live in a better world. It is also dedicated to everyone who has suffered or perished due to practices like these. May these "tactics" someday become so obvious that they no longer work.

Thanks go to all the leaders who provided us with such rich material to draw from. And thank you as well to everyone who contributed by pointing out techniques and tactics worth investigating or case studies that provided valuable insight into the current practice. Obviously we can't thank you by name, or you'd find yourselves cast into prison for further 'questioning.' Suffice it to say we're grateful, and will think kindly on your contributions from our *own* verminous prison cells.

Our grumpy little dictator dude character, Richard M. ("Dick") Tater, was drawn by HappyToast.[3] The cover was designed and drawn by Heidi Jordan at Detail 37.[4]

Disclaimer

In an era where nothing "goes without saying," we must say it expressly: The views expressed here are solely those of the authors in their private capacity and do not in any way represent the views of the authors' employers, colleagues, family, or friends. The opinions expressed in this book were compiled on the basis of publicly documented information and the personal experience and creative talent of the authors. The contents of this book are not the official opinion of any government or any government agency, and do not represent the view of any government or government institution. This book is not an official publication of any government, has been endorsed by no government or institution thereof, and has been neither approved nor authorized by any government, our employers, or our lovely wives. Mention of a person in this book does not expressly mean that person is a dictator; omission does not mean that person is not. This book focuses on the methods of dictators and makes no express judgment as to who *is* and *is not* a dictator, tyrant, autocrat, and so on. If you are mentioned in this book as having employed some of the methods of dictators, please accept our heartfelt thanks for the material, rather than sending your thugs out to beat us mercilessly.

---

[3] http://happytoast.co.uk
[4] http://detail37.weebly.com/graphics.html

Visit Us Online

This book isn't – and never will be – complete. In fact, relevant anecdotes filled the daily news even as this went to press. The book chooses representative examples, leaves some people unmentioned, and makes no attempt to catalog every example of the practices mentioned within. This book is just the beginning. Once you've read the Handbook, join us at `http://www.dictatorshandbook.net` to join the conversation. Here we're watching the world's leaders put these tips in practice, spotting new techniques in action, and generally making a nuisance of ourselves to our fearless leaders. Is "that guy" employing a move straight out of the *Dictator's Handbook*? He probably is!

About the Authors

Randall Wood, author, engineer, and teacher, has lived in Asia, Africa, and Latin America for most of his adult life, working in engineering, construction, agronomy, diplomacy, and teaching. Much of the inspiration for this book came from personal experience and observation. He writes, "Time and time again, when the media would report some new political atrocity, I would mutter, 'Well, that's a move straight out of the *Dictator's Handbook*.' If I said to myself, 'Next, the president will insist on constitutional reform,' I was too frequently right. Finally, I began to wonder if there truly was some sort of Handbook these political clowns were using to organize their governments and plot their next moves. And now, finally, there is." Writing this book has been a sort of personal catharsis. He is the author of two other books and several technical manuals. His website is `www.therandymon.com`.

Carmine DeLuca, writer and history enthusiast, has long cultivated an interest in the authoritarians of every stripe. In part this fascination stems from his personal life – a Bonapartist father, an aunt named after the Battle of Adowa, and a grandfather and great uncle in Mussolini's army. Two decades of reading and thinking on the historical significance of "great" men plus a fantastic library of books on the Romans, Facists, Napoleon, Greeks, and beyond have prepared him for the writing of this book.

Chapter 1

Getting to Power

I would rather be first here than second in Rome.

Julius Caesar, ca. 61 BC

1.1 Introduction

DICTATOR wasn't always a term of opprobrium, a pejorative used to scare the masses and attract power worshipers of every stripe to the ascendant regime. The term dates from the Roman republic, and it referred to the constitutionally-sanctioned granting of political/military power to a single individual for a limited period of time for the purpose of getting a job done. Roman leader Quintus Fabius Maximus Verrucosus Cunctator was one not-so-famous example. The Roman Senate declared him Dictator so he could do whatever was necessary to oppose the seemingly unstoppable Hannibal, who was then advancing on and planning to annihilate Rome. Cunctator means "the delayer" and that's what he did. Employing scorched earth and harassment tactics, he kept Hannibal from engaging him in a battle Cunctator's forces would surely lose, while simultaneously forcing Hannibal and the Carthaginians to squander their resources fighting.[430] The Senate's mandate allowed Cunctator to call the shots, cast off an otherwise lethargic government bureaucracy, and get stuff done. It allowed him to *dictate*. But when the fight was over and his term expired, Cunctator resigned and more or less went back to normal political life. What an amateur! Clearly, this was an opportunity that remained unexploited.

Many years later, towards the end of the Republic, Julius Caesar took the practice a step further and became something that more closely resembles the modern autocrats we know and love. In 44 B.C. he had himself declared "Dictator for Life" (a conspirator's knife ensured that would nonetheless not be too long a reign) in order to benefit from a rule with few checks and bounds. But it took his heir, Octavian (who became Augustus Caesar), to really pull it all together and show how a truly great dictator rolls. As Tacitus explains, "When the world was wearied by strife [he] subjected it to empire under the title of 'Prince.' ... Augustus won over the soldiers with gifts, the populace with cheap corn, and all men with the sweets of repose, and so grew greater by degrees while he concentrated in himself the functions of the Senate, the magistrates, and the laws."[453] For the aspiring dictator, those are words to live by. Centuries later, the methods remain the same, and it's just the implementation of the theory that has changed from practitioner to practitioner. After all, if you are the one mandating, the world can be your oyster. Read on for the practical details.

1.2   Coming to Power Through Your Family

Your first order of business is to install yourself at the top, and the easiest way to come into power is the old fashioned way: by inheriting it from your old man. This scenario means dad was probably a bit of a power broker himself, employing some of the techniques in this book to stave off enemies and guarantee the right to name his successor. On the plus side, you can argue your lineage has either a genetic, more likely a divine, right to rule, making your own power grab expected, inevitable, and pre-ordained. Pass on the good luck then: as you get older, groom one of your sons – or daughters – to take the reins after you're gone (but not *before* you're gone, dammit!) This is easiest in a monarchy, where the son is expected to follow the father. But a monarchy is hardly required for this mechanism to work, and if your father is amenable to you taking over behind the wheel, there are many mechanisms – legal, constitutional, and er, creative – he can use to ease your way in. This book covers many of them. Rise to the occasion without shame! Many leaders install their sons, well-groomed to continue on the family legacy, as a matter of course: Syria's Bashar al Assad inherited power from his father Hafez al Assad after the latter's 30 year rule.[72] Gabon's Ali Ben Bongo Ondimba came to power in essentially the same way when his long-ruling father, Omar Bongo, passed away. But first, the nation of Gabon took the time to go through the formality of holding a sham election that Bongo won easily. See the next section for more about how a little sham election can help legitimize your rule.[321]

In lieu of a national election, sometimes the military can facilitate the passing of power from a father to son. Togo's first president was assassinated, and Eyadéma Gnassingbe went on to rule Togo from 1967 until 2005. But when he died in 2005, the Togolese military wordlessly handed power directly over to son Eyadéma's son Faure.[1] This reinforces the importance of

---

[1] Thanks, dad (and generals)!

maintaining good relations with the military, and ensuring they understand at all times their role is like the butler's: to just pass it on.

One man rule does not have to be a father-son enterprise; nor does keeping it in the family necessarily mean you will inherit power without using force. In fact, if you happen to be born into a powerful family, it may be in your interest to keep an eye out for weak or vulnerable relatives who wield the power you crave. Such was the case in Equatorial Guinea, where young Teodoro Obiang Nguema's uncle was the wealthy but vulnerable leader of the nation in the 1960s. Obiang seized the opportunity, gathered a small force of political and military supporters and put the squeeze on his uncle, who was forced into exile. The unlucky uncle was later captured and, just to be sure, executed by firing squad. No hard feelings, uncle, it's just business! Obiang has been the leader of Equatorial Guinea ever since.[47][6]

It's a lovely twist when nature and circumstances force you, reluctantly, into power. In 2001, when the Democratic Republic of Congo's Laurent Désiré Kabila was murdered, his grieving son Joseph was forced to step up into the presidency and take over.[361] Buck up and dry your tears, tender young tyrant, it's part of the job and Dad would have wanted it this way! Furthermore, taking over for a murdered relative affords you the chance of assuming power with both the sympathy of the nation and a ready-made rallying cry: avenge your father's killers! And since that's going to take money and time, you had better just settle in and figure out how to ensure the next election keeps you in power, for starters.

1.3   Elections

The advantages of getting elected far outweigh the challenge of making it happen. They are the best legitimizing mechanism on the planet these days. Not only have the people spoken, but your detractors will be forced to quiet down and accept the will of the nation. Furthermore, you can insist that further political change happen only through similar elections, and then spend your time – and the state's money – making sure future elections guarantee your future victory. Since you've come to power this way, you'll know what to look for and will be able to identify (and neutralize) others who might seek to rise through the ballot (and if you don't, have a look at chapter 12). Finally, elections make the Americans and Europeans happy and happy Westerners are unlikely to clamor for regime change at the United Nations. In the final analysis, an election legitimizes your administration before your people and the Western world, and if the West recognizes your leadership it will be more difficult for them to deny funding when you come calling, sooner or later (and it will probably be sooner). If you get to power this way you're in the company of Peru's Alberto Fujimori, who came to power at the polls and worked his way through the rest of this book before resigning in disgrace.

Nicaragua's Daniel Ortega provides a good example of why this mechanism is so enjoyable. His Sandinista Revolution came to an abrupt halt in 1991 when his party finally conceded to hold elections – and lost. He gracefully stepped down from power[2] and ran unsuccessfully in the next three elections. In 2006 he got his chance[3] and won at the polls. The United States and other governments had cast their lots with the opposition and were clearly disappointed in Ortega's victory. But Ortega's legitimate win at the ballot boxes ended their protests. Any leader knows how that must feel: damned good! [44]

1.4   External Support

If you are very fortunate, a superpower or two will come along and facilitate your rise to power. When you're a hungry and ambitious general or an on-the-rise parliamentarian with a disdain for democracy, be on the lookout for agents from the hegemonic power next door. Once you identify them, make contacts, let it be know that you hate their enemies, and soon the logic of "my enemy's enemy" will work its magic. Americans and Europeans often have a special fondness for leader-candidates who can come across as intellectuals or technocrats with multiple advanced degrees from Western Universities, fluency in English, and the ability to speak eloquently about democracy and moderation. Develop these traits when you are "courting" the West and watch them fall in line to support you, as they did Ahmad Chalabi (Iraq), Said al Islam (Iraq), Hacim Thaci (Kosovo), Hamid Karzai (Afghanistan), Ibrahim al-Jaafari (Iraq), and Isaias Afawerki (Eritrea).[346]

That's one side of the story. The other side, of course, is that there are very few Western leaders who seem to be able to resist a powerful, brutal *generalissimo*. Usually the general in question is also a staunch enemy of the most recent American or European bugbear (the fights against communism and terrorism have both led to some political installations). Suppose you are an ambitious general chafing under the authority of a democratically-elected paper-pusher. Put a fly in the ear of a Western ambassador, meet with a foreign intelligence officer, and develop a cadre of fighters funded and trained by foreign cash. When the time comes, rise up and send the Professor packing. Augusto Pinochet's rise to power in Chile was simply a variation on this script: A staunch anti-communist, he seized power in the 1973 coup with help from the CIA, mainly through his underling, Colonel Manuel Contreras. It was the beginning of a beautiful friendship, as they say, and Pinochet, with CIA support, infamously disposed of thousands of his "enemies" in the name of anti-communism.[484]

---

[2] Well, not *that* gracefully: the Sandinistas privatized in their names everything worth owning on the way out.[282]

[3] Again, not a lucky chance but careful scheming we'll cover in chapter 12.

Chad's Hissene Habre, who went on to earn the moniker "Africa's Pinochet"[4] was nevertheless suspected of earning CIA support in the 1980s, when he was a bulwark against the encroachments of neighboring Mohammar Khadaffi. [45] In 2003, François Bozizé was helped to power in the Central African Republic because neighboring Chad's Idriss Déby took a liking to him and helped broker his ascension.[493] And Idriss Déby himself allegedly had a little help from a buddy, in this case the French Secret Service, who helped him orchestrate the overthrow of his predecessor Hissene Habre, former friend and mentor.[321]

There is a downside. No one installs you in power solely because they like your speeches. Rather, you are henceforth a bought man, and your superpower friends believe you are in the presidency to at least partially do their bidding. Furthermore, your legitimacy before your people is diminished if they understand you have been somewhat "imposed" on them. Should your practices bring you into disfavor, that lingering resentment may eventually strengthen their will to overthrow you, as was the case for Mohammad Reza Shah Pahlavi. The Shah of Iran from the 1940s through the 1970s, he came to power with aid of the CIA in one their most successful coups. A generation later, his progressively unpopular regime was overthrown in the Iranian Revolution, and you'd better believe his former benefactors made little effort to save his hide then.[484]

1.5   Through the Party

You can work your way to the top if you're careful, methodical, and earnest, but do not underestimate the importance of an organized political party, which can make everything an order of magnitude easier and ensure the road to the presidency is lined with impassioned speeches and crisp, white shirts rather than muddy campsites and rifle fire. Going it alone is often a recipe for oblivion, but if you can dominate a political party your rise has the chance to be swift, while your career will likely be durable since you'll have a steady if not growing stream of supporters.

Romania's Nicolae Ceausescu was nothing more than the Communist Party regional secretary of his home province after Romania fell to the Soviets in World War II. But rigged elections permitted him to become a member of the Grand National Assembly. From there he became deputy minister of the armed forces, and nominee member of the Central Committee, a primary Communist planning organization. At that point, a gentleman by the name of Gheorghiu-Dej became the Communist party leader and Ceausescu the deputy in 1952, but thirteen years later when Gheorghiu-Dej died of pneumonia, Ceausescu became leader of the Romanian Communist Party and leader of the nation. Welcome to your new office, sir: shall we begin rewrit-

---

[4]He's at least ahead of Idi Amin, who got stuck with the nickname "Hitler in Africa."

ing the Constitution today?[5][236].

Serbia's Slobodan Milosevic also rose through the Communist Party: his friend and classmate Ivan Stambolic appointed him Party Leader of the city of Belgrade in 1984, but two years later when Stambolic became president, Milosevic rose to become Party Leader for all of Serbia. A year later, Milosevic loudly denounced Stambolic for anti-Communist and anti-Serbian policies, forced his friend's resignation and became president himself.[381]

A better example still is Adolf Hitler, whose meteoric rise began in 1919 when he joined the old German Workers Party (the germ of the National Socialist German Workers Party, i.e. the Nazis). Early on he used the absence of the party founder at a meeting to thrust himself into the limelight, speaking to a raucous beer-hall and uniting his audience with his oratory. This was a beginning, and when Hitler describes this little scene in *Mein Kampf* there is little doubt that it is the seed of an ambitious proto-dictator aligning himself with a political party (for the time being). By 1921 he was the leading figure in the movement, which he was to re-organize into the National Socialist German Workers Party (NSDAP) or more familiarly, the Nazis.[277]

The NSDAP allowed Hitler to make contacts with powerful groups who were opposed to Weimar Germany, it exposed his oratorical talents to a wider audience and allowed him to access and capitalize on a growing organization for the dissemination of propaganda: within a year of its existence the party expanded from 30,000 to 100,000 members and would expand to over 200,000 by 1923; in 1920, still the early days and nothing like what was to come, the NSDAP distributed nearly 8 million pamphlets and 5 million hand bills promoting their cause.[277] As a get-out-the-vote mechanism nothing is as time-tested as a political party. After joining the NSDAP and serving several years as an increasingly in-demand political speaker, and after gaining notoriety and then jail time for the failed beer hall putsch, Hitler emerged in the late twenties as the master of the party, having eclipsed or otherwise removed his rivals. The NSDAP was Hitler, or his exclusive creation.[6] He had in his hands a superior political organization primed to rally the mass vote in a way that humbled the capacities of the competing social democrat parties.[230] In a way Hitler was already dictator of a state within a state, and with hindsight we can all see how that experience served him well in later years.

Josef Stalin's rise through the communist party ranks during the early days of the Soviet Union further illustrates the power in party politics. After the October Revolution he gradually acquired more responsibilities and positions within the communist party, eventually, for example, being named commissar of the Workers' and Peasants' Inspectorate (the Rabkrin). But rather than be satisfied with this position (even though it enabled him to ensure compliance with Central Committee dictates), he quickly added to his

---

[5]In fact, reworking the Constitution was exactly what he did upon taking office.
[6]Never mind the NSDAP predated him; before long he and the party were synonymous.

responsibilities and within the next few years was appointed General Secretary after the Eleventh Party Congress. This allowed him to entrench his power in nearly every organ of the government infrastructure.[120]

This kind of power is not to be confused with celebrity. In hindsight it's clear that Stalin's great rival, Leon Trotsky, was the more visible, popular, and famous exemplar of the Bolshevik Revolution, but that his power was a function of his fame. Stalin developed *his* power by proving useful to the party (and Lenin) as an enforcer and implementer of Politburo decrees, by developing contacts and molding protégés at all levels of the government, and by increasing his influence over regional and local Communist party representatives who further expanded his power base. It's no surprise that when he and Trotsky clashed, Stalin easily emerged victorious. Rising through the party may seem a more circuitous route to one-man-rule, but it may be less risky than an uncertain coup d'etat.

Lastly, Iraq's Saddam Hussein was a well-respected member of the Ba'ath Party when the party seized control in 1968, and Hussein became a powerful backstop to his cousin, the president and chairman of the new Revolutionary Command Council. Before long he was Vice Chair of the Council and thus Vice President of Iraq. The Ba'ath party served Hussein's interests well, for people thought Saddam would become the charismatic leader of a movement seeking egalitarianism and justice. The Ba'ath party was made up of the intellectual elite of a generation, and Hussein seemed to have a mastery of both the goals and the methods. But when the moment was right, he struck.

That moment was his attempted assassination by party leadership worried about Hussein's ambition. He foiled the attempt on his life, and staged a public and fearful, televised event in which the leader (tortured beforehand) confessed and named his accomplices. One by one they were escorted from the audience by the military – some protesting their innocence – and executed. The remaining people present, grateful they'd been spared, realized their very salvation depended on throwing their support behind Saddam. At the same time they realized Saddam had not been with the party because he believed in its goals, but because the party gave him the power to pursue goals of his own.[112]

1.6 Through the Military

This is what every low-ranking officer knows: it's a very short step from General to King. Rise quickly through the ranks, emerge as a war hero beloved by the masses, and then, once your military career has reached its apogee, make the leap.

Follow the trajectory of the Dominican Republic's Rafael Trujillo. He enlisted in the national police at the tender age of 27, and was sent to officer's school, where over the next seven years he was quickly promoted to captain, then inspector, major-commander, lieutenant-colonel, chief-of-staff, colonel, and eventually commander-in-chief of the police. The Police were then transformed into the National Army, and Trujillo rose again to the rank of brigadier-general. As popular frustration increased over then president Vásquez' removal of constitutional term limits, political leader Rafael Estrella struck a deal with Trujillo in which Estrella would seize power and call for elections, and Trujillo would ensure the army didn't interfere. The plan worked almost perfectly. But what Estrella hadn't counted on was that when elections were announced, the military would intervene systematically against every other potential candidate, until the only opposition candidate remaining was Trujillo himself. Trujillo won easily and seized the presidency, where he would remain for another 31 years.[239]

Another famous Latino strongman, Paraguay's Alfredo Stroessner, followed a similar track. Entering military school at a young age and advancing through the ranks, Stroessner participated in several war efforts and eventually wound up leading military brigades that would support but eventually betray sitting Paraguayan presidents. Six presidents were overthrown from 1948 and 1954, by which time he was chief of the army. And then it was his turn: with a "surgical coup" that cost the life of just one man, Stroessner became the nation's leader, where he too remained for three decades.[424]

Likewise, in 1942, Indonesia's Suharto entered military school as a sergeant at the age of 21 and rose to battalion commander during the Japanese occupation of World War II. He fought the Dutch during the struggle for independence, distinguishing himself in battle. By 1957 he was a colonel, by 1960 a brigadier general, by 1963 commander of a special alert force, and by 1965 he was commander of the entire army. On September 30, 1965, competing factions of the military put down each other's coups. Suharto led the massacre of pro-Communist forces, leading to nearly a million deaths, including the military supporters of then-president Sukarno. At the end, Sukarno had been both politically and military isolated, and he transferred the presidency to Suharto, where he remained for the next thirty years.[237]

1.7 Unfortunate Circumstances of your Predecessor

Let's face it, if you spend your time climbing the party ladder and waiting for the "right" moment, you run the risk of having to wait a very long time. Maybe the party will choose you as the nation's next leader, and maybe they won't. That's why it's nice when fate intervenes. And when fate lingers, you can still sometimes work it so fate intervenes on your behalf. For the impatient among you, it may be the most realistic way forward.

Natural Causes and Accidents: Consider yourself fortunate if your boss falls ill and dies, allowing you to move in and take over. Such was the case for José Eduardo dos Santos (Angola) who assumed power when Angola's first president died of cancer.[47] [104] Likewise, Cameroon's Paul Biya became president when the nation's first post-independence leader, Ahmadou Ahidjo, began suffering from ill health. Biya, who was Prime Minister at the time, proudly stepped up and into the limelight, and has been there ever since.[47]

The best example is without doubt Syria's Bashar al Assad, who would probably be an obscure optometrist today had his older brother Basil, who their father was grooming for the presidency, had not been killed in an automobile crash in 1994.[72] There are automobile accidents, however, and then there are:

"Unnatural" Causes and "Accidents":   Sometimes you don't have the luck of a cancerous predecessor or a drunk-driving elder brother. In this case you will need to make your own good fortune, and often a little shove is all that's required. Let's look at the rise of Slobodan Milosevic from another angle. Serbia's Ivan Stambolic, who was denounced as a traitor and ousted by his friend and colleague Slobodan Milosevic once said, "When somebody looks at your back for 25 years, it is understandable that he gets the desire to put a knife in it at some point." In Stambolic's case, it was two bullets instead of a knife, but by that point Milosevic had become the President of Serbia, where he would outlast Stambolic's short year as president by an order of magnitude.[442]

Zine Al-Abidine Ben Ali (Tunisia) took power from his predecessor, Habib Bourguiba, not because Bourguiba was killed but rather because he was able to claim the former leader was increasingly senile and no longer fit to govern.[7][47] There's a lesson here, and it's simple: while you sharpen your knives and assemble your supporters, do your best to encourage your boss take up chain-smoking, develop an addiction to fatty foods and a sedentary lifestyle, drink heavily, and practice dangerous sports, preferably in remote locations. And then just wait for your day.

1.8 Revolution, Guerrilla Warfare, and Force

Force is sometimes a necessary adjunct to power. This is particularly true if you happen to be an ambitious general or opposition leader in a country where the current president is making his own power grab. If that is the case, waiting for elections is not advised; and if there are elections scheduled, the incumbent has probably already read chapter 12 of this book, and is probably rigging them against you. Your response to this dead-end scenario is obvious and obligatory: assemble your men in a quiet, overlooked territory, begin attacking government troops and government offices, out-running or out-foxing the generals and their men, and enjoy the hit-and-run lifestyle of guerrilla warfare. In sum, let the glorious revolution begin. It will be civil war before too long, but there are many examples, including that of Mao Tse Tung, that show a protracted guerilla conflict can be won.[472] And once the incumbent's forces have been humiliated, demoralized, or simply out-gunned, your victory will be absolute.

Cuba's Fidel Castro began his career as a sweaty grunt running insurgency missions out of the forests surrounding Havana. And Nicaragua's Daniel Ortega overthrew Anastasio Somoza under the same circumstances: no political parties or campaign speeches were necessary, when superior military strategy, grit, and determination made the difference between victory and defeat. Likewise, Mohammar Khadaffi (Libya) led a group of young military officers in a coup d'etat in September 1969.[47] And in 1986, Yoweri Museveni (Uganda) did the same, leading his National Resistance Army into the capital and seizing power.[47] In fact, there are too many examples of successful coups d'etat to bother listing: it was practically the only way to power in Latin America for three decades, and many African nations experience coups as a matter of course.

---

[7]In 2011, protesters rose up and booted Ben Ali from power during violent protests, claiming after 23 years, Ben Ali was no longer fit either.

An important part of this strategy is impressing upon the business community the importance they back you (hopefully financially, but at least in spirit) as your revolution begins. They will want to make sure they bet on the right side of the revolution, for they can ensure your swift economic vengeance should they back the status quo and the leader you oust. It's equally important to win the hearts of the struggling masses. They can provide an endless reserve of troops, actionable intelligence, and serve as a background into which your guerrilla warriors can melt if pressed by the establishment powers. And if the masses don't support your little revolution, you're off to a shaky start[472]

Zaire's Mobutu came to power via coup in 1965, and that's a pretty common route for future autocrats. But it's important, if you go the route of the coup d'etat, to make sure dead men tell no tales. In 1960, still just a colonel in the military, Mobutu temporarily suspended the nation's institutions while his military encircled embattled president Patrice Lumumba, who took refuge in the United Nations mission in Leopoldville. When Lumumba was captured, Mobutu's men delivered him to his arch-enemy, the Katanga Moise Tshombe (after a bit of torture, of course). Lumumba was killed in mysterious circumstances, and his body was never found. Five years later, Mobutu was a lieutenant general, and strife between Zairian president Kasavubu and prime minister Tshombe led Mobutu to intervene. Tshombe was captured and exiled to Algeria, where he too died in mysterious circumstances. By that time, Mobutu was in power, and he'd stay there for the next three decades.[212].

Likewise, Nigeria's general Sani Abacha seized power in 1993 after canceling presidential elections and jailing the presumed winner, Chief Moshood Abiola. He proceeded to promise the country would be returned to democratic civilian rule, but never quite got around to doing so, as his multiple purges of the military and restrictions on civilian activity kept Nigeria a police state until his death five years later.

Weigh the pros and cons of guerilla war or a coup before jumping in:
Disadvantages:

1. You arrive in power owing lots of favors, such as to the president of the neighboring country that permitted you to stockpile arms and assemble your men on his territory, to the military that supported you, and to the business and economic elite (if they supported, see below). These commitments can limit your ability to govern, cost you more money than you are able to provide, and even compromise your government.

2. Death of your men.

3. Ensuing chaos. High levels of instability related to dramatic changes in economic development and social mores, tend to lead to coups, revolutions, and other opportunities to seize state power. Coups – even if conducted against aging, alienated, senile leaders – usually lead to

continuing unrest, a contracting economy in the post-coup years, further attempts at rebellion (copy-cat coups?), or civil wars, to name just a few disadvantages. If you are going to use a coup to take power, be prepared to lock it down, fast.

Advantages:

1. There is absolutely no doubt who is the boss now.

2. Death of your opponents' men.

3. Uniform: Nothing says "leader" or "victory" better than a heavily-starched uniform replete with gold epaulettes and as many medals as you can fit on the chest. Spiffy!

1.9   A Little of Everything

Ultimately, you may find what's required is a strategy that takes into consideration all of the above. You can't just set up camp in the mountains and begin your guerrilla war; nor can you probably just work your way up through the party and wait. With the single exception of your father-the-president's untimely death, you will have to work multiple angles at once.

Panamanian Manuel Noriega, born to a poor family with Colombian roots, entered the army and before long was the most feared man in Panama, allegedly responsible for hundreds of disappearances of Panamanian opposition figures. He became chief of staff of the military in the early 1980s, serving under Ruben Dario Paredes del Rio. But he soon eclipsed even Paredes and by 1983 had consolidated power and become Panama's military strongman leader. A close friend of Panama's de-facto leader from 1968–1981, Oscar Torrijos, Noriega was later implicated in the mysterious plane crash that claimed Torrijos' life.[458]

But whatever strategy you decide to pursue in your quest for power, ensure the most important criterion is met: it should be durable. Once you've elevated yourself and settled into the presidential suite, get to work immediately on ensuring your revolution lasts. And watch your back, in case some of your followers have been watching you, and learning. So get cracking: Seize the presidential palace, dissolve state institutions, have your guys fire a couple of volleys into the houses of potential political opponents or the presidential family, and call for the establishment of a "National Transition Council," headed up by yours truly. If you're feeling chummy, call for "immediate elections" you know you'll never get around to organizing, and then make yourself comfortable: you are going to be here for a long while. You've got the whole rest of your life ahead of you now, and twelve more chapters in this book to show you how to make sure that life is a happy and wealthy one.

Chapter 2

Inimitable You

> This is the epitaph I want on my tomb: "Here
> lies one of the most intelligent animals who
> ever appeared on the face of the earth."
>
> Benito Mussolini

REMEMBER this: It's all about you. Fundamental to your rule, your struggle against external and internal enemies, your grinding path against
judicial, military, and political obstacles, is the unshakeable conviction that
you alone are capable of leading the nation, and that under anyone else's
leadership your people will flounder in disgrace. This self-confidence has
been common to countless autocrats, living and dead. In other words, a little
megalomania goes a long way. 'Dictator' is not a job for wall-flowers or
meek intellectuals, and you know from experience that only the strong inherit anything other than the sleep of the grave. Some might question your
enormous self-belief. Don't let them get you down, and above all, be persistent.

That sense of conviction explains many newspaper headlines, and the
determination of many a heavy-handed leader, and even some ousted leaders who brave unspeakable difficulty to reclaim what they believe is theirs.
That was the story for Pakistan's General Pervez Musharraf, who returned to
his country at the risk of being arrested[1], understood that endurance is sometimes more important than the will of the people, and that if you hang around
long enough good things will happen.[14] Paraguay's Alfredo Stroessner
was a strong man, but his ascension to power ended 27 years of coups,
rebellions, and non-democratic government transitions between presidents
who barely lasted a year each. In fact, perhaps you and your strong, fatherly

---

[1]Other hurdles for General Musharraf: a hostile judiciary, the Pakistani army intent on defending President Zardari, a gamut of political parties who would all benefit from attacking him,
and the Pakistani people, who nearly universally disliked him.

guidance are the only things holding your nation together. Many would argue that Saddam Hussein was the only thing preventing Iraq from splitting into factions. It may be true: Iraq's sectarian violence certainly took a pretty dramatic upturn the afternoon the American troops left.[2][347] Same goes for Libya under Mohammar Khadaffi. Khadaffi's body was still warm in the grave when Libya began to splinter into competing, rival factions, and regions declaring their immediate autonomy.[316] [88]

Learn the arts of self-promotion, since you can hardly expect a nation to follow you blindly if they're only minimally aware of your greatness. But regardless of how you promote yourself, make sure that you also have the skills to back your advertising. These include the arts of persuasion, plain-speaking, organizational skills, and a forceful, boisterous personality. Use charm and charisma to seduce your benefactors and funders, whether they be the pro-democratic West, religious radicals, or the ethnic business class of your nation.[346] You must be able to translate vision into reality, and straddle the fine line between "generous, benevolent father" and "the iron fist." And all times, keep your beatific presence at the center of the national conversation.

2.1   You Are the State

Just as there is more to leadership than simply being able to persuade and lead, there is more to the state than just infrastructure. When your persona and nation mingle and become inextricable, you have transcended simple humanity and joined the ranks of those who personified their nations or movements. Think of it this way: if savior, redeemer, and the shining link between God and nation does not describe you, then you've got some work to do. Everyone in the nation should assume you are a demi-god. Says author Blaine Harden [232]:

> "If you took a quarter-century worth of His Excellencies the African leader and tossed them in a blender, you would come up with a Big Man who looks like this:
>
> "His face is on the money. His photograph hangs in every office in his realm. His ministers wear gold pins with tiny photographs of Him on the lapels of their tailored pin-striped suits. He names streets, football stadiums, hospitals, and universities after himself. He carries a silver-inlaid ivory mace or an ornately carved walking stick or a fly whisk or a chiefly stool. He insists on being called 'Doctor' or 'the big elephant' or 'the number-one peasant' or 'the wise old man' or 'the national miracle' or 'the most popular leader in the world.' His every pronouncement is

---

[2]No points to Nouri al-Maliki, Iraq's Prime Minister, for subtlety, that's for sure.

reported on the front page. He sleeps with the wives and daughters of powerful men in his government..."

Obviously, this is just a starting point, and applies not just to African
"Big Men." Here are the top 10 things to do just to make sure everyone
knows who their daddy is:

- Build statues: the bigger and bolder, the better, and preferably with
  your face looking out over sea, frowning over the city, and contemplating the horizon (over which you've got your foreign accounts, probably). This is such an important subject it deserves its own section. See
  section 2.2.6.

- Require your picture, front and center, in every government office in
  the nation.

- Require your picture, front and center, in every business whose owner
  doesn't want to get shut down.

- Put your picture on currency and coins. Coins last nearly forever
  (imagine the future archaeology student who digs one one up and marvels at your scowling profile on the obverse) but in the meantime are a
  tangible reminder of your omnipresence. They're also a fun obstacle
  to impose on your successor, who will have to deal with changing the
  currency should you ever be removed. And until he does, his pockets
  will jingle with your smiling mug. Or, if you're ambitious, super-
  impose your face on nature itself. There can be little argument with
  the man whose silhouette blots out a mountain face or gorge, as does
  Mussolini's.[22]

- Name things after yourself: ball parks, stadiums, bridges, schools,
  universities, neighborhoods, even weapons. Idi Amin renamed Lake
  Albert to Lake Mobutu Sese Seko, and Lake Edward to Lake Idi Amin
  Dada.[489] The Dominican Republic's Rafael Trujillo named the capital Ciudad Trujillo and the highest mountain Pico Trujillo.[239]

- Make your birthday, your wife's birthday, or your mother's birthday a
  national holiday. You can potentially do as Turkmenistan's Saparmurat Niyazov did and even rename the days of the week after your family members as well. North Korea's Kim Il Sung had the national calendar re-calibrated so that 1912 – the year of his birth – became Juche
  1.[235] Niyazov's successor, Gurbanguly Berdymukhammedov, upon
  taking office, not long after his predecessor's death, began naming all
  that stuff after *his* family members.[349]

- Insist on a half hour's time on every television network in the nation.
  Use the time to talk favorably about yourself and cast aspersions on

your enemies, remind the people they are lucky to have you and remind your enemies they will be crushed and pulverized; lastly, insinuate imminent danger from somewhere nearby, to ensure their continued political support (see 9.3.2 for much more on this subject).

- Rename the streets after your friends and supporters and members of your ethnic group.

- Inaugurate things. Ribbon cuttings are a constant source of amusement, as it is likely the factory or mine you're inaugurating will lead to your personal enrichment, the new airport will fund your party, and the new port will ensure your ethnic group's incursion into the territory of some other ethnicity. This has the added advantage of propping up the illusion that the economy is actually working for the benefit the people.

- Host international events, conferences, symposia, and festivals, all bearing your name, your slogan or mantra, or your image. Bonus points if, like Iranian President Mahmoud Ahmedinejad, you can use an event like this to publicly threaten to extinguish your enemies (Iran's Ahmedinejad to Jews at a Holocaust conference: "Israel will soon be wiped out.").[432]

2.2   Building your Cult of Personality

What's the best part of leading the nation: crippling your enemies? Repelling potential coups? Getting rich? We'd argue one of the most enjoyable aspects of leadership is becoming larger than life. And it pays political dividends as well. In fact, you may well find it's an essential part of keeping your thumb on the nation. Ideally, you are popularly perceived as invincible, untouchable, semi-divine, all-knowing, the best and the greatest. Without you, the nation is nothing; without your blessing, nothing happens. Who would dare replace you then?

Nicaragua's General Anastasio Somoza Debayle is a good case study. In a telegram published August 1973 in La Prensa (a moderate opposition daily), author Antonio García Cruz and H. Martinez address the General as

> "Leader, flagbearer, prominent one, guide, inspired and illustrious one, savior, supreme ruler, benefactor, unique leader, glorious one, talented one, man of destiny, counselor, illuminator, wise, virtuous, upstanding, inspiring, intelligent, regal, serene, prudent, builder, creator, hurricane of peace, negotiator, future president, referee, arbiter of justice, supreme commander, general in chief, famous one, magnanimous and generous one, his excellency, most excellent one, judge, predestined, distinguished, renowned, chosen, victorious, brilliant, strong personality, clever,

fabulous, magnetic, west pointer, strategist, organizer, protector, statesman, comforter of the afflicted, statistician, winner, sword, pacifier, polar star, morning star, genius, restorer, emancipator, liberator, idealist, liberal, planner, solid academic background, man of science, engineer, helmsman, pilot, captain, director of industry, bastion, bulwark, fortress, beacon, the man, paladin, patriot, democrat, savior of the republic, giant, first taxi driver (and all "firsts" ever known or imaginable), sacrificed to his people, altruistic, doctor honoris causa, bachelor ad honorem, chief of chiefs, indisputable chief, sustenance of democracy, supporter of Latin America and great friend of Nixon."[3][332]

The authors of that lengthy quote were being facetious, of course. But it's a list of titles and qualifications Somoza used to describe himself; the authors had simply kept a thorough list. But by modern standards, Somoza was an amateur. To wit:

Turkmenistan's Saparmurat Niyazov called himself "Turkmenbashi," ("Leader of the Turkmen") so Gurbanguly Berdymukhammedov had the Council of Elders name him "Arkadag" ("The Protector").[349]

Kim Il Sung was known as "the 'iron-willed, ever-victorious commander', the 'great sun and great man', the 'great leader', the 'great father', the 'sun of the nation', the 'clairvoyant', 'the supreme brain of the nation', a 'matchless patriot' and 'national hero' and 'one of the genius leaders of the international communist movement and workers' movement.' " He and his state media ceaselessly promote a fabricated biography of him that present him as an infallible genius; North Koreans come to understand him as a semi-divine emperor, and post-humously the constitution was amended to make him "Leader for Eternity."[235] But you can top it.

The Dominican Republic's Rafael Trujillo awarded himself so many medals he grew to be called "Bottle Caps" behind his back. He called himself the 'Great Benefactor of the Nation' and 'Father of the New Dominion.' When he took power in 1931 he had parliament issue an official proclamation that the 'Era of Trujillo' had begun[4][322]

Uganda's Idi Amin called himself "His Excellency, President for Life, Field Marshal Al Hadji Doctor Idi Amin Dada, VC, DSO, MC, Conqueror of the British Empire in Africa in General and Uganda in Particular"[5][95]

In Zaire, the general formerly known as Joseph Desiré Mobutu became "Mobutu Sese Seko Kuku Ngbendu waza Banga," typically translated as "the all-powerful warrior who, because of his endurance and inflexible will to win, will go from conquest to conquest leaving fire in his wake." That's

---

[3]The telegram goes on to ask sardonically, "In the name of any of these offices of qualities, we would like to ask you to do something to stop the price of consumer goods from increasing, and to make the rain fall. – Your humble servants, workers of the city of Managua."

[4]It had begun, indeed, and would last 31 years.

[5]It's perhaps not necessary to be quite so specific.

the kind of title that commands respect, although it's a bit tough to get onto a business card. No matter – dictators don't *need* to hand out business cards.

Equatorial Guinea's Teodoro Obiang Nguema Mbasongo has claimed through state radio to be a "God,"[321] whereas Gambia's erratic Yahya Jammeh insists on being called "His Excellency the President Sheikh Professor Alhaji Dr Yahya Abdul-Azziz Jemus Junkung Jammeh."[6]. Since 2010 he has been pushing to become king as well, sending traditional chiefs and tribal elders fanning out across the Gambia to promote his coronation. It could very well happen![321]

But why stop there? "God" wasn't too much of a stretch for Mohammar Khadaffi, who ensured he was named "king of kings" by a meeting of Africa's traditional rulers.[47] He also repeatedly compared himself to Jesus Christ and the Prophet Muhammad, while taking the name Imam of All Muslims.[117] Hard to imagine how he handled all that responsibility.

Haitian president François Duvalier worked hard to portray himself as a Voodoo sorcerer, semidivine, "the embodiment of the Haitian nation, a voodoo Jesus Christ." In 1963 he proclaimed, "I am the Haitian flag. He who is my enemy is the enemy of the fatherland."[238]

2.2.1   Finding Religion

The above examples clearly show that it helps to infuse your personality cult with a sense of spirituality or mystic feeling in order to exploit the genuine religious fervor found in many of your fellow countrymen. Gravitating toward a dominant religion is a twist on this tactic that serves several purposes: it can increase your popularity with the majority of believers, associate your cult with the popularity of a proselytizing faith, and lead to practical benefits in consolidating your rule and running the country.

For example, in Uganda in the 1970s, Idi Amin cultivated a religious aura, using it in many cases to further intensify the public's affection for him. Although he previously did not emphasize his Muslim faith, upon taking power he made it clear that he was doing Allah's good work and began to frequent mosques and patronize Islamic organizations. He peppered his speeches with references to God and encouraged a growing public perception of him as a kind of Kalashnikov-toting prophet. God spoke to him often in dreams, advising him on policy decisions, he claimed. Many Ugandans responded positively to these measures and felt they were the signs of someone who was destined to rule.[333]

Adopting religion can benefit those of you inclined to build empires. It provides an undeniably popular cause to which your co-religionists can rally, and the result is often imperial expansion and conquest, providing convenient justification for wars of aggression.[391]

---

[6]Not bad for a gentleman whose reading ability has frequently been questioned.

2.2.2 Getting some Western Polish

You can do wonders for your image – both at home and abroad – by schedul-ing some important meetings with western leaders. Back home, it will ap-pear as if you are accepted, or at least tolerated, by foreign governments. You reduce the suspicion that you are an outcast and your nation an outcast because they elected you. Get some nice photos shaking hands with smiling partners, and make sure your national press pushes them in the front of every one of your people during their breakfast: you are a legitimate leader.[132]

2.2.3 How you Suffer

It's not your fault that you are omnipotent: your nation needs you, and you alone are qualified for the job. Paraguay's Alfredo Stroessner used to com-plain that he would have prefered to retire to a life of fishing and hunting, but that his country needed him.[424] And Turkmenistan's Saparmurat Niyazov once complained, "I'm personally against seeing my pictures and statues in the streets ... But it's what the people want."[200]

2.2.4   Advocate a National Ideology

This is your chance to reorganize the world and grandstand for personal issues that dovetail with a popular or growing ideology. The goal here should be to inhabit the cause or ideological position the way a ghost haunts a house: when your subjects think of the cause, they will think of you.

Kim Jong Il developed a Marxist-Leninist political ideology he called "Juche," a self-congratulatory philosophy that demands total loyalty to the supreme leader and the 'religion of Kim Il Sungism' (Kim Il Sung Chuui) and stresses the benefits of sacrifice, austerity, discipline, dedication, unity and patriotism. It is typically described as "encyclopedic thought which provides a complete answer to any question that arises in the struggle for national liberation and class emancipation, in the building of socialism and communism."[235]

Libya's Mohammar Khadaffi showed how to invent and manipulate an ideology by authoring the *Green Book*, an infamous three volume meditation on "politics, economics, and everything from the evils of mechanized poultry farming to the importance of owning one's car."[32] Though derided by some as the ramblings of a scatter-brained autocrat, or a collection of aphorisms, the 21,000 word volume does describe the particular world view that Khadaffi espoused the entire time he was the leader of Libya. And he did see himself as equal parts philosopher and statesman.

The *Green Book* is a mix of utopian socialism, Arab nationalism and the Third World revolutionary ideology that came out of the late 1970s and early 1980s. For good measure, he adds in a bit of Bedouin supremecism.[32] Khadaffi's "Third Solution" to the ills of both Capitalism and Communism was what he believed to be democracy in its purest form: a panoply of peoples' committees that replaces the functions of governments and permits popular self-rule; in 1977 he resigned from all official government positions to become the "Guide to the Era of the Masses." Here he showed his true colors, for the peoples' committees, when convoked, were controlled by him and his cronies, and served only to rubber stamp Khadaffi's own ideas and proclamations.[32] Promoting, studying, and exalting the edicts of the Green Book became a (well funded) industry in itself, with its epicenter in the World Center for the Study and Research of the Green Book. This Tripoli think tank employed a staff of over a hundred, had international subsidiaries outside of Libya, and oversaw the production of over 140 studies and academic papers about the Green Book.[7][32]

Turkmenistan's Saparmurat Niyazov wrote a similar book, the *Ruhnama*. Completed in 2001, he considered it the final, authoritative word on all things

---

[7]This is not one of them.

Turkmen, from the history he traces from Ögüz Khan to the Turkmen people of present, to his philosophy of what it means to be Turkmen, and his own poetry.[8][345] . His successor Gurbanguly Berdymukhammedov then decided to write a book of his own, reportedly to be called either *Turkmennama* ("the book for Turkmen") or *Adamnama* ("the book for Humanity").[349]

Indonesia's Sukarno developed a political philosophy during his run to power that combined elements of socialism, nationalism, and monotheism. Called *Pancasila*, it was a mystical hybrid of then-popular ideas – a useful trinity when attempting to unite a population behind your rule.[444][211] Venezuela's Hugo Chávez didn't develop such a robust ideology *per se*, though his governing style came to be known as *Chavismo*, a vaguely nationalist, pro-Latin America movement that he used to position Venezuela as a strategic counterweight to the hegemony of the United States.[256]

While *Pancasila* was arguably a successful and even positive, guiding force on Indonesian society, Yugoslavia under Josip Broz Tito grew under an ideology later called *Titoism*, a blend of Communism with free market forces and certain, limited freedoms (like the ability to travel mostly unimpeded). It was a clever administration that permitted limited pleasure and required the sacrifice of neither principle nor honor.[18] Lauded for uniquely being cast out of the Soviet bloc in 1948 for "boundless ambition, arrogance, and conceit," Tito is to this day admired for having not flinched before Josef Stalin. And *Titoism* remains pretty well respected as well.[18] He wins; Burma's Ne Win loses. Ne Win's 28 point manifesto, *The Burmese Way to Socialism*, was instead a roadmap to poverty. Although it promised freedom from a "pernicious" economic system through political and economic mysticism, there was little mystery in it: it prescribed a one party state, nationalization of foreign assets, and a near-total lockdown of the political opposition. Protests on the day he retired led to an estimated 10,000 killed as Burma/Myanmar continued its slide into isolation and bitter (pernicious) poverty.[38]

Few national philophies are better known and emulated than the famous "Authenticity" promoted by Zaire's Mobutu Sese Seko. It promoted a pro-African nationalist, anti-colonialist pride (in the years following Belgium's exit from Africa, who could blame him?) emulated by many other African nations. Authenticity meant banning of Western names, the bleaching of hair or listening to foreign music on the radio. Instead of 'Mr.' and 'Mrs.' Zairians were expected to call each other "citizen." The movement even came with a uniform of its own, the infamous, low-collared *"abacost,"* a two piece pants-and-tunic ensemble patterned after the Mao suits of Mao Tse Tung. The nationalist stripe of authenticity also meant, and led to, rampant nationalization of formerly Belgian enterprises and businesses. We'll see how this plays out in section 11.4. Authenticity furthermore meant a rapid erasure of the colonial period in a fit of renaming. The capital, Leopoldville, became Kinshasa, and the nation, formerly the Congo, became Zaire. And

---

[8]Writer Paul Theroux excoriated it during his visit to Turkmenistan in early 2006, describing it as silly and a symbol of Niyazov's weak mind.[463]

of course Mobutu himself became "the all powerful warrior."[212]

2.2.5   Connect Yourself to a Historical National Hero

Why not use a corpse to promote your greatness? Assuming your own personality is somewhat lacking, drape yourself in the cloak of a national father.
In Roman times, Augustus Caesar fueled his rise by aligning himself with
his murdered adoptive father, the very popular Julius. But this is a technique
that has proven to be valuable through the centuries, right up to the present.

Hugo Chávez found his long-deceased hero, Simón Bolívar, suddenly
politically useful in 2010 and had the old Latin politician exhumed to determine beyond doubt if he had truly been poisoned by Colombians in the 19th
century.[487] The episode, which fully televised a weeping Chávez mourning the death of a national hero, provided a convenient distraction at a time
Chávez was suffering criticism of his administration; rising inflation; looming economic recession; and crime, and provided additional justification for
the hatred he was attempting to foster against the nation of Colombia.[129]
Teary president Chávez posted to Twitter, "I confess that we have wept, we
have sworn. I tell you: that glorious skeleton must be Bolívar, because his
flame can be felt."[9][370]

Nicaragua's Daniel Ortega followed suit not long after, vowing to find
the remains of Augusto Sandino, a rebel soldier whose political philosophy and guerrilla tactics inspired the nascent Sandinista guerrillas 40 years
after Sandino's death. His iconization was largely a work of revisionist
history, but it worked so spectacularly as the Sandinista movement gained
strength through the 1970s and 1980s that Sandino eventually did truly become, posthumously, the "father" of the Sandinista movement. Twenty years
later, to shore up flagging cultural support from a Nicaraguan populace little-
enamored of a president increasingly turning autocratic, Daniel Ortega, former head of the Sandinistas, followed Chávez' lead. He vowed to find the
remains of Sandino, thus strengthening his cultural association with the well-
loved national hero, and provoking Nicaragua's sense of nationality.[426]
This clever bit of false nationalism helpfully overlooked not only the fact
that Sandino would have abhorred Ortega the politician, but also the fact
that the Sandinista government under Ortega led to a decade-long civil war,
millions of casualties, and the continued impoverishment of the nation.

Saddam Hussein, who understood the tribal nature of the Iraqi Muslims,
took it a step further. He had genealogists construct a plausible family tree
linking him back to Fatima, the daughter of the Prophet Mohammed. The
symbolism of the blood line linking Hussein to the Prophet was epitomized
in a 600 page hand-lettered copy of the Koran that was written with Saddam's own blood.[112]

---

[9]A year later, Bolívar's remains were encased in a coffin encrusted with diamonds, pearls,
and gold stars.[82] One wonders if the old man would rather have just been left alone to rest
rather than dragged into this mess.

2.2.6   Erect Statues

What do you call a bronze bust of your frowning face in every city square in the nation? A good start! Putting up statues and monuments is extremely important as it builds your legitimacy, solidifies your image, defines public space, and offers an unmistakable point of reference in city squares throughout the country. Each time you raise a new ostentatious statue, the press will cover the event and your potential opponents will have lost another propaganda battle. Not long after assuming power, statues of both Joseph Stalin and Vladimir Lenin adorned just about every public space in the Soviet Union. North Korea's Kim Jong Il, a Stalinist by nature, set out to top it: by the 1980s, Kim Jong Il had erected over 34,000 monuments to himself and ensured his portrait was in public spaces throughout the nation.[235]

Turkmenistan is having a tough time keeping its statues current. Former president Saparmurat Niyazov had monuments built in his image across the countryside, but when he died, his successor, Gurbanguly Berdymukhammedov, set to work having them removed. After five years, and during his second term, Berdymukhammedov finally had his own statue built: a white equestrian pose, in which he is represented in traditional attire with a dove (a Turkmen symbol of luck) near his right hand.[307]

But your statues don't have to be of your own image, if you are working on associating your legacy with some sort of national ideology (see section 2.2.4). Venezuela's Hugo Chávez began construction of an enormous mausoleum for the remains of recently-exhumed Simón Bolívar, who will have a nice view of Caracas' slums from his final resting place.[390] And though Paraguay's Alfredo Stroessner wasn't a "statue" sort of guy, he ordered the construction of an enormous, neon sign that flashed his name over sleeping Asunción during most of his reign. And of course he dominated television and news coverage during that whole time.[424]

The downside is that any statue so intimately connected to you becomes a magnet for marches, riots, and even vandalism by your detractors. Be prepared to use the military to protect your likenesses because the people, once riled, will take great pleasure in trashing your masterpiece. Note: 24 hour illumination of your statue during a lengthy blackout of the capital city is a bad idea, as it will remind everyone your priority is illuminating your masterpiece, not allowing the masses to watch the football match, and your lovely work of art will become a tempting target for violence and mischief.

If bronze busts aren't your style, follow the lead of Hamad Bin Hamdan Al Ahyan, who had work crews dig channels in his private island so that the in-flowing water would spell out the letters of his name. The earthen graffito was of a scale immense enough the letters can now be seen from space.[10][498]

---

[10] Technically, Al Ahyan is just a wealthy person, not a dictator. But his work reflects what you can do if you've got the money and power.

2.2.7   Keep it Quiet

Interestingly, Cuba's Fidel Castro chose a bolder route than you probably will: the man who led Cuba for five decades refused that entire time to develop a cult of personality around himself, preferring to shift emphasis to his political and social revolution. As such, you won't find a single statue dedicated to Castro on the island of Cuba (although you *will* find the occasional tribute to quotidian things he touched or used, like a monument in Playa Gión that permits you to admire a hole puncher Castro once used).[171] What a missed opportunity! Cambodia's notorious Pol Pot also chose to operate from the shadows. One of history's most determined recluses, he didn't even bother to declare himself to the Cambodian people as their leader until nearly two years into his administration (the Cambodians believed themselves to be governed until then by an anonymous organization by the name of "Angkar"). He rarely gave speeches or interviews. Needless to say, statues were out of the question.[455] Likewise, Spain's *Generalissimo* Francisco Franco made little use of the media. An unprepossessing 5'3" tall, with spectacles and a high, lispy speaking voice, his television addresses consisted generally of video footage of recent events, set to the dictator's voice-over. Aloof and chilling, his coldness was well-known and understood.[466]

2.3   Lifestyle of a Leader

Shakespeare wrote "uneasy lies the head that wears a crown," and who are we to argue? It's not easy being an autocrat: the culmination of the state is often surprisingly alone. Says author Mark Bowden:

> The tyrant must steal sleep. He must vary the locations and times. He never sleeps in his palaces. He moves from secret bed to secret bed. ... It is too dangerous to be predictable, and whenever he shuts his eyes, the nation drifts. His iron grip slackens. Plots congeal in the shadows. For those hours he must trust someone, and nothing is more dangerous to the tyrant than trust.[112]

Your day job will necessarily consume your personal life as well: such is the strain of being number one. If you were penniless and powerless you could go and do as you pleased; but once you seize the throne the entire fate of your nation and people depend on your every decision. You will no longer be able to travel without a security entourage. The press will gawk at your every bite of food, your opponents will attempt to divine weakness in your every move, and the vulturous sycophants who surround and depend on you will annoy you from sun up until sun down.[112]

2.3.1 Your Public Appearance

It's essential that every aspect of your physical and public appearance bolster a consistent performance of strength and determination. The starched epaulettes are no joke: they portray military might – and right. Stay in good physical shape and avoid the appearance of aging by whatever chemical means necessary. If your enemies catch you hunched over, limping, graying, wrinkled, or dozing off in a conference, they will infer weakness. And weakness invites attack. If your eyes weaken, have your aides print your speeches in 20 point font rather than resort to reading glasses; if you limp, make sure you are not seen walking in public. [112] If you need to, see the plastic surgeon, particularly if you want to look good on television.[39]

Your presence in the media – from your smiling (or frowning) face on state television to your booming voice on the radio to your every last word on the Internet, should be covered in adulatory detail. See the entirety of chapter 9 for much more on this essential subject.

2.3.2 Your Palaces

If you are worried about personal attack, it's a good strategy to keep your opponents guessing. Iraq's Saddam Hussein had more than twenty palaces, each fully staffed, and three meals a day were prepared for him daily in each palace to avoid anyone deducing in which he was expected.[112]

As an autocrat, you have near total freedom to do what you want on earth. Unfortunately, where your palatial decor is concerned, that lack of restraint may lead you astray. Peter York, who has visited and cataloged dozens of dictators' mansions, has come up with tenets of decorating that will keep you in line with your colleagues.[11] Despot decor aims to impress upon you the leader's unbridled power, and by contrast, the visitor's total impotence. The message must be communicated instantaneously, and the palaces serve more as a medium of communication than as a place to live. You shouldn't be hanging pictures of your children on the stairwell, of course.[496] It's also safe to presume that Silvio Berlusconi did not hang portraits of his wife at the 154-room mansion at Arcore outside Milan, epicenter of the infamous bunga-bunga parties.[374]

Some more tips, all courtesy of Peter York:[496]

- Choose things that are too big to be practical.

- Give preference to having gold everywhere, from mouldings to furniture to the ceiling.

---

[11]He writes, "The premise was absolute style – what happens when people with absolute power and absolute resources have their way with their buildings and interiors. My going-in point was ironic, frivolous and, frankly, rather snobbish. I was hoping the interiors would turn out to be completely over the top. I wasn't disappointed."

- Buy modern reproduction of classic looks, not shoddy and worn antiques.

- "Reproduction French" is always in style. Otherwise, be influenced by big city hotels.

- Marble and glass are your friends.

- Prefer large oil paintings of yourself, doing heroic things.

- Prefer global luxury brand names in every aspect, from your car to your designer sunglasses.

- Animal prints: always a winner. Marble lions, golden eagles: a page out of Napoleon's notes.

It seems Spain's Francisco Franco took that advice to heart. He lived and worked out of a 16th century palace a few miles outside of Madrid. Its spacious office was outfitted with Aubusson carpets, velvet draperies, and gilt-inlaid furtniture. The photos on the walls changed with his political convictions: portraits of Mussolini and Hitler were later replaced with Dwight D. Eisenhower and finally by Pope Paul VI.[466]

2.3.3   Your Transport

Needless to say, you should have a fleet of the latest luxury car. As your presidential caravan transports you through the streets of the capital, security forces – immense, jackbooted men riding enormous BMW motorcycles behind mirrored sunglasses – should clear the way for you with blaring sirens and lights. Ernest Bai Koroma's motorcade in Sierra Leone is valued at about $400,000 (the nation's GDP per capita is $325), but is nothing next to Uganda's presidential motorcade, consisting of eight or nine cars, some mine-resistant South African armored personnel carriers, and a Mercedes truck toting a portable lavatory.[187] Since your city's traffic is probably unbearably congested and difficult, this serves two purposes, getting your important self to wherever you are headed, and helping you remain skeptical of any traffic problem at all. If you don't see or experience it, it doesn't exist.

You can take it a step further, as did Kim Jong Il, who built a network of 19 private, luxury train stations for his exclusive use throughout the countryside. His private fleet of trains afforded him the utmost comfort while ensuring he was forced to endure no contact at all with the common, North Korean peasants.[457]

Finally, your routes themselves should be as luxurious and ostentatious as someone of your stature merits. See the section of public works (section 4.7.1) for more details, but in sum: make sure the routes you frequent are nicer than any other in the nation, so you are not uncomfortable. For starters, make sure the routes from the Presidential Palace to the airport and the National Assembly, and from the National Assembly to the Supreme Court, and so on, are lovely. It's hard to believe you'll go anywhere else, and as for the people using the rest of the nation's rotted, rutted, routes: who cares?

2.3.4 Your Food

Eat well, and copiously. You are the king, after all. Saddam Hussein had fresh food flown in for him twice a week: lobster, shrimp, lots of lean meat, and plenty of dairy – not bad for a desert nation. All of it was immediately and thoroughly inspected by his nuclear scientists, who x-rayed and tested the food for radiation and poison.[112]

2.3.5 Your Sexual Prowess and Manly Virtues

As leader of the nation and the strongest, most powerful, most well-loved man in creation whose very presence is a gift of God to your people, you should naturally be the world's best lover – or at least the most prolific. You want women to quiver in your presence, young men to aspire to your level of sexual competence, and bespectacled opposition leaders to grind their teeth with jealously over your priapic adventures. At the same time, it's a good idea to cultivate the manly arts: hunting, fishing, and sports, to name a few.[12]

Idi Amin, for example, otherwise a portly autocrat, emphasized his history as a boxer and former light-heavyweight champion, encouraging his supporters to emulate him and smash their enemies. "I would like to speak as the heavyweight champion of Uganda ... The only chance to defeat [those] who are against you or against the country is to win by knockout. This is the only thing," he said once to an adoring audience who had gathered to watch him receive one of his many honors[427] Beyond that, he made sure the masses knew of his love of physical competition, and one endlessly recycled news clip showed him challenging and soundly defeating pretenders during an impromptu swimming contest. In it, he emerges from the water, grinning, proclaiming himself a champion.[333] Winning such contests, you will find, is the easy part, because it's likely no one will try too hard to defeat you. Delighting in sports and physical activity can help popularize you and your regime, build and extend your cult of personality, and generally provide balm for tough times and economic woes.

Learn from autocrats throughout history who have cultivated an image as sportsmen and lovers. Benito Mussolini, for example, cultivated both, and was portrayed as a vigorous swimmer, fencer, aviator, equestrian, and champion of the *boudoir* (through his numerous not-so-secret affairs). Via official state organs, he was commonly characterized as a bronzed and muscled athlete in vigorous health, one who typically rose at seven in the morning and, after bathing in cold water and drinking lots of chilled milk for breakfast,

---

[12]Things to avoid: playing with computers, writing boring books, and building web sites.

proceeded to an early morning horse ride, followed by a fencing contest. As a fencer, the readers were assured, Il Duce ("Leader," from Latin *Dux*) would always use the most potent weapon – a saber – and engage his opponent with a ruthless, aggressive style. State journals characterized Mussolini as 'the first sportsman of Italy.'[111]

The Duce's amorous activities were similarly used to project an image of Latin sexual prowess and win converts to his personality cult. Letters from adoring females attest to the success of this strategy. One young woman wrote to him admiringly, putting him on the level of Christ during the Eucharist at mass:[103]

> "Both of you will be there on my tongue, will repose on my breast, will rest on my poor heart. How good you will be!"

Further fueling this image of Mussolini as an all-powerful Lothario was his barely hidden affair with Claretta Petacci, which included seaside vacations with adjoining houses for family and mistress, and rampant media speculation on clandestine contacts between the lovers.[111]

Silvio Berlusconi will probably be better remembered for his flawless complexion (the result of lots of plastic surgery) and his seemingly endless exploits with young and mostly gorgeous women than for his woeful public policy record.[481] Indeed, his lasting image is one of a broad smile, not a scowl: he was the perfect image of happiness and health. On the other hand, the Dominican Republic's Rafael Trujillo managed to mix both sexual bravado with the running of his government. Author and full-time political critic Mario Vargas Llosa once wrote that Trujillo routinely slept with the wives of his enemies and political opponents.[328] That's certainly one way to dominate your cabinet both at work and home.

Vladimir Putin is another contender for the prize of macho heart throb. Already, Putin's image is emblazoned over T-shirts, Moscovite billboards portray him as a masculine action hero/crime fighter, and a Siberian cult worships him as the reincarnation of Saint Paul. But a 2011 video disseminated over the Internet showed young, nubile women ripping open their shirts for him, and encouraging others to do the same. The thumping hip-hop beat, the derisive anti-opponent lyrics, and the bubbling, adolescent sexuality deliver an unmistakable message in red lipstick: "I rip for Putin." The video is consistent with a calendar published in 2010 on Putin's 58th birthday portraying 12 female university students posing in lingerie under a banner stating, "We love you Vladimir Vladimirovich." And the sexual theme corresponds with publicity that has sought to portray Putin as a swashbuckling man of action through carefully choreographed activities: sedating a polar bear, peeling out in a Formula I race car, scoring a quick goal in a hockey game.[417] Turkmenistan's Gurbanguli Berdymukhamedov obviously got the message: He dropped by Turkmenistan's first auto race in April 2012, and "on a whim," decided to compete at the last minute. And won! Now that's a man of action worth rallying behind.[94] And note: sex and politics *do* mix. Quoth a party member in Moscow's City Duma, "Why do we never see successful, pretty girls in the opposition?" Easy: because the opposition apparently never gets laid.[28]

2.3.6   Release the Creative Muse

You wouldn't be the first dictator to use the liberty of the nation's power throne to crank out some literature. And we're not talking about political treatises. Author Paul Theroux noted that Turkmenistan's Saparmurat Niyazov thought himself an accomplished writer ("a clear sign of madness in anyone")[463]. And Saddam Hussein dabbled in writing fiction, and appears to have written and published two romantic fables about a gloried Middle East, a misunderstood king, and so on. Mark Bowden noted, "Before publishing the books, Saddam distributes them quietly to professional writers in Iraq for comments and suggestions. No one dares to be candid – the writing is said to be woefully amateurish, marred by a stern pedantic strain – but everyone tries to be helpful, sending him gentle suggestions for minor improvements."[112]

To be brief, your talents likely lie elsewhere. Still, if you are that rare autocrat who has a penchant for the entertainer's life, why not cultivate this talent, and use it when trying to build a consensus? Jacob Zuma of South Africa famously publicly sang "Bring Me My Machine Gun" before and after taking office, and this anthem soon became a rallying cry for his supporters and the nation.[259] Another music lover, Silvio Berlusconi released an album of love songs, "Il vero amore," ("True Love") which showcased his talents as a songwriter.[13][383] Don't delay or soft-peddle this kind of thing like Silvio did – release it the day you are sworn into office, sing and play every instrument on the record, and go on an intimate theater tour. Then build your brand among the lonely housewives of your nation.

2.3.7   Be Eccentric

Tread lightly here, but be aware that many before you allowed their limitless power and influence to throw off the shackles of decorum and diplomacy. As you are a demi-God, however, don't be afraid to be yourself. Turkmenistan's Gurbanguly Berdymukhammedov had a fetish for all things white, and insisted by decree on things like a "National Week of Health and Happiness" starring theater events called "The Inspirational Era of Happiness" and "The Era of Power Illuminated by Happiness." He mandated exercise for all government employees, and established a national holiday to celebrate his favorite breed of horse.[307] [349]

Idi Amin declared himself the "uncrowned king of Scotland" in 1976 and once bizarrely wrote to the Queen of England requesting an invitation

---

[13]Though not as a cruise-ship crooner, his former job.

to Scotland, Ireland, and Wales, so he could meet with the "heads of revolutionary movements fighting against your imperialist oppression." He is reported to have later sent her a Telex that read, "Dear Liz, if you want to know a real man, come to Kampala."[95]

'Papa Doc' Duvalier was intensely superstitious, even by Haitian standards. He held the number 22 in high regard, believing on the 22nd of each month his voodoo spirits guarded him; he would frequently venture outside the presidential palace only on that date, and organized ceremonies and significant life events to happen on the 22nd of the month. Having put a voodoo hex on American president John F. Kennedy, he was delighted when the latter was killed on November 22nd.[33] His superstitions led him to other extremes as well, such as having all black dogs killed.[322] Burma's Ne Win was similarly preoccupied with the spiritual portent of numbers. In 1962, he decided that 9 being an auspicious number, the currency would be recast so bills of 45 and 90 kyat could be made available - divisible by 9. Their predecessors, bills of 50 and 100 kyat, were simultaneously deemed worthless, rendering many a Burmese savings account null and void. He also liked the number 8, and chose to retire from government on August 8, 1988.[14]

Gambia's Yahya Jammeh is among the more colorful African leaders, with self-proclaimed mystical powers that permit him to cure AIDS and asthma with "single-dose herbal treatments and a banana-rich diet,"[321] neither of which has been confirmed by the scientific community but served to distract the media from other subjects and reinforce his demi-God status among many of Gambians. Or, if you are the more negative type, try banning random things, like beards, ballet, and gold teeth, like Turkmenistan's Saparmurat Niyazov (then rename the days of the week after your mother, father, and your recently published book).[463]

North Korea's Kim Jong Il (at the time still son of the dictator, not yet dictator himself), interested in improving the films being produced by North Koreans in the 1980s, had a noted South Korean film maker kidnaped and transported over the border, where he was forced to produce films for the North.[15][66]

Mohammar Khadaffi: Wow, where to begin? He declared war on Switzerland, claiming the nation had been destroying mosques.[16] He came to an international conference in Manhattan and insisted on land on which he could pitch his desert tent (he was denied). He once publicly slapped an aide for taking him to the wrong venue at a conference. Opening the Africa-EU summit, he stated bluntly "The partnership has failed." His wardrobe has provided infinite discussion: from starched-epaulet bleach-white mil-

---

[14]Before you laugh, 8 was Elvis' lucky number too, and many an American kept a peeled eye that day in hopes he'd return from the Great Beyond.

[15]Said Kim Jong Il in 1987 about film, "No production of high ideological and artistic value can evolve out of a creative group whose members are not united ideologically and in which discipline and order have not been established." A fitting quote for a future autocrat.

[16]In reality, Switzerland had voted against the construction of minarets, but why interfere with a great battle cry?

itary uniforms festooned with a constellation of medals and awards (they seemed to multiply in number over time; who presented him these awards and for what?), to flowing Bedouin robes with matching headgear. For a conference of the G-8 in Paris he was reported to have "channeled Saturday Night Fever" via his shiny outfit[378]. He favored printed fabrics festooned with the portraits of African leaders, and shiny Western suits.[340] But never mind the wardrobe: he once transported a camel to Paris for an event.[378] And in 2011, as NATO warplanes bombed Tripoli, he complained he would go bomb Europe's homes, factories, and families, since that's what the nations of the G8 were doing to him.[61] In sum, he commanded attention at every venue, as should you.

2.3.8   Or Just Be "The Man"

Hats off to Silvio Berlusconi, who has blended eccentricity with charm more appealingly (to his constituents) than any leader of modern times. With a smile, a song, money and near total domination of the media, he was able to stay in power through crises that would have humbled many a leader elsewhere. Historian David Gilmour has noted the way *il Cavaliere* projected a seductive, vivacious image, contrasting sharply with the somewhat rougher-edged Mussolini. This image has helped Berlusconi weather a number of personal scandals and maintain an appearance that baffled the rest of the world:

> "Berlusconi had a hold over the Italian people as no politician had had since Mussolini. Of course the allure of the fascist leader had been very different, for women as well as for men. He had not been one for serenades and lingering siestas: he liked to take women roughly and briskly, on the floor or up against a wall. Berlusconi by contrast was a seducer and a caresser, an archetypal giver of chocolates and pearl necklaces. A smiler rather than a scowler, he appeased his narcissism with a face-lift and a hair transplant and by surrounding himself with gaggles of young women, to some of whom he gave political careers and occasionally a post in his government. He liked making remarks that were crass, sexist, and insensitive, as they were when he advised an unemployed young woman to marry someone like him, but most women forgave him. He was an Italian male.
>
> Berlusconi's message to men was equally simple: I am like you, and you can be like me if you try; you too can be famous, rich, and seductive even if (like me) you are small and not very handsome. ... They did not seem to mind if he made gaffes, told lies, betrayed his wife or faced criminal charges."[218]

2.3.9   Be a Hero

Much of the above describes how to make a reputation for yourself if you're otherwise not very exciting. But if you are already made of iron, your reputation will grow naturally. No better example of this exists than King Hassan II of Morocco, who we can only respectfully suppose must have had balls of steel. He survived several attempted coups, but two bear mentioning. In the first, a thousand mutinous troops attacked his presidential palace during the celebration of his 42nd birthday. In the spray of gunfire, nearly 100 guests were killed and another 125 were wounded. The King hid, and then emerged from his palace only to find himself face to face with a gun-toting rebel commander. Keeping eye contact, King Hassan II recited the opening verse of the Koran. The rebel dropped to his knees and kissed the king's hand.[17]

About a year later, the King was returning from Paris on his private Boeing 727 when a squadron of Royal Moroccan Air Force fighters began strafing his jet. King Hassan, himself a pilot, grabbed the radio as the plane descended to the runway, ordering, "Hold your fire; the tyrant is dead!" The rebels, fooled, stupidly obeyed. Hours later, the rebel leaders were rounded up, arrested, and shot.[225] If you've got this kind of *cojones*, forget the rest of this chapter: you don't need to worry about creating your own legend.

2.3.10   For Richer or Poorer: Your Spouse

For the most part, the spouse of a dictator stays out of the spotlight and lets her husband tend to slaughtering the opposition on his own. It's difficult to imagine Lyudmila Aleksandrovna troubling Vladimir Putin terribly, and Muhammad Zia-ul-Haq, the *generalissimo* of 1980s Pakistan did not seem to seek the counsel of wife Shafiq Jahan before taking action.

But if your significant other shares your values and works with you, consider your partnership an asset. For example, Serbia's Slobodan Milosevic and Mira Markovic used their twin talents to positive effect. Both devoted Communists, Mira was more sophisticated and cosmopolitan, blunting Slobodan's street-tough image. During Milosevic's climb to power Mira was an ardent supporter and fellow traveler in political ambition, while later, particularly after the start of the Yugoslav civil war, she emerged as a visible and unabashed partner in the aborted rise of Greater Serbia. It has been claimed that Mira helped to arrange the action against Stambolic that characterized Milosevic's early rise. During his (their) reign she kept the couple's ideological focus from flagging by persistently stressing their socialist credentials in articles such as "The Left Will Rise, You'll See" and "Socialism Has Raised the Oppressed from Their Knees." Her presence alongside Slobodan kept the focus on their intellectual and philosophical goals – Communism – providing context and "enlightenment" to her husband's often heavy-handed tactics.[155]

---

[17]Not long after, loyal troops crushed the revolt, captured 900 rebels and killed another 150.

This may effectively turn one-man-rule into rule by the power couple. In Milosevic's case, Mira's intellectual pretensions led Slobodan to frequently and unselfconsciously parrot her thoughts and support her recommendations. [156] With Milosevic's blessing, Mira formed her own political party, the Communist Yugoslav United Left (JUL). Realizing that Mira could help spread his influence to groups that otherwise would never align themselves with him, Slobodan let the JUL soar, and the combined political appeal of both strengthened Slobodan's hand immensely.[440]

While no one can accuse Nicaragua's Daniel Ortega of overtly taking orders from his wife Rosario Murillo, popularly reviled as "la bruja" ("the witch"), it is widely suspected she calls the shots from behind in the role of (extremely) trusted advisor. In the 1990s when Ortega was being accused of repeatedly raping his stepdaughter Zoilamerica, Ms. Murillo had an opportunity to defend her daughter. Rather, she recognized the opportunity implicit in helping propel her husband back to power. Zoilamerica's legal case thus went nowhere, and Murillo became power broker to her husband, re-fashioning his struggling political campaign in vivid pink and yellow hues[96] and helping him win the presidency in 2006. Once Ortega won, she continued to guide his every move and public appearance, and was at one time the head of the political party's media organization.[344] No wonder she is roundly despised even by former Sandinista insiders[126] and is perceived by the Nicaraguan public as a quasi-witch with jangly jewelry and a penchant for the arcane.

Prefer to go it alone? Despair not: Many of your fellow dictators are solitary men who disdain the company of women, and oftentimes for good reason: Phillip II of Macedon, at the height of his power, just as he was crowning himself king of the Greeks, was assassinated while his powerful and ambitious wife Olympias looked on. It's thought that she, and their son Alexander ("the Great"), had orchestrated the killing.[495] Similarly, some historians portray Livia Drusilla as poisoner-in-chief, ruthlessly eliminating all of Augustus Caesar's chosen heirs so her son Tiberius could inherit the Roman Empire[18].[453]

But for God's sake, keep your spouse(s) under control! Nothing is more potentially damaging to your reputation as a demi-God than the public finding out your wife is sleeping with someone else; worse still if the guy cuckolding you is part of your government! His Majesty Mswati III of Swaziland was somewhat publicly chagrined when it was discovered his 12th wife was having an affair with Mswati's Minister of Justice.[456] Similarly, Robert Mugabe of Zimbabwe learned to his chagrin his wife Grace was sleeping with the president of the Central Bank.[321] And the Philippines' Ferdinand Marcos, no matter what else his authoritarian rule accomplished, will be most easily remembered for the excesses of his wife Imelda, whose palaces were found to contain over a thousand pairs of shoes, 888 handbags, 71 pairs

---

[18]"Thanks, mom!"

of sunglasses and 65 parasols, for starters. You've got your reputation and legacy to think about, and your significant other's closets shouldn't be a part of it.[226]

2.4   Enjoying the Privileged Life

Your people undoubtedly have found that your country is an extremely uncomfortable place to live. The roads are in tatters, the electricity cuts out daily, and the water is undrinkable. The streets run with sewage when it rains, the traffic is tied up in knots until mid-morning, and accomplishing even basic chores, like paying the phone bill, takes an eternity. Too bad for them!

You on the other hand should not have to suffer, and neither should your closest cadre of advisors and supporters, the sycophants who hang from your teat and from your every word. It's one of the perks. This mandate applies obviously to your day-to-day lifestyle in whatever flea bitten capital city you live in, but applies equally to your traveling lifestyle, and the way you are maintained overseas, from shopping trips in Milan and Nice to real estate on the best beaches around the world. As leader of the nation, you are expected to live a life of luxury, and who are you to argue with popular expectations?

Living Well at Home: Because your country spends close to nothing on the educational system, your schools are probably an abomination. Fortunately, you send your own children overseas to elite private schools. Because your police force is ill-trained, ill-equipped, and under-educated, crime and violence are likely a problem. Hire foreign, private bodyguards for your family, and pay them handsomely to make sure they're not tempted by your enemies. Because your electrical system is ancient, unreliable, and grossly inadequate to meet your nation's needs, ensure enormous diesel generators are available to power your palaces. Who cares if it takes money to live well in your country: you've got money.

Invest in Real Estate and Open Savings Accounts: If cash alone doesn't satisfy you, there is always land. Indonesia's Suharto is alleged to have embezzled between US$15B and US$35B dollars, making him the world's most corrupt political leader, according to Transparency International. But he also wound up with 3.6M hectares of real estate, 100,000 sq. meters of prime Jakarta office space, and nearly 40% of the land in Timor.[237] And the CIA estimates that Kim Jong Il, who also owns six villas in Europe, one in Russia, and one in China, has also absconded over US $4B, stored in Swiss bank accounts.[19][235]

---

[19]Despite chronic famine that is reported to have killed several million.

Cameroon's Paul Biya is also accused of running government finances like a personal petty cash fund, and stories abound of splashy casino nights in posh French resorts and suitcases containing millions of Swiss Francs. In 2011, Biya faced a French probe for illegally commandeering state funds and stashing them overseas. Likewise, Gabon's Ali Ben Bongo Ondimba and the Republic of Congo's Denis Sassou-Nguesso are under similar investigation. Sassou-Nguesso's spending habits are regularly criticized, and he has amassed a sizeable number of properties in France.[321] Russia's Vladimir Putin hasn't done badly for himself either: a Russian political analyst reported to German periodical *Die Welt* that Putin had amassed a fortune worth more than $40 billion during his tenure as president.[256]

Party Hearty: Living the good life doesn't have to translate into mansions, cars, and opulent possessions, either. You can enjoy lavish parties, and enjoy watching beautiful, desperate people do as you bid because you've paid them well. Chechnya's Ramzan Kadyrov celebrated his 35th birthday party the way anyone with a looming mid-life crisis and a thick wallet would: by inviting Hollywood's bold and beautiful to join him. Shakira, Eva Mendes, and Kevin Costner all declined, but Seal, Jean Claude Van Damme, Vanessa Mae, and Hilary Swank all attended[20] and Swank, despite an appeal from Human Rights Watch, took center stage for some flirting and face time. Well paid? Who are we to suggest it?[439] Nor do you need to rush for anyone or anything: you are expected to live the good, unhurried life. Nicaraguan president Arnoldo Alemán was in the midst of a lavish wedding – his own – in Miami, when Hurricane Mitch struck Nicaragua the last week of October, 1998. He eventually returned to Nicaragua to get to work, but not until the party was over. Georgia's Mikheil Saakashvili did much the same thing in 2012, leaving behind flood-stricken Georgia for a round of high-end shopping in Milan.[308]

Zaire's Mobutu Sese Seko is perhaps the undisputed king of living the good life, something his phenomenally wealthy nation permitted him to do with ease. He collected luxurious mansions around the world, traveled on extended vacations to the world's hot spots, and permitted himself extended shopping trips in destinations like Disneyworld and Paris, traveling with an entourage of relatives and courtiers on specially chartered Boeing 747s.[212]

Such a public display of extravagant consumption becomes more important if your regime is in jeopardy. In February 2011, despite crippling food shortages that put approximately 5 million North Koreans at risk of famine, North Korea staged an opulent festival to celebrate Kim Jong Il's 69th birthday. State media reported a 'solar halo' had been observed over Kim's mythical birthplace, Mount Paedku, and that 'pride and joy' had pervaded the nation.[208]

---

[20]Who knew those actors were so interested in Caucasus politics?

Take up Sailing: When in doubt about how to spend, buy a big boat. In 2011, Equatorial Guinea's Teodorin Obiang, son of president Teodoro, commissioned the world's second most expensive luxury yacht for his personal use.[21] At 387 feet and $387M, it boasts a cinema, restaurants, a swimming pool and a bar. Teodorin also owns a mansion in Malibu, California, a private jet, and a collection of expensive, fancy cars (including 7 Ferraris, five Bentleys, 4 Rolls Royce, 2 Lamborghinis, 2 Porches, 2 Maybachs, and an Aston Martin) valued at over $10M. He reportedly chooses his car to match his suit.[441] Not bad for a country where the average lifespan is 50 years and decreasing.[373]. Obiang's lifestyle is impressive: traveling on a diplomatic passport with bags of cash, he was a frequent visitor to Las Vegas, Miami, Bermuda, Paris, and Nice, staying regularly in hotels like the Four Seasons at $5000 per night. Who can blame him? It's important to be comfortable.[441]

Take Good Care of the Family: As leader of the nation, you may be in the game for the power and glory alone, not the money. Don't count on your family to follow suit. Saddam Hussein professed little interest in wealth, but his wife Sajida engaged in million-dollar shopping sprees in New York and London, while his son Uday favored expensive cars and custom-tailored suits (self-designed).[112] The wife of Indonesia's Suharto was lambasted as "Madame Ten Percent" on the basis of the commission she allegedly demanded from business deals.[237] If these examples describe your kin, make sure to remember their greed and avarice when it comes time to write your will.

2.5   Don't Take Any Flack

Finally, something that should be self-evident. You are unequaled; you are the supreme leader; you are the soul of the nation. You shouldn't have to listen to anything else, or frankly, anything you don't feel like hearing. In Belarus, it is illegal to "insult the personal dignity and honor of the President." In Russia, while it's not technically illegal, in practice, insulting the president will get you fired or maybe injured, as two executives at the Kommersant publishing group discovered after they published an unflattering picture of Vladimir Putin.[143] In 2011, Zimbabwean legislator Lilian Kirenyi learned the same is true in her nation, when she was arrested for having accused President Mugabe of homosexuality.[359] Perhaps she reconsidered her opinion while languishing in jail. The Central African Republic's Jean-Bedel Bokassa once killed one hundred school children when they had the temerity to complain about school uniforms made in his government fac-

---

[21]Curious? The largest yacht belongs to Russian tycoon Roman Abramovich.

tory,[22][489] as did, reportedly, school children in Khadaffi's Libya.

Project your strength and confidence by using your time before the camera to trash-talk just about anyone you'd like. Speeches are a great opportunity to take some pot shots at your enemies. Addressing the U.N. General Assembly after George W. Bush, Venezuela's Hugo Chávez once infamously said, "The devil came here yesterday ... It still smells like sulphur today." Just in case, he went on to inform the U.N. its system was worthless and its actions neither legitimate nor effective.[42] About a year later at the Iberio-American summit in Santiago, Chile, Chávez called Spanish Prime Minister José María Aznar a fascist, and interrupted him so many times that moderators eventually shut off Chávez' microphone. Exasperated, Spanish King Juan Carlos finally muttered to Chávez, "Why don't you just shut up?"[46] Chavistas in Venezuela responded with a T-shirt campaign proclaiming, "Shut Up Your Mother!" Not very mature, but typical of Chávez.

Interestingly, Paraguay's Alfredo Stroessner disliked and took offense at the word 'dictator.' Never mind his government is mentioned repeatedly throughout this book. And he frequently complained the international press overlooked his contributions to the nation of Paraguay. An official biography published in 1968 and distributed to foreign embassies offered a complete catalog of state visits, prizes, and elections won (including statistics). His heavy-handed style was just that, the cost of doing business, and hardly what he considered the mark of a dictator.

But as leader of the nation, the final word on any subject is yours alone. Use it then simply to ensure no one is laughing behind your back.

---

[22]The authors don't recommend this as a great example of how to be eccentric. Better would be ensuring each school uniform is emblazoned with your picture and party seal, and insist they wear a silly hat.

Chapter 3

Building and Managing Your Government

> For Hitler's originality lay in his realization that effective revolutions, in modern conditions, are carried out with, and not against, the power of the State: the correct order of events was first to secure access to that power and then begin his revolution.

Alan Bullock

3.1 Democracy or Something Else?

ZAIRE'S Mobutu Sese Seko once famously declared, "Democracy is not for Africa." [450] And of course, as long as he was president, that was exactly correct. Turns out, there's no reason to believe democracy is the logical endpoint of human social and political organization. It might even just be a passing fad! In the meantime, dictatorship is an evolving art, with principles that remain unchallenged since the Roman Empire (and probably before that). But beyond the classic Roman autocrats, the Emperors and Khans of the 15th – 19th centuries, and the totalitarians of the early 20th century, the means and mechanisms of modern-day autocracy are evolving, and so are its practitioners. Witness the nation of Iran, governed largely by a body of Shiite Muslim clerics, modern Russia, ruled by kleptocrats evoking Soviet nostalgia and right-wing nationalism, Venezuela, ruled by a modern Latin *caudillo* espousing a faux-socialist ideology, and Pakistan, teetering between military rule and radical, Muslim insurgency. Clearly, there is lots of political space for experimentation and nuance.[256] In fact, autocracy no longer implies a Nazi-like administration of absolutes. In an age where it's important to

espouse democratic principles, it's equally easy to ensure democratic institutions and principles are manipulated sufficiently to ensure you the same
control you'd have had otherwise: you are a wolf in sheep's clothing! In the
words of Osvaldo Hurtado, former president of Ecuador,[228]

> "In an age in which the democratic values have become uni-
> versal, the dictatorships of the 21st century are hidden under-
> neath constitutional garb, a pretense that gets the OAS [Orga-
> nization of American States] and its member states to turn the
> other cheek."

Obviously, this should get the rest of the international community to turn
its cheeks, too: it presents another target for you to slap! The point is this:
in an age when "democracy" is supposed to mean participatory elections,
balance of powers between executive and legislative, rule of law, and protection of basic freedoms, understand (and we know you do) that you can easily
have a "democracy" while doing away with everything but elections.[497]

3.1.1 The Case Against Democracy

The way the word 'democracy' is bandied about you may be tempted to
think the days of strong-handed *caudillos*, autocrats, and tyrants is behind
us. Economics, anecdotal evidence, and common sense says otherwise. Furthermore, who's to say democracy is the answer to your nation's ills? Nevertheless, you will endure endless entreaties to be more democratic and it's
good to have a ready defense for why democracy is not the magic pixie dust
most advocates seem to believe. In fact, democracy is full of weaknesses.
Enjoy mentioning them the next time a foreign nation's ambassador gets on
your nerves.

- Crime Demands a Strong Man: A 2001 poll conducted throughout
  Latin America revealed diminished support for democracy and increasing support for stronger leadership unfettered by the perceived
  shortcomings of democracy and dialogue. The reason is simple: the
  failure of democracies to produce viable, concrete results for the people over the 1990s. Increased crime, civil violence, the privatization
  of state resources (this latter part of the classic package of neo-liberal
  reforms that presage loan packages by international donors) have all
  been distasteful to Latinos, who increasingly reflect with nostalgia on
  the days of stronger-handed leadership.[159] In Guatemala, they went
  so far as to elect president a former top general, Otto Perez Molina,
  in hopes his military background would help curb the influence of
  drug gangs and similar scourges.[110] A similar, modern nostalgia for
  the "good old days" under Communism increasingly pervades the ex-
  Soviet states too (particularly the Ukraine, where in 2009 only 32% of
  those surveyed approved of the move to a multi-party system).[384]

Over 60% of Russians regret the breakup of the Soviet Union, and Vladimir Putin himself has called it "the greatest geopolitical catastrophe of the 20th century."[271]

- The People aren't Necessarily Fit to Govern: Direct democracy means elected officials can be removed before their term is complete; citizen referendums mean uninformed citizens can reject legislation that took years to create, and special initiatives lead to a mass of conflicting interests proposing one-off laws that benefit them alone. Often such initiatives have no budgetary backing; it's a mess in which the hens are ruling the henhouse. Strong leadership is necessary to guide the uneducated masses toward decisions that benefit the nation. Even America's founding fathers recognized the dangers of mob rule and the threat of minority factions seizing and overwhelming the democratic process.[179] And a 2012 study by researchers at Cornell University concluded that your average citizen isn't smart enough to make the choices a democracy requires in order to function: people lacking a skill are inherently unable to judge the competence of others in that skill; as a result, no amount of "information" will permit a voter to accurately assess a candidate's qualities. As such, democracies rarely or never elect the best leaders, serving instead "only to prevent lower-than-average candidates from becoming leaders." [491] Your people need you.

- Democracy Leads to Ethnic Violence and Anarchy: Democracy might empower the ethnic minority in your country while marginalizing the minority that keeps the economy running. Your firm hand might be required to protect them and stabilize the economy: remove your benevolent leadership and ethnic conflagration will tear your poor nation asunder.[141] Democracy in Sudan in the mid-1980s was an unmitigated anarchy which led to a military regime prone to violence and barbarism.[270]

- Democracies Aren't Nimble: Your nation requires leadership, not protracted negotiation, in order to address its difficulties. Democracy's requirements of transparency and consensus make it hard for a government to make fast decisions, particularly where matters of security are concerned. In countries with slipping security conditions, the people very often wish for strong, decisive government while democracies generally fail to provide one.[133]

- Democracy isn't Necessarily the First Step: Many economists and political scientists suspect that democracies grow organically once the economy is rolling and the society reaches a level of complexity and sophistication where the middle and upper classes then require greater services than an autocracy can necessarily provide. One doesn't simply start up a democracy in hopes it will be the secret sauce of prosperity, and until those underlying conditions are met, insisting on participatory government leads to more trouble, not less. The world is full of examples.[270]

This is instructive, and provides two obvious conclusions for you: First, a flagging economy under democratic leadership may instill a longing for a heavy-handed ruler like you, and permit easier acceptance of your results-based authoritarian style. So might increasing violence, ethnic strife, rising prices, or even simply crime. People look to their leaders to fix problems that get in the way with their enjoyment of life, and democracies are not necessarily the best equipped to solve problems. But the other shoe fits too: your administration must be capable of showing economic results, decreased civil crime, better market prices, and better perceived opportunity. Since life is going to be easier for you if you call yourself a democracy, you might as well do so. That gives you the freedom to go about governing as you please while maintaining the ruse. Here's how to go about it:

3.1.2 Redefining Democracy

First, get people to re-interpret what they expect from a democracy. There are nuances, as any strong-handed leader knows. Let it be known at home and abroad, that while your country is truly a democracy, it is democratic according to the parameters established by you. Increasingly, the heavy-handed governments of China, Venezuela, Russia, and other nations, are engaging in an overt re-education campaign to pervert the popular understanding of the word "democracy." This is clever and useful, for many of those clamoring for increased "democracy" have only the vaguest notion of what that means, or even what they want. Redefining the notion of democracy compromises their goals and provides you additional negotiation space.

For starters, insist on nuancing the discussion by calling it "Western" democracy, intimating it is not the same thing as "sovereign democracy," a meaningless term you can flesh out as you wish. "Sovereign Democracy" is defined by the Russian government as "the right of the people to make its own choice relying on its own traditions and the law." The Chinese Communist Party has similarly usurped the word "democracy;" President Hu Jintao used it over 60 times in 2009, in ways that make the concept of democracy more, not less, vague.[256] The government of Iran frequently discusses "genuine Islamic democracy," implying this is somehow distinct from democracy elsewhere. It is supposed to better protect the interests of the underclass (*mostazafan*), unlike the "bogus, bourgeois" democracy of the West, which is derided as the tool of the rich (*mostakbarin*, "the arrogant ones"). To this end, Iran has taken great advantage of the American war in Iraq to strengthen its disparaging of Western democracy, and taken near-pleasure at publicizing the effects of the 2010–2012 financial crisis.[256] Equatorial Guinea's Teodoro Obiang has done much the same. While reforming the constitution in 2011 (Obiang's 32nd year in power!), he exclaimed, "Here, we are developing a democracy in our way. Here, no one has to come to give us a lesson in democracy. Democracy as we understand it is not a product for importation."[6]

3.1.3 Other Government Models

Regardless of how you shape the term "democracy," there are alternatives you may consider.

God's Right Hand Man: Theocracy

Consider the following scenario: you've just assumed power as a military dictator of a weak nation-state that has experienced several waves of unrest followed each time by a coup. You are the most recent beneficiary of this pattern, but you know full well that continued unrest might encourage a pretender to strike a blow. How do you calm the unrest or at least lower the tension and strengthen the state enough so you can consolidate power and keep potential rivals occupied with non-threatening duties? Both of these are prerequisites for a long reign.

This was the exact scenario faced by General Zia ul-Haq in Pakistan in 1977. Immediately after his coup he had wanted to restore some kind of democratic state (he promised to hold elections within 90 days) but it quickly became apparent that Pakistan could only tenuously be considered a nation at all. In fact, tribal and ethnic tensions plus the presence of a large neighboring enemy (India) created the chaotic conditions that General Zia recognized could destabilize his rule. Because he in part came to power through aligning himself with Islamic zealots he saw that a deepening of this alliance – turning Pakistan into a military-run Islamic state, in effect – could be the glue that, however gingerly, could keep his rule in place. The deep Islamization of Pakistan began with Zia ul-Haq in the 1970s, and he expertly used youth to change the face of his country. Schools were encouraged to teach that Pakistan was an outpost of Islam in a sea of nefarious Hindus bent on the fatherland's destruction.[231] Schoolbooks were rewritten from an Islamist point of view; in fact, some researchers have noted that the madrassa phenomenon in Pakistan flourished under General Zia, and the religious schools reciprocated, sending the general radicalized youth to fill the ranks of his army.[389] After Zia's death, the idea of Pakistan as the vanguard of Islam did not melt away, but was rather buoyed by the army of youth that had passed through the state educational system. They were ripe for further radicalization during the Soviet invasion of Afghanistan, and arguably Zia's vision continued to form the guiding light of Pakistan to the present day.

Within a year of seizing power he was quoted as saying that he was on a mission to "purify and to cleanse Pakistan," declaring himself a firm believer in God, and stating that he would rule as long as Allah willed it. That year also saw the introduction of a general tone of Islamic piety in all government institutions. State employees were encouraged to have pious Islamic backgrounds, and increasingly Islamists were filling the ranks of the judiciary, military, and intelligence services. By 1979 this merging of Islam with the institutions of the state was more or less complete, as symbolized by the support Zia received from the radical group Jamaat-e-Islami during the trial and execution of former President Zulfikar Ali Bhutto. General Zia would go on to rule for 11 years, the longest tenure of any military ruler in Pakistan's history.[231]

The lesson here is to claim the mandate given by the Almighty to act through you, and use it to shape institutions and processes that facilitate your longevity in power.

Military Dictatorships

There was a time when it was getting hard to distinguish dictatorships from military dictatorships, as so many of Africa's and Latin America's leaders not only led with an autocratic style, but had either the full support of the military, a complicit military sharing the decision-making process, or had come to power through military channels. Military dictatorships were once the law of the land through much of Latin America in the 1970s, Africa sporadically from the 1960s onward, Asia, and even Europe. Don't think their day in the sun is over. Their advantages include the fact that the guys toting the heavy weaponry are implicitly on your side, and the fact that military decision-making processes are more about subordinates blindly following orders than questioning authority. If that appeals to you, applying this style to the nation at large is the way to go, and inviting the military to become the government is a straightforward way to make that happen. You may look to Paraguay, Chile, Nicaragua, Brazil, Nigeria, North Korea, Ghana, the Gambia, Egypt, and Mali for inspiration, as well as many, many more. Their disadvantages include the fact that in the 21st century they are somewhat out of vogue (but, like hem lengths, fashion changes and interest may again be on the rise). They are further weakened by the fact that – let's face it – some of your generals aren't the sharpest knives in the drawer. They're prone to easy bickering among themselves, and to developing rival factions you will be obliged to reconcile by force. Finally, should your generals decide to go against you, everyone in the room has a gun except you.

3.1.4 One Man Rule

But let's face it: this book isn't about choosing what type of government you might impose. You've already made that decision, so let's cut to the chase! There's no reason for an enormous government and all of its management challenges if you alone, or with a small cadre, can achieve your goals. You will avoid time wasted debating and can efficiently achieve whatever it is you want.

Kudos, then, to Zimbabwe's Robert Mugabe, who even after a power-sharing deal with Morgan Tsvangirai, remained Head of State, Head of the Cabinet, and Head of the Armed Forces. [53] And Romania's Nicolae Ceausescu was, by late in his career (1989), head of state, the head of the Communist Party, the head of the armed forces, chairman of the Supreme Council for Economic and Social Development, president of the National Council of Working People, and chairman of the Socialist Democracy and Unity Front.[236] Similarly, if you are simultaneously involved in, and the leader of, everything that matters you can be assured you will have your way. Nicaragua's General Anastasio Somoza Debayle was at one point the head of so many organizations that he was at once: General, Head of the National Guard, Supreme Commander of the Armed Forces, President of the National Emergency Committee, President of the Agricultural Committee, Delegate to the Central American Common Market, Leader of the National Liberal Party, Head of the Foreign Finance Committee, Grand Master of the Order of "Ruben Dario," Senator for Life, President of Lanica Airlines, President of Mamenic Shipping Line, Chairman of the National Cement Company, Chief Executive of "El Porvenir" Plantation, and Chief Executive of "Central de Ingenios" Refinery.[494] North Korea's venerable old leader, Kim Il Sung, "held every important post in the country, including General Secretary of the Central Committee of the Workers' Party of Korea, its one party, and president of the country."[422]

Zaire's Mobutu Sese Seko took it a step further, having his one-man rule actually enshrined in the Constitution. He was declared the "embodiment of the nation," and his decisions were exempted from the checks and balances that had been written into the document to otherwise curb the limits of presidential power.[212]

If this is the route you choose, look no further than the utility of imposing a lengthy term of martial law. And then do as you please. Ferdinand Marcos, frustrated with the frailty and inefficiency of democratic governance, finally declared martial law in 1972, and kept it in place until 1981. That done, the next steps were obvious and inevitable: appoint yourself Prime Minister under the new constitution, President under the old, and "Absolute Ruler" under both, suspend the Legislature and rule by decree, and beef up the military to defend your decisions. Finally, force into exile just about anyone who opposes you. And that's the way it worked for twenty years.[369]

3.2 Your Administration

3.2.1 Size and Relations With Your Administration

How big to keep your administration is a difficult question to answer, as each additional ministry or department you create leads inexorably to bureaucrats and demands for salaries, office space, equipment, vehicles, and the like, all of which is expensive and may require you going to the donors for help. Furthermore, the IMF, if it has helped you steady your economy in any way, will require you to keep the size of your government limited. That's a real shame, because hiring and expanding the size of the government – even if you're hiring people who won't do much – is a time-honored way of providing jobs (i.e. opportunities for patronage), influencing people, and expanding the size of the team who is directly dependent on you for support (you had better believe every one of your government employees will be campaigning for you, because if you lose they are history). Ideally, you want a tight-knit group of supporters, but you – like many others before you – will probably fall into the trap of keeping people around as "technical advisors" long after they've stopped being useful. That spreads the pork of cushy government jobs to people you need on your side, but will instantly cause your government to bloat. Make sure, at a minimum, they pay you back in loyalty, votes, and more. That way, if they sleep all day at the office, you've at least gotten what you need most from them.

Now that you've got a staff, put them to work. But keep them on their toes. If your greatest threats are internal, you will want to keep even your ministers and government staff guessing at all times, and furthermore you will want to keep them at arm's length. Why? They are potentially planning your ouster even as you talk, and will shamelessly get together to discuss how deeply to stick the knife in your back, the moment they think they can accomplish it.

No one knew this better than Saddam Hussein, who maintained multiple offices, and never told anyone from which he would be working. During meetings, if need arose, he would adjourn to a side room for a quick nap while the other attendees waited quietly and patiently at the table for him. He would often drop in, unannounced, on parts of his government to see what they were doing and how they were doing it. No wonder he was tired – he slept poorly even at night, given the constant threats to his life from the inside and from elsewhere.[112] Surprising his underlings was the best way to check up on who was plotting what. Saddam Hussein's administration tried to feed him a steady stream of doctored and falsified information, and his bureaucrats schemed at length to ensure he was peppered with good news about their performance, and that he saw only what they wanted him to see. Confronted with a fountain of excrement and seemingly endless good news, the dictator was forced to resort to subterfuge in order to gauge the truth.[112] You will face the same challenge, from sycophants eager to get on your good side, and from plotters busy detailing which alliances will be necessary to engineer your death.

The following anecdote is exemplary of how Hussein would arrange a meeting with a member of his military staff. Use it to inspire your security planning, if the threats from within are sufficient to warrant such precautions:

"Major Sabah Khalifa Khodada, a career officer in the Iraqi army, was summoned from his duties ... for an important meeting. It was nighttime. He drove to his command center ... where he and some other military officers were told to strip to their underwear. ... Each of the officers, in his underwear, was searched and passed through a metal detector. ... The clothing was then laundered, sterilized, and x-rayed. Each was instructed to wash his hands in a disinfecting permanganate solution. They ... were then transported in buses with blackened windows ... and then were searched again as they filed off. They had arrived at an official-looking building. Khodada did not know where. ... They were instructed not to talk, just to listen. When Saddam entered they were to rise and show him respect. They were not to approach or touch him. For all but his closest aides, the protocol for meeting with the dictator is simple. *He dictates.*"[112]

3.2.2 Getting What you Want

As the top man in your government, you should be able to get what you want, and you have all the means at your disposal necessary to ensure your government administration serves your purposes. Be inspired by Niger's president Mamadou Tandja, who needed a referendum that would permit him to run for office a (constitutionally-prohibited) third time. His constitutional court ruled three times that the referendum plan was illegal. This was clearly not the right answer, so President Tandja dismissed the entire court and appointed a new one, composed of three hand-picked nominees, three magistrates chosen by (his) minister of justice, and a university professor. He posed the same question to the new court, who ruled, not surprisingly, that a referendum would be just fine.[48] This is a fine example of making sure the presence of various "institutions of state power" don't get in the way of the only institution that matters: you.

Ecuador's Rafael Correa understood that lesson perfectly. Elected president on a platform of social and economic reform, Correa used that mandate to ensure his administration complied with his directives. Once, he called for a constituent assembly; when Congress questioned it he dismissed opposition lawmakers; and when a constitutional tribunal declared the dismissals illegal, he dismissed the tribunal's members.[228] Likewise, Nicaragua's Daniel Ortega used the same logic to extend the periods of 23 top judges and magistrates whose terms would have otherwise come to an end as prescribed in the Constitution, claiming the change was necessary to satisfy his constitutional obligation to provide stability to the country and prevent chaos. [410]

And Paraguay's Alfredo Stroessner took this a step further, ensuring his team consisted of compromised men on whom he could count fully. A former American ambassador recalled how the Paraguayan ambassador to Buenos Aires had gambled away the embassy's entire budget. Stroessner scooped him up and forced him to sign a confession, and then promoted him to foreign minister. "He could never have an independent thought or deed after that," the American ambassador recalled.[424] Spain's infamous dictator, Francisco Franco, personally hired and fired all cabinet ministers, the 50-odd provincial governors, the mayors of all large cities, all military commanders, all bishops, and the heads of the 24 major workers' unions.[466] And leave it to North Korea to take the strategy and run it to its inevitable conclusion: there, bureaucrats perceived to have "failed the regime," regardless of whether they were simply carrying out some other paper-pusher's orders, are routinely either executed or fall victim to inevitable traffic accidents.[1][419]

It doesn't always work. Peru's Alberto Fujimori is famous for two things: being the first Latino president of Asian heritage, and his "auto-coup" of 1992. Faced with an opposition congress, Fujimori in one fell swoop suspended the constitution, purged the judiciary, and closed congress. Executed

---

[1]Did someone say something about the importance of promoting efficiency in government?

in the name of overcoming bureaucratic hurdles to his pursuit of the Shining Path insurgency, it became obviously clear soon after it was nothing more than an attempt to seize dictatorial powers. And when his chief of security was implicated in a vote-buying scandal, the lid blew off his presidency, revealing networks of corruption, shady financial deals, trafficking of drugs and arms, and illegal enrichment. When Fujimori was unable to arrest his chief of security, it only made him look hapless. Fujimori fled to Japan, from where he faxed in his resignation in disgrace.[2][37]

The lesson is: make sure your administration serves you; that's what they're there for.

3.2.3 Rotation of your Staff

In the next chapter you'll learn the sixth fundamental rule of successful autocracy is keeping people on their toes. Any government predicated on the strength of its leader's personality and the premise of patronage will require constant shuffling. Rotate them around in different positions, pit them against each other, fire them and re-hire them in other roles. Place them in positions where they are unqualified and won't be able to produce results, then if you need a scapegoat to keep the NGOs or the political opposition happy, rail against that minister's astonishing incompetence, and sack him. Anyone who becomes a threat must be removed, and sometimes you will simply need to give somebody else a bite at the apple (i.e. a chance to command the political and economic benefits that come with participation in part of your government). But this implies a lot of staff turnover. Who cares? People are cheap and abundant.

There are too many examples to mention here, but they all look like this: Venezuela's Hugo Chávez's government from 1999 to 2008 had 6 vice-presidents, 6 foreign ministers, 9 interior ministers, 12 secretaries of the presidency, 7 finance ministers, 9 ministers of industry and commerce, 6 ministers of health, and 7 ministers of infrastructure.[256] Chávez' case is far from unique, and even Western European nations follow suit in a system where the only constant is the president, while everyone below him or her floats. In countries like this, ministers joke about arriving for work the first day with two speeches in hand: their acceptance and welcome speech, and their farewell speech ready for the following week. At first glance from the outside, the shuffling looks like a president demanding efficiency and results from his government. But look under the cover and it's something else. So start the roulette wheel spinning! Your goals are as follows:

- Keep people who do your bidding.

- Move on the people who get too comfortable, start building a constituency of their own, overshadow or threaten you, or who just do poor work.

---

[2]The Peruvian Congress rejected his resignation, firing him instead.

- Move people into position when you need to "throw them a bone." Then move them on when they've had a good-enough opportunity to gnaw the meat from it, and it's time to give someone else a chance to eat.

But it can work in the other direction, too. Hungary's Viktor Orban ensured the constitution he passed in 2011 permitted *longer* terms for his political appointees, to ensure his people would remain in place for longer and be harder to remove, even by successor governments.[286]

The idea here, obviously, is to use the duration of appointments to further your goals while frustrating everyone else's. It's not hard to do, if you simply pay careful attention to your team and what they are up to.

3.2.4 Ministries and Ministers

Keep the lines of authority straight: they should all lead to you. Your ministries should report to you, not to your Congress or National Assembly.[249] It's important to have not just the right number of ministers working under you, but for them to have the right composition, and for each individual minister to have the right qualities to serve you. Specifically, don't worry about the technical ability of your appointed ministers to do whatever task that ministry is responsible for. That's not usually their purpose, and the lower level technical people are responsible for getting the real work done anyway. Rather, choose ministers who can provide for you the following:

- **Votes:** Your ministers should be responsible for bringing to your administration the votes necessary to keep you in power; having you in power keeps them in power. They should be willing to lobby on your behalf among their ethnic group, their region, their church and social group, and so on.

- **Devotion and Loyalty:** Do not trust any minister who is not willing to stage a massive support rally in your name, personally leading the parade with a banner bearing your picture. Your ministers should devote themselves wholeheartedly to helping you search out and destroy your political enemies, availing themselves of all the tools their ministry makes available, their personal connections, and even their own money, if necessary.

- **Money:** Your ministers should be managing the industries and institutions they oversee to maximize the amount of money that gets directed to you and your supporters. Ineffective ministers are those who can't keep the pressure on those institutions, who are unable to creatively channel it, or who get tempted to turn the siphon to their *own* pockets, which is unacceptable.

- Peace: It's easier living when special interest- or ethnic groups leave you alone because one of *theirs* is (temporarily) in office. That might mean ensuring your cabinet is composed of one minister from each ethnic group or region. As a bonus, you can claim you are running an "inclusive" government; it's just that you alone decide who gets included – and for how long. If you can't manage to squeeze in every ethnicity, you may be forced to create additional ministries for the purpose of appeasing these groups and keeping things quiet.

- Acceptable Incompetence: There's nothing worse than a competent minister who eventually becomes well-liked or associated with progress and reform. Your ministers should, under no circumstance, upstage you. And that means they should be somewhat ineffective, unless their actions are directly attributable to you. Remember that any minister who is too successful, too able to produce concrete results, or complete projects the people want, becomes a political threat as his own success may contrast with yours. Be careful to ensure your ministers remain somewhat ineffective to prevent their eventual candidacy.

Your ministers should *not* be raising money to fund their own eventual campaigns, criticize you publicly or privately, question your decisions, show disloyalty in any form, or take more than you deem they should from whatever revenue stream they're managing. Failure to abide by the above tenets will require you to throw your minister to the wolves.[3] While you probably won't be able to resort to any of the techniques listed in section 5.4, you can allow due judicial process to actually run its course in this case, and let journalists, the police and the judicial system do what they do best (and when you allow them): try and convict the guilty. The result? A foreign-reported news article like the following:[398]

> "so-and-so indited over misuse of aid ... Minister so-and-so, who has always said he would defend himself against the charges [i.e., thought he would be protected from the system by his contacts and connections but was not] was in court but asked not to plead [i.e. recognized his ship had sunk] ... other people including senior staffs of the ... ministry have been arrested [which reveals they too were involved in a complicated, jointly-complicit project of fraud and corruption] have been arrested [i.e. you have been forced to throw several people to the wolves, to save donor funding] ... the charges include misuse of public property, embezzlement, fraud, collusion to commit fraud, favouritism amongst others ... [i.e. the same thing that goes on regularly, but under strict condition of your blessing and your personal benefit]."

---

[3] It's a figure of speech (probably)!

At the conclusion of such a scandal, two things have happened: the outside world is disappointed that a donor-financed project has been compromised by theft and deviation of funding. The government has reacted, identified the guilty parties via a serious investigation, and punished them accordingly. The inside world has realized that the judicial system works *when you want or need it to* and if they lose favor with you, they will be punished for doing what they, you, and all of your corrupt economic and political elite likely do on a regular basis anyway.

Note: as leader of the nation, you owe lots of favors and your family members are all chomping at the bit for their turn at the trough. It is however somewhat bad form to nominate family members to be part of your government. Not only is it too blatant, but you more than anyone know their incompetence. Furthermore, you are much better served by a non-relative eager to have your approval (and whom you can easily do away with, shame, jail, and so on – see section 5.4) than a family member you can not do those things to, and who will either try to build his/her own fiefdom, or simply be ineffective. No style points are due Malawi's Bingu Wa Mutharika for nominating his wife as Minister of the Interior, but there are lots of brothers and cousins on government payrolls out there and you can guarantee the day you seize power your own long, lost second cousin will show up on your doorstep looking for a job.[339]

3.2.5 Courts and Judiciary

Your judicial branch is essential, as much of your political shenanigans will entail clever (shall we say "judicious"?) interpretation of the rules. Nowhere more than in your courts and judiciary does the concept of one man rule hold true. If you control them, you control much of the government's ability to maneuver. As such, you should be empowered to appoint judges and magistrates yourself.[249] Indonesia's Suharto hand picked all judges. In Myanmar, the ruling military junta does too, and they proceed to adjudicate cases according to the junta's decrees.[248] The process is called 'court packing,' and it means ensuring the courts are packed with *your* people. If you can't pack it with your people, just do it yourself: In Cuba, the Council of State, presided over by president Raul Castro, serves as a *de facto* judiciary, and controls not just the judiciary but the court system as a whole.[248]

Your courts should be empowered to grant instant injunctions against anyone, when instructed to do so: this permits you to attack your political enemies with little warning.[362] Ensure your judiciary lacks the safeguards – legal and personal – for them to render independent decisions; they will be thus forced to look to you to know which decision to render, as they should.[364] Better yet, place all your judges under the oversight of a single person (belonging not just to your political party but to your inner circle, of course) who holds them accountable – not to the law, but to you.[325] If you have crusty old judges whose loyalty is suspect or who fail to fully implement your mandate, you can move them out by means of mandatory (i.e. mandated) retirement on the basis of their advanced age.[325] You may also have a Constitutional Court that judges decisions on the basis of their conformity with the constitution. Fair enough: but make sure it's staffed with your own party's people as well, as did Viktor Orban in Hungary.[286] You'll see the utility of this practice when we look at winning elections (chapter 12).

3.2.6 National Assembly

Your relations with your National Assembly or equivalent will require your most adept maneuvers. Ideally, it is a rubber stamp congress that simply validates your decisions "in the name" of the regions they represent; it is composed primarily of members of your party, on whom you can rely on to pass laws – even propose them – that favor your next move (like an extra-constitutional third term, for example). If your national assembly doesn't fall into lockstep behind you, you need to make sure some heads roll. Hugo Chávez, accustomed to a generally supportive relationship with his National Assembly, was forced to react in 2010 when a new Assembly was elected in which his political opposition had the majority: just before the new Assembly took power, he ensured laws were passed that permitted Chávez to rule by decree for 18 months, required the new Assembly to meet no more frequently than 4 days per month, put all parliamentary commissions under the control of the government (i.e., the executive), limited speeches to no more than 15 minutes per member, required all televised coverage to be transmitted by official government channels only, and curbed the risk of political defection by prohibiting members from changing parties once elected.[168] Consider that a very short leash.

Your constitution, if properly written, can entrench your party's power by reserving a guaranteed number of seats for your supporters, as does Myanmar's. [227] Nicaragua's *Pacto* guaranteed the two majority party leaders a seat in the National Assembly for life.[494] If it doesn't guarantee your representation, you can at least easily make sure that's the way it works out. In Equatorial Guinea, 99 of the 100 seats in the "House of People's Representatives" are held by President Obiang's ruling coalition.[248] One way to do this is to pass legislation that requires the government, i.e. *you*, to directly appoint some or most of its members. In Indonesia under Suharto, fully one third of Parliamentary members were appointed by the government, which just happened to be controlled by Golkar – Suharto's party – and thus by Suharto himself.[237]

3.2.7 Other

As long as you are hand picking your government and the leaders of important institutions, you may as well go all the way. Indonesia's Suharto hand-picked the governor of the central bank, the board of directors for all state-owned companies, and the chairman of the Security and Exchange Commission. That represents not just a long list of allies, but as well a long list of people who depend on you for their employment.[237]

3.2.8 Foreign Ministry and Embassies

Your own embassies can be effective points of control for your nation's expatriates. At a minimum, use them to keep an eye on and inform you about the activities of your overseas citizens. The administration of Rwanda's Paul Kagame made death threats to prominent Rwandan refugees living in the United Kingdom in 2011, forcing the British Metropolitan Police of London (after discovering credible evidence of the threats) to warn the immigrants their lives were at danger from the Rwandan government.[151] The Eritrean government likewise keeps close tabs on Eritreans living overseas through its foreign embassies.[392] But as long as you're at it, why not take the opportunity to collect a tax on them as well? Eritrea furthermore charges a 2% tax on overseas Eritreans and threatens and intimidates the families that don't pay.[392] Lastly, your foreign embassies can also be distribution points if you happen to be in the illicit trade business: North Korea under Kim Jong Il was once busted for smuggling heroin into the West on the bodies of its diplomats. But you are smarter than that, hopefully.[29]

3.2.9 The Civil Service

Upon taking power, purge the administration of the former administration's employees. It's unlikely your country has civil service code that requires the bureaucrats and administrative staff stay in place, and *you* certainly won't be developing such a code, because it's counter to your interests. Why clean out the government? Because the old employees probably weren't that productive, being composed of lots of lackeys the former government paid to buy support. Furthermore, those employees may still have bonds of loyalty to your predecessor, and you cannot be sure they won't undermine you, spy on you, sabotage your plans, or otherwise make a mockery of you. They are better off on the outside where they can starve, so if you eventually decide to re-hire any of them you can ensure their loyalty to you will be total.

This loyalty will indeed be valuable: government workers will absolutely vote for you, and can be pressured to ensure their friends and family will support you as well. Simply let it be known that job tenure is dependent on pro-government political participation (see section 6.1.4). State employees were an important support to Hugo Chávez when he called for a referendum to lift term limits. This Statism is an important part of any self-respecting autocracy, as it further entrenches the administration, who answers to you.[256]

Note that this is an important reason to maintain control of important national industries, as it provides you with broader opportunities to distribute political patronage through jobs: this is arguably the most effective form of patronage as the benefits – and thus the loyalty – are long lasting. Venezuela's Hugo Chávez was able to stuff supporters into the state-owned oil production company Petroleos de Venezuela, where despite flagging production and near-zero capital investment, employment swelled by 50% from 1999–2009.[256]

One last trick: it can be beneficial to make employment by the government mandatory, even if there isn't much work for them to do. Eritrea mandates an 18 month obligatory national service period, during which time employees are paid a pittance. But the real advantage to the government isn't the employment; it's subsequently mandating that any government employee "behave." Government employees in Eritrea can be jailed for questioning government policy, reading the bible, trying to flee the army, or calling for democracy, and other sweeping restrictions on political dissent and religion follow in the same vein.[392] But even if you don't mandate national government employment, at least mandate all members of your government join your political party. Indonesia's Suharto required all government employees to join the Golkar party and compelled them to vote for Golkar in elections, making the party all but unassailable.[237]

3.3 Governance and Legislation

3.3.1 Legal Framework

Starting with your nation's constitution and working down through even low-level, municipal legislation, your nation is organized by a legal framework that sets out the balance of power. Recognizing that balance is the first step in identifying how to redress it in your favor. The basics:

- Executive vs. Legislative: Does the constitution tilt the balance of power in your direction? Ideally, the Constitution should vest most of its power in you, the president, relegating the National Assembly to the role of rubber-stamper. It should allow your presidential decrees to have a greater weight than the nation's laws, as is the case in Belarus.[248]

- Term Limits: Ideally, you should have no limits on how long you may remain as president. If that's not the case, address it: see section 12.2.

- Libel Laws: Making libel an imprisonable offense frees your hand when dealing with journalists, as you can seriously crimp their style if they ever dare speak out.

- Media Oversight: If you have the ultimate say in what gets said, you win (see section 9.2).

- Financial Disclosure: Neither you nor your handpicked appointees should be required to disclose any personal financial information at any moment (personal wealth, sources of income, similar). Neither should government procedures facilitate an audit trail that discloses how money moves.[364]

But beyond those basics, your legal framework should provide you with a complex attack mechanism. Every civilized country, including yours, has a large body of laws that regulate affairs. But contrary to what foreigners might think, your legislation isn't designed to describe *what* you can and cannot do, but rather *who* can and cannot do it.

An example: your property laws state that no one can build a house whose edge is closer than one meter from the property line. But no one pays much attention to the rule, and it's rarely enforced. You now have lots of people who have broken the law and if pressed, will do what it takes to regularize their situation. You also have a new weapon to use against your political enemies, one that is much more subtle than more obvious means of persuasion. If a challenger to your throne arises, it's easy to have your ministries do an audit of your challenger's life, find the transgressions, and tie him up in endless legal battles that cost him a personal fortune, exhausting his funds, his patience, and his stamina to fight you. The entry points for such an attack are numerous: did he pay his taxes? declare his household staff and pay their salaries and benefits, including his contribution to their state-run social welfare account? Is his car inspected, insured, registered, and was it imported through legal channels that obliged him to pay your nation's 100% tax on luxury goods? Does he drive while wearing a seat belt? This is where it begins, and if you and your ministers are clever you can make this last as long as you need to.

This strategy works for other reasons as well. Because all laws become breakable if permission is granted and enforceable otherwise, the system of patronage that ultimately leads to you is immensely strengthened (see chapter 4). For fear of prosecution, everyone will inevitably seek the approval of their superior and eventually you. Because political connections will be essential they will also become expensive; as loyalty becomes a matter of prime importance, your role as ultimate and supreme ruler will become unshakeable.[4]

3.3.2   Introducing Legislation

Introducing questionable legislation to your administration for approval is somewhat of an art form. Specific tricks:

---

[4]It also tends to drive the economy to a standstill, since no one can get anything done without endless permissions and bribes, and your government personnel are all scared to make a decision since it may not be the one their superior agrees with.

- Give it a happy name: Your land grab along national borders is the "Border Security Act," the law which permits the restitution of a national military draft is the "Law of National Defense," and the law which gives you the ability to silence the media is the "National Security Law." [412] A favorite: Myanmar's "Roadmap to Democracy," in 2010, a program intended, rather, to achieve quite the opposite: the solidification of party power.[248]

- Introduce it at the last minute and under duress: Shorten the discussion by introducing your legislation at the last minute before a national holiday or political deadline.[412]

- Urge Efficient Review: stress the national urgency of the legislation, intimating the threat of foreign or internal enemies (see section 6.2).

3.3.3 Dodging Oversight

It's not hard to develop the framework of transparency, oversight, and popular reform, without reforming anything. For a worthwhile example, look no farther than the government of New York, where a bill introduced in 2011 to improve political transparency fell far short of the mark instead. The bill proposed a 14 member Joint Commission on Public Ethics to monitor elected officials, legislators, and lobbyists. As written, it would have rather protected those in office. The members of the Commission would be appointed by the governor in office and by the legislative leaders, split among the two parties. But any investigation would require consent from at least eight of the fourteen members, including two from the party of the accused. That loophole would give the legislative leaders the opportunity to ensure no investigation ever threatened their party members, and as such, the Commission was useless. Neither did the proposal deal with issues of campaign finance or the designation of voting districts by an independent committee in order to prevent gerrymandering. Ta-da! Ethics reform that accomplishes nothing. Take note.[190]

Similar tricks are easy to invent and spring upon an unwary government. Indonesia's Suharto once appointed a commission to investigate corruption in the government. Apparently misunderstanding what was expected from them, they diligently found quite a bit of it. Naturally, Suharto shut them down.[237] If your own commission is smarter, keep them poking their noses into the file cabinets and offices you choose, namely intrusive foreign NGOs, your political opposition, and anyone who dares threaten your power, including your own ministers, if they get out of line. Ensure your oversight institutions answer directly to, or receive their funding from, you, and if possible, see to it that their leaders are your personal appointees.

3.4 Alternative Mechanisms for Governing

3.4.1 Referendums

If you're headed down the populist trail anyway (hint: are you heading up a "Popular Revolution"? Do you make regular reference to your mandate from "the People"?) you can bypass an obstructive National Assembly or unsupportive political opposition by eschewing traditional government for direct governance through referendums. They are an easy way to get what you want and though they're cumbersome and slow, are far easier to manipulate to your advantage. The advantage of going straight to the people is that they are probably not that smart, are more easily convinced of your super powers, and more afraid of the consequences for them if you don't get what you want. They may not understand the question, are more easily bullied by your local supporters, youth wing, and hired thugs, or can be pushed into abstaining through classic intimidation if necessary. President Manuel Correa neutralized Ecuador's traditionally lethargic and closed political system by going straight to the people with such a referendum, focusing on solutions that would free his hand to make decisions directly without recourse to Ecuador's National Assembly. The referendum, when successfully passed, granted the president increased control over the media and the judiciary, authorized the appointment of an ad-hoc committee that appoints judges to the judicial system, and created a new administrative body that oversees the media.[228] Well done, and bonus points for striking all those blows with one fell swoop.

Follow Hungary's Viktor Orban, who employed a Referendum to smooth the passage of a new constitution in 2011 that radically consolidated the power of his political party. Says Robert Marquand, "Orban, with a supermajority in parliament, was preparing to rewrite the nation's governing document. Enclosed were 12 questions seeking citizen feedback. Should a constitution protect future generations and family values? One asked about life prison sentences, another about biodiversity. None dealt with basic questions about how power is ordered and checked in a modern democracy. In the end, it didn't matter. Two weeks after the mailing, a single-draft constitution emerged ... By April 19, without debate on any other draft, the parliament ratified a radical new charter, saying it would go into effect Jan. 1 as something demanded by the people." The two tricks to learn here are to mismatch the questions with the solution, and to identify the solution as something the people demanded.[325]

3.4.2 Local Structures

Go ahead and "decentralize government." At face value, the donors love it and you can make lofty promises of ensuring the people take greater control over decisions that affect them. Meanwhile, set up local civilian structures that will be dominated by your party, which will become local centers for information gathering, pork-distribution, and local political manipulation.

Nicaragua's Daniel Ortega took such an approach for the second time shortly after regaining power in Nicaragua in 2006. His "Revolutionary" government, ostensibly aiming to empower the disenfranchised, established *"consejos populares ciudadanos"* (citizen governing counsels) across the nation. At face value simple neighborhood committees that permit citizen participation in government, it is immediately obvious they serve an additional purpose. Controlled and organized under Ortega's Sandinista party, Nicaragua's own National Assembly had voted against them. No wonder: they permit Ortega to bypass the National Assembly entirely and distribute patronage through the CPCs directly to supporters – who are, by definition, party members. The CPCs further usurp the role of the national government by taking on government responsibilities and by being organized with a portfolio that mirrors the organization of government ministries. For bonus points, Ortega's wife runs the whole system.[5] They decide which stores will distribute subsidized foods, who will receive state loans, administer vaccinations and offer literacy classes. Their funding is totally opaque and their management is party-specific. [266]

If the CPC sounds familiar, it's because they are just a modern incarnation of Cuba's *Comites de Defensa de la Revolución* (Committees for the Defense of the Revolution), from where the idea probably sprang. Venezuela and Ecuador have implemented similar models, and Nicaragua under Ortega had similar *Comites de Defensa Sandinista* (Committees for the Defense of *Sandinismo*) in the 1980s. Cuba's were – and are today – the self-styled "Eyes and Ears" of the Revolution, i.e. the government, reporting on local dissident activity, and explaining at the local level the decisions of the government, even when they are distasteful.[421]

---

[5] To be fair, that complaint bolsters Ortega's explanation that it permits neighborhoods to have more control, as previous central governments had mostly forgotten "the people."

Chapter 4

Running the Nation

> When you have an efficient government, you
> have a dictatorship.

Harry S. Truman

UNLESS you've inherited your presidential palace from dad, you've probably had to fight your way to the top. But the hard work starts now: the
delicate dance of running the nation and consolidating power while keeping
your enemies off balance, your critics silent, and your people mostly happy
(or at least pacified). This is also the time to preserve or even enhance your
reputation, ensuring that some day you are revered as the nation's kindly father, benefactor of the people, a tireless and valiant leader without whom life
wouldn't be worth living and the nation would cease to exist. And if all goes
well, you'd like to remain in power for the length of your days, ceding it to
your son as you near death, as the nation is overcome with mourning. Finally, given the chance, it would be useful if your fortune and fame multiply
immensely, propelling your family into permanent prominence and authority. That's a challenge, to say the least: consolidating your power while
running even the most backward nation means walking a tightrope.[1] How
exactly to stay in power without falling off that tightrope is covered in detail below, so for important rules, pointers, and your daily task list, read on.
Once in power you must:

- Consolidate power, ensuring that your government consists of perfectly loyal toadies, your political party of hacks wholly obsequious
  to you who fawn over your every proposition, and the populace at
  large convinced either they want you or dare not consider the idea of
  anyone other than you (see section 3.2),

---

[1] Fortunately, you have just the skills required (not to mention this book).

- Reward the loyalty of both those who helped propel you into power and those who help sustain you there. From trinkets to cars to perks to plumb jobs, you must consistently spread good will to those who may otherwise conspire against you, as it is hard to stamp out your remaining enemies if your inner circle is not trustworthy (4.1.4).

- Run the nation in a way that maximizes economic inputs and outputs, whether that means investing in industry (see section 4.4) or kissing up to the international donors (see section 10), to ensure your people see immediate benefit of your leadership.

- Ensure that said revenue also accrues to your government and consequently to you and your family, financing your opulent lifestyle and political campaign needs, while greasing the wheels of government/politics by providing you with the means to distribute benefits to those who support you and deny them to those who don't (see section 4.5),

- Divide, delay, deflate, or destroy your political enemies, ensuring they remain incapable of organizing against you and rallying sufficient support to their cause, or so excluded from politics and civil society that they pose no threat (see section 6),

- Silence your critics, or at least neutralize their criticism and reduce their ability to project their voices (see section 9),

- Quell any riots, uprisings, or disturbances before they gather steam and lead to your ouster, but not at the expense of tarnishing your reputation[2] (see section 8). Otherwise, infiltrate your opponents' and critics' networks to learn who's involved and what trouble they are capable of causing you (see section 8.4),

- Maintain warm relations with the international community to encourage their investment in your projects. The projects will bolster your image as cooperative and concerned benefactor to your people, while making available funding sources that if used cleverly will further line your pockets (see section 10), and

- All this while carefully maintaining yourself at the exact nexus of all economic, political, and social activity, ensuring nothing happens without your express approval and probably under conditions that strengthen you politically, financially, or both.

---

[2] Well, not at first, anyway. It's interesting how soon after taking power most autocrats stop caring about how negative events reflect on them, and simply do whatever they please. Wouldn't you say, Mr. Bashar al Assad (Syria)?

4.1 Basic Tenets of Leadership

4.1.1 Think Long Term

If you manage these inter-related and conflicting tasks, you will be around for a long, long time, like the recently-departed Mohammar Qaddafi, who was somewhat of a master of these skills until his death in 2011. Qaddafi came to power in 1969 via a coup d'etat and remained there until 2011; he would probably still be there today were it not for NATO's support of an "Arab Spring" rebellion he was otherwise poised to crush. But even his rule pales beside that of Cuba's Fidel Castro, who overthrew predecessor Fulgencio Batista's dictatorship in 1959 and has been there ever since, like fungus.[147] These two gentlemen get points for longevity, but many others are not far behind (see table 4.1).

Omar Bongo was president of Gabon for 42 years: a generation! From 1967 when he took power, he kept his enemies at bay for four decades, succumbing only to death in 2009 for health reasons. Had he eaten more vegetables he'd probably still be the president (instead, it's his son, Ali Bongo Ondimba).[47] Other African states have their strong men too. In 2011, on the 32nd anniversary of his usurpation of power, Equatorial Guinea's Teodoro Obiang Nguema declared, "The day you are tired of me, I will retire." Those are nice words, and perhaps refreshing after his uninterrupted 32 years in power, but if they ring false it's because the Equatorial Guineans have lived for decades in a brutal police state where no one would dare raise his voice to suggest any such thing (see section 5 for more on imposing such a state).

4.1.2 Rule 1: Nothing Happens Without You

Start with the basics: be omnipresent. Maybe not physically, but financially and politically. If there's a deal, you're part of it, if there's profit to be made, it goes to your companies, if there's a political arrangement, it happens between your party and another, not between two other parties that exclude you. Construction projects happen because you desire them and ensure your government follows through, roundtables are held only because you host them, and contracts get signed because your family, your inner circle, your political cronies, and your political supporters at large will benefit. If you're not part of something, it doesn't exist, and never will. If you don't benefit from it politically, economically, or both, it won't happen at all.

Fortunately, you are well equipped to be at the nexus of the universe. Your party is the only one whose presence is obligatory. Your government is the responsible party in negotiations with foreign donors or capital funds that will finance your new airport, and that puts your team – including your family in a privileged position to know the value and extent of the work, which properties will increase in value as a result, and who will participate

Leader	Nation	In Power
Fidel Castro	Cuba	1959 – 2008 (49y)
Kim Il Sung	North Korea	1945 – 1994 (49y)
Mohammar Qaddafi	Libya	1969 – 2011 (44y)
Omar Bongo	Gabon	1967 – 2009 (42y)
Eyadéma Gnassingbe	Togo	1967 – 2005 (38y)
Alfredo Stroessner	Paraguay	1954 – 1989 (35y)
Teodoro Obiang N.	Equatorial Guinea	1979 – present (33+y)
Jose E. dos Santos	Angola	1979 – present (33+y)
Suharto	Indonesia	1967 – 1998 (31y)
Mobutu	Zaire	1965 – 1996 (31y)
Rafael Trujillo	Dominican Rep.	1930 – 1961 (31y)
Robert Mugabe	Zimbabwe	1981 – present (31+y)
Hosni Mubarak	Egypt	1981 – 2011 (30y)
Paul Biya	Cameroon	1982 – present (30+y)
Yoweri Museveni	Uganda	1986 – present (26+y)
King Mswati III	Swaziland	1986 – present (26+y)
Blaise Compaore	Burkina Faso	1987 – present (25+y)
Zine Ben Ali	Tunisia	1987 – 2011 (25+y)
Islam Karimov	Uzbekistan	1989 – present (23+y)
Kim Jong Il	North Korea	1994 – 2011 (17y)

Table 4.1: Longest Serving Leaders

in the evaluation panel that decides which firm gets the contract. You are uniquely suited to channel resources, make decisions, stop or start projects, and spend the government's money. How could it possibly be any different?

4.1.3   Rule 2: The Principle of Double Purpose

Now that you are at the center of the economic and political universe, absolutely everything you do should serve at least two purposes. Your goals should be to act in ways that a) benefit you personally by either weakening your opposition, consolidating your power, or enriching your party or family, while at the same time b) furthering at least the illusion that your nation is growing, advancing, or developing along a path to greatness. If your government breaks ground for a shopping center, your family's cement factory should get the contract for the cement and an entrepreneur who is also a political supporter should get the right to run it. If your government negotiates with a donor to implement a "Government Decentralization" program, it should enable you to place your supporters at the local level and ensure your next victory. If your government starts to build a highway, it should run straight through your political opposition's territory, fragmenting them geographically, or next to your own farms, increasing their value and crushing their economic competition. If your country takes on reform of the customs system, it should not only attract donor financing but provide a new source of revenue for your political party, and ideally, be led by a technical consultant from your own ethnicity. The principle of Double Purpose thus allows you to have your cake and eat it, an exceedingly rare thing.

4.1.4 Rule 3: A Chicken in the Pots You Choose

Never forget this: your people need to eat. If they are so badly off that they can't put food on the table, they will begin to look for alternatives to you. But if you can provide them a minimal standard of living, they will probably settle for that. And if you can provide them that, as well as the opportunity – real or perceived – for a bit more, they will likely spend their energy striving for the next level, and leave you alone. In fact, as dictator, you can easily afford to stifle political expression and opposition, but you can't afford to stifle economic activity. If your people begin to suffer too greatly it will lead to determined organization against you. So make your offer to the people an either-or offer: you will provide basic economic growth, provide the conditions for some to find jobs and put food on the table. But the benefits accrue only in exchange for a tacit understanding that the system will only distribute benefits under your watch and in your presence. Let them work, earn, and save what they can, but strike them down mercilessly if they organize politically against you (or even simply *without* you). Once your people learn the limits of your patience, they will mostly likely content themselves with their working class wages and jobs that barely cover their expenses and put food on the table. And they'll be too busy working to riot, and may just concede, "It's not a lot but it's better than nothing." Bingo – you will be left alone for the long term.

This rule is the basis for most regimes in the Middle East, although the Chinese have applied it successfully as well: prohibit popular participation in politics in any public forum, including participation in civil society. Clamp down on activism in all forms. Then take control of the economy by whatever means necessary, from direct investment, expropriation, or simply getting involved in – and assuming control of – key industries. Once the revenue starts to flow through you, you will be well placed to let some of the scraps trickle down as you see fit.

Likewise, meticulously-selected political reforms can go a long way to keeping you in power. These actions are substantial propaganda coups as well, as they permit you to more easily refute accusations of autocracy. Follow the lead of Morocco's King Mohammed: Upon taking the throne in 1999, he moved quickly to undo some of the egregious human rights abuses perpetrated by his father, King Hassan. His first official speech as head of state described the king's plans for economic liberalism, constitutional monarchy, regionalism, decentralization, and a political field that permitted multiple parties. He permitted the repatriation of a Marxist political exile, liberated the imprisoned leader of a banned Islamic group, and established an Equity and Reconciliation Commission to investigate disappearances and torture under his father. And he institutionalized the presence of women in government. But these things said, Mohammed kept journalists on a tight leash, cracked down hard on demonstrators hoping to legalize a banned Islamic party, and did little to improve levels of literacy and poverty; furthermore, his record on dealing with issues of corruption has been irregular.[288] Does this make King Mohammed a dictator? No, it makes him a savvy politician who understands you can give up some things in order to preserve others. Here we see the success of the king's strategy: permit some freedoms, and work against others, while flaunting your credentials as a modernizer and liberator. You would be wise to follow suit.

4.1.5   Rule 4: The Iron Fist in the Velvet Glove

As an overt political ideal, totalitarianism is, for the moment at least, out of fashion; dictatorships *per se* are distasteful. But it is possible to run a nominal "democracy" while enjoying most, if not all, of the benefits of an autocracy. The trick is simply to be nuanced, exerting a careful but calculating grip on the issues that matter.

It's no longer to control the minutiae of your people's daily life. Rather, offer limited economic and political freedoms, as well as increased but controlled or filtered access to information (including international information, if you're careful). Modern Russians and Chinese enjoy freedoms and luxuries like international vacations, Internet access, and consumer goods of all types, that would have stunned their compatriots from a generation ago – but the price for this economic florescence has been the entrenchment in power of folks like the Chinese Communist Party, or Russia's Vladimir Putin.

Modern autocracies instead tend to achieve political control through a combination of influence over ruling elites, control of the military, and strong influence or overt control over economic actors. Any group willing to recognize that power and avoid antagonizing or threatening the ruling coalition should be permitted to operate in peace. If you can manage it, the degree to which people can exercise and enjoy freedoms such as travel or access to financial resources should depend not on the rule of law but rather on their personal relationship with you or other members of the ruling elite.[256]

That said, from time to time the velvet glove will have to come off so the iron fist can do some smashing. See chapter 5 on the stick that accompanies the carrot, and chapter 8 for more on what to do when push comes eventually to shove.

4.1.6   Rule 5: Bread and Circuses

The more disengaged (that is, "entertained") you can keep your citizenry, the less likely it is that you will need to crack down or deal with unrest. One of

Old School	Cool Running
Build a wall around the nation to prevent escape.	Make travel documents difficult and expensive to obtain.
Prohibit use of private automobiles.	Make auto ownership a privilege available only to your party members.
Cut off all access to Internet.	Allow limited Internet access, but use it for espionage.
Mandatory communal labor camps	Private employment in factories owned by you.

Table 4.2: Nuanced Control

the more famous examples is the idea of "bread and circuses" current under the Roman Empire. A same-day satirist pointed out that this had the effect of keeping a formerly engaged, civically responsible class of Roman citizens distracted by free food and gory entertainment – leaving the rulers in peace to do as they wished.[268]

You no longer need bear pits and gladiator races to woo the crowds in the age of television and the Internet. Focus on controlling the content, but throw your full support behind a bevy of fun and vapid programs, reality TV shows, chat programs, movie downloads, and easy access to entertainment. That may lead to rampant piracy of copyrighted materials: who cares? Those guys are wealthy already. You will be surprised how quickly your people will quiet down and stop grousing about politics if they're home pirating Hollywood's latest and surfing the latest gossip sites. Focus simply on ensuring these channels don't foster political organization. Ensure access to all that low cost entertainment comes at the expense of refraining from engaging political debate using those channels, and the debate will be on your terms. This means drowning out opposing viewpoints with content that mirrors your own philosophy or programming that entertains/distracts/deflects.[106] This is an insight that Italy's Silvio Berlusconi understood well, but he's in good company among many, many leaders who are increasingly realizing they can not only control public debate in the media but simultaneously use TV and the Internet to keep everyone home, parked in their cushy, well-worn sofas.

4.1.7 Rule 6: Keep Everyone On Their Toes

Keep your team productive, but not so productive they become a threat. Don't let anyone – particularly your ministers or heads of key industries – stay long enough to build a political coalition that might eventually pose a threat. Move people around at your whim, either to please cranky donors who want "change," punish would-be pretenders to your throne, or keep your underlings working hard by making them fear failure in their new position.

Shuffle friends into the lucrative jobs, then remove them when they displease you or when, in your opinion, they've had their fill at the trough. Above all, use uncertainty to remind everyone, everywhere, that you are the supreme, unreproachable leader. You'll see this in the chapters on running your administration (chapter 3), your political party (chapter 6) and your educational system (section 6.4.4). It should be your mantra.

4.1.8   Rule 7: Look Over your Shoulder

No one knows better than you what's at stake, or how easy betrayal comes to ambitious underlings. Sadly, this is another area where the fawning public generally underestimates the difficulty and the loneliness of being the nation's leader. You must be suspicious of everyone, everywhere, all the time. Your ministers may be plotting against you, your chief of staff conspiring with the donors to release torture photos that will smear your name. Even your family is suspect, and you've probably got a brother somewhere who wouldn't mind sitting in your throne. The military should be your greatest asset but is instead a constant threat, and it's headed by arrogant generals who need a paddling from time to time to prevent them from thinking you work for them, instead of the reverse (see section 7 for more on how to manage the military).

A coup probably propelled you into power (section 1.8), so ensure your own would-be successor isn't developing a similar strategy. Watch out for capable, ambitious generals, your closest political allies, ministers, and highest ranking government servants. All of them are close enough to you to know your weaknesses, and are studying your every move. Needless to say, you should equally watch out for the remaining members of your family, and in particular any half-siblings. Togo's Faure Gnassingbe has had to keep his half-brothers under close scrutiny for decades, and for good reason: they are a coup waiting to happen. Nor do they wait: in April 2009, a general in the Togolese military tried to launch a coup d'etat against Faure; he was supported by Faure's half brother and then Minister of Defense Kpatcha Gnassingbe, and Colonel Rock Gnassingbe, another half-brother.[5] The lesson here is clear.

4.2   The Inevitable Interlocutor

Autocrats since time eternal have found the secret to staying in power is the art of remaining in the center of things, and being, in a way, all things to all people. King Hassan II of Morocco played this role expertly, becoming an intermediary between the Middle East and the West with regard to diplomacy and peacekeeping, but also managing expertly the complex dynamics of Morocco's internal, social context. He satisfied the Moroccan elite with royal patronage and limited market reforms that led to a comfortable middle class, pleased the Islamic faithful with grandiose plans that glorified Islam, and deeply understood the "tribal mentality of Morocco and the importance of the throne as a unifying force."[225] He alternated cleverly between reforms that would please the workers and reforms that would please the elite, thus ensuring he was popular with both. And when Saddam Hussein invaded Kuwait, he sent Moroccan troops to Saudi Arabia to support the West, while expressing sympathy for the plight of Iraqis suffering under U.N. sanctions.[225] But he also used ruthless divide-and-rule tactics that enfeebled the country's political class while ensuring the monarch remained at the center of society.[160] All in all, the picture of cleverness.[225]

Russia's Vladimir Putin chose a slightly more divisive strategy, an inevitable choice, perhaps, given the Kremlin's clannish politics and high-stakes oligarchal economy. Nikolai Petrov of the Moscow Carnegie Center proposes that Putin has imposed a system of managed conflict, in which different clans within the ruling elite compete for resources, attention, and power, leaving Putin free to play the role of arbiter who keeps them in balance. Because he can neutralize any of them, removing them from power and arresting their ability to enrich themselves, the system does not turn unless he is present – just as it should be.[486]

4.3 The Dict-o-Meter

What kind of dictator are you today? It's a specific question because, though it would be fun to pick one personality early in your career and stay with it, that's not the way it usually plays out. Rather, you will find yourself sliding from one end of the spectrum to the other as the years pass, and different circumstances will warrant different responses from you, causing further variation in your 'personality.'

At one end of the spectrum, you are superhuman, even divine. The people dread the day you are called to claim your throne in the Afterworld, because the sun may stop shining and human civilization may come to an end. If you are really lucky you will be extolled by posterity as well as by your immediate followers, as was the case for both Alexander the Great and Augustus Caesar.

Even if your aura isn't superhuman, perhaps you are viewed as the savior/father of your nation. Your people fawn over and worship your every utterance.[3] North Korea's Kim Il Sung falls into this category. His son Kim Jong Il (though he and his followers worked nobly to achieve the same recognition) has probably been too cantankerous and easily-mocked to be viewed in a similar fashion.[4] In that case, better then to shoot for 'wily heir and despot,' someone mortal but important to the nation, though not as indis-

---

[3]The international community is probably not so impressed by you, but who cares what they think?

[4]Let's see if history is kind to him after his death in 2011.

pensable to national culture as the father. But when you die, even nature will mourn for you in the form of supernatural events reported by government media.[65]

Towards the middle of the spectrum you are the clever, master politician, neither revered nor despised but firmly at the center of the universe, delegating power, firing ministers, arranging deals, taking a cut, inaugurating projects and posing for a photo op with the poor. Bereft of adulation and whispers of immortality, this persona may sound somewhat prosaic, but it's actually a somewhat enviable position to be in, as it permits your cunning and ruthlessness to continue unabated as part of the nation's daily rhythm, and permits you to earn a lot of money.

As you approach the other end of the spectrum you are in a position where you command much or all of the power, but now lack some or much of the popular support. The people oppose you either subtly or overtly, and as the situation worsens they begin to organize against you. You are now forced to use the means at your disposal – the security forces and military (see chapter 7) to quell the disturbances, remind the people not just of your authority but of your *inevitability*, and maintain civil order. As the violence against your administration increases, so do the means you employ, and you head eventually to the final notch on the spectrum.

At that end, you are seen as – and probably are – a ruthless, bloodthirsty tyrant, a thug who doesn't hesitate to draw the blood of his own people, sacrifice families for the sake of maintaining power, destroy human lives via indefinite prison sentences in hellish, undeclared warehouse dungeons, and torture enemies and traitors using techniques that would raise the eyebrows of someone from the Middle Ages. You may still have the power at this point, but your grasp is failing, and as you delve deeper into barbarity the one thing that will outlast you – your legacy – is slipping through your fingers (see chapter 13).

4.4   Prosperity and Growth

4.4.1   A Strong Economy

Successful economic development is a challenge even for legitimate rulers, but if you don't master this concept and provide some sort of economic benefits for the masses they will eventually rise up and remove you. But we are not advocating a free market, by any means. Too much economic development will destabilize your regime: a growing economy will provide jobs and opportunities through channels other than yours; a wealthier populace will grow better educated (abroad, probably) and push for reforms of the types they see overseas or read about. Ideally, you should provide just enough economic progress to garner political support and establish the basis for your legacy, but not enough that it will weaken the political bonds of patronage that make you an indispensable element of your nation's economy and your people's world.

It is essential that in some ways you provide employment and limited prosperity for your people. The old adage, "no king is more than two missed meals away from a revolution" is absolutely true. Hosni Mubarak's case in 2011 should prove a warning, as his failure to share the spoils of Egypt's decent economic growth led to unrest. The principal reasons for the dissatisfaction? Unemployed youth (85–90% of the unemployed are younger than 30), and rampant poverty (40% of Egyptians live on less than $2 per day). Add inflated food prices and reduced food subsidies for basic products, and you are on shaky ground.[5][317] A University of Adelaide study of civil conflict in 120 countries over 40 years found that in low-income countries, increases in food prices lead to a significant deterioration of democratic institutions and a significant increase in anti-government demonstrations. The same is not true of wealthier countries."[21]

4.4.2 Government Works

Chapter 11 discusses other concepts of financial fitness, mechanisms for personal enrichment, and ways to rig a national economy to your benefit, but the benefits begin to accumulate long before they hit your bank account. A healthy economy can help spark some economic development and more importantly, emerge as a vehicle for spreading pork and strengthening your political hand. But as far as the public knows, your decisions are for the sole, benevolent purpose of "improving the lives of the people." That means your government should be heavily invested in building, moving, shaping, changing, and lifting, all of which makes the money flow in the name of

---

[5]Right, Mr. Mubarak?

something no one can dispute. Your government should be building roads, bridges, schools, clinics, hospitals, airports, marine ports, and industrial infrastructure. Keep in mind, bold, capital-intensive and invasive construction projects permit you to:

1. *Get the money flowing.* Once the purse strings are loosened, you can get some of that money for yourself, or to spend on your supporters. Governments that don't spend money are of no use to anybody.

2. *Distribute wealth to your supporters.* Make sure those contracts go to your friends, advocates, and supporters, while your adversaries and their businesses are left to wither on the vine. In Spain, Francisco Franco's victory in the Civil War allowed him to do just that, and reinforced the idea of a two-tiered society in which his supporters were enriched and his enemies impoverished. The Spanish left, including the working class (the vanguard of opposition against Franco) became a second-class citizenry. Blue collar sections of Spanish cities were denied official support and allowed to degenerate into slums prone to state-sanctioned violence and hunger, while Franco's supporters lived a pampered life.[246] The impact of this on Spanish society? Thousands of executions, starvation, and a high suicide rate – but Franco remained in power until the mid-1970s, and that is the metric you should be looking at.

3. *Keep your people employed.* If possible, you should provide jobs wherever and however possible, even if that makes your projects more expensive and unwieldy. It's worth it if it permits you to put some money in the pockets of the little people: uprisings and manifestations are frequently manned by the bored and unemployed who have little better to do. If an angry young man perceives that leaving work to go participate in a rally would mean the end of his employment, he will not go. As such, prioritize local employment over every other consideration. If you're building a road, make sure a different local company gets a contract for each kilometer: who cares if that means a hundred different contracts and a road 15 times more expensive than planned? It puts people to work, distributes some benefits, and you get the road as a bonus.[6]

4. *Draw attention to your leadership.* Every project should have large signs on all sides that make explicit whose idea it was, and to whom credit should be given. Lots of public works projects can be named after you (see section 4.4), but even if the highway/school/airport doesn't bear your name, there should be no doubt in anyone's mind who made it happen. Don't hesitate to use annoyance as a tool to achieve this

[6]And the super-bonus is getting the development community to finance it for you. You win three times!

goal: roads can and should lead to deviations, re-routing, and road blocks. Ensure vast, invasive construction projects are manned during daylight hours so no one misses the site of the swarming construction crews building your dream. As your people sit in their cars in horrendous stop-and-go traffic, they can't help but be aware of your project, rather than driving blindly past it. Nicaragua's Arnoldo Alemán took it one step further, by placing signs reading "Please excuse the disturbance, but we are replacing bad quality roads built by the previous administration."

5. *All of the above.* It's not unusual to combine your cult of personality, affectionate allegiance to the people of your home region, and the resources of the state. Zaire's Mobutu Sese Seko converted his previously sleepy, ancestral forest village of Gbadolite into a multi-million dollar public works project that saw to the construction of three white marble palaces, a high rise luxury hotel and conference center, numerous broad boulevards, and an international airport. The town's population, responding to the availability of employment, exploded in population, going from about 2,000 to 30,000 inhabitants in twenty years. The upside of this strategy is the numerous opportunities it provides you to distribute favors, sign contracts, and benefit "your" people. The downside however is the aftermath, should you depart. Upon Mobutu's ouster in 1997, Gbadolite returned almost immediately to its earlier state of "dreamy irrelevance," as the palaces crumbled into dust and the roads rutted in the tropical rains.[467]

4.4.3 Dealing with Downturns

Finally, given the importance of putting chickens in people's pots, you had better scramble if your economy starts to run out of steam. You might consider economic reform, loosening the reins on requirements for businesses held by anyone other than your friends, or letting international foreign companies run key industries. But you probably won't. So take the easy route, instead: To the extent possible, blame your former colonial master, or international institutions like the World Bank and International Monetary Fund (IMF) for your troubles. These two find themselves frequently the target of abuse. They're not just accustomed to it; they are expecting it! Don't disapoint them, then, and do your best to convince your people their every economic worry is the result of onerous requirements imposed on poor, loveable you, by cruel, international bureaucratic organizations.[273] See section 10.2.3 for more on this rich subject.

4.5   Clientelism

One of your main responsibilities as dictator will be to decide who will prosper and who will not. You choose who gets the lucrative but shortlived career as customs inspector, judge, or tax official, and who gets the lengthy prison sentence. This naturally forms the linchpin of a client-patron relationship. When clientelism becomes the cornerstone of national development, all actions – economic, military, possibly religious – have to go through you or your chosen delegates. Entrench this system by removing or discouraging any meritocratic organizations that would make your absence possible; instead, replace them with a system of personal networks that eventually lead to you.

Take this example from Russia, at the moment when Dmitry Medvedev announced his withdrawal from the presidency and Vladimir Putin's return to the same. The Economist noted: "The applause from bureaucrats whose only concern is to stay close to the rent-distributing centre grew louder when Mr Putin and Mr Medvedev told them ..."[181] It doesn't matter what the two speakers went on to say; it only matters that agreeing vigorously with them was essential for all those unimportant and easily-discarded politicians, government functionaries, and petty bureaucrats interested in keeping their jobs and making money. In your nation, *who* you know is the only thing that's important.

All power networks should eventually connect to you, and your distributive coalition (all structures or parties capable of providing wealth and wellbeing) should be closely associated with you. All of your economic work, your development programs, your construction projects, and things you inaugurate should be relentless identifiable as your doing. Take that opportunity to portray your actions as paternalistic or just benevolent, but make sure everyone knows whose hand is on the ladle, dishing it out. Here are the advantages to you and your clients:

- *Economic Protection* The government has the ability to protect key industries from a sometimes chaotic marketplace (The fact that you and your friends own those key industries is inconsequential). Governments who do so frequently need to set higher exchange rates for higher currency to maintain the competitiveness of those firms, making the possession of foreign currency a premium, since there's not enough to go around. Those who possess that currency are suddenly in a much stronger position to reward political followers and supporters, increase wealth, and build a political network.[30]. Your industrial magnates understand this perfectly and should need little reminding; their first move in supporting your beneficial stewardship of their livelihood should be a quick trip to your campaign office's treasurer, checkbook in hand.

- *Co-Opting* While the strengthening of an economic middle class frequently – or at least historically – has led to a class that eventually challenges authority, in China the newly wealthy have also been economically co-opted by the ruling party; as such the new business elite has as much reason to support the status quo as the ruling elite, and have strong economic incentives to suppress "instability" of any sort (including ethnic).[256]

- *Reinforcing Benefits of the Party* Promoting economic and social disorder in places your opponents have the upper hand is effective use of "the people" against the opposition: political connections to you should be the sole guarantee for private property, prosperity, and security. Hugo Chávez has encouraged workers' strikes in private firms that have expressed disloyalty, denied funds and decision making authority to opposition led political districts, and passed a law that permits the executive branch – i.e., Chávez – to "reverse" monetary transfers to Venezuelan states. Presumably, he invokes this privilege only in states where the opposition is in the majority. He has likewise nationalized ports in opposition-led states, denying those regions of financial resources.[256]

- *Personal Finances* Indonesia's Suharto amassed one of the largest personal fortunes known to humankind during his 32 years in office (as can you: see chapter 11). But the political strategy that permitted him to do so was spotless: ensure people eat and have jobs, and ensure there is slow economic growth, so the people forgive you for or even overlook how much you take for yourself. Suharto ensured that through the 60s, 70s, and 80s, the number of Indonesians living in absolute poverty dropped from 60% to 14% and economic conditions improved dramatically. Not coincidentally, Suharto's own "poverty" dropped significantly over the same period of time.[237]

4.6 Outright Populism

You can take it further, if you want or need to personally play the role of patron of the masses. This subject has little to do with construction and everything to do with popular fervor. But there's much to be said about portraying your administration as the vanguard of a popular revolution whose mandate is to undo the wrongs committed by the former political elite, former colonialists, or foreign oppressors. As support swells, tap into the energy and channel it into neutralizing the opposition just as you'd do with your youth wingers, your political party, or your military. If you're lucky, some musicians will be overcome with inspiration by your lofty rhetoric and provide you with the soundtrack that rouses the masses.[7][287]

---

[7] And if you're unlucky those same musicians will turn against you, prohibiting you from using their music later for purposes of your own when you need the crowds to continue swooning

The key to populist rule, once you've established your "popular revolution" is a simple matter of condescending to your people directly with
superficial gifts. Start by appealing directly to the impoverished, making
them your political base. Deliberately and consistently, paint a picture for
your nation in which foreign governments are their enemy and you are their
savior. Or, the existing political elite (who predates your government and is
not the result of your government's largesse) is the enemy, and only by ad-
hering faithfully to your patronistic self can your poor topple the injustices
before them. Create programs that will raise them from the miserable existence they have known to a slightly less-miserable plane (and no higher) and
it's possible you will become a kind of messiah to them, the hero who has
led them up from dire poverty into a sometimes working underclass. Their
gratitude will have the potential to last an entire lifetime.

In fact, developing and executing social projects, that is, projects whose
benefits accrue directly to the poor and disenfranchised is a good thing, and
will enormously increase your popular appeal, your personal reputation and
legacy, and your standing among the international and donor community.
They can be used at the same time to reorganize the socio-economic fabric
of your nation to your political advantage, to redress ills engendered by your
nation's colonial past, or just to frame your ongoing "reforms" in a more
positive light.

Venezuela's Hugo Chávez and Bolivia's Evo Morales are notable practitioners, and not because their projects were of any better quality or provided
any better results than the donor- or government-funded projects in any other
country. Both were able to formulate their social projects in the context
of a greater reawakening and reorganization of their countries. In Chávez'
case it was his much-lauded Bolivarian Revolution, and Morales was able
to emulate it, partially riding Chávez' coat tails. Hugo Chávez' economic
"missions," run from his own office, were no less than a welfare distribution
mechanism run parallel to the state, consisting of social programs in health,
education, and citizen mobilization targeted at key sectors of the population. The missions increased political loyalty of the beneficiaries (the poor)
through the benefits themselves and through better access to jobs and other
forms of patronage to Chavista supporters.[256]

Chávez was lucky: he was able to take advantage of record oil prices to
access significant funding streams, and he was able to spend almost at will.
He thus channeled significant amounts to the military, subsidized certain
businesses and agricultural processes, augmented the payroll of government
workers whenever necessary, and still had cash left over to target the poor
via specific projects. In fact, Chávez was able to stimulate impressive (8-9%)
economic growth from 2004-2007, which bolstered his personal popularity
despite worsening public services over all. The lesson is this: populism
works well (in the short term): The political boost those programs gave

---

over your.

Chávez was strongest among four important sectors: those who received social benefits directly (i.e., the poor), those who joined the government apparatus (i.e., new government employees, of which there were many as the government increased by 50% over 10 years), the rent-seeking private sector, who benefitted from lucrative government contracts, and the military, who behaved like the rent-seeking private sector.[256]

Another decent – if amateur – example is Nicaragua's first ice skating rink, erected in 95 degree tropical heat under a climate-controlled plastic tent. Hardly an example of social awakening or reorganization, it was a simple sop to Nicaragua's poor. The rink was the brainchild of first lady Rosario Murillo and funded entirely out of personal and undeclared accounts. "The park is for the children, because they were born to be happy ... All children have the right to learn how to skate on ice," she explained.[409] They potentially have a right to an occasional meal, too, but that wasn't the point here. Ice in the tropics is an obvious and surprising "gift" and such gifts strengthen your reputation as the nation's ultimate and only benefactor. Similarly, Venezuela's Hugo Chávez organized and managed his infamous economic "missions" straight out of his own office to ensure there was no doubt who was responsible for distributing their benefits, or what failure to support his presidency would engender.[256]

Note, these social projects, if they involve large-scale institutional reform, are often a money-maker for you personally. Look at Zimbabwe, where over 30 years, Robert Mugabe's administration confiscated white-owned farms and made them available to poor blacks. A hero? Sort of: the Commercial Farmers' Union notes that Mugabe kept 39 of those farms for himself. Job perk![400]

Directly subsidizing economic well-being or at least contentment is extremely important. Consider it if your nation is wealthy enough. Iran has lavished its oil money on the people in the form of economic subsidies for everything from bread and sugar to gasoline and electricity. Such investments – reportedly $70B – $100B per year – can be used to keep the people economically satisfied with your administration.[256]

Lastly, never underestimate the power of personal gifts, especially expensive ones, in countries where luxury goods are not available, and especially where they're a sign of political or economic connection. In North Korea, ruling party officials can expect additional ration cards for rice and corn, and senior officials reportedly receive gifts like Rolex watches, Armani suits and Gucci handbags.[208]

4.7 Building a National Brand

Once the economy is growing and your people are tasting the crumbs of prosperity (with the lion's share reserved for you), it's time to think about those conspicuous projects that can be used to ensure continued economic success, enhance your reputation at home and abroad, and lay the foundation for your legacy. These large-scale initiatives tend to be a mix of substance and style that will cement your national coalition if done properly. Think of yourself as a salesman pushing an authoritarian product; this is what you'll need to do to build a brand:

4.7.1   Public Works

Being supreme leader offers boundless opportunities for channeling money to the right sycophant, building support among the lower orders, and manipulating information to your advantage during election or riot season. And being number one is useful when there are large public works to be done. Public works do more than show you consuming conspicuously – they can improve the functioning of a growing (if inegalitarian) nation and offer your subjects an obvious point of reference. "Life is better now that we can get across town on the Richard M. Tater Highway," they may say, as they pay the extortionate toll and creep around the smog-shrouded traffic circle.

Funding these endeavors is more feasible if you're managing the nation's finances properly. It makes the government the only actor with pockets deep enough to fund big development projects. And in a happy complement, only the government is able to make the decisions that make high-expense projects necessary. You should use these two things to your advantage. But if your government does not have the budget to enact these sort of programs on its own, you will inevitably wind up dealing with the donor community and the International Banks (see section 10.3 for lessons on how to deal with them). While you ponder the funding issue, here are a few examples of prominent and useful development projects to favor:

Airports and State Airlines

Only the government is able to do something like build a new, international airport to replace an older/smaller one. That puts you and your supporters in an advantageous position as you will be responsible for choosing the new site, buying out the existing owners (you and your friends will be the existing owners, of course), and securing funding not only for its construction but for the subsequent projects: highways to take passengers to the new airport, restaurants and gift shops within, and so on. And your government will probably have control one way or another over the ensuing opportunities in the neighborhood: hotels and restaurants, for starters. Every single one of these aspects is an opportunity to enrich yourself, while providing an opportunity for your people to admire you for bringing to them a shiny, new airport.

Establishing a state-owned, flagship airline should be a badge of honor for any dictator in charge of a developing country who desires more than mere regional respect. Don't know anything about aviation? Don't worry; find an eager entrepreneur or enlist the services of an established airline company that can provide your national airline with all the vessels, flight crews, pilots, ground crews and maintenance staff you'll need. The really first class dictator however will want to have a personal hand in selecting flight attendants. Make sure they emphasize the superior, natural beauty of your people. Never mind that you can't keep the lights on, feed your people, or develop an industry that produces anything more complex than pottery: take to the skies and the world will say 'Now there is a leader of men!'

Additionally, having a national airline may offer an opportunity to enhance your strategic relationships. Nicaragua's proposed Air Nicaragua will provide connections to friends and sponsors such as Venezuela, Mexico, and Russia (via Cuba), which says more about Nicaraguan geopolitical goals than its economic ones.[8][189]

However, just as an airline can make a nation's reputation, it can also ruin it – so avoid catastrophic crashes that will only serve to fuel the self-assured grimaces of smug Western leaders. This may entail making sure the airline is well run, which in turns means you may not be able to meddle with the finances and hire and fire staff as you'd like. But if the urge to meddle proves too strong, and you find your flagship carrier has a substandard safety record and risks being banned from lucrative international routes, cut your losses and stay local.[3] In the final analysis avoiding the embarrassment of international exposure allows you to keep your national airline and reap at least some of its benefits.

Roads and Bridges

The Romans built their empire on the back of a highly impressive network of paved roads that linked far-off regions and promoted trade.[207] Road building should be important to you too, but not for the same reasons. They involve large sums of money (often provided by foreign donors), have a dramatic and noticeable effect on your people's lives, give you something extremely obvious to point to as standing testament to your largesse and generosity, and will probably last for several decades.[9] The highways that link distant cities will lead to economic revolutions at both ends, and commerce will hopefully flourish alongside them.

But city road projects are useful too, especially in the capital, where you will benefit personally from an easier ride to the office. Here, focus on building as many traffic circles as possible. They eliminate the need for traffic lights (since your electrical system is probably in shambles) but furthermore provide convenient stages throughout the capital for the erection of billboards, statues, and personal propaganda of many types. Each day,

---

[8] It may also say something about Nicaragua's creative use of media outreach and journalism. The article appeared in an otherwise unheard of journal among articles of questionable journalistic merit.

[9] Actually, the roads won't last more than a few years if you don't maintain them; this requires a robust and well funded administration to look after roads infrastructure. See if you can convince the donors to help you get one without imposing taxes of any sort.

people will be forced to drive past four or five of your traffic circles, slowly perambulating statues to your prowess and virility, the superior physical attributes of your ethnicity, and the marvels of your rule.

Ensure, too, that the routes you personally travel frequently are the loveliest in the nation. Normally that means the routes linking your Presidential Palace to the National Assembly, the airport, and the Supreme Court. The road to your summer cottage should be exquisitely paved even if the surrounding countryside remains a morass of muddy cart tracks (the paved road to former Nicaraguan president Arnoldo Alemán's Laguna de Tiscapa summer cottage leads right to his driveway, omitting the final remaining 50 meters of road which consist to this day of sand and mud). Spend the time and money to ensure those routes are lined with swaying palm trees (even if your semi-arid climate requires a water truck to irrigate your hibiscus and palm tree gardens every 4 days in front of thirsty street children), and ensure the mayor's street cleaners prioritize your routes over the rest of the nation.

Monumentalist Architecture

Nothing brings the nation together like a towering monument that reminds the Hoi polloi of their station while glorifying the apex of power (that would be you). The Arc de Triomphe, The Motherland Calls monument in Volgograd, the Coliseum, the Pantheon, Franco's monstrous "Valley of the Fallen" and many other simple reminders of what a mass of marble and concrete can do for a ruler who needs to visibly demonstrate the moment when a nation flowers under the hand of an expert gardener. Hitler's plan for a new German capital over the old Berlin – 'Germania' – was chock-full of such overweening glories meant to cap the initiation of the new Thousand-Year Reich.[342] The trend of "bigger means more powerful" continues into the present in places like Tajikistan, where president Emomali Rahmon built a state library so big they didn't have enough books to fill it, and was forced to requisition reading material from students under duress.[407]

4.8   Bad Ideas for You and the Nation

It's fair to say most bad ideas start with the word "radical." So take it easy, keep the money flowing, and don't rock the boat. That's not easy for a natural-born leader like yourself, so take warning from those who erred on the side of extremism:

Military Hubris   You might be a demi-god, but your military may not match your divine prowess, and nothing will dampen your nation's enthusiasm for your rule than an ill-timed or expensive war.[10] Saddam Hussein's belligerent confrontation with Iran in 1979 was an unmitigated disaster that

---

[10] Ain't that right, George W. Bush?

ended eight years later with hundreds of thousands dead, and economic devastation throughout Iraq far greater than the billions the war had cost. His invasion of Kuwait in 1990 was "one of the great military miscalculations of modern history ... He gambled that the world would not care, and he was wrong."[112]

Radical Social Experimentation Nicolae Ceausescu decided in 1966 that the Romanian nation would benefit if there were more Romanians, and introduced sweeping policy changes that outlawed contraception, taxed childless couples at a higher rate, and prohibited sex education. While the birth rate in Romania increased, so did the number of infant deaths and the number of handicapped, poor, or abandoned children that became the ward of the state in clandestine orphanages. Their discovery upon his death became his unwitting legacy.[236]

Indonesia's "Transmigrasi" (Transmigration) program saw the resettlement of ethnic Javanese from their own, overpopulated island to all over the rest of the archipelago, from Sunda to Irian Jaya to Sumatra. Decades later, the record is spotty: the transplanted Javanese led to lots of ethnic strife, marginal economic improvement, and questionable over all benefit. But it cost the Indonesian government a fortune.[11]

Radical Economic Hardship Nicolae Ceausescu similarly decided that his nation would pay off in their entirety, substantial international debts provided by the Western world. Doing so engendered draconian austerity programs, food and fuel rationing, and a nation that exported rather than ate. An impoverished and angry nation eventually rose up against him in 1989, and he and his family were summarily executed.[236]

Ethnic Purification and Genocide The history of violence against ethnic minorities is lengthy and no corner of the world has avoided it. That doesn't necessarily make it a good idea. Beyond the utility of demonizing ethnic minorities (see section 6.2.2, many regimes take it a step further, forcibly "integrating" groups who pose a threat of secession from the nation. Such forced integration escalates inexorably to massacres, wanton sexual assault, and worse, none of which benefits you either politically or morally. Be it the Guatemalan persecution of the Mayan people, the Chinese persecution of the Tibetan and Uyghurs, the Burmese persecution of the Karen, or the Dominican persecution of Haitians, hardly anything has ever come of forcing an ethnic group to integrate at gunpoint, and the possibilities that such a tactic will lead you towards unwitting genocide, war crimes, or just waste a lot of money, make this an activity not obviously worth persuing.

---

[11] Eager PhD candidates benefitted to the tune of hundreds of theses and dissertations (which also counts as a questionable benefit.)

Other than perhaps Adolf Hitler, only the Cambodian Khmer Rouge leader Pol Pot manages to dramatically exemplify all of these bad ideas in one, four year administration. After 19 years at the head of the Khmer Rouge guerrilla movement, his team seized the capital, Phnom Penh, in 1975. And then they went nuts: Pot outlawed money, abolished religion, closed schools, sent the children into the fields to participate in a "Worker Revolution," and relentlessly persecuted anyone even vaguely ethnically foreign – or even just those who exhibited "foreign" traits. Sensing the capital city was filled with supporters of the preceding administration, he turned everyone out of the capital and into the fields. Anyone with any sort of valuable skill – doctors, for example – was killed. By 1979, an estimated 2 million Cambodians (fully a quarter of the population) had succumbed to torture, starvation, disease, or been executed.[468]

You've got your legacy to think about, and this kind of planning won't reflect favorably on how people look back on your government. Forget about your ethnic pogrom project. Focus instead on getting wealthy, cornering the economy, and cueing up your son to continue the trend. You will soon see, at any rate, that keeping your ethnic minority around provides you political benefits of another sort. Keep reading!

Chapter 5

The Culture of Fear

One death is a tragedy; one million is a statistic.

Joseph Stalin

UNFETTERED liberty to work; learn; and relax, a people totally free to associate with peers, express itself in any forum and through any media, organize itself along any criteria, respond thoughtfully to the decisions of your administration and participate in the process of governing. Sound good? Not really! The last thing you need is unsolicited criticism, popular political movements, and a vocal press questioning your motives, lambasting your administration, and evoking resentment of your fatherhood of the nation. And if your people are 'free' they are implicitly free to organize against you. Who wants that? And so you too will instead opt for a regime that curtails these liberties, individually or *en masse*, to ensure your word is final, your decisions the law, and your opinion the only one worth knowing. But how far should you take it? Read on.

Welcome to the culture of fear, a lifestyle in which the peasant, student, and laborer lives in terror of you, those connected to you, and those doing your bidding. In a heartbeat, the wrong word can evaporate his job, his savings, his life, and the lives of his family. He will do anything to avoid that, draw as little attention to himself as possible, avoid challenging, threatening, or competing with you. He will thank you for what you provide, and remain silent about what you do not. His greatest worry is that your police, secret police, or body guards will ask for his name, and write it down in their little notebooks. You'd like to think you are above this, that your people will look upon your government gratefully and appreciate your heartfelt benevolence. But life isn't like that, and as your people get unruly, you too will find the culture of fear to be an impressively pragmatic solution to your growing problems. And you will follow a long pedigree of rulers who have done the same, from Egypt's Hosni Mubarak and his military, Mohammar Khadaffi in Libya, not to mention such esteemed organizations as East Germany's

Stasi and Iran's Revolutionary Guard. All have been responsible for making the locals sweat in their sleep, think twice before opening their mouths, and look over their shoulders. Wives and sons whisper the words when father goes missing. And would-be authors, critics, and pundits step back from the keyboard and the microphone.

The culture of fear is not just useful for silencing your enemies. Maintaining a steady, low-grade level of political and social instability through sectarian or other means is a clever strategy for cementing or justifying your rule. Nothing encourages the people to cling to their political leadership like a feeling of creeping malaise and danger. Help them come to that same conclusion simply by providing the malaise and danger, and then insist that only you and your strong leadership will be capable of restoring peace and prosperity. Furthermore, it may be that you and your strong, fatherly guidance are the only things holding your nation together. Many would argue that Saddam Hussein was the only thing preventing Iraq from splitting into factions. It may be true: Iraq's sectarian violence certainly took a pretty dramatic upturn the afternoon the American troops left.[1][347]

Following the fall of Hosni Mubarak, the Egyptian military was accused of implementing just that strategy to provide justification for a lengthy stay in power. It wouldn't have been the first time. In October 2011, a Christian church was burned; when Christians turned out to protest, the Army crushed the demonstration, killing 24 and stoking the flames of sectarian chest-thumping across the nation.[138] Later, the military blamed the Christians themselves for the violence.[136] This was one, single incident. But it gives you the idea of how easy it is to provoke disorder, disturbance, and death. The solution to disorder is to impose order, of course, and that requires a heavy hand: *yours.*

5.1 The Range of Repression

5.1.1 Formal vs. Informal Surveillance

The grubby little crew-cut man in cheap, anonymous clothing, recording every unorthodox thought and action. This is the image of state functionary assigned to watching the citizenry and reporting all the squalid details back to you. During the Cold War the East German Stasi were exemplars of this kind of surveillance, and their records were used to smash any spark of thought and hope while keeping the People's Revolution on track. This is how the Stasi followed one East German dissenter who had attracted their attention, and reveals just a glimpse of their methods:[152]

> "Sometimes they took pictures of her on the sidewalk, or they piled into a white sedan and drove 6 feet behind her as

---

[1] No points to Nouri al-Maliki, Iraq's Prime Minister, for subtlety, that's for sure.

> she walked down the street. Officers waited around the clock
> in cars parked outside her top-floor apartment. After one of her
> neighbors tipped her off, she found a bug drilled from the attic
> of the building into the ceiling plaster of her living room."

Never mind the extensive archives, the files, the agents, the listening
devices, and the men who asked uncomfortable questions of people with
whom you just spoke. The Stasi were an organized, state structure that op-
erated with full recognition of the East German government. Likewise, the
distrust and suspicion permeating the streets of Equatorial Guinea is impressive. "Strolling in the wrong neighborhood lands you at the police station.
A visit to Parliament's lone opposition member in his crumbling downtown
walk-up is quickly known to the security services, bringing stern warnings
from the information minister. The government publishes the only newspaper, and it is five months out of date at the leading hotel, a former torture
center. ..."[358] But you can take the clandestine route too. Khadaffi's
legion of unofficial-but-paid informers was legendary. Experts believe as
much as 10 – 20% of Libyan society was composed of paid informants supplying the government with detailed information on the movement and activities of the Libyan people.[117] The benefit of this off-the-books system
is that no one can be sure if their neighbor is taking notes, cataloging their
coming-and-going, or listening to their phone calls; such fear makes popular organization extremely difficult, and thus unlikely (Who's going to say,
"Hey, let's get a group together to discuss how we can get rid of this guy"
under such circumstances?)

5.1.2   Overt vs. Subtle Repression

What to do with all that information, all those tips about the misdeeds of
your people? Mark Bowden writes:

> Cruelty is the tyrant's art. He studies and embraces it. His rule
> is based on fear, but fear is not enough to stop everyone. Some
> men and women have great courage ... But the tyrant has ways
> of countering even this. Among those who do not fear death,
> some fear torture, disgrace, or humiliation. And even those
> who do not fear these things for themselves may fear them for
> their fathers, mothers, brothers, sisters, wives, and children. The
> tyrant uses all these tools. He commands not just acts of cruelty
> but cruel spectacle ... Pain and humiliation and death become
> public theater. Ultimately, guilt or innocence doesn't matter,
> because there is no law or value beyond the tyrant's will: if
> he wants someone arrested, tortured, tried, and executed, that is
> sufficient. The exercise not only serves as warning, punishment,
> or purge but also advertises to his subjects, his enemies, and his
> potential rivals that he is strong. Compassion, fairness, concern

for due process or the law, are all signs of indecision. Indecision
means weakness. Cruelty asserts strength.[112]

Cruelty was the name of the game in Uganda under Idi Amin in the
1970s. Amin and his military, working hand-in-hand ensured that uncertainty and suspicion permeated every level of society, and relied on random
violence, torture, beatings, kidnapings, disappearances and of course murder
to make sure there were no misunderstandings. Subtlety was not in Amin's
nature: bodies floating in the Nile and enemy corpses dangling in nooses
from tree limbs were the symbolic messages of his terror campaign. Nor
did Amin rely expressly on the military. He formed special military groups,
including the Public Safety Unit and the Bureau of State Research, both
of whom carried out many killings. These organizations were designed to
spread fear and eliminate undesirables. These undesirables came from all
walks of life: former politicians, farmers, priests, hotel managers, judges,
students, *anybody*. Blanket persecution of your populace ensures no one
considers himself "safe" enough to contemplate your ouster.[2] [334]

Equatorial Guinea provides another example. Listed among the world's
worst abusers of human rights, decades of systematic torture have led to a
culture of fear and repression that make the incredible commonplace. Man-
fred Norwak, UN Special Rapporteur on torture, complained after a visit to
the nation, "They don't even hide the torture instruments. It was just on the
table."[358]

Egypt's infamous State Security Investigations, Mubarak's feared secret
police, were revealed to have employed systematic use of torture when dealing with informants, opposition forces, and dissidents. When Mubarak was
pushed from power witnesses came forward with stories of whipping, beating, being left to hang in the air for long periods, electric shocks – especially
to the genitals – and more. According to Dr. Mona Hamed, psychiatrist,
"Torture is a wide-spread, systemic, routine policy in Egypt through the last
30 years. It is everywhere and in every place in Egypt."[292] Ethiopia in
the time of Mengistu Haile Mariam and the Derg (1974-1987) worked in the
same way: parents were frequently imprisoned with their children and forced
to watch while their kids' fingernails were ripped off or their feet beaten to
pulp. Parents that avoided that fate could look forward to their children's
tortured, bloody corpses turning up on display near their homes. There is no
limit to cruelty, and no lack of examples from which to draw.[255]

But beatings and murder are frankly, not the most effective weapon in
your arsenal, as the dead make lousy witnesses and can no longer help spread
the message ("Watch out!"). Instead, the dead catalyze intense resentment
and strengthen popular will to undo your administration. Rather than cutting straight to the chase, focus your efforts on the non-lethal means that
keep people unwilling to raise their voices, travel, organize, or complain.

---

[2]And, in the case of Amin, will earn you the moniker "Hitler in Africa." Perhaps the overt
approach isn't the greatest?

Other features of Amin's rule of fear included the random use of roadblocks, the persistent presence of armed guards in public places, the withholding of identification papers with little or no reason, and the imprisonment of foreigners. The diversity of these methods may also help achieve your goal of cowing a populace via methods of terror: relying exclusively on heavy-handed military tactics may bring short-term gains at the expense of sustained levels of fear in your country.

Paraguay's Alfredo Stroessner, with a military background and a penchant for cultivating just this atmosphere of cold sweats and shifty eyes, excelled at steeping Paraguay in a fear that lasted for decades. Headless bodies were frequently seen floating down the Parana river. In fact, writes Diana Schemo,

> Paraguay's security forces became so efficient at intimidating potential opposition figures that eventually fear itself – fear of arrest, torture, exile, and murder – became one of his prime levers for staying in power.[424]

Once fear outpaces your actual imposition of repression, you have succeeded.

5.1.3   Targeted Elimination

These days, you get the most bang for your buck by eliminating a particular nuisance in a way that your government can't be directly identified, and allowing sufficient press coverage to ensure everyone listening to the evening news vows to do whatever it takes to avoid a similar fate. The Litvinenko Affair of 2006 in Russia is a good example: When the Russian expatriate Alexander Litvinenko began to suggest state complicity in the terrorist bombings that led to the second Chechen war, he died soon after from an overdose of polonium. Though many suspected and even blamed the Russian intelligence services, no direct link was ever established.[162] Such a public execution sent an unmistakable message to whistle blowers and critics of Putin's regime: open your mouth at your peril. The Litvinenko affair followed the mysterious murder of journalist and author Anna Politkovskaya and the dismemberment of the powerful Yukos oil company (whose president had been an outspoken critic of Putin's).[161] [233] These acts contributed to a burgeoning sense of dread among those inclined to disagree with state policy. The wide publicity these events received also helped spread the message so widely that even the most obtuse of Putin's critics could see what would follow should they keep complaining about freedom of the press or democratic transparency. Andrei Ilarinov, Putin's former economic advisor has noted that:

> "The destruction of Mikhail Khodorkovsky's Yukos oil company, the murder of journalist Anna Politkovskaya, the polonium poisoning of former agent Alexander Litvinenko – the

goal in each of these cases is to keep society in a state of constant fear. That makes it easier to control the people. This is the only reason the state-controlled media are allowed to report at length on these cases. It contributes to the climate of fear."[448]

5.1.4 Self-Censorship

Ideally, the undercurrent of menace convinces your people to keep their opinions to themselves. Rather than actively searching out and annihilating unwanted messages, publications, broadcasts, and printed works (i.e. traditional, official censorship), take the subtle approach. It is more effective but takes more time and creativity to impose, and involves teaching your people what not to discuss, write, or think, and requiring them to muster the self-discipline to comply. Draconian punishments are helpful in that regard.

The Chinese under Mao, for example, evoked broad categories of prohibited topics, like "criticism of Confucius" without much detail of how that proscription would be interpreted. The government established narrow boundaries of accepted speech, and prohibited most of the rest. Modern China has inversed the trend, permitting more open conversation but strictly prohibiting several specific topics, including the famines under the "Great Leap Forward," corruption of top party officials, Taiwan independence, Uyghur or Tibetan autonomy, the Falungong movement, and other "incorrect" views on national or international affairs such as attribution of the blame for the current economic slump to the government or Communist party.[256]

The self-censorship model delegates the enforcement to local authorities (who may interpret directives slightly differently). Party officials and their hired thugs enforce the party line in an escalation from verbal warnings to electronic surveillance, job loss and blacklisting, labor camp, prison, torture, and execution. Citizens who toe the line may never encounter the authorities at all, but everyone knows exactly what happens if you incite the authorities against you.[256] This local delegation of authority furthermore reinforces popular interest in being a party member, where you can be the enforcer rather than the enforced.

5.1.5 Limited Freedom of Association

It's better if you prevent people from getting together, forming groups, and plotting against you. That's especially important for your local NGOs and other civil society groups (see section 6.4.5), but is equally important for your population in general. In Cuba, "Limited rights of assembly and association are permitted under the constitution. However, as with other constitutional rights, they may not be 'exercised against the existence and objectives of the Socialist State.' The unauthorized assembly of more than three people is punishable by up to three months' prison and a fine." Furthermore, beyond simply preventing citizens from leaving the island (see section 7.1.5), Cuban law makes it extremely difficult for individuals to choose their own residence, place of employment, or even travel easily.[248]

Further examples of this tactic are listed in "Discouraging Assembly" (section 8.2), as limiting this freedom is one of the most important ways to prevent unrest before it starts.

5.1.6   State of Siege

But if you're going to prevent people from getting together, you may as well just go ahead and declare a state of siege. Paraguay's Alfredo Stroessner kept that declaration in place from his arrival to power in 1930 until basically the end of his administration. At one point in 1959, he briefly considered restoring some constitutional liberties. But when student protesters started marching to protest the price of trolley fare, that was the end of that (it was essentially the end of the protesters, too, many of whom were arrested and tortured).[424]

5.2   The Crackdown (The Sweep)

It's counter productive to get to power and simply begin repressing. Nor is it necessary to start off with a public declaration of the end of liberty. Ideally, your increasingly heavy hand should be perceived as the response to some threat, menace, or movement that threatens the very fabric of your society. Thus will some people come to understand (maybe even appreciate?) your methods.[3] What you need is the pretext for a crackdown that not only permits you to eliminate the "national threat" but provides the context for a new societal framework. Best effectuated immediately upon taking power, or immediately after an extraordinary crisis, a "sweep" is a comprehensive and ruthless removal of multiple enemies, usually with the aid of of your most trusted security forces. It takes a man of vision and guts to implement a sweep, and this strategy is not for anyone.

Enter Josef Stalin with an example: In the early 1930s, Josef Stalin had more or less consolidated his rule of the Soviet Union; his political opposition was demoralized and disjointed. Sergei Kirov, leader of the Communist Party in Leningrad and advisor to the Politburo, had by that time become a leader of Stalin's opposition. In late 1934 Stalin made his move: he ordered the assassination of Kirov, and blamed the murder on "enemies of the state." It permitted him to draft an emergency decree that simply stated that "all terrorists were to be tried as quickly as possible, and executed without appeals being considered."[150] It was terrifying, terrible, and terrific. It was indeed the blueprint for all Terrors to follow.

---

[3] Probably not the ones you're beating.

Not only did the Kirov murder and Terrorism decree implicate the main opposition leaders in a political assassination, but Stalin also used this event to launch a process that would end in their deaths and the removal (deportation or death) of millions whom Stalin had characterized as political rivals, supposed fifth columnists, army intriguers, intellectuals, and other enemies of the state. It was a long campaign of show trials, forced betrayals, public decrees announcing draconian penalties, and secret executions that turned neighbor against neighbor, children against their parents, and professional rivals against each other. The NKVD and their informers were ubiquitous, and ordinary people were fearful of giving the least impression of dissent. When considering this option, be prepared to purge those who've helped you conduct the purge itself. Nikolai Yezhov, the leader of the NKVD and one of Stalin's main enforcers during the purges was arrested in 1939 and later executed.[121]

In the end, Stalin's Terror demolished both the opposition and any hint of explicit independent thought among Soviet citizens for a generation. The result was a relatively comfortable near decade in power, until exogenous forces intervened: the German invasion in 1942.[150]

Stalin is just one example; other dictators have been arguably as ruthless if a little less thorough. After the September 1973 coup in Chile, Augusto Pinochet sent his security forces on a tour of provincial cities in Southern Chile. Armed with knives, grenades and guns, and traveling by helicopter, this so-called "Caravan of Death" performed scores of ruthless extrajudicial killings and cemented Pinochet's grip on power.[36] In Ethiopia in the 1970s, the Marxist, military junta called the "Derg," under Mengistu Haile Mariam, began the "Red Terror."[4] The Red Terror swept up pro-democracy protesters, detained and tortured them, and then deposited their bloody corpses on the street in front of their families' homes, often with a little red "Red Terror" sign pinned to their chests.[255]

Iraq's Saddam Hussein used similar methods. In 1979, when he decided to consolidate power once and for all, he took an approach like Stalin's. He called a conference of leading Ba'athists and, once they had assembled at a conference hall in Baghdad, he announced the discovery of a variety of sinister plots. This triggered a series of frantic confessions and accusations, the removal of identified traitors by the security forces, and the requisite liquidations that resulted in a much smaller (and presumably more loyal) group of fellow travelers. To seal the deal, Saddam ensured the purge was lovingly videotaped and distributed to inquisitive minds throughout the country.[112] Not only did Saddam very publicly remove at least of third of his rivals on the Revolutionary Command Council, but he squelched much of the remaining dissent, and sent an unequivocal message to everyone. The openness of this purge offers another didactic opportunity. By removing your enemies in so obvious a way (and recording it for posterity) you may be able to get

---

[4]Hint: if your program has a name, it's a sweep. Doubly so if the word "Terror" is an explicit part of the title.

away with killing as few as is reasonably possible. "Less is more," it turns out, is advice applicable not just to writers and businessmen.

Cuba, the world's most notorious island-prison is yet another obvious example. Since the 1960s as Fidel Castro's Revolution took shape, dissidents have been summarily rounded up and either executed or detained for lengthy periods – even indefinitely. The crackdown in March 2003 was exemplary but by no means unique: within three weeks, Castro had rounded up and tried 45 dissidents and imposed jail terms on them that averaged 20 years.[5][105]

---

[5]Pundits wonder if the crackdown, which happened just as the United States was entering Iraq to topple Saddam Hussein, was timed to take advantage of the USA being distracted elsewhere, to preemptively fend off a similar incursion by a hawkish America into Cuba, or simply to prevent a rapprochement by the American government, as having the USA as a political enemy has been useful to Castro for decades. Ask the guys who are *still* in prison what they think.

But the South Americans might win the award for providing the best example of both the Sweep and the concept of international cooperation. The security forces of Chile, Bolivia, Brazil, Uruguay, Argentina, and Paraguay all banded together in what is now known as "Operation Condor" to root out their political opposition and those clamoring for greater democracy – er, officially to root out Marxist and terrorist threats to South America – in the 1970s and 1980s.[424] Who says you can't rely on your friends?

Key to a good sweep is setting the context of vaguely defined, internal and external enemies (see the lengthy section 6.2 if you have any doubt about the importance of nationalism and enemies). Your legal framework with regard to treason, dissent, and freedom of speech comes into play here. Fortunately, the Western world's sudden focus on terrorism potentially provides the cultural recognition necessary for you to clamp down on civil liberties in the name of thwarting would-be terrorists. Follow Saudi Arabia, who proposed a law in 2011 that permits lengthy detentions without trial, restricted legal access, and the use of the death penalty. Like Saudi Arabia, your law should broaden the definition of terrorism to include any action "deemed to be harming the reputation of the state or endangering national unity." Those two provide you not only the right to self-define the offenses, but to punish them severely.[6][55]

5.3   Learning to Love the Militarized Society

Autocrats have historically been of the military persuasion: admit it, those spit-shined boots and chest-full of medals give you a tingling feeling that only true love or a hidden slush fund can approximate. And having a cohort or two ready to crush your enemies at your say so certainly makes the martial lifestyle that much more edifying. At times you may itch to go all the way, particularly if, over time, recurring protests make you rue the day you agreed to have writing taught in schools. If this sounds like your dilemma, then a little bit of focused thought will lead you to an undoubtedly brilliant theory – if you militarize society, then the nation will respond to you the way your security services do, with fawning 'yeses' and crisp salutes. Of course they will. And they will also fight for you more efficiently and effectively, forming the cogs of a smoothly functioning war machine whose very name will make those treacherous neighboring states tremble and agree to all your territorial demands without the bother of an actual shooting war.

The best reason to consider this option is that, over time, you will be able to starve grass-roots protest movements of personnel by indoctrinating the younger generation. The mechanics of societal militarization are simple,

---

[6]Much of the Western World, including the United States, is struggling – and failing – to define and crack down on "terrorism" without defining such an undefinable subject in a way that permits you the dictator to impose a similar law as a method to crack down on your opposition. Fun times!

so take these very basic tenets to heart: compulsory military service for both sexes through age 30, compulsory reserves after 30, make barracks life the law of the land, and encourage paramilitary organizations to recruit those no longer on active service. Stress the primacy of martial music and military-themed festivals over family life. As the years go on, you can militarize the schools and encourage everyone to wear a uniform all the time. Think of how impressed your subjects will be when their gynecologist or tax lawyer starts reports for work in a crisp army tunic – only to return home and see their children playing charming war games or "Guess Who's the Spy."

Perhaps the first (and probably most complete) militarization of society occurred in ancient Sparta. The Spartans pioneered many of the techniques described above, and used them to carefully construct a culture that thought of duty to the state first and last.[7] When developing this kind of society it's best to begin right away and not get caught up with any sentimental focus on family life – so consider doing what the Spartans did, and have newborns checked for any physical defects. You can't have cripples and asthmatics serving in your army's vanguard, can you? Then, take them away from their parents before the age of 7 to enjoy life in the barracks: sport, training, thin gruel for food and exposure to the elements. This should certainly toughen them up and prepare them for the rigorous military training of their preteen years, during which they will be endlessly drilled and taught how to use weapons, murder slaves, think clearly under fire, and most importantly obey, obey, obey. Then more of life in the barracks, as much as they can stomach, up to and including communal meals even after marriage.[262] It was just such a system that built the finest fighting force of archaic and (most of) classical Greece. In the end though it wasn't enough, and despite defeating their main rival Athens during the Peloponnesian war Sparta only enjoyed a brief hegemony, as subsequently their political tone deafness and overconfidence in arms led to their destruction at the hands of internal and external foes.

If you decide to turn your nation into a militarized state, you should consider its main drawback – an overly simplistic trust in your armed might – and learn from the mistakes of your predecessors. North Korea's reputation as the most militarized society of the early 21st century is well-earned: North Korea typically allocates a greater proportions of national income per share of population toward military spending than any other nation. While this undoubtedly allowed Kim Jong Il to satisfy his totalitarian yearnings, this skewed economic construction also led to the deaths of at least 600,000 of his fellow citizens during a 1990s famine that was exacerbated by having an economy designed to massively overproduce military goods and services at the expense of food and fuel.[355]

A fully militarized society might cause you to smile and salute, but don't shine those medals just yet. In translating the military ethos to civilian life you may just empower your army to the point where they decide their gen-

---

[7] That sentence has a nice, soothing ring, does it not? Doesn't it bring a tear to your eye?

erals – and not you – should be running things. No one knows better the risk of an irrationally over-authorized military – and the ensuing risk of a coup d'etat every morning you go to work – then the Pakistanis. President Ali Zardari's administration broke ranks with the military by asking the USA for help subduing the military, and the Army responded with ire. Prime Minister Yousuf Gilani suggested to journalists the military response had been unconstitutional, and the military, now clearly vehement, declared those allegations would have "very serious ramifications with potentially grievous consequences" for the nation, a characteristic but unusually direct warning the military would remove the civil government if it felt threatened.[118] You are absolutely in an uncomfortable position the moment the military decides you work for them, and not the reverse.

5.4   Strategies of Suppression: Dealing with Enemies

Investigating Them   You can't always prevent enemies from emerging, but if you recognize the threat they pose to your rule then you can deal with them effectively – and use your security forces to do so. Remember, an informed autocrat is a safe one. If for example you are forced to deal with diplomatic representatives from an unfriendly state, task one of your security agents with investigating the diplomat in question. You may find incriminating information that may allow you to discredit them and embarrass the rival nation. Of course, you may need to doctor your surveillance to actually make your charges stick, but that shouldn't be a problem for your black ops cadres. Moreover, you can then use the results of the investigation as propaganda. This strategy was employed under the Sandinista regime in Nicaragua to discredit political enemies, including Catholic clergy and U.S. diplomats. From a report given in Nicaragua in the late 1980s:

> "For the last two years, I had been assigned on various occasions to tape, follow, photograph, and bug political officers and other diplomats of the U.S. Embassy in conversations with different political, church, and independent union leaders in Managua. The idea for propaganda was to show the links between these officers and the different local leaders. In particular, I was in charge of following U.S. political officer Linda Pfeifel from June to December of last year. I was able to learn everything about her. We were ordered to do a number of films of her activities and edit the film to show a conspiracy against the revolution. We would provoke American double agents, telling the agents to lead 'the Americans into forming a group in opposition to the regime. In this manner we could frame diplomats and expose them as CIA agents, completing the internal propaganda

campaign in efforts of getting support from the populace and proving their propaganda correct.' "[209]

Such techniques are used throughout the world, and in Belarus investigative reporter Irina Khalip had her apartment raided by a dozen uniformed security officers, who ransacked and carried off their computer, DVDs, and other media for investigation. In this case, the blatant nature of the investigation sent a clear message.[351]

Harassing and Menacing Them   Continued, low-grade harassment is useful for two reasons. First, it keeps your enemies on the defensive, and hopefully occupies time and money they'd otherwise have available to harass you. Secondly, it keeps them in the press, where their impotence and vulnerability will be available for everyone to see. Keep it simple, like Sheikh Hasina, the Prime Minister of Bangladesh, who noted her political rival, Khaleda Zia, was living in a home with an irregular lease, and had her publicly evicted.[169]

It's an equally impressive display of force to simply pick up your enemies for a good talking to via a forced abduction that reinforces for the victim how easily you could worsen his situation. Witness former Belarusian opposition candidate Vital Rymasheuski, who was organizing a protest on the one year anniversary of the 2010 protest that led to the arrest of several opposition candidates. His work was interrupted by his sudden 'abduction' by unidentified and un-uniformed men.[8][306]

Discrediting Them   In seeking to discredit your enemies, endeavor either to show the person is not who he is popularly believed to be, is unworthy of the popular praise he receives, or is secretly allied with the people's (i.e. the state's) enemies.

Let's say you've got a well-liked character in town who is slowly gathering a constituency, making the headlines as director of a development program that is making meaningful differences in the lives of the poor, and is slowly rising in visibility. He appears to be contemplating a candidacy in the upcoming presidential elections, and the way things are going, you estimate he'd be a popular candidate. Clearly, that's not acceptable. First you have the government audit his previous projects to check for misallocated funds or equivalent. Then you have state security read his email and look for unflattering – even treasonous – messages. Finally, perhaps you concoct a letter, ostensibly written by him, in which he requests funding for his political campaign from a foreign source while simultaneously slandering you offensively. Then you ensure this letter is "discovered" and revealed to the press. Shortly thereafter, when the audit turns up allegations of corruption and graft, you have him imprisoned pending charges. It doesn't matter what

---

[8] As of the writing of this book, he had not been heard from again.

that person did or did not do: even if the allegations turn out to be spurious, his political campaign is sunk, and doubly so if he was planning to run on a platform of honesty, transparency, and the like.

In Nicaragua in 1982, Father Carballo, the pastor of the Church of San Miguel, was invited to lunch at the house of one of his parishioners. While there, another man forced his way into the house, began beating Father Carballo, and forced him to remove his clothes. The Sandinista police arrived at the right moment, and dragged him out of the house, where Sandinista reporters photographed the scene. The newspapers duly alleged a homosexual relationship between the pastor and his parishioner, soiling the man's reputation and impeding his ability to criticize the Sandinista government.[9]

You can use their "own words" against them if your administration has access to the phone company and/or a state monopoly on Internet access (i.e., all Internet service providers are forced through your state-owned entity). Simply have the appropriate administration find the person's email account and password, and hack in long enough to send some politically damaging email. For example, any message insinuating potential disloyalty, treason, or personal lack of ethics or morals will keep your enemy tied up for ages, and can smear his name irreparably.

It's even more entertaining, and not that hard, to attack your opponents on moral or legal grounds in ways that not only tie them up in endless legal battles but erode their reputation or diminish their charisma. Malaysia's Anwar Ibrahim lost three years to jail and legal wrangling over charges he'd engaged in sodomy (illegal in the Muslim nation).[371]

Removing Them from Power   Early on, get a handle on how to get people you don't like out of their position of power, whether they be a member of the National Assembly, the Election Board, or a particularly irksome mayor. It's a skill you will come to rely on throughout your rule.

No one said being a dictator in a country that pays lip service to democratic ideals was going to be easy. If this describes your situation, then you may be faced from time to time with troublesome elected officials. Sometimes killing them is not an option, even when your secret police are itching for something to do on weekends. How then, do you remove people you don't like from their positions of power, whether they are members of the National Assembly or parliament, an election board, or a particularly irksome mayor? When your hands are tied, and violent action is unwise, be bold and public, and show no hesitation in dissolving offices or governmental institutions. You've got the power, the fetters of so-called democracy notwithstanding. This is what Niger's President Tandja did during a constitutional crisis in 2009. He publicly dissolved the National Assembly when it increasingly appeared that his hold on power was slipping; then, after further

---

[9]Be careful: this example backfired because of clumsy execution, and strengthened support for the Catholic Church.[11]

conflict with the courts, he simply announced he would rule by decree. [48] Even if this only exacerbates a political crisis, at least you will know in the aftermath who's on your side and who belongs to the opposition.

Co-opting Them   Certain enemies can be best dealt with by bringing them into the fold. Your loudest political agitators will in most circumstances shut up immediately after you offer them a job in your administration, and they simultaneously deal themselves a political death blow by behaving in a way that reveals the shallowness of their ideological and political convictions. Once you've bought them out, you can use that fact against them for the rest of their non-existent political careers. Use this option carefully to ensure your detractors don't use their position "on the inside" to spy on you, gain access to sensitive information, or worse.

Arresting and Imprisoning Them   An arrest every now and then is a good thing: it shows you are serious. Put someone in jail every now and again, and let them fight a bit; if they are later declared innocent, bully for them! But you can bet it increases their respect for you!

For maximum effectiveness, make sure the arrest goes smoothly and in your favor. Make your arrest when you have the strength in numbers and when your adversary is unlikely to be able to find support from neighbors, friends, family, or allies. Catch them in their apartments early in the morning when they're groggy and have barely had time to button their trousers, on trains in foreign places. If necessary, send them other places so they will be more vulnerable. In the Soviet Union, it wasn't uncommon to reassign someone to a new job in a foreign city for the explicit purpose of leaving them defenseless at the moment you arrest them. [446]

Keeping your political enemies in prison is effective but will draw the attention of the international world. But it works. Charismatic Russian oil baron Mikhail Khodorkovsky, once Russia's wealthiest individual and there-fore a clear political threat to Vladimir Putin, was arrested in 2003 and jailed in 2005 for embezzlement and money laundering (from his own firm). His sentence was extended in 2010 for another six years, as "he could only be reformed by being isolated from society."[10][50]   Political opponent Boris Nemtsov made a comment in support of Khodorkovsky, and was arrested the next day. That will teach him to keep his opinions to himself![178] Sim-ilarly, former Prime Minister of Ukraine Yulia Tymoshenko found herself in court defending deals she made as Prime Minister. The Ukrainian gov-ernment claims they were harmful to Ukraine's national interest; and when convicted she faced up to ten years in prison. Tymoshenko posited the fact she has emerged as the Ukraine's most prominent opposition politician is the real reason she has been attacked, noting the travel ban the government

---

[10]The fact those six years take Russia safely past the next presidential election are pure coin-cidence

had levied against her turned into an arrest warrant because of questions she asked alleging corruption of other officials.[403]

Former Belarusian Minister of Foreign Economic Affairs Mikhail Marinich bid unsuccessfully to unseat incumbent Alexander Lukashenko in 2001, and was jailed afterwards to five years in prison. There, he was denied his medicine and suffered a stroke as a result.[351] Belarus provides further examples here, like forbidding prisoners access to their lawyers (the case of Zmitser Dashkevich, 2011)[300], and jailing the family when they protest the imprisoning of their loved one (here, Dashkevich's fiancee, who spent 12 days in jail)[299]

Once your enemies are behind bars, you are free to have a little fun with them, make them a bit uncomfortable, drive in the spikes. Tymoshenko was subjected to a no-wound form of physical torture: total deprivation of personal privacy and a 24-hour lights-on policy that made it hard for her to get restful sleep.[315] The Egyptian military took the liberty of imposing 'virginity tests' on female inmates, ostensibly to deny them the opportunity of claiming they were raped, but probably just for a chance to see what was under that dress.[58]

Having Them Committed   You don't have to rely on your jail system if you have mental institutions that will perform the same role. The editor in chief of the Tajik journal "Turkmen World" was dismissed from his position and briefly committed to a Tajik psychiatric hospital in Ashgabat for eight days. Civic activist Amangelen Shapudakov spent 43 days in a psychiatric hospital, and upon release the village leaders warned him to stop criticizing the authorities. It could have been worse: 69 year old Kakabay Tejenov was admitted to a psychiatric hospital in January 2006; a month later the government officially denied he had been detained or confined to any mental institution. Months later another "patient," upon release, confirmed the detainment. His crime? Requesting authorization to hold a peaceful political demonstration, clearly a sign of insanity in any authoritarian state.[20]

Humiliating Them   It's said Saddam Hussein particularly resented the sophistication and education of Tahir Yahya, former prime minister of Iraq. So upon taking power he ensured Yahya was sent to prison. There, Hussein negotiated so that Yahya was assigned the prison task of carting a wheelbarrow from cell to cell to pick up the prisoners' slop buckets. The former prime minister's degradation and humiliation pleased Hussein to no end, and he would recount the story, giggling, until the day Yahya died, still in prison.[112]

Torturing them   Torture is surprisingly effective: there's a valid reason the practice didn't disappear with the Middle Ages. And it works with both your adversary and their families. Kazakh opposition journalist Gulzhan Ergalieva learned this to her dismay in 2001, when a group of masked men broke into her Almaty apartment, beat her and tied her up, before proceeding to torture her husband before her eyes for several hours; to this day he is crippled.[11][302] Said Levi Rufinelli, leader of the Paraguayan opposition liberal party – who had been imprisoned 19 times and tortured six by 1975, "Most of the time I did not know what they wanted ... They did not even know what they wanted. But when they put the needles under your fingernails, you tell them anything. You denounce everybody, and then they say: 'See, you were lying to us all the time.' "[424]

Making Them Disappear   Once your opponents are imprisoned, you can make them mostly disappear. When jailed opposition candidate Andrey Sannikau wrote a letter[12] claiming his life was in danger, the Belarusian authorities ordered him placed in total isolation with no contact from anybody – even his lawyer – to protect him from all such threats to his life, while an inquiry into his situation was conducted. The inquiry was expected to last six months.[310] Similarly, former opposition candidate Mikola Stratkevich was given three years in a 'closed regime,' which is little different.[304]

Killing Them   While it's well within your power to simply ensure pesky journalists suffer unfortunate accidents, this technique is increasingly viewed as clumsy and un-creative. Nicaragua's president Anastasio Somoza Debayle was widely credited with ordering gunmen to kill journalist Pedro Joachin Chamorro in 1978. Chamorro was killed as he drove to work on a Managua highway. The popular outcry over Chamorro's murder, which was quickly identified as politically-motivated, intensified the opposition to Somoza, which led eventually to civil war and Somoza's ouster.[265] So either ensure your planned hit is a lot smoother and harder to identify as an assassination, and make sure you can not be personally linked to it, or try a more subtle approach, liking making sure they suffer deaths from natural causes, like car accidents, heart attacks, and similar. And in Belarus, the campaign manager for opposition candidate Andrei Sannikov was found hanged in his apartment. Apparently a suicide, his otherwise happy home life leads many to suspect it was the work of the administration of incumbent Alexander Lukashenko.[351]

Be careful, though, of martyring a charismatic leader whose death will catalyze the rebels who supported him, as they will be able to redefine his story in the context of his humble rebellion and your vicious dictatorship's brutal murder of him. In such a case, even slandering him before his death will strengthen him at your expense.[411] Be careful, too, of deaths that will cause you even more trouble down the road. Liberia's Samuel Doe unleashed a wave of extrajudicial killings, but one of them – the son of the

---

[11]Note the attack didn't sway her resolve; she went on to found an opposition web portal in 2011, which still "unknown attackers" were forced to neutralize using cyber warfare.

[12]Who's to say he even actually wrote the letter?

former president – was poorly chosen. The son, Adolfus Benedictus Tolbert, had married the daughter of the neighboring Côte d'Ivoire's ruling party's founder, who appealed personally for clemency for Tolbert. Another family link connected Côte d'Ivoire to Burkina Faso. Once Tolbert had been assassinated, Doe found himself "encircled by regional rivals who had very personal scores to settle with him."[376]

Targeting Their Families   Exactly how much of a bastard are you? Potentially worse than killing a dissenter is subjecting them to a life of misery, except it permits them to retain their voice and definitely sharpens their hatred for you. But it's a chillingly effective maneuver: the Taliban, when spurned by a police officer who failed to meet their demands, kidnaped and killed the man's 8 year old son.[433] Or, you might just eliminate your enemy and send his or her family a frightening token of your enmity. In Hitler's Germany in the 1930s, crusading journalist Franz Gerlich was murdered by the SS after publishing one too many negative articles on the Führer; his blood splattered spectacles were then delivered to his grieving wife.[415] Paraguay's Alfredo Stroessner's security agents once played a tape for a schoolteacher: the sounds of her husband's screams while being tortured.[13][424]

---

[13]Ironically, she died under the strain, while the husband survived the torture and went on to discover government documents now called the Archives of Terror, unveiling some of the government's efforts to impose the state of terror.

Chapter 6

Politics and the Party

> "Worshiping a dictator is such a pain in the ass."
>
> Chinua Achebe

INSOFAR as anyone can tell, your nation is an erstwhile democracy, so besides the other trappings like a "free" press and periodic elections, you can expect to have a few opposition political parties kicking around. That's not the end of the world as it's easier to deflect accusations of autocracy if you can point to a (somewhat) vocal opposition engaged in (controlled) criticism of your government. But furthermore, the framework of party politics can serve both to strengthen your cult of personality and reinforce the links of patronism that make your government tick. So embrace it: make party politics a strength, not a liability.

6.1 Managing Political Parties

6.1.1 The One Party System

First of all, it's relatively easy to do away with the political opposition entirely, if your initial political mandate is strong enough: such is often the case with a "Revolutionary" government, as is the case in Cuba. In Cuba, Fidel Castro's Communist party (PCC) is the only legitimate party, and it controls all government entities from the national to local level. All other political organization is illegal, and dissent of nearly any form merits lengthy prison sentences, including for dissidents who speak rather than write.[248] But even if you lack a revolution, this option is open to you.

The Dominican Republic's Rafael Trujillo outlawed all parties other than his own, the Partido Dominicano, of which he was the head. Likewise, Zaire's Mobutu founded his Popular Movement of the Revolution (MPR) and required that all Zairians become obligatory members; by 1971, the party was effectively a state within a state.[212] Imitation is the best flattery: the Democratic Republic of the Congo's Laurant Kabila imitated Mobutu – a predecessor – and outlawed political activity by any party other than his own. As a result, leading opposition leader Etienne Tshisekedi was rounded up by authorities and put on "internal exile," where he was given some seed and told to go out and learn to farm: not a bad day's work. A single party system is also *de rigeur* in Turkmenistan, where the Democratic Party of Turkmenistan has essentially had free reign since independence. In 2012 plans were drawn up to create an agrarian party and a pro-business party.[313]

The fact that Turkmenistan's ruling party has decided to create additional parties, neither of which is likely to have much autonomy or present any real opposition leads you to recognize the logical next step, which is a multi-party system in which no other party matters. Nigeria's military strongman Sani Abacha provided his creative touch to the burgeoning science of democractic re-invention by creating five different political parties, and then ensuring each of them approved his unopposed candidacy for an elected presidency.[35]

6.1.2   Obligatory Party Membership

Loyalty to your party and to you is important. And if it doesn't come naturally, you can try to force it. It's useful to make membership in the incumbent party a necessity for the matters of daily life and for personal, economic, or political well-being. In doing so – letting the party permeate every aspect of society and the economy – you save time and energy politicking around the nation convincing people to vote for you or support your party. Instead, people will choose to become a member willingly, and in doing so be quietly co-opted, as they are now "part of the system" whether they like it or not. You dramatically weaken the opposition this way, as being a member of any other party brings few benefits, and it may risk being a liability. Indonesia's Suharto required all government employees to join the Golkar party and then compelled them to vote for Golkar in elections, making the party all but unassailable for decades.[237]

Personal Necessity

In 1970, the president's UNIP party of Zambia resolved that "the UNIP membership card should be made a legal document for the purpose of identification and holders of the card should be given preferential treatment over non-holders in such spheres as employment, promotions, markets, loans, business, housing and all socio-economic activities." Suddenly, ordinary citizens found they needed a party membership card to complete quotidian tasks like crossing bridges, boarding buses, or dealing in the city markets, and otherwise qualified citizens were ineligible for jobs, housing allowances, or travel overseas unless they were a member.[291]

Thirty years later, this same tactic is equally effective. Daniel Ortega used this trick to great advantage in Nicaragua after 2005. Having a San-dinista party card opened up all sorts of opportunities and made life outside the party exasperating and difficult. Students with party cards received their grades first while everyone else was forced to wait in line; job opportunities typically required you to show your card before proceeding. Certain shops offered you lower prices if you were "a member," and others turned a cold shoulder to you unless you had a card.[1]

Political Impunity

In the same vein, selective enforcement of requirements – such as anti-corruption laws – develops an effective culture of impunity in which you are either protected on the basis of your loyalty, or you are exposed. In Venezuela, a culture of impunity has been an effective political tool. While corruption is rampant, state prosecution of the accused happens on the basis of political merit: supporters are given access to the opportunities to engage in corruption while opponents are denied the same. It is a mechanism that distributes a new form of patronage, cultivates supporters who rightly see the opportunities for economic improvement this provides, and dramatically increases the loyalty of those involved, as suddenly the success of the ad-ministration means an impact on their personal well-being as well.[256]

6.1.3   The Youth Wing

Ah, youth – idealistic, energetic, impassioned. Also, volatile, reckless, oc-casionally violent, and easily-manipulated. The fact is[2] the youth of your nation, particularly if they're unemployed, restless, and disenfranchised, are going to rise up and rally anyway. So you'd be better off if they were rallying on your side instead of on the opposition's. Your political party is the only one that matters, and reaching out to pull adolescents into the fold is a smart move for several reasons:

1. They grow up believing in your party, your ideology, and your mech-anisms, thus sustaining the role of your party for the next generation.

2. Becoming part of your system, they are no longer available to the op-position, who is looking for support.

---

[1]Good thing party membership provides some economic benefits, as it also requires you to turn up at the next rally dressed in your official party-colors outfit for some public support (see 6.1.4)

[2]Actually, the fact is. prefixing a statement with "The fact is" does not necessarily make it the fact.

3. They can be relied upon to spray paint your slogan all over the capital's walls, rough up journalists, activists, NGO-workers, and anyone else whose roughing-up can't be directly attributed to you.

4. They help you keep tabs on the university system, who might otherwise be organizing against you.

5. They can help you sow a little disorder here and there, cowing those who think peace and stability are going to persist in your absence, menacing ethnicities you choose (Hitler's youth wing played a serious role in the destruction and looting of Jewish property in the 1930s [278]), reminding the wealthy elite how much they need your protection, and so on.

To encourage their participation in "the machine," make sure party benefits – the "get out of jail free" card – apply equally to them: ensure party youth get easy access to government school loans and party member graduates get easy access to government jobs. Ensure youth that want passports can acquire them more easily if they are members, and permit them to more easily skip obligatory military service when the time comes. Once they're members, put them to work harassing the opposition.

6.1.4 Organizing Effective Support Rallies

An occasional mass demonstration can be a powerful tool in your foreign relations arsenal, if the grand public turns out either to support you or to denounce a foreign power (and, for example, its intervention in your affairs).

But the demonstration must be correctly handled for it to work, and will make you look foolish if there are too few people. This is a surprisingly effective way to ensure your plaza is filled to the point of overflowing with your supporters, each of whom has been properly coached in the right slogans to shout.

Embattled Syrian president Bashar al Assad used this tactic with stunning precision on 12 October, 2011, after seven months of relentlessly pounding a growing rebel movement with his military, and steadfastly ignoring international criticism of his administration and its brutalities. Nearly three thousand Syrians had already been killed by the Syrian military as it tried to quell the rebellion. And then suddenly, like the sun parting the clouds, tens of thousands of Syrians gathered in Damascus' Sabaa Bahrat Square in a show of support for the dictator. "Today's rally is a message for the West and the Arab World to let them know that the president is legitimate," said a representative. "Assad represents economic and security stability. He's our guardian. We don't know how the next president will be." Televised reports showed demonstrators raising Syrian flags and pictures of Assad and his father (a real, autocratic father-son team). Signs read "The army and people with you, Bashar al-Assad" and "Syria is our country and Assad our president." What they did not say, but can be directly inferred, was this: "Europe and America: shut up and leave our patron alone."[27] Extremely well done. You too can have a rally of support, whether your administration has been massacring the protesters and needs a little support, or you just need a nice, full, plaza of chanting followers to praise you before the national and foreign media. Follow the examples of Nicaragua and Cuba to ensure a good rally:

1. Establish a cadre of key rally organizers.

2. Alert the foreign press so they know to film it and distribute the images back home.

3. Through your ministries and government offices let it be known that all employees of the government are expected to show their full, heartfelt, and dedicated support to you at the planned rally. That means they will dress in party colors.

4. Have each organizer show up at a government office the morning of the rally to pick up "any willing employee interested in participating." Get those employees onto the bus. But before leaving the building, inspect every corner of it, and get the names of every single person that did not get on the bus.

5. On the day of the rally, provide transport, logistics, snacks, and a small stipend. Give everybody matching flags, baseball caps, t-shirts, etc.

6. The day after the rally, ensure those people not present at the rally lose their employment or worse.

7. Televise the rally to the maximum extent possible.

Here it is in practice in Nicaragua, April 2011:

> Exhaustive planning by the organizers, however, proved no match
> for Ortega's political machinery which leverages government
> assets to bribe supporters and intimidate opponents. ... First,
> he mobilized the Sandanista [sic] Youth Movement to sponsor a
> counter protest for which he coerced state employees (by threat-
> ening their jobs) and high school students (by threatening grade
> point reductions) to participate. Still unsatisfied, Ortega's un-
> derlings bullied the country's bus owners into canceling charters
> to transport opposition groups into Managua. He then height-
> ened tensions between the Sandanista [sic] Youth Movement
> and opposition groups to lay the groundwork for police inter-
> vention. On Saturday, those bus owners that did decide to trans-
> port demonstrators to the capital for the march had their buses
> stopped south of the city, making it impossible for their passen-
> gers to participate. On the one hand, the four thousand activists
> that were able to congregate were met by police in full riot gear
> and barricades that effectively blocked the agreed to route. On
> the other hand, Ortega, through questionable financing, was able
> to bring busloads of "supporters" into the city, drape them in
> pro-regime t-shirts and arm them with propaganda. They were
> allowed to move freely past barricades throughout the city.[338]

6.1.5   Power Sharing Agreements

Your opposition parties may simply be too entrenched, have too historical a
presence, or be too strong to eliminate entirely. But perhaps you can work
with them. Don't underestimate the power of the gentleman's deal to smooth
your way to power. Nicaragua's *Pacto* allowed two ostensible enemies from
opposing political parties to not only ensure their own personal survival, but
to divide up the institutions of government between them for further exploitation and political longevity. In the months prior to Nicaragua's 2001 elections, Nicaragua's embattled, incumbent president Arnoldo Alemán (under
investigation for the embezzlement of over $100M dollars during his pres-
idency) and pretender to the throne Daniel Ortega (under investigation for
sexual abuse of his stepdaughter) signed an infamous agreement that protected both, derailed politics and divvied up the government between their
two parties. [205] It granted political impunity to both ex-presidents and
guaranteed seats-for-life in the National Assembly. It replaced the Controller
General with a trio representing both their political parties and divided up the
principal positions of both the Supreme Court and the Electoral Commission.
It enlarged all government institutions and staffed them with an equal number of each man's party members, and enacted more stringent regulations

to ensure other political parties couldn't join in the festivities. In one fell swoop they had eviscerated and politicized the structures of government to their mutual advantage.[210][494]

But in the long term, power sharing agreements aren't a great solution. That was the case for Kenya's president Mwai Kibaki, whose electoral loss led to near civil war and hundreds of deaths. The violence ended when he agreed to let opponent Raila Odinga become the Prime Minister, in a sort of power sharing agreement. That led not to consensus building and constructive governance but rather to a simple division of the political and economic spoils.[3] So while Odinga went on to implicate himself in a maize-trading scandal, Kibaki and his party were implicated in questionable petroleum dealings. From the point of view of a single leader, this is obviously disappointing, as both deals would have otherwise belonged to the victor.[4] [16]

6.2   Nationalism and Enemies

6.2.1   Nationalist Pride

A sense of nationalism is a stirring political force that has propelled many an autocrat to power and facilitated the most barbaric of acts.

Ethnic Grudges   A dormant Serbian nationalism in the fractured, post-Communist Balkans allowed Slobodan Milosevic to strengthen his hand sufficiently to propel the Serbs into several successive wars against the Croats, the Slovenes, the Bosnians, the Albanians of Kosovo, and eventually the forces of the NATO alliance. His appeals to a Greater Serbia and his careful exploitation of historical, ethnic grudges were exactly what it took to lay the groundwork for the conflicts he later engendered. Even the Serbian intelligentsia was seduced.[442] He seized on Serbia's own "lost cause" myth, the Battle of Kosovo in 1389, and used this to incite the budding nationalism of the 1980s that heated the Yugoslav republics to a violent boil.

The original battle, against the Ottoman Turks, was a Pyrrhic draw that led to the defeat and eclipse of Serbia under Muslim rule.[98] It was perennially portrayed as glorious and doomed last-stand, a defeat that seeded generations of resistance against the Turks. When, in the aftermath of Tito's death, the Serbian media began to advocate national causes at the expense of a federated Yugoslavia, Milosevic seized this moment to raise the ghost of 1389. In April 1986 he attended a gathering of local Serbs at Kosovo

---

[3]That alone reveals that both men have read and are actively working out of this book. Bravo, gentlemen!

[4]Meanwhile, the Kenyan people agreed that after a full year in power, the combined government had achieved nothing, and the ministers were running amok positioning themselves for their own future political careers. That says power sharing agreements aren't good for you or for anybody at all.

Polje (the site of the battle) and, after listening to their grievances, passionately took up their cause by invoking the martyrs of 1389. He claimed that Serbs in Kosovo had been the victims of genocide and that, now that they were awakened and with his support, they would never be defeated again. This was one of the first overt appeals to the nationalistic myth of Serbia the "glorious loser," and it was a harbinger of media campaigns that would subsequently characterize Milosevic's rise to power and much of the rhetoric that accompanies the breakdown of Yugoslavia in the 1990s.[99]

Revisionist Jingoism   There are many examples that prove you can promote your career by using a misunderstood or mythic event from a country's past as a kind of political shorthand to let your supporters know where you stand or, better yet, inflame your existing and hopefully very vociferous base. In an American context circa 2010 you would have said that you hoped to restore a belief in the Constitution or the Founding Fathers, or that you supported a new American Revolution aimed at restoring the original principles upon which the republic was founded. Remember: keep the actual details few and vague, as these are not important and may only serve as ammunition for intellectuals when they (inevitably) attack you for demagoguery.

Blind National Pride   Iran's Mahmoud Ahmedinejad has tapped into Iranian frustration and made nationalism and Iranian pride a significant political force. In particular, he has made Iran's development of nuclear capabilities a matter of national pride, and the West's opposition to Iranian nuclear capability an example of foreign meddling in Iranian sovereign affairs.[256]

6.2.2   Enemies

Always ensure the nation has an enemy or some sort, and if possible, have an external enemy. They're useful for two reasons: first, having someone to rail against gives you an opportunity to show your leadership, "guiding" your people away from danger. Secondly, you can use them to pin blame for just about anything, including things that are your own fault. People are inherently binary, and want to think in terms of "us vs. them" or "good vs. bad." Help them do so by positioning yourself as "us/good" and let them draw their own conclusions about everybody else. George W. Bush's "Axis of Evil" is a fantastic example, but this tactic is present everywhere. The Nicaraguans and Costa Ricans are unfriendly to each other, the Hondurans and Salvadorans occasionally bristle, and Cuba has spent decades railing against the United States. North and South Korea seem to be perpetually at the point of armed conflict, and North Korea has worked hard to portray the United States as a permanent enemy.

Promoting the notion that forces are afoot to destabilize the nation, and that you are a source of protection, can lead to immediate political support out of an unconscious human sense of sympathy (*this* is why you've been cultivating a popular fear of outside forces and unspoken enemies – see chapter 5). An attempted-but-ultimately-fruitless coup d'etat, in which your security forces capture the evil-doers, can be a publicity bonanza, and lead to increased popular support for you: your target here is the common country folk, the grandmothers and grandfathers that think it's wrong for someone to try to assassinate their president on ethical grounds (note: this ploy won't work if you yourself rose to power via an assassination, or you can be somewhat easily be accused of having organized assassinations of your own). Make sure it's a credible attempt, however. If all you've got is a couple of students planning to riot, and your minister of justice wrongly inflates it into an attempted coup attempt, you will both look foolish.[203]

Imperialism, Capitalism, and Colonialism   If you have no other options, it's always convenient – and easy – to infer the United States is plotting against you. Evo Morales, beleaguered in Bolivia, let the press know in July 2011 that he was afraid to fly to the United States for an international conference on water, for fear the US government would plant cocaine on his plane as a pretext for his arrest.[7] Bolivia of course has gotten tremendous mileage out of planting fears that the US government is "secretly trying to destabilize Bolivia by plotting ..." The USA, having actually done those sort of things in the 1960s and 1970s, of course is powerless to protest.

Venezuela's Hugo Chávez was well known for the same battery of (often baseless) accusations, all carefully gauged for a receptive local audience. As he recovered from cancer, and reacting to the news that neighboring Argentinian president Cristina Fernandez had also been diagnosed with cancer, a bloated and bald Chávez mused out loud that perhaps the United States had found a way to induce the illness, and was using its new power to infect presidents in countries whose leaders they disliked.[5][296]. Venezuela's increasingly strident anti-American approach may serve the purpose of attracting an international coterie of radical backers, but it equally attempts to goad the United States into a drastic action that confirms its enemy status and would justify a further draconian crackdown on dissent within Venezuela; it also promotes a culture of fear. While the United States has mostly resisted Venezuela's insistent goading, Chávez has filled the gap by supplying as many conspiracy theories as required to position the United States as an enemy.[6]

Finally, don't forget grievances that date to the colonial period! Ghana's Kwame Nkrumah rejected democracy as an "imperialist dogma" despite

---

[5]Never mind the fact that rather than "sending" Osama bin Laden a lingering bodily ailment they assassinated him at gunpoint.

[6]The US recognition of the coup that briefly overthrew Chávez was a notable, regrettable exception, as it served to bolster Chávez' subsequent, outrageous claims. At any rate, the US government's intervention in Latin America during the past 40 years or longer means most conspiracy theories find fertile ground regardless of their accuracy or plausibility.

Africa's long tradition of something remarkably similar. It made a convenient excuse to scapegoat Great Britain and by extension, the United States.[26] Zimbabwe's Robert Mugabe turned a blind eye to his country's horrid economic mismanagement and blamed instead sabotage by Great Britain. [53]

Neighboring Country   If you are so lucky to have a neighboring country that is your people's historical enemy, you have many options available to you. If you are not so blessed, it's not too hard to create an enemy out of your neighbors anyway. In either case, the presence of an enemy on the doorstep is a powerful incentive for your people to rally around you, and many presidents in times of distress have found it useful to provoke the neighbors in order to remind the people how lucky they are to have such a fearless leader at the helm.

Kim Jong Il and his father, Kim Il Sung, have used South Korea as a threat and foreign enemy for decades, and American economic and military support of South Korea has made the U.S.A. a logical target and scapegoat as well. In fact, any country that supports your neighbor and ethnic near-relatives but not you must obligatorily be made an enemy, for reasons of pride alone. On numerous occasions, North Korea has justified its nuclear program or its immense, standing army on the grounds that national sovereignty is threatened by a bellicose and dangerous America.[235]

Nicaragua has such an antagonistic relationship with Costa Rica, a wealthier and better-organized country just to the south. In 2010, a dredging team (headed by a former Sandinista general allied with the president and with intimate knowledge of the region[7] set up camp on the Costa Rican side of the river, with a contingent of soldiers "for their safety." The Costa Ricans responded with the obligatory and predictable police response, and Nicaragua's president Ortega suddenly found himself on a lovely wave of increasing popularity. As indignant Nicaraguans shouted "The San Juan River is 100% Nicaraguan, you sons of bitches!" the general responsible for the gaffe blamed the error on Google maps. Better still, Google went on to apologize on behalf of Western Imperialism. Nice![167]

Other Ethnicities   Says economist and author Paul Collier, "The politics of hatred has a long and, electorally speaking, pretty successful pedigree." Indeed, you don't have to look far for examples, from the Ivoriens who blame Burkinabe immigrants, the Congolese of the DRC who blame the Tutsi, and the Zimbabweans, who love to blame the whites. Most Southeast Asians distrust the Chinese, the Chinese mistrust minority ethnicities at home, and the list rapidly delves into nuances among peoples outsiders would struggle to distinguish. [148]

---

[7]Coincidence? Of course not! Good planning!

This is a slippery slope that leads rapidly in the direction of ethnic cleansing, if you're not cautious. But the Dominican Republic's Rafael Trujillo didn't think twice before ordering the massacre of at least 20,000 Haitians living in the western part of the Dominican Republic in 1937. The "Parsley Massacre," so called because people were asked to pronounce the word *perejil* ("parsley") to see if they were native Spanish speakers, led to the butchery of French Haitians unable to produce a good, rolled "R." The massacre solidified a somewhat permeable border separating the two nations and eventually led to to payment of war reparations.[239] But the massacre, and related programs of anti-Haitianism strengthened Trujillo and increased his popularity back home.

Foreigners in Idi Amin's Uganda fared little better. In the early 1970's the Uganda economy was foundering and Amin's solution was to scapegoat the Asian minority. These ethnic Indians, Pakistanis, and Bengali were small-scale traders and shop-keepers for the most part, but comprised a notable, urban, ethnic minority. But Amin "had a dream" in which God directed his servant to expel all Asians without Ugandan citizenship within 3 months.[8] Amin knew that Ugandans identified the Asians as aloof, unfriendly, and an economic drain, and knew that by expelling them he could deflect attention from the true cause of Uganda's pending economic collapse: corruption and lavish state spending on the military. The Asians were forcefully expelled, including some who had legitimate papers to stay; others who met the criteria for Uganda citizenship were rounded up and transferred to distant districts, and their businesses were seized. Before the transports left, Amin himself addressed a crowd of Ugandans who had gathered to watch the Asians go: "Be kind to them," he said, "and teach them ways to dig hard and seriously." All in all Amin had achieved his objectives: he diverted attention from a poor and mismanaged economy, focused resentment and anger on a visible ethnic minority, and strengthened his rapport with the masses.[9][335]

Other Religions Ever since 11 September, 2011, when New York's Twin Towers fell, the word "terrorism" has come to mean very little, and protecting your nation from "terrorists," "radical movements" and "evil" has become accepted. For the sitting tyrant, consider it a godsend. Uzbekistan's Islam Karimov has used the pretext of "radical Islam" to engage in often brutal sweeps across the nation.[19] Critics complained it untied the military's hands from prudent peacekeeping: they could now simply shoot someone, then fill out paperwork that claimed the dead was a "terrorist." No civilian had any right to question this characterization.[420] Western nations have been little more altruistic, inclusive, or gentle. Surprisingly[10] Iraq's Nouri al-Maliki used the charge of terrorism against his own vice-president Tareq

---

[8]Funny dude, God.

[9]Oh yeah: the Ugandan elite – mostly the military – got to keep the abandoned shops the Asians left behind.

[10]Or, not.

al-Hashemi. Al-Hashemi fled to Kurdistan, while pundits opined whether
Maliki's power grab would lead to open civil war.[347]

6.3 Your Political Opposition

The best way of controlling the outcome of an election is controlling who
participates. If your opponent isn't eligible to run on account of where he
was born, where he lives, or where he has been, the political threat has been
neutralized. And your creativity is the limit here.

6.3.1 Tactics of Exclusion

On Legal Grounds   Myanmar's ruling junta passed the 2010 Political Parties Registration Law, prohibiting anyone currently serving a prison sentence
from being a member of a political party; this barred Aung San Suu Kyi and
many others.[227]

On Grounds of Birthplace and Nationality   In the 70s, Kenneth Kaunda
in Zambia and Alassane Ouattara in Cote d'Ivoire were each denied the right
to run for office on the grounds they had been born to immigrant parents and
were thus not nationals.[30]

But the Zambian opposition party tried something similar in 2011 to prevent incumbent president Rupiah Banda from taking part in the September
elections: Zambia's constitution requires both parents of a presidential candidate to be Zambian by birth, but Banda's father was born in what is now
Malawi. A technicality? Perhaps, but a technicality that may ultimately
disqualify.[399]

Georgia's president Mikheil Saakashvili used a similar trick to great effect in late 2011. When billionaire Bidzina Ivanishvili declared his political intention to run as an opposition candidate in the upcoming presidential
election, he made the mistake of doing so before renouncing his other citi-
zenships (he had simultaneously French, Russian, and Georgian citizenship).
No worries then, the Georgian judiciary system struck in four days, stripping
him of his Georgian citizenship. And suddenly, not only was he no longer a
candidate, he was no longer even a citizen: Game over![298]

On Grounds of Geography   In representative government, the national
territory is divided into districts, each of which represents a portion of the
population, usually on a geographical basis, for the purpose of electing local representatives. Daniel Ortega and Arnold Alemán used this to great
advantage in 2000 to exclude a potential political candidate vying from a
non-incumbent party for position of mayor of Managua (a job that typically serves as a launching point for the presidency). The candidate, Pedro
Solórzano, was already well on his way to becoming the favorite candidate

for the position, when suddenly he found the map of the capital had been redrawn, and he no longer lived there. No small coincidence that candidacy required living in the capital for at least two years, and his plan B – a law permitting candidacy on the basis of a minimum number of signatures on a petition – was simultaneously revoked! Solórzano's candidacy was torpedoed.[11] [157]

Brute Dissuasion Under the right circumstances, your opponents might discover that their appetite for politics has waned. You can help strengthen their resolve to pursue other activities with just enough violence or physical harm to remind them of what awaits them if their political campaign advances. Such was the case for Ukrainian opposition leader Viktor Yuschchenko, who suddenly became gravely ill in 2004 as he campaigned for disputed elections later declared invalid due to irregularities. Doctors determined his body contained levels of a poison called dioxin 1000 times above normal levels. A soluble substance, it could easily have been administered dissolved into something like soup. His face was completely disfigured and his hair went from chestnut-colored to ashen; his skin tone matched.[40]

Uganda's Yoweri Museveni's administration took a similar approach. In the context of rising gas prices, opposition candidates began very publicly walking to work as a publicity stunt. Their stunt backfired however when they were beaten on their way to the office. Pretty soon, a life in politics starts to look awfully painful.[416]

Otherwise, almost all the tactics listed in "Strategies of Suppression: Dealing with Enemies" (section 5.4) come into play here: Throw them in jail, have them arrested, have their companies, ministries, and personal accounts audited, investigate their background, find a suitable scandal in which they are potentially implicated. A particularly enjoyable strategy is accusing your opponents of corruption. Says Paul Collier, "After all, it is likely to be true. A delicious added benefit is that because donors are always urging me to be tougher on corruption, they can scarcely object." [148]

Physical Isolation You may count your predecessor among your most bitter rivals, if he aspires to a return and hasn't been killed. By all means, keep him away until your power has consolidated and he's picked up a fun hobby instead. Madagascar's Andry Rajoelina thwarted the attempted return of exiled former president Marc Ravalomanana by simply closing off national airspace in 2011 and blocking the former president's airplane from entering.[393] The fact that Madagascar is an island makes this advantage particular to the likes of Cuba, Haiti, and similar, but if your terrestrial borders are adequately sealed (get your military on the case: see section 7.1.5),

---

[11]His political career was not. He became Minister for Transport and Infrastructure not long afterward, where he went on to allegedly misappropriate $6.5M of government funds.[214]

you can accomplish this inland as well. Former presidents arrive in enormous, protected motorcades; they don't typically sneak over the border in chicken buses, and so they're relatively easy to spot. It's hard for them to run if they're not around, and the fact you prevent their arrival is a not-so-subtle reminder to your populace of who *does* and *no longer does* "call the shots around here."

6.3.2   Beating them in the Contest

Ideally, you will have enough political opposition to deter any international or national cries of autocracy, while ensuring they remain too weak, disorganized, and riven with internal divisions and petty power struggles to pose much of a challenge to you. Your goal is not to prevent the existence of political opposition but rather to maintain it in an inchoate, disorganized, and ineffective state, while erecting the necessary barriers to entry to prevent real threats from arising to your power. Fortunately, this is not difficult to do, and is fully part of being a 'democracy:' in fact, most of the following tactics are practiced regularly by the political parties in the the Western World.

Start by ensuring your political opposition remains hopelessly, terminally, insufferably divided. Good points of division include: class, ethnicity, age, religious preference, and economic status.

Beat the Strawman   Arrange for someone to run against you, agreeing to lose. That Trojan horse candidate will take some but not all of the opposition vote, easing your way to victory. That candidate will not become president, but you will reward him richly for having assured your win.[241]

Co-opt the Opposition   You can frequently decimate your competition by hiring/nominating your most outspoken opponent to be part of your government. Not only do you shut that loudmouth up, but you reveal him for the hollow mouthpiece he is. In accepting your job, their credibility immediately plummets.

Divide and Conquer   Your opposition best serves you when they are rife with internal divisions. If the only thing that binds them is their hatred of you, this becomes much easier. Your research should be able to identify political differences of opinion, or fractures of allegiance. Push against them to let the fissures open up. Let's say your opposition is composed of a mix of business interests and religious fundamentalists. Propose a law that progressive business-people would approve of but the religious fundamentalists will oppose, such as a law that allows school children's parents to review religious school teacher performance and fire non-performing teachers. The two sides will turn against each other, and leave you alone. Do you care about non-performing religious school teachers? Not at all: the issue is simply the wedge that divides your opposition. Divide and conquer is a well-worn chestnut because it works so well and so frequently.

Look at the example of Josef Stalin, who used the technique throughout his career. While working through the party bureaucracy after Lenin's death, he rarely challenged his enemies outright, preferring instead a more subtle game where he cultivated the aura of moderate "centrist" in the Politburo and positioned himself squarely in the center of his colleagues' rival factions. Before he achieved supreme status, this maneuvering kept him safe from rival attacks. When Trotsky tried to have him removed from his post of general secretary before the 13th party congress in 1924, a rival group led by Grigory Zinoviev and Lev Kamenev rushed to aid, lest his removal benefit Trotsky; this culminated with Kamenev calling for Trotsky to be ousted from the party in 1925, while Stalin demurred. Turnabout being fair play, Trotsky subsequently refused to side with the duo after Stalin moved to eclipse his new partners by building support with other forces within the party. By the time Trotsky, Kamenev, and Zinoviev realized the prudence of joining in opposition to Stalin it was too late: Stalin had acquired enough power to expel all three of them from the party, which led eventually to a more permanent kind of expulsion.[122]

Venezuela's Hugo Chávez employed a similar strategy to keep his political opposition off balance. Rather than compromising with a rising tide of protesters in 2002 Chávez hardened his position and grew rhetorically more abusive (even vulgar, even by Latin American standards: his speech is frequently laced with expletives, unfounded accusations, and carefully gauged personal insults in order to incite the opposition to retaliate with an extreme response. By barreling down the center of your opposition's political platform you divide it into two halves, each of which must harden its position to distinguish itself. Frequently, these hardened positions are of reduced appeal to supporters.[256]

Gerrymandering Weakens the Opposition   Secondly, with careful manipulation of these district boundaries on the basis of historical voting records, ethnic makeup, or historical loyalties, you can ensure they are constructed in a way that the opposition is at a disadvantage. Increasingly sophisticated computer software now exists to help you achieve that goal.[192] Look no farther than the bastion of democracy, the United States, for inspiration, where Congressional Representatives are chosen by district, and the incumbent party gets to determine the district boundaries. The resulting districts, each chosen to maximize the ability of the incumbent to remain unchallenged, is extraordinary. Some of the districts generated automatically are so bizarrely shaped their purpose and origin are obvious, and they attract names: "the Ribbon of Shame" (California, 23rd Congressional District and California 46th Congressional District), "Rabbit on a Skateboard"

(Illinois), and "Upside Down Chinese Dragon" (Pennsylvania)[12].[330] Hungary's Prime Minister Viktor Orban and his Fidusz party likewise employed gerrymandering effectively and to Fidusz' advantage in 2011.[325]

The process of redistricting may also lead to the creation of new districts. If so, appoint their leaders yourself, using the process in essence to bolster your over all majority. To ensure your party's ability to control the shape of districts – and thus the outcome of local elections – ensure the process is run by your incumbent party rather than by a neutral party; if an outside party is chosen to run the process make sure its members are appointed by you or your party. Gerrymandering leads to other benefits come election-time, when potential voters will be unsure of where they need to go to cast their ballot; assuming these are people who would otherwise have supported your opposition, their rejected ballots help tilt the score in your favor (section 12.4.5).

Consequential Economic Hardship You may weaken your opposition's resolve to continue the fight if challenging you means personal economic hardship. In Belarus, when the father of Pavel Marinich decided to run against Alexander Lukashenko, Pavel's business opportunities collapsed, as authorities closed all his avenues for trade.[351] And when General Valery Fralou, former member of Belarusian parliament, helped form a coalition supporting measures Prime Minister Lukashenko disapproved of, he left government. Fralou and the others then found they'd been blacklisted, unable to find employment with any state company.[351] Suddenly, putting on the "Opposition" ball cap starts looking like a phenomenally bad idea.

6.4 Special Interest Groups

A large part of dealing with your own and other political parties is negotiating with, placating, or neutralizing special interest groups. Sometimes you will be able to co-opt them, other times you can convince them loyalty to your party, or participation in your distributive coalition, is the key to satisfaction of their demands. Other times you will want to torpedo them so they leave you in peace to govern. But each group will require its own approach and a bit of finesse.

6.4.1 Intelligentsia

Your writers, journalists, potentially professors, as well as the nation's organizers, rabble-rousers, and would-be political opposition candidates will all try to attack you if given the chance. An occasional crackdown will become necessary to remind them where in society they are expected to remain. Follow China's example: worried that the Jasmine Revolution sweep-

---

[12]Have a look at some of them for yourself: [502]

ing the Middle East would eventually spread to China, the authorities began rounding up "dissidents" like human rights lawyer Teng Biao and five others, blogger Zhang Jiannan, and Ran Yufei, a writer and blogger. Each essentially disappeared, victim of extra-legal detentions that doubtlessly reminded them and their families that dissent is not necessarily tolerated.[492]. Other writers were restricted in other ways, such as Liao Yiwu, poet, author, and musician who was denied travel authorization to attend a festival in Australia (and who had received four years' jail time for having written an unflattering poem about Tiananmen Square).[113]

Similarly, prevent these people from traveling overseas if they are to receive a reward of some sort, as their doing so ultimately strengthens both their personal prestige and the force of their argument. China wisely blocked dissident Liu Xiaobo in 2010 when he was to travel to Oslo to receive the Nobel Peace Prize.[113]

6.4.2   The Political and Business Elite

The whole rest of this book deals somewhat with the question of satisfying the political and economic elite, namely you and your cronies. But let it be said that this interest group, especially if it extends beyond the reach of your personal power, is dangerous and powerful. Their participation in the electoral process seeks only to preserve their traditional power of patronage over a largely poor countryside, and to ensure the privileges to which they are accustomed remain firmly in place. Their land holdings will stymie any legitimate cadastre or land registration reform; their traditional rights of import will prevent you from opening new or closing old markets, and their wealth permits them to back candidates against you if you are not careful.

6.4.3   The Religious Community

Nicaragua's Daniel Ortega had a troubled relationship with the Catholic church. As head of the left-wing Sandinista party in the 1980s Ortega's administration was a relentless opponent and critic of the Catholic church. But in 2006, sensing throwing a bone to the Catholic population would shore up support for his 4th bid for the presidency, his party passed a law outright banning the practice of abortion in any form.[43] Wrote Nicaraguan feminist and staunch Ortega critic Gioconda Belli, "Obtaining the complicity of the Catholic church and his one time nemesis, Cardinal Obando y Bravo – who Ortega managed to protect from a scandal of misused funds in a church's non-profit organization of which the cardinal is president – this time he might be able to convince voters that he's a changed man."[96] And perhaps it worked: Ortega squeaked through that election with a percentage that won him the presidency.

You can take the opposite approach as well: In Haiti, Papa Doc Duvalier recognized the Roman Catholic Church as a legitimate political threat, but neutralized it by encouraging Voodoo as religion, and by expelling the Archbishop in 1969.[33] As a result, he was excommunicated by the Vatican for the next two years.[238] The Dominican Republic's Rafael Trujillo also took the route of antagonism in 1960, and arrested and deported Catholic priests he believed were assisting rebel groups intent on his ouster.[239] And in Cuba to this day, the Church is highly suspect. It is not permitted to conduct any activities deemed "educational" and all publications of the Church are subject to censorship by the Office of Religious Affairs.[248]

6.4.4   The Universities and Student Body

The university system is a hotbed of potential opposition, if you're not careful. And because they are institutions of learning, they are equally institutions of indoctrination. Hugo Chávez's government in Venezuela took the challenge head-on and reacted by passing a law entitling the entire staff of a university – blue collar staff as well as academics – to choose their new rectors, ensuring Chávez working-class supporters would prevent radicals from taking the helm of the educational system.[168] Another way to ensure the school system in general is subservient to your administration is to rigidly structure what they do and do not teach. Italy's notorious strongman Benito Mussolini once boasted, "At every hour of every day, I can tell you on which page of which book each school child in Italy is studying."[469]

A bolder move is to hold teachers responsible for the political activities of their students, as in Myanmar.[248] In fact, Myanmar took even greater precautions after the student pro-democracy uprisings of 1988, relocating many college campuses to remote areas to ensure the student population is dispersed and to interfere with their ability to organize.[248]

The Cuban government prides itself on its educational system, and indeed Cuba has produced well-trained doctors it has sent around the world on "peacekeeping" missions. But all teaching materials – including for subjects like mathematics and and literature – must include ideological content favorable to the Cuban "revolution."[248] The Nicaraguan government took great inspiration from the Cuban amalgam of education and ideology, and incorporated the same tenets into the literacy campaign the Sandinistas oversaw in the 1980s. Then, math books taught counting of rifles and tanks, and reading books extolled the virtues of the Sandinista revolution while demonizing the United States and foreign capitalism.[282]

6.4.5   Civil Society

Civil society should be weak by any measure.[249] While it's acceptable to have watchdog groups and groups that organize public opinion (their presence facilitates your being able to justify a pluricultural political system operating in transparency) you should keep them under your thumb. For starters, make sure their funding stream is at least partially government-controlled. If you have an agency that monitors public procurements, ensure their funding – a percentage of any public procurement, for example – is managed by the Ministry of Finance, who provides it to them on an allotment basis. This permits periodic review of the agency's performance, and provides some face time for your minister before he writes the check.

You can further tighten your grip on power by ensuring you yourself are the head of significant civil society groups. Ali Ben Bongo Ondimba (Gabon) invited senior French Freemasons to Gabon shortly after taking power. They named him Grandmaster of the Grand Lodge in Gabon as well as of the Grand Equatorial Rite, the nation's top French Freemasonic organizations. Needless to say, these are now two organizations that support, fully, the Gabonese leader.[321] The Chinese government takes a dim view of civil society in any form, and has mostly neutered it by prohibiting the formation of any group larger than 10–20 people (basically, anything bigger than a birthday party, and no balloons). It furthermore ensures all NGOs are subject to the Communist Party.[256]

The persecution of civil society groups over all is on the up-tick these days, just as political freedoms are generally on the decline. Under particular attack are those NGOs that advocate for political issues, defend human rights, press for the de-marginalization of special interest groups, or defend the press. So feel free to jump on the band wagon. The trick is as follows: leave the non-political NGOs alone. They will continue to provide health services, teach literacy, improve agriculture, build schools, and the like. But get aggressive with the rest:[385]

- Pass laws that allow them to raise funds under very strict conditions and solely under your authority.

- Prohibit fundraising from countries other than yours. If they can't get financed by European or American sources they are as good as dead in the water.

- Fine NGO directors personally when their NGOs transgress your regulations. Make it hit home!

- Occasionally raid NGO offices: seize computers, files, archives, so you can "inspect" them for hints they are engaged in espionage, covert political activity, or subterfuge. These investigations take time, so proceed at the pace of your choosing while they wait to recuperate their belongings.

- Inspect their buildings for code violations: sealed doorways, shaky stair cases. If in doubt, condemn the building until necessary repairs are made.

- Arrest NGO workers for espionage, subterfuge, and the like. Put them through a show trial: even if you eventually let them go, their public

humiliation and their obvious fear will dump a bucket of cold water
on the aspirations of any recent graduate looking forward to a job promoting democracy in your country. Well done!

6.5   Natural Disasters: Political Benefits

Natural disasters are a good opportunity to strengthen your hand by insisting on the freedoms, authorities, or powers you need to act with impunity.
Simply insist the people demand your rapid response, and belittle the ability
of the National Assembly or similar to be able to react in time. Yes, a major
flood, hurricane, or typhoon is a tragedy. But it's a great opportunity for you
personally.

For starters, coordinate the recovery and aid efforts yourself, or through
an office that answers directly to you. Ensure that aid gets delivered to
"your" districts first, and when opposition-controlled regions come crying
for help, invite them to sit down at the negotiation table and strike a deal.

Then, grant yourself some new powers. Hugo Chávez did this in December 2010 to respond to the devastation of high flood waters that had inundated
some regions of Venezuela, and earthquakes that had left 40 dead and over a
hundred thousand Venezuelans homeless. The National Assembly, stacked
with his supporters, granted him the power to rule by decree for 18 months
(6 more than he'd requested).[13][52] You can imagine the tears in his eyes as
he gazed out over the rubble and floodwaters: they were tears of joy.

---

[13]and just in time, as just months later the composition of the Assembly would be composed
of more representatives of the political opposition.

Chapter 7

Military, Security, and Intelligence Forces

> Terrorism is the best political weapon for nothing drives people harder than a fear of sudden death.
>
> Adolf Hitler

SECURITY forces come in many shapes and sizes, from large blunt instruments like a conscript army, to more subtle and lethal tools such as secret police, and black ops cadres. A truly successful autocrat will use them wisely, unleashing unanswerable force in one instance and, when the circumstances change, decide on a subtler application of state security. Intelligence services, for example, can engage in subtle covert operations to confuse, scatter, or undercut your enemies at a fraction of the cost associated with more traditional arms. Police agents, likewise, are probably more effective as suppressors of internal dissent. Your military, police, and espionage resources should be large, powerful, and flexible components in the machinery of your absolute rule. Keep them oiled, make sure they're working properly, and replace any defective parts. Letting them idle for any length of time can be hazardous, so keep them busy (and it's likely that you will have a very long to-do list.)

7.1 Your Military

The traditional military (army, air force, navy) is your strongest asset and potentially your most tenacious enemy; in all probability, your relationship with the men with guns will define your administration. Look at the trajectory of the "Arab Spring" revolutions of 2011: Tunisia, Egypt, Bahrain,

Syria, and Libya. In Tunisia and Egypt the presidents were forced to step down, while in Bahrain and Syria the uprising led to protracted combat but not to a change in leadership. The distinction is the role the military played. It was widely noted that Egypt's military refused to intervene against protesters, strengthening the hand of the opposition and weakening the hand of President Hosni Mubarak. In Syria however the military supported President Bashar al Assad with fervor, and the "revolution" failed to consolidate.[1]

And in Myanmar in 1988, as demonstrations threatened to consume the nation, the military stepped in and ensured the failure of the would-be revolution. How? By being "prepared to kill as many people as it took to thwart it."[166] This is what they do best, so make sure their guns are pointed in the right direction (i.e. not at you).

It may be that the military runs the country, as they seem to do in Pakistan regardless of how elections turn out. This eventuality may arise from and amplify a belligerent relationship with your near neighbors (India and to a lesser degree, Afghanistan, in Pakistan's case). If you head the military and the military runs the country, then congratulations. Otherwise, take care, as the military – being somewhat less fit than other structures for solving legitimate societal problems – can also be the cause of significant economic and social challenges. In Pakistan's case, the military's pursuit of a policy supporting the Taliban affected the nation in other, significant ways.[256]

Even good generals can become complacent or corrupt, and of course you might just have a bad day and decide to remove the deadwood (as supreme ruler, it's your perogative). Rot can easily spread to the rank and file, and you must nip this phenomenon in the bud. Deal with unruly regiments by sacking the leadership and placing yourself at the head. Learn from Blaise Compaore in Burkina Faso. After a military uprising over unpaid benefits, President Compaore fired his entire cabinet and top military personnel, naming himself Minister of Defense in April 2011.[397] Once you start however, you'll find it hard to stop, and as we recommend in chapter 4 and again in section 3.2.4, it's important to keep shaking up your leadership before they take on more strength than you desire. It's no surprise then that seven months after Compaore changed his military leadership, he did it again: repeat as often as it takes to configure things they way you require them![257]

7.1.1 Independence

If your military sees itself as a separate entity not directly linked to your administration, then you clearly have a problem. In such cases the military may attempt to preserve its integrity and reputation in times of conflict and choose not to soil its hands with the blood of fellow citizens, "manage" a protest rather than squelch it, and hand you over to your ignominious fate. The military will see a future for itself beyond your administration. Worse,

---

[1] As of early 2012. Stay tuned ...

any military with too distinct a "corporate" identity runs the risk of pushing your government to praetorianism with a military that controls the president instead of the reverse. Egypt's Hosni Mubarak might agree with this.[263]

You are far better off with a military so bound to you that their very existence is threatened if you are overthrown; ethnic considerations are one of the better bonds to consider. Syria's military is overwhelmingly drawn from the ruling minority clan and organized under the leadership of president Bashar al-Assad. If he goes down, so will they, and their will to fight for him is strengthened immeasurably as a consequence.

Better still is a military you control fully. Indonesia's Suharto, not long after taking power, placed all the divisions of the armed forces under his direct control.[237] There are many examples of this, but Suharto's long staying power should make this option a leading one if you have confidence in your ability to make military decisions, should it come to that.

7.1.2   Unity vs. Balkanization

For maximum efficacy under your personal control, your military should be cohesive and professional: if you fail to instill these essential traits your armed forces may splinter under stress, with some units defecting or other units combining in local allegiances that convert your national military into a patchwork of militias [263] . . .

. . . unless a patchwork is what you prefer. If your own military is your greatest political threat, you're better off splitting it into rival groups, and cultivating ambitious, competitive leaders for each. Soon they will be fighting each other within the government bureaucracy and will have been neutralized as a threat. President Mobutu of Zaire did this to great initial success.[149] Liberia's Samuel Doe took this route to prevent a military coup of the sort common to that country. By managing the military as separate units, he ensured no single military, police, intelligence, or militia faction would have strength sufficient enough to challenge him. Individual security units remained loyal to their immediate commander and to the President, but nothing resembling a formal chain of command existed. The Minister of Defense had close to no authority before his troops whatsoever, and more often than not it was individual militias who took the lead in managing field operations. Doe likewise developed a laundry list of parallel military structures with overlapping and confusing mandates rather than relying on his military: the Anti-Terrorist Unit that guarded the presidential palace, the Special Operations Division, the Special Security Forces, myriad militia groups that supplemented the police and finally, an extremely weak military proper.[376]. Prudence is called for however, because this strategy can also backfire if pushed beyond certain limits, and in the case of Zaire the military was stretched so thin it became ineffective as a force for repression.[149]

7.1.3 Ethnicity

Military units who, for reasons of religion, geography, nationality, or language, see themselves as different from the people they are sent to put down, will do so more willingly – and perhaps more violently, if necessary – than military personnel who identify with their victims. The 1989 crackdown in China's Tiananmen Square is the best-known example of this: the People's Liberation Army's 27th unit was at the front of the crackdown; hailing mostly from the northern Shaanxi Province and speaking a different dialect, they were far more apt to fire upon the protesters.[263]

Bahrain and Libya understood this point long ago. Bahrain built a military out of imported Sunni Muslims from Pakistan, who had no qualms about firing on Bahraini Shia protesters. In Iraq under Saddam Hussein the military was mostly Sunni and was effective against the 1991 Shia and Kurdish uprisings, while the Syrian army is mostly Christian and Druze, more than happy to attack Sunni Muslims.[263] And the United Arab Emirates, working with a well-known American security firm, has built a training base and recruited hired mercenaries – mostly from Colombia – to ensure Muslim targets pose no problem.[326] Lastly, Mohammar Khadaffi built an anti-insurgency unit out of hired mercenaries from across Africa. Having no allegiance to or affiliation with the rest of Libyan citizens, they were more reliable in times of conflict, and Khadaffi relied heavily on them to quash dissent in the military in 2011. The question of ethnicity is doubly true for your military's leadership, who will make the decisions the foot soldiers then follow.

7.1.4 Professionalism and Brawn vs. Brains

If your government is a poorly educated military junta unaccustomed to wealth and privilege, then it's easy for your military to get out of control. In Liberia, the Samuel Doe military junta of the 1980s was an unabashed disaster partly because the humble, poorly educated soldiers of the junta suddenly found themselves in a position of unprecedented power. Like puppies off the leash, they wrecked the government's fleet of Mercedes Benz vehicles, detained wealthy Liberians at gunpoint for ransoms of petty cash, and worse. Their lack of professionalism and immaturity doomed the Doe administration and appalled most of the world.[2] Writes John-Peter Pham, "One unfortunate merchant, having paid off the officer holding him was walking out of prison when he was sighted by another *putschist* and rearrested on a different set of trumped-up charges. By the end of their rule, it was estimated that Doe and his surviving colleagues had looted the national treasury of some $300M in public funds."[376]

We don't mean to suggest that all your fighting men should be bright:

---

[2]Not the Americans, however. Because the Ronald Reagan administration saw Liberia as an ally against Communism, it fawned over Liberia regardless of its immature and dangerous antics.

You don't need Nobel laureates to smash skulls at a protest march and you certainly don't want the rank-and-file to question their orders when an angry mob is approaching your presidential palace. Nor will patient reflection help when you need rough treatment for opposition leaders. Rather, ensure that thugs, criminals, and other high school dropouts fill the ranks. Their penchant for violence and cruelty is useful. But they need to have good judgment, a fact you'll remember when it's too late. Nothing will hasten your own demise than jackbooted goons getting caught on video (as did the Egyptian military in 2012) stripping and stomping on a half nude female protester after tearing open her burka.[59]

That said, be prepared to weather any unprofessionalism, as it's essential to keep the military on your side. In addition, you want to make sure they are staffed properly. Start with the basics:

1. *Choose the head of the military carefully.* Look for a combination of loyalty, (just enough) ambition, and ability in equal measures. Make sure your generals are effective military leaders so they can defend you and your interests when necessary while also ensuring that they support you fully, regardless of the ebb and flow of given conflict or any personal strains. Edward Gibbon's description of the Emperor Justinian's most famous general, Belisarius, is instructive: "Belisarius was chaste and sober. In the license of a military life, none could boast that they had seen him intoxicated with wine. The most beautiful captives of Gothic or Vandal race were offered to his embraces; but he turned aside from their charms, and ... was never suspected of violating the laws of conjugal fidelity ... amidst the perils of war, he was daring without rashness, prudent without fear, slow or rapid according to the exigencies of the moment; that in the deepest distress he was animated by real or apparent hope, but that he was modest and humble in the most prosperous fortune. By these virtues, he equaled or excelled the ancient masters of the military art. Victory, by sea and land, attended his arms. He subdued Africa, Italy, and the adjacent islands ... In his fame and merit, in wealth and power, he remained without a rival, the first of the Roman subjects ..."[216] Sound like a wet blanket? He nearly reconquered half of the Roman Empire – don't mess with him!

   Good choices for your top general are people not well enough liked to topple you, or on whom you have some significant leverage. Bad choices include your brothers or immediate family members, including your sons, who may eventually get too ambitious for their own good. Make sure to prevent the formation of officer cliques, as their thoughts will turn eventually to dreams of a world where they out-rule you. Augusto Pinochet's rise and role in the September coup in Chile in 1973 can be seen both as a model for you and as a warning. Remember, there's only one job better than head of the military, and it's yours.

2. *Feed the Beast.* A wealthy army is a prosperous one. The Dominican Republic's Rafael Trujillo, a military man himself, ensured the military received generous pay raises and enjoyed special privileges. A good way to keep the generals cognizant of the benefits of loyalty is to slip them the occasional bone. For example, whenever they remove an enemy of yours, allow them to keep that person's home for themselves. You'd be surprised how fast this trick works for your loyalty issues. You can also grant them important territory to be administered under their control, such as the fifteen kilometer border strip proposed by Nicaragua's Daniel Ortega.[412] Such income and control keeps the Military happy and on your side.

3. *Keep your generals guessing.* Nowhere is the trick of rotating your leaders on an erratic or unpredictable basis more useful than here. If any particular general criticizes you publicly or otherwise questions your leadership, either put into practice the harassment routine (see section 5.4) or appoint someone else to take their place. Under no circumstances, give that person a chance to become a hero; rather, make sure he spends a year or two washing your car for you, while the press covers his plight in excruciating detail. Rather than promoting young, capable commanders until they rise through the ranks and eventually target you, instead, select the weak, elderly, retiring, or incompetent military leaders and start shuffling them. Soon the rising superstar may find himself laboring under an aging, senile general, 'promoted' to a position where he will be inundated by mindless paperwork, or forced to work with an equally ruthless rival. And you will have neutralized a potential threat. Such actions may also force the hand of eager general contemplating your overthrow, and once they show their plans these conspirators are easily dealt with. No one better mastered the military re-org than Spain's General Francisco Franco, who kept his generals in a state of constant rotation via swift, un-announced, and often subtle changes in position and authority. In the 1940s, upon learning of a coup being plotted by one General Muñoz Grandes, he pulled Grandes from power, later counterintuitively placing him in a prestigious but less powerful position.[246]

4. *Remove the Dead Wood.* Haiti's François Duvalier survived an unsuccessful coup attempt in 1958 and responded immediately by re-shaping the military. He replaced senior officers with younger and more loyal men, reduced the size of the army, and closed the military academy.[238]

But watch out for angry, recently-fired deadwood. In Guinea, former military leader Nouhou Thioam returned with a battery of heavy artillery, and shelled the president's residence in apparent retribution for having been removed.[3] [9]

5. *Watch your Back*. If the military is your greatest asset, it is also potentially your greatest liability. Watch out for attempted coups led by disaffected military leaders. In Niger, a group of military leaders – among them, one commander and a lieutenant – tried to overthrow President Mahamadou Issoufou in July 2011. Investigators found documents describing the establishment of a "Popular Committee for the Establishment of Popular Democracy" on one of the accused's computers. But Issoufou had *been* popularly elected, and his presidency had been recognized by both Europe and the USA. Furthermore, as Issoufou was in the process of investigating corruption within the military, it seems clear they were just eager to maintain their economic livelihood.[10] [464] Worse still was the fate of Mali's Amadou Toumani Toure in 2012: as Tuareg forces fighting for regional autonomy continued to batter the Malian army[4], army leaders finally attacked their own presidential palace, ousting the president in frustration with their government's failure to better supply the army with weapons.[89]

Perhaps to stymie any similar misfortune at the hands of his military, Paraguay's Alfredo Stroessner made a habit of showing up every Thursday at the general staff headquarters of the armed forces over the years. It was a none-too-subtle reminder that he too had a military background, and as president had ultimate authority over the military. He lost to a coup anyway, ousted by a military faction led by a general who sensed he was losing his standing in the battle for succession and pounced when he got the chance.[424]

6. *Politicize the Machine* In the Soviet Union's Red Army, every battalion contained a political commissar who had the unique right to countermand any order made by the unit commander if he deemed the order contrary to the interests of the Communist party. That subverts the role of your military to your political party, which you control, and reinforces your authority over the armed forces.

After learning these basics you might carefully reconsider your longer-term relationship with the military. On his deathbed, the Roman emperor Septimus Severus had some advice for his heirs: "Be harmonious, enrich the soldiers, and scorn all other men." This gets to the heart of the rapport between autocrats and their armies.[131] There are many useful techniques for keeping this relationship healthy and like a good marriage it may require some work on your part. Though certainly more tedious than stringing up your rivals, spending time with your security forces is worth the bother. The

---

[3]President Conde survived, two presidential guards were injured and one killed, and Thiam was captured.

[4]It's no small accident the Tuaregs were winning: many of them were recently returned from Libya where they'd been trained and armed over the years by Mohammar Khadaffi.

military can place you in the seat of power and remove you from it quite forcefully, so learning how to manage them is an essential part of the dictator's tool kit. Don't let your vigilance wane! Even the most successful chief can grow soft or lazy, and such behavior invites the attention of power-hungry generals.

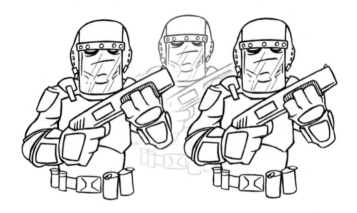

Once again Adolf Hitler provides a successful example of how to accomodate the military establishment. In his case it was a gift even the most critical suitor couldn't fail to appreciate. First the necessary background: Leading up to his seizure of power in 1933 Hitler had used his private paramilitary group, the SA, as an effective tool to cow the opposition and dose the populace with a sprinkling of terror around election time. Street brawlers, disgruntled veterans seeking violent affirmation, criminals and perverts, by the time of Hitler's chancellorship the SA numbers had swelled, changing the organization from a loyal group of enforcers to a dangerous mini-army with an increasingly independent streak. Certainly Ernst Röhm, their leader, had taken the idea of revolution to heart and by 1934 was advocating for the German army to be neutered and eclipsed by the SA with Röhm as the *generalissimo* answerable only to Hitler. Röhm's antagonism toward the army had served Hitler well up to that point, but once it became apparent that the military hierarchy was no longer amused, it was time for his good friend Röhm to go. He and at least 80 others were dispatched during the infamous "Night of Long Knives" and the army got the message: Hitler was on their side.[204] The brutal public executions in June and July of 1934 reassured the generals that they were not to be supplanted by a tub-thumping street revolutionary like Röhm and made Hitler's bond with his military that much closer. It cemented his rule in another way as well: by placating the army he neutralized the only institution in Germany that could have threatened his power.

Other autocrats, like Hosni Mubarak, apparently forgot that lesson after years of living by it, and the events in early 2011 confirm that an unhappy military and one man rule are generally incompatible. The importance of recognizing disgruntled soldiers and scheming generals can't be stressed enough. In retrospect, Mubarak failed to see that the military's offer of a drawn-out lame duck period for his regime (the mysteriously titled Communiqué Number Two, proposed in February of 2011) was not a sign that they were throwing in with him; rather, it was a lifeline, an invitation to buy time and weather the wrath of the protests until an accommodation could be reached. But that accommodation never included Mubarak once his generals saw that the future was not with him but rather with the protesters that had flooded Tahrir Square.[177] Mubarak's case is certainly a warning against letting your guard down, while also clarifying the choices available to despots during such a critical stage in their lives. When you suspect your generals are wavering in their support, it's time to sweeten the pot – or get out of the way. If not you may share Mubarak's fate, or possibly invite a more unpleasant one. After months of military defections Mohammar Khadaffi was left with few competent supporters in the face of a increasingly powerful rebellion, and this torrent of deserting rats fled the sinking ship of the Colonel's regime.[293]

7.1.5 Role of the Military

Now that you have a nice shiny military with debt-financed hardware, how do you use it? We've detailed elsewhere how to claw your way to, consolidate or maintain your power through the military, but the fact remains that you can't always send out the tanks to crush your enemies – and you'd better find something constructive for the army to do lest they start grumbling about back pay, sick time, and pensions. Here are a few activities that might keep the grunts too busy to think about your wars against personal freedoms and transparent elections.

Fight Wars

Yes, technically, it's true, but it's more likely your enemies will be internal, not external. Also, if your military is not managed properly they will put you in the history books forever, as did the Salvadoran military in December, 1981. Deeply mired in a bloody civil war, the now-outlawed semi-independent Atlacatl battalion entered the village of El Mozote (accused of collaborating with the rebels) and killed a thousand civilians, half of them children, in what is now recognized as the single worst massacre of Latin American citizens in contemporary history. You can imagine the military vowing to teach those villagers a lesson they'd never forget. The effect was arguably the opposite.[86] Go read the section on the professionalism of your military again (section 7.1.4).

Maintain the Border

It is helpful to keep your people where they are. It's even more helpful to keep dangerous foreigners and their democratic ideals away from your gullible subjects. To help achieve these ends there is no better tool than a well-drilled army. First, mobilize: send the troops to the border, string the barbed wire, and make border-crossing punishable by sniper's justice. Then build an infrastructure, an impermeable line of concrete bunkers, thick walls, and electrified fences. Finally, have the army enforce strict compliance with laws demanding appropriate papers for all those entering or leaving the country. This will keep them busy when there isn't a war or insurrection to fight, and if the more unscrupulous members of the army skim a little contraband then congratulate them on their entrepreneurial initiative (while keeping an eye on them, of course).

Eritrean president Esaias Afawerki has apparently followed these instructions very carefully. The borders of Eritrea are mined, and patrolled by soldiers with "shoot-to-kill" orders, both to protect incursions by the neighbor-enemy Ethiopia but also to ensure Eritreans do not try to escape. Escapees are furthermore frequently returned to Eritrea from places like Malta, Libya, Sudan, Egypt, and even Britain. Once returned, these people are viewed as guilty of treason and subject to jail, torture, and potentially death.[392] Afawerki has also made travel permits and exit visas mandatory for domestic and foreign travel, respectively.

Not to be out-done, Daniel Ortega proposed legislation in late 2010 that would make a fifteen kilometer strip along the Nicaraguan national borders the administrative domain of the army. In addition, a five kilometer strip directly on the border was declared a "border security zone" in which all property belonged inalienably to the state.[412] That's easy to propose when you're drumming for armed conflict with a neighbor, or when you intend to prevent the people living within that strip from supporting the same neighbor.[5]

Naturally, such comprehensive border enforcement is easier if your nation is an island. For decades, Cuba has been somewhat of a maritime prison, and it is illegal – and subject to harsh punishment and prison terms – to attempt to leave the island without permission.[248]

Defend your Nation from Foreign Invaders

Ha ha, just kidding! With *very* infrequent exceptions, the typical nation faces few threats from neighboring countries that are not more easily resolved through diplomacy. Traditionally in countries like yours, the role of the military is to maintain a trained, weapons-bearing force that will crush

---

[5]In Nicaragua's case, in the 1980s, such a declaration led to the 1981 'Red Christmas' in which indigenous communities were displaced en masse, and many individuals were killed, in the name of preventing their defection to, or support of, Contra troops operating out of neighboring Honduras.

your political opposition, terrorize your minorities, and if push comes to shove, save your bacon from internal uprisings born of discontent with your rule. See chapter 8.

Fend for Themselves

Your military will eventually grow to be big enough you can scarcely afford to feed them. Whip out your capitalist credentials and make your military a money earner. Myanmar's military force is one of the nation's biggest black market economic forces as well, controlling huge tracts of land and commanding a privileged economic role in the farmlands outside of the nation's two big cities. There, they cultivate opium poppies, outlaw products that compete with their own farms (like local farm chickens), and clear cutting teak forest. And you thought they were only good for putting down your rioters.[185]

7.2   Your Police Force

Local and regional police forces are your ears to the ground and your eyes in the homes of your citizens. No one knows the local troublemakers like they do, and they should be trained not only to keep the daily peace but also to spot undesirables (e.g., anyone who disagrees with you in public). You don't need to recruit the smartest individuals; here, brawn will do over brains.

Your police should also be empowered to conduct searches without a warrant or prior notification. [362] However, every member of the police force should be intimately aware of the risk to their own personal security should they investigate the "wrong" cases, such as those involving you and your narcotrafficking financiers. Sadly, sometimes you need to remove cops who rise above their station. The murder of uncooperative or overly-ambitious/curious law enforcement personnel sends a strong signal to the rest of the force that their role is to make sure purse-snatchers don't bother the citizenry very much, keep your opposition in line, and turn a blind eye to you and your cronies.[364]

The police have an important role in defining the benefits of your political support and the misery that awaits your opposition. You will dramatically undermine your enemies if opposition-led areas become lawless, dangerous areas of town. Hugo Chávez ensured Venezuelan regions that preferred opposition candidates in 2008 were denied the funding required to maintain law and order. Crime waves ensued. The moral is: physical security should be the direct consequence of support for you, whereas lack of support should be accompanied by repercussions.[256] Who better to enforce consequences than the men in blue?

7.3 Subtle Hammers: Secret Police, Elite Units and Spies

Although the temptation to fire-bomb your detractors back to the stone age will admittedly be difficult to resist, don't push the button just yet. You have finer, more subtle tools available, and as detailed in this and other chapters (see chapter 8) your intelligence services are more than capable of defusing a potential danger when necessary. Think of them as your subtle hammers; not as obvious as sending in the tanks, and usually just as effective.

Intelligence services, paramilitary orders, secret police, elite units, black ops cadres: they come in many names and have many overlapping functions. This is good, because a Byzantine conglomeration of rival spy agencies and special forces means that no one group becomes so powerful that you need fear them toppling your regime. Generally though, their responsibilities can be divided between those devoted exclusively to domestic security and those whose responsibilities are broader. Secret police usually fall in the former camp, and are usually an elite security organ with a hierarchy outside the traditional local police forces. Such organizations handle the the daily tasks of domestic security, surveillance of enemies, and general suppression of dissent. Smaller, elite police units may be charged with the ruthless elimination of internal enemies and probably answer only to the president. Larger state organs or local forces can retain the public face of law and order (investigating fraud, traffic tickets). In either case, a wise dictator will lean on them heavily, because they will be his best and most fanatical supporters.

Elite security units will often do the dirty work for which a conscript army is ill-suited. For example, within five years of independence, Zimbabwe's Robert Mugabe had established the infamous Fifth Brigade, which unleashed a wave of terror in opposition areas. Ghana's Kwame Krumah had the President's Own Guard Regiment (POGR), also known as the president's "private army." But Zaire under Mobutu had a number of redundant and extra-systemic military forces, including the Civil Guard (commanded by the President's brother in law), the Special Research and Surveillance Brigade (also related to the president by marriage), the Special Action Forces (a paramilitary unit, commanded by Mobutu's chief of intelligence), and the Special Presidential Division (the most effective of the units, and commanded by a close relative of Mobutu).[31]

It is no longer fashionable to have quite so many extra-systemic police/military units. But you will probably want one secret police force to do your bidding. Your secret police should be fanatically loyal and ruthlessly efficient, as they were in Khadaffi's Libya.[459] One way to counter the threat of a powerful oppositional military is to ensure that your secret police vastly outnumber them, as did Papa Doc Duvalier and his *Tontons Macoutes* in Haiti.[33]

- National Intelligence Directorate (DINA) (Chile). Responsible for a reign of terror under Augusto Pinochet and the assassination – even abroad – of political opponents.

- Stasi (East Germany): The Ministry for State Security, also known as the Stasi was responsible for the suppression and identification of internal enemies, the elimination of dissidents, and covert operations with an international reach. The Stasi were notorious for using sexual intrigue to entrap and blackmail Western diplomats or soldiers in West Berlin; this technique was such a favorite that a Stasi-run brothel was established in that city. The Stasi also facilitated the East German government in their support of terrorist groups who struck targets in the West, such as the Red Army Faction of Ilich Ramirez Sanchez (Carlos the Jackal).[194]

- State Security Investigations (SSI) (Egypt). The SSI was the coercive arm of the Hosni Mubarak administration, fully authorized and entitled to acts of brutality in order to keep the machine rolling. They had great sway over institutions like Cairo University, where one SSI director chose the dean of the school, which professors to hire, promote, or fire, and which students would be denied the right to continued education. The SSI was also responsible for detentions, kidnapings, disappearances, systematic torture and rape, and managed a set of underground prisons whose methods were all exposed in 2011 when Mubarak fell.[6][62] Given their power, ruthlessness, and autonomy, Egyptians were rightfully terrified of the SSI, and Mubarak rightly made it a central pillar of his regime.

- Tontons Macoutes (Haiti): More thugs than secret police, the Tontons were a brutal private militia that helped both Papa and Baby Doc Duvalier squelch dissent; an estimated 30,000 Haitians died at their hands
  .

- Documentation and Security Directorate (DDS) (Chad): Under Hissene Habre, the DDS committed atrocities at a scale only Chile's Augusto Pinochet could fathom. A board of inquiry has attributed over 40,000 politically-motivated murders and about 200,000 cases of torture to the DDS. The abuse targeted minority ethnicities and the cruelty of the DDS' methods is the stuff of legends today: electric shocks, asphyxiation, death by starvation, and the like.[45]

- Iranian Revolutionary Guard Corps (IRGC) (Iran): 125,000 members strong and distributed throughout the nation. Hardly secret, the IRGC

---

[6]Once Mubarak fell, protesters ransacked the SSI offices, videotaping and publishing evidence of secret graveyards, medieval-like dungeons, the files of dissidents held for more than a decade, lists of informants.[62]. As you run your security apparatus, think about what protesters will find and publish about you, if they succeed in pushing you from power. Invest in a paper shredder; your legacy depends on it.

is rightly-feared and economically unassailable. Ahmedinejad was, himself, a member. Originally charged with defending the nation against foreign enemies, the IRGC has increasingly has been put to use eliminating domestic foes and political threats to the Ahmedinejad administration; as such it has been reorganized on a geographical basis, and the district commanders now directly oversee the two- to five-million members of the Basij, Iran's gang-like militia.[256] The broad mandate of geographic presence of the IRGC prepares it well for regional uprisings or popular revolt. The IRGC enforces adherence to the Islamic faith and has sole jurisdiction over patrols of Iran; its Quds Force has exported the means of warfare – missiles, land mines – to Hezbollah and Hamas, and is widely involved in Iranian domestic economic and political affairs. It oversees the Basij Resistance Force, founded by Ayatollah Ruhollah Khomeini in 1979: a voluntary paramilitary organization responsible for defense from external threats.[256] Importantly, membership in the IRGC is both politically and economically rewarding: President Mahmoud Ahmedinejad is a veteran of the organization, and has used his authority over them accordingly. Two thirds of the President's cabinet are IRGC commanders, and 80 former IRGC officers hold seats in parliament. IRGC members have ties to more than 100 Iranian companies, are involved in lucrative gas and engineering contracts, have won government contracts, and earn between $12 and 15 billion per year in business, construction, and engineering.[256]

- Military Intelligence Service (SIM) (Dominican Republic): responsible for cowing the Dominican opposition for three decades.

Finally, special mention should be made of the Okhrana, or the Department for Protecting the Public Security and Order, the Czarist secret police established in Russian in 1880. Until the 1917 revolution, these loyal servants of the Czar infiltrated and subverted labor movements, removed enemies of the crown, spied on suspect citizens, and most notoriously forged "The Protocols of the Elders of Zion," the pamphlet purporting to be the blueprint of an international Jewish conspiracy. More importantly, the Okhrana has been seen as the prototype for totalitarian police systems that followed, partly because of their ability to turn captured radicals into well-placed agents within opposition groups.[462]

7.4 Spy Agencies

Although in many cases secret police and spy agencies may share overlapping responsibilities, or be integrated into one unit (e.g., the KGB), a few points of distinction are warranted. First, although black ops may be an attractive side hobby, never forget that spy agencies function best when they focus on developing sources of information on internal and external enemies. This is where agencies such as the Stasi and KGB shined, and where the alert dictator can pick up many pointers. Always try to plant your men in the spy agencies of other nations first, and you will never be surprised by a military incursion or late night bombing raid. The NKVD/KGB famously recruited British spy Kim Philby in the 1930s, and Philby went on to provide decades of valuable information to Stalin and his successors in their ideological struggle against the West.[195]

Second, always appoint someone you trust as your spy-master. Unlike other cabinet ministers or chiefs of staff, intelligence chiefs have access to sensitive, classified information, and unless you have no secrets to hide (and since you're supreme ruler, you likely do) make sure that your appointee is loyal to the regime. If not, the more ambitious master spies may neglect to inform you of plots against your life or of imminent attacks, and rush to step in once you are removed from power. Worse, if they are eventually implicated in scandals attributable directly to you, they will precipitate your almost immediate downfall, as Vladimiro Montesinos did for Peruvian ex-president Alberto Fujimori.[37]

Lastly – and this is arguably the most important tenet – your spy agencies are most useful when they are totally covert and operating in the midst of your other institutions and the military and police in particular. Think about it: many of your most immediate threats originate from your armed forces. They will find it much harder to organize and plot against you if they do not know – and are deathly fearful of – hidden spies among their ranks. Ensuring that no one truly knows who is working for your secret, personal intelligence services will have a profound impact on the rest of your government's loyalty, enthusiasm, and dedication.

7.5 Using Your Security Tools

You have your army fully staffed, your secret police are well-placed across the land, and your spies are collecting important and actionable intelligence. What next? Beyond the obvious (start a war, arrest troublemakers), there are several tasks that might be considered, and each of them will help you achieve your goal – staying in power.

7.5.1 No spark, no fire

Poverty may help precipitate a revolution, but it rarely leads to one by itself. Provide a spark though, something around which angry people can organize, and the fire may soon burn down your regime. It's worthwhile to look at a few precise events that have stirred unrest and eventually sparked revolutions. They are frequently violent death, often directly attributable to the dictator or his secret police, or ruinous financial policies.

Nation	Year	Event
Tunisia	2010	Self-Immolation of fruit seller
Iran	1978	Burning of hundreds in cinema, attributed to Shah's Secret Police
Indonesia	1998	4 dead protesters led to larger protests and 1000 dead

Table 7.1: Sparks that set off Revolutions

In the aftermath, pressure builds until the military is forced to choose whether it is better to back the dictator or the people. Avoid this uncomfortable moment by re-reading the section on economic development (section 4.4) to ensure the people see some benefit in your administration; then do whatever you can to ensure your military will support you in the time of need; and finally, if you can, move quickly to snuff out any militant spark before it becomes a rallying point for public outrage and causes crowds to assemble.[63]

7.5.2   Prisons

Think of your penal system as the hard infrastructure of your security state. Just as highways must be maintained by an army of workers, your network of prisons must be kept sufficiently terrible by the security forces, and in this case the more terrible the better. A truly fearsome prison does wonders for the courage of rebels and dissidents. It dissolves courage wonderfully, like acid. But what, in this day and age, makes a good (or bad) prison?

First, other than the basic *accoutrements* like barbed wire, vicious dogs, and sniper towers, you must establish fact one: anyone entering your prisons is likely never to leave again. Broadcast the fact that every other Sunday is execution day; then, for the smug bastard who is due to be released on Wednesday, move the date up a week. It's no good letting anyone think they can cheat fate, and the unpredictability will spread fear among your actual and would-be enemies. In fact, it might prevent the latter from raising a peep, which is the point in the first place. During the presidency of Saddam Hussein and long before the Americans put it on the cover of *Newsweek*, Abu Ghraib prison was already an infamous hellhole of a detention center, with regular mass killings of jailed political undesirables, particularly when enemies of the state were most readily identifiable after the Shiite uprising in the wake of the first Gulf War.[24]

In light of this, it's unwise to place your prison system under the management of non-military government agencies. Such groups, which may include your department of the interior or justice, may have a soft spot for the incarcerated and gradually agitate for more liberal prisons. This kind of laxity could lead to general unrest, prison riots, and in the worst case give you a reputation for softness. A safer bet is to let your military run them, as was done in Kazakhstan in 2011. Not surprisingly, their military had a much lower tolerance for disorder. Complaining that military control of Kazakh prisons has led to widespread abuses of human rights, Susan Corke of Freedom House International said,

> While conditions for prisoners in Kazakhstan remain atrocious even under civilian control, the involvement of civil society at least provided a valuable watchdog that could advocate for greater progress and more humane treatment of prisoners.

Thanks Susan; putting the military behind the wheel was intended to do exactly that.[251]

Have a look at North Korea then, where the horrors you thought ended when Josef Stalin died continue right up to the present. North Korea's gulag prison system is home to multiple generations of offenders, most of whom are never released. There, the race to the bottom of human rights offenses continues. Consider:

> "The gulag's captives are not told of their crimes, though torture usually produces a 'confession' – which might admit to defacing an image of the 'Great Leader' or listening to a foreign broadcast. There is no defence, trial, judge or sentence, though most inmates remain in the camps for life, unless they escape. They are victims of forced disappearances, in that neighbours, colleagues and distant family members know nothing about the fate of those who vanish. Inmates are held incommunicado, without visits, food parcels, letters or radio. Chronically malnourished, they work in mines, quarries and logging camps, with one rest-day a month. Infractions of camp rules, such as stealing food meant for livestock, damaging equipment or having unauthorised sexual liaisons are punished with beatings and torture. Guards rape women prisoners, leading to forced abortions for the pregnant, or infanticide. Inmates are under pressure to snitch. Executions are routine – and fellow prisoners must often watch.

> "Consider the case of Shin Dong-hyuk, the subject of a new book ("Escape from Camp 14"). He was born of "model" prisoner parents in Camp 14, Kaechon in 1982 and spent his first 22 years inside. As punishment for dropping a sewing machine, his finger was cut off. He was also suspended over a fire, and a hook was thrust through his belly, to make him 'confess' to joining an escape supposedly being planned by his mother and brother. He was then made to witness their executions."[186]

7.5.3 Infiltrating the Opposition

It's important to have your people on the inside of your opposition parties and movements. You can record and note their decisions and strategies, using them when appropriate. For example, Georgian authorities put down a protest movement in 2011 with what some considered excessive force. After absorbing some criticisms they released a video of the opposition leaders discussing how to provoke the police to use violence; further video evidence includes members of the group speaking of a plot to storm and burn government buildings).[428]

7.6 Keeping Tabs on the International Community

You have lots of internal enemies; that's well-understood. But you also host many foreign diplomats, technocrats, and development workers, and their opinions can influence their government's willingness to fund your increasingly voracious regime. And because they have diplomatic immunity, the Vienna Convention prevents you from the overt use of your tested methods of persuasion. That crimps your style, but doesn't prevent you from being able to get a sense for what they are thinking and reacting appropriately.

It's not hard to find out what your foreign embassies are thinking. Frequently you can just ask them. In other circumstances you have to be clever. In general, you can count on your Westerners to believe they're an elite clique monitoring and helping you; put enough of them together in a room and they'll all begin to talk. Is the waiter on your payroll? He should be. Invite your diplomats to a meeting, huddle them together in a waiting room with a waiter and some wine and cheese, and take notes. You'll be surprised how indiscrete they can be.

You have many other forms of espionage available, and of course your nation's people are employed within those embassies as well. Some of them may be willing to help you by providing a list of phone numbers, helping you learn the ambassador's schedule, and so on. For example, if the French Ambassador is suddenly meeting the Chinese Ambassador frequently, perhaps you'll want to schedule some time with the Chinese Ambassador as well.

Your international community typically lives in large town houses with spacious gardens, and lives in fear of burglary, banditry, and petty violence. They've hired minimum-wage security guards on contract to sit outside their houses. But those security guards are easily brought over to your side on an individual basis, and since they typically earn a wage that barely permits them to feed their families, will probably be happy to provide you with the information you need in exchange for some money. Does the occupant make telephone calls with the window open? Do your own people visit on occasion? Who are they, and what are their license plate numbers? This is basic information gathering, and costs very little.

Members of the international community notoriously frequent a limited number of restaurants and watering holes, preferably those where their native language is understood, and where they can cry into their beer about your government's intransigence and incompetence. Place a few waiters on the staff to get an idea of what they're discussing. Open up a Café Americano with your slush fund money and show football games on large screen televisions, hire voluptuous waitresses, and watch the tables fill with loose-lipped functionaries. Or, send in your agents, preferably comely women and handsome men, and see which international diplomat sends over a round of drinks. Then, once the your plant leaves the satisfied mark in a post-orgasmic daze at the motel, send your enforcers in to snap the incriminating photos. Before long you will have a growing cadre of cowed informants working for you within the international community. Entrapment and blackmail may sound farfetched – the provenance of bad television thrillers – but they were techniques used with much success by the East German Stasi and its notorious chief, Markus Wolf.[194]

Chapter 8

Unrest, Demonstrations, Riots

The truth is that men are tired of liberty.

Benito Mussolini

YOU'VE assumed power, dispersed your rivals, scattered your enemies, and subsequently legitimized your rule in the eyes of the international community. Your family is happy and not doing anything to embarrass you; the generals are pleased with your compliments, an infusion of high-tech military hardware, and those shiny gold epaulets you've fastened on their uniforms. The business community is in equally high spirits ever since you mandated unfair trade practices that have generated a windfall of cash for their formerly sputtering enterprises. And you've just won a limited war with those vermin in the adjoining country, annexing an oil field or two for good measure. In short, the gods have smiled on your authoritarian adventure, and all should be right with the world. But wait a moment: some blogger is complaining, somewhere, about your record on human rights; a crowd in a public square starts chanting dangerously political slogans after the victory of the national soccer team, and the supporters of a defeated rival you've failed to imprison organize a peaceful march (with candles, flowers, and "Freedom" signs in tow) protesting your increasingly hard-line tactics. What a mess. Civil unrest, political demonstrations, and rioting are useful in small doses as sedatives for an unruly citizenry, but let them proceed unchecked and they can and will topple your regime or at least sow the seeds of revolution. Happily, these expressions of public anger can be prevented, managed, and in a pinch put down ruthlessly, and you should consider all three options if you expect to have a lengthy and uneventful rule.

141

8.1   Overview of Riot Management

Rule number one: move quickly and decisively. A riot quickly becomes a revolution, and a revolution is a 24-hour-a-day event. You have no time to pause and take stock. The Shah of Iran, fatigued by his ongoing battle against cancer, was slow to react and was ousted in 1978; Indonesia's Suharto, aging and out-of-shape after decades in power, was neither quick to respond to protests nor agile enough to react appropriately, and was ousted in ten days.[63] A corollary of rule one is that you should always try to anticipate unrest, as this involves preparation and intrinsically allows you to move fast when the signs of turmoil are evident.

Rule number two: know your enemy. Have a look at *From Dictatorship to Democracy*([435]); this is the manual that your opponents are increasingly using to develop their strategies. For example, many pro-democracy agitators may shun negotiation to avoid falling into a cycle of never-ending talks, and seek to embrace nonviolent methods to increase media exposure for their cause. You might consider countering these tactics with precise, violent strikes and/or by insisting on intensive (but meaningless) "dialogue" between your regime and the protesters.

8.2   Preventing Unrest Before it Starts

The Charm Offensive   Sometimes nice guys don't finish last. As distasteful as it might seem, you may need to develop a strategy of beneficence in order to keep your subjects happy, distracted, and impervious to discontent. This can consist of many things, from generous entitlement programs to tax breaks or cash giveaways every other Friday, but whatever the form, it's a strategy with a long and impressive pedigree.

The benefits of charm are obvious: If you make your move with sufficient anticipation, you may be able to appease your people before the urge to rise up overwhelms them (and you). In 2011 the Algerian government under Abdelaziz Bouteflika, watching the wave of protests spread through North Africa, took dramatic steps to keep people satisfied: a revised national budget with an emphasis on workers' salaries and subsidies for basic foods (flour, milk, sugar, oil), pay raises of up to 34% for civil servants, and several programs aimed at helping the youth open businesses and find reasonably-priced housing. It lifted a 19 year old law forbidding demonstrations and restricting the formation of political associations, released Islamists from prison (many held since 1992), and launched an ambitious reform agenda to culminate in a revised constitution. In some areas, the police have been told not to collect taxes from shop keepers. In sum, it has gone against almost all the other advice in this book and its own inclinations when it saw the writing on the wall.[64] You may not like this strategy, or feel it's a betrayal of your core principles, but at least it keeps you in power in the short term. Think of it this way – once the streets are calm and your people go back to playing online poker, you can tighten the screws once more.

A note of caution, however. When you prepare your seduction of the nation, be careful not to over-reach, as being too permissive might only encourage the protesters and bring your regime to the tipping point. There is also the danger of forgetting to leave well enough alone. When in the late 1980s Mikhail Gorbachev introduced the market-like reforms under the banner of *Perestroika*, it helped to stir a troubled but relatively quiet citizenry that, once agitated, only clamored for more democratic reforms. Gorbachev had no intention of dismantling the Soviet Union or abolishing communism, but the instability unleashed by *perestroika* led to the eventual collapse of the USSR and has become an example of what mass demonstrations can accomplish in the modern era.[222] You should always remember that an exaggerated degree of openness and freedom might spark the very fire you're seeking to smother, so be frugal with your charms.

Discouraging Assembly: Curfews, Criminalization, Barricades Limit your opposition groups outright (and ahead of time) by legislation that makes any 'unauthorized' gathering illegal. Then arrest the opposition leaders, or at least break up their rallies, for holding 'illegal gatherings,' like in Kazakhstan.[311]

Keeping people off the streets will prevent them from massing and causing more trouble. Declare a curfew, for the capital at least, if not everywhere, and keep people in their homes after dark. Otherwise, take it a step further and declare martial law. Alert your military and security services, and ensure they are enforcing the curfew. Anyone out and about is likely rallying supporters against you: bring them in for questioning.

Curfew might seem like a bold admission of your intentions. If you'd prefer something more subtle, simply prevent people from congregating in groups that might lead to more organized demonstrations. As the Belarusians became more subtle in their protest techniques, president Lukashenko clamped down, producing draft legislation that would criminalize the gathering of a group "for a previously planned action *or inaction.*"[144] Bravo. This quick bit of policy work made protests illegal and turned protesters into criminals, a very useful turn of events. Such an approach also legitimizes your next step – bringing in your security forces to crush the demonstration – and sets up the protesters for being considered responsible for their own rotten fate (as happened in Tunisia).[386] You can just as easily ban the rally, if you're careful and if you don't do it too often (otherwise your reaction will be correctly identified as an attempt to squelch dissent). On the grounds that yours is a society that dislikes chaos and violence, insist on the state's right and obligation to ensure order; if you are unable to provide it, declare the proposed rally or protest illegal.

You can also simply make things difficult for the protesters and discourage them from assembling downtown and launching a rally. Supporters of the Ukraine's Yulia Tymoshenko (who was imprisoned) found the tents with which they'd established a wintery sit-in forcibly removed from the site, ostensibly because the site was to undergo "repairs."[314] [303] That's funny! When supporters of the Armenian National Congress opposition party began camping out in Yerevan's Liberty Square to stage a 24-hour sit-in protest, the government simply closed down all the public toilets and curtailed transportation between Yerevan and the countryside (note: there's at least one obvious way the toilet trick might backfire against you, but it's worth a try and will at least be momentarily funny to watch your constipated opposition rage against you, knees tightly crossed. Maybe offer them a free cup of coffee, while you're at it?).[295]

Finally, if these methods seem too esoteric, you might consider some old-fashioned but effective methods for anticipating and deflating a planned protest. It's simple: keep additional people from joining. Put up barricades, string out the razor wire, and place tanks at strategic urban intersections. The military has probably been well-trained to do this, and you've got lots of soldiers eager to try out what they've studied. By cordoning off the city into easily managed sectors, you can prevent the flow of people from one zone to another; effectively you are depriving the protest of the oxygen it needs to burn. This time-honored tactic was used in 2011 by the Syrian army to keep pressure on the demonstrators.[78]

Decapitation: Disrupting or Detaining Leaders   When in doubt over how to best defuse growing unrest, go for the jugular. Disrupt the organization of the protests by arresting the leaders and as many others as you can, up front. Bring them all in for questioning and see how anxious they are to ascend the soapbox with electrodes hooked up to uncomfortable places. Even if you don't glean any useful intelligence from the round up, you've sent a message, at least, and it will likely delay or prevent them from assembling, organizing, and striking out.[500] Belarus' Alexander Lukashenko has used this technique repeatedly. Reports Radio Free Europe/Radio Liberty: "Like every Wednesday for the past nine weeks, hundreds of disgruntled Belarusians gathered across the country for so-called 'silent protests' … And like on previous occasions, security forces violently dispersed the rallies and detained dozens of prisoners." The Belarusian government detained over 1500 protesters over a nine week period, sentencing many to fines or brief stays in prison.[401] The Chinese government takes this to its logical conclusion and simply executes the leaders on the spot, as they did with two ethnic Uyghurs they suspected of participating in an attack on the city of Kashi, and of having received training in jihad, explosives, and firearms in Pakistani terrorist camps.[297] The one drawback to this degree of enthusiasm is that you risk creating a martyr (and martyrs are like zombies: once they're dead they come back harder to kill).

The Gentle Threat   You can put the fear of God into your protesters without necessarily resorting to violence. Three women of the Belarusian "Femen" movement (renowned for its naked or topless, female protesters) were abducted and taken by force to the woods where they were stripped naked, doused with oil, and threatened. A knife was pressed to their throats and their hair was cut off before they were allowed to find their way, still naked, back to the village.[80]

Preventing Inspiration from Revolutions Elsewhere   There may be other political movements around you that serve as inspiration for would-be revolutionaries. Nip that inspiration in the bud with a few choice arrests. Zimbabweans who clearly found the Arab Spring of 2011 a source of inspiration met to discuss "What can be learnt" by the events, i.e. how Zimbabweans could incite something similar. Strongman Robert Mugabe responded by having the conference leaders arrested for treason; if convicted they face the death penalty.[1] [84]

8.3   Crippling and Containing The Protest Movement

If protests do gain traction in your country, don't panic. Usually they start small – a few unemployed losers toting signs and chanting – before swelling to sizes that can make even the most hardened autocrat think twice about spending another night in his bed. Curb their appeal during early stages before the middle classes and respectable professionals have joined the movement, by portraying them as unwashed heathen.

Arrest the Leaders   Assuming you weren't able to arrest the leaders before the opposition rally begins, it's not too late to do so once they're on the streets. Do so strategically and within measure, though, and watch out your security team doesn't resort to excessive violence. In Malaysia, the Najib Razak administration overlooked this second tenet, and not only arrested 1600 protesters, but resorted to violence that was often captured on videotape: not only was the opposition political leader physically injured himself but the police appeared to fire water cannons and tear gas at a mass of protesters taking refuge in a hospital. Now that these tactics come under greater scrutiny, they clearly are not easy to explain or defend in the glare of the media. Furthermore, in the age of smart phones and digital cameras, there are a lot of cameras out there that can capture and publish your actions (see the chapter on suppressing access to the Internet to deal with this latter aspect: section 9).[183]

---

[1]Mugabe appears to have answered their question, if you think about it. Hope they were listening.

One variation of this tactic that works quite well is the now common "house arrest." The term conjures images of protest leaders in pajamas, lounging on their couches watching television while state security yawns outside their door. This comic, prosaic image works to your benefit by deflating the prestige that usually surrounds the leaders of protest movements. No one will take Mr. Human Rights quite as seriously if they think he's at home watching the Simpsons in his jockey shorts (unless it's Aung San Suu Kyi, for whom house arrest has led to no diminuition of her political strength or popular appeal whatsoever). The other great advantage to this approach is that you keep the movement on a knife's edge, particularly if you use it repeatedly. Whenever trouble seems to be brewing, confine the opposition leader to his apartment or (better yet), his country house (in the latter case, he won't be able to claim solidarity with the working class any longer, and will be away from population centers and out of communication with agitators in the capital). Out of sight out of mind: a cliché but a valid strategy for keeping a protest movement leaderless during (rigged) elections or (illegal) wars. The Iranian government has used this approach frequently of late, and their on-again/off-again house arrests of MirHossein Mousavi has succeeded so far in keeping the opposition protests at a manageable level.[173]

Then Arrest Those Who Complain   The initial round of arrests will lead to a public outcry over your government's heavy-handedness. But it doesn't have to. Once you complete the initial round of arrests, set a precedent that will affect all future protests by immediately arresting anyone who complains about the first round. Iran and Belarus provide the best examples here: In Iran, after the 2011 demonstrations that President Ahmedinejad brutally put down, a group called the "Mothers of Laleh Park" appeared, composed of the mothers of activists killed or detained in the demonstrations. Ahmedinejad proceeded to put the moms in jail too.[2][196]

Discredit or Dismiss the Protesters   If your intelligence forces are speedy, you can quickly research the protesters' motives and resources (use the information and networking information you glean from hacking their email accounts: see section 9.8) and use any relevant findings to discredit them and undercut the movement. The Moroccan government in 2011 uncovered alleged alcohol abuse (strictly taboo under Islam) and ties to Saharan activists and Christian groups, i.e. facts that would indicate they are treasonous, weak Muslims.[288] You can upload videos to services like YouTube that ostensibly show the opposition in unflattering situations, like attacking government troops (shows them as violent and extremist, potentially alienating the middle class), or with prostitutes or using drugs (morally unfit).[437] In many places of the world, if you can convince the people that the opposition is

---

[2]Clearly the act of a man who has no mother of his own, being instead spawned from the unholy union between two, probably unpleasant things.

aligned with America or Israel, you've taken a great step toward blackening their names in eyes of the citizenry.[354]

In public appearances, dismiss the protesters as paid lackeys of the opposition, as thugs, as the stooges of foreign powers, as imbeciles and hoodlums devoid of any moral authority or legitimate grievance (Vladimir Putin after the December 2011 pre-election protests: "at least they will make some money."[242]). Syria's brutal crackdown in 2011–2012 under Bashar al-Assad was, to listen to Assad, the result of "armed terrorist groups." "No political dialogue or political activity can succeed while [they] are operating and spreading chaos and instability," he vowed to visiting UN-Arab League envoy Koffi Annan.[3][90]

The Cocoon: Restrict Access   You are under no obligation to listen to your detractors. If you are appearing at a public event and your detractors are planning to mass along your route to slander you, do something about it. George W. Bush was subject to this experience on numerous occasions but did not suffer from his detractors, thanks to careful team planning: the parade route was announced late and the crowd was cordoned off so they couldn't get within blocks of where he would travel. Security forces blocked off certain areas beforehand, and ensured detractors and protesters were forced to remain in those areas. To get to the front lines, spectators needed to provide proof they were party members, ensuring the crowd along the route was not only supportive but also well-behaved. This is yet another reason to exploit party membership (see section 6.1.2). Or, you might consider shunning contact with the public altogether (except for pre-planned events with heavy state security presence). Although he normally had little to fear from protesters, Kim Jong Il nevertheless constructed a private and inaccessible travel infrastructure in North Korea, the centerpiece of which is 19 private, high-tech train stations, allowing him unimpeded travel across the country, and little to fear from street-level unrest. Autocrats, start taking notes.[457]

Dislodge the Protest   If the circumstances are right – if you are faced with an isolated, somewhat limited protest – then it is possible to simply break it up as violently as possible. Still, you'd be wise to make this decision carefully, as its benefit (cowing the demonstrators through a display of ruthlessness and superior force) may occasionally be outweighed by its detriment (increasing the protesters' anger, drawing attention to their cause, or presenting yourself as unreasonable, overly cruel, and/or disconnected). The odds are, though, that you will be able to clear the streets without too much trouble. One scenario in particular is worth considering – what if your "new" government has been swept into power on the strength of public demonstrations, and now that the old autocrat (your predecessor) is gone, the problem

---

[3]Naturally, Syria's strategy for inviting those same terrorist groups to the negotiating table was to blast the city of Homs (and elsewhere) to rubble, killing at least 7500 civilians.

of public order remains? A thorny problem to be sure. But in 2011, the post-Mubarak caretakers in Egypt did not hesitate to end a three-week long sit-in in Tahrir Square by sending in hundreds of security troops and police. Protest over, gentlemen.[4]

Another time to consider sweeping the protests away is when the demonstrations have the potential to evolve into something that threatens your rule. A classic example is the crackdown in Tiananmen Square in 1989. As the demonstrations built and built during that spring, the leaders of Chinese Communist Party had reached an impasse. Although the protests had been peaceful, they were large, and growing, and to allow them to blossom into an organized protest movement with a sense of impunity could have sowed the seeds of civil war – particularly since many members of the Party (and by extension, the People's Army) supported aspects of the protest movement. This was intolerable to Deng Xiaoping, and he ordered the army to clear the streets.[337] As Deng knew, when dislodging a protest, half measures are for amateurs. The army advanced on the student protesters with automatic weapons, tanks, armored personnel carriers, and heavy weaponry.[406]

Cow the Media   As things heat up (hopefully, before then), pull the journalists in for a quick talking-to, and warn them of what will happen if they foment trouble. You want all possible forces pushing in the direction of smaller, less effective protests.[459] For that matter, shorten the leash of the local diplomatic community, as well, since they talk too. Syria, during the riots in 2011, warned the American Ambassador he would be expelled if he left Damascus, after he met with the opposition in the "flash point city of Hama."[501]

Encourage Factions Among the Protesters   If your country is already riven with internal divisions – religious, class, ethnic, or other – now is the time for your *agents provocateurs* to feed the fire. If you can sow dissent within the dissenters, they may potentially start to attack each other instead of you, freeing your hand to propose a "solution" while the two halves (more, if possible) exacerbate each other's weaknesses. Many accuse the Syrian government of doing just this in 2011.[499]

Interrupt Communication Channels   Your protesters are going to suffer mightily if they can't communicate or coordinate with each other. And, it's not too complicated to arrange: have the state telephone company cancel service, disrupt the electrical grid, hack the Internet and all forms of social media. Do this and the riot, though worrisome, will proceed blindly, allowing your security forces the time they need to identify leaders, intercept them, and mobilize the ranks for street fighting. The added benefit of this tactic is that, once the demonstrations are brought back down to a manageable level, you can still use your expertise to spy on, infiltrate, and otherwise frustrate the ambitions of the opposition, preventing future unrest. Recent evidence suggests that in the aftermath of the 2009 protests the Iranian regimen initiated a cyber-attack that possibly allowed them to surveil their own citizens through Google, Yahoo, Facebook, and other sites. (See chapter 9 for more on this strategy).[114]

Stage Your Own Demonstration If you or your supporters are feeling besieged by the protesters in your midst, you might consider employing a kind of political jujitsu. Assuming your enemies have already loudly declared they won't back down or be intimidated by heavy-handed thuggery, publicly announce that you had no intention of breaking up their public protest, that your regime has always been supportive of free expression. Then, about a week later, hold your own protest. But make sure it's well attended by criminals, street toughs, drug addicts, perverts, and religious fanatics of all shapes and sizes. Make doubly sure they are supplied with grim-looking weapons and placards bearing your beaming yet stern face. You'll have the media's loving eye for the next news cycle, you'll have eclipsed your rivals, and you'll have reminded any timid fence-sitters that, should they side with the opposition there's a good chance you'll unleash the thugs the next time around. You also get bonus points for turning your enemies' tactics around on them. Consider the example of Hezbollah in Lebanon, which responded to a series of protests against Syrian influence in that country with a massive demonstration of their own.[202] In the context of ongoing tension between Syria and their Lebanese satellite, this was clearly a move designed to ease the pressure on President Assad while issuing a warning to the reformers in Lebanon; namely, that Hezbollah and their formidable paramilitary were firmly in Assad's camp, and could be counted on should the Cedar Revolutionaries go too far.

Likewise, embattled Hungarian Prime Minister Viktor Orban was able to rally 100,000 people in Budapest to defend his administration amid criticism his new Constitution was undemocratic and his administration hell-bent on entrenching a one party state. For bonus points, the protesters carried signs written to be understandable by the European Union and IMF, who had demanded reform. And crucially, the 100,000 supporters outnumbered the preceding opposition rally, which had only mustered 70,000: an impressive show of force.[93]

The Kitchen Sink When the streets are threatening to get beyond your control, then you must consider a combination of many of the techniques noted above. Once again, the aftermath of the election protests in Iran in 2009 are instructive in this regard. The clerical leadership:

- unleashed a wave of violence to cow the demonstrators;

- curbed the use of electronic media where possible;

- publicly claimed to have "addressed" any irregularities observed during the election and, once this was announced,

- made it clear that no further protests would be tolerated; and

- arranged a large counter-demonstration that interrupted the momentum of the those protesting the election results.

- Placed the leaders of the protest movement under house arrest and continuously derided them as foreign toadies responsible for a "spurious and deviant movement aligned to American and Zionist goals."[354]

8.4   Benefitting from Disorder

Never let a good riot go to waste; they are practically a gift. Sooner or later you will cross somebody's line in the sand, and they will organize demonstrations against you. Fantastic: here are several ways you can use a good riot to your advantage.

Remind the Upper Class   If your iron-fisted rule has been responsible for keeping a multi-ethnic or socio-economically divided nation together, riots may be an opportunity to remind people – particularly the wealthy – how important you are. Exacerbate the class divisions, encourage a little looting and pillaging, and see if there isn't a sudden surge in financial support for your heavy-handed methods among the business class who suddenly realize the protection you've been providing them.[285] Your society may be repressive, but it has benefitted a certain class of people, and if you let them get a little bit scared they will certainly rally to your side. It always helps remember the parable: A rich man will part with 99% of his money rather than lose all of it to the bastard who shines his shoes.

Knowledge is Power   You've got your secret service agents working around the clock, anyway, but now is a great chance for them to hone in on the most valuable information without the hassle of listening in on phone calls and hacking email accounts. Your information gatherers, undercover, should attend a rally and pay close attention to who's chanting what, who is standing next to whom, who arrives with whom, and so on. Your opponents expose themselves when they rally, and you should seize the moment to improve your knowledge of who they are and how they are organized. Your plain-clothes security forces can easily mingle with the rabble rousers, and get a full report.

Who are the leaders? Do they really believe all their claptrap about human rights and free trade, or are they just looking to push a personal agenda that will benefit them personally, like giving their family's company a competitive edge? Are they easily compromised or discredited due to unorthodox practices (alcohol consumption in a traditional society, or similar)? Lastly, are there discernible fractures in their composition? You couldn't ask for a better research opportunity, and the information will provide you with the seeds of their ultimate fragmentation and destruction. All you have to do is listen.

Attack the Attackable   There are countless benefits in having angry, unruly, and somewhat violent crowds at your disposal, particularly when they attack a group whose persecution benefits you politically. In many cases you don't have to build these groups; they will form spontaneously, and all you have to do is allow them to proceed somewhat un-hindered, perhaps providing enough of an official government response to exculpate your administration without hindering the mobs' performance.

In Nazi Germany, the attempted assassination of the German ambassador to France by a German Jew permitted Adolf Hitler's Chief of Propaganda to decry the conspiratorial attack of "International Jewry" against the Reich and, by extension, against the Führer himself. On 9 and 10 November 1939, gangs of Nazi youth ran amok through Jewish neighborhoods, burning and looting Jewish businesses and burning synagogues. 101 synagogues and about 7500 businesses were destroyed. Of the many Jews physically attacked, 91 died. Officially, the German government denied any involvement in these "spontaneous outbursts," but it was later discovered that Hitler had instructed his party officials that such demonstrations were not to be prepared or organized, but neither were they to be stopped. The event is now known as "Kristallnacht."[25]

Blaming your Political Opposition   If the protests are being organized by your political opposition candidates themselves, you have a special opportunity to blame them personally for the unrest and have them put away. Former Belarusian opposition candidate Mikola Stratkevich was accused of organizing mass disturbances in 2010 when 15,000 demonstrators protested alleged vote fraud in the December election. He was given three years in a 'closed regime' prison that removed him totally from the limelight, potentially ending his political career permanently.[304]

8.5   Political Spin and Psychological Operations

Be prepared to spin events to your advantage, plant doubt in the minds of your enemies, and hijack the news cycle so it serves your ends.

The Issue is Security, not Politics   One of the best tactics you can employ is to treat the riots in the time-honored way – as a civil disturbance (i.e., a police/security matter) as opposed to a political matter (i.e., one in which the demonstrators have a message of any sort or a legitimate right to be heard). Offer no immediate concessions, since there is nothing to concede. If you stress that your only concern is to keep order, then the public will be more inclined to tolerate your use of security forces should you decide to use them.

Play the Blame Game   Then, remember to blame anyone you can: foreigners, exiles, drug addicts, extremists of any sort, or (especially) the media.[68] This is effective in a divide-and-conquer strategy, when you have one minister blame foreign provocateurs while another denies there's any issue to talk about.[288] It also alleviates the pressure on you and forces the opposition to scramble to deal with your claims.

Issue Warnings   Immediately let it be known protesters will suffer mightily if they continue, as the battle and foe they've chosen are beyond their abilities. As protesters rallied for the ouster of Mohammar Khadaffi, his son vowed "we will fight to the last minute, until the last bullet."[68] Malawi's Bingu Wa Mutharika chose this path as well in 2011, threatening to "smoke out" the opposition, who responded by immediately going into hiding: "Even God knows that I have been the most patient president on the continent. Enough is enough. You wanted to take the government by force, which is against the laws of the land. This time I will follow you into your homes."[272]

Or, if warning the opposition doesn't work, you can often isolate the protesters by convincing the rest of the nation that the protesters themselves are a menace to society, and that should the protesters succeed, your nation will be "rent asunder," "cast back to colonial times," or "irreparably divided into a land of clashing tribes in permanent warfare." Seif al-Islam Qaddafi warned Libyans, "the nation's oil wealth will be burned."[68] Elaborate as you see fit, but ensure your nation understands the protesters will do more harm than good. They will surely support your crackdown.

Nix any Talk of Trends Be aware of the danger of revolution season ("revolutionary contagion"). If your rioters are following on the tails of a recent uprising elsewhere, publicly state that your nation is unique and exceptional, that revolt has no place in such an enlightened society. The last thing you want is for your protest to be part of a pattern or a trend, when in fact it's a bunch of thugs up to no good.

The Statistics Game In your public statements, downplay the number of rioters in the streets, as well as the number of them your security forces have killed. Emphasize the number of government troops or innocent bystanders killed as a result of the uprising, to criminalize them. If you've prevented any foreign media sources in the country, it will be hard for anyone to verify or dispute *anyone's* numbers, and you know the rebels will be exaggerating in the other direction; your counter numbers will force everyone down to a reasonable average.[77]

Deny it Until the End Psychology is half the battle, and you control the airwaves. Use them to your advantage, painting a picture of your administration's strength and health, and the weakness, desperation, and defeat of your enemy. What better example than Mohammed Saeed al-Sahaf, the Iraqi Minister of Information, who remained on air until the end of Saddam Hussein's Iraq, declaring "I triple guarantee you, there are no American soldiers in Baghdad," "We have them surrounded in their tanks," "Now even the American command is under siege. We are hitting it from the north, east, south and west. We chase them here and they chase us there. But at the end we are the people who are laying siege to them. And it is not them who are besieging us" and "There are no American infidels in Baghdad. Never!" Saeed al-Sahaf did such a fun job of rallying the troops despite overwhelming odds that he became somewhat of a popular (and well-liked) figure even after the fall of Baghdad.[253]

Mohammar Khadaffi carried this out in expert form, well into the NATO strikes pummeling his Republican Guard and government palaces: "We only

have one choice. This is our country and we shall stay here till the end –
dead, alive, victorious. It doesn't matter. We shall not leave. We shall not
surrender. We shall not sell it," he added. "We welcome death. Martyrdom
is a million times better. We are stronger than your missiles, stronger than
your planes and the voice of the Libyan people is louder than explosions.
The Libyan people will march, in the direction of the east or the west, or to
any place where there are armed gangs to strip them of their arms without
fighting." Addressing NATO, he added: "Your planes will not be able to stop
these marches of the millions, nor will the armed gangs that you support be
able to resist for even a minute in the face of these marches."[67] All great
quotes from a guy who was later confined to a bunker as the rest of his
military deserted him and fled to Niger.

Control Information for the Outside   Lastly, clamp down on the press,
Internet, and citizen journalists to ensure the outside world is forced to rely
on your official accounts of what's happening. See chapter 9 for much more
on this subject. Unfortunately, in an age where every local yokel is sport-
ing a smart phone with video-upload capacity, this is getting tougher. But
Syria's Bashar al-Assad gave it his best in 2011–2012, slaughtering journalists, cutting off the Internet, bombing safe havens where known foreign
correspondents were reporting on the carnage of his crackdown, and detaining citizen bloggers and correspondents.[109]

8.6   Security Forces: Use Them or No?

Security forces are a big hammer. You should think carefully before applying
them to a small nail, as satisfying as that might be. Review some of the pros
and cons about using military force to manage unrest, below:

Pros   If the military is on your side then using them to quell unrest may be
a quick and relatively painless option (for you). But are you sure of their
loyalty? Have you been paying them well? If it gets to the point to where
they desert you in the face of rioting, your political longevity will plummet.
The 2011 riots in Egypt were not decisively a popular victory until the moment a uniformed military spokesperson announced to the public they would
not use force against the people, and that the military both understood the legitimacy of the demands and affirmed freedom of expression for everybody.
That statement made Mubarak's subsequent capitulation almost obligatory:
the balance of power had shifted against him.[283]

In Yemen, President Ali Abdullah Saleh chose this route, and his security forces opened fire with live ammo and tear gas on protesters, killing
several.[83][387] This option may also stiffen your resolve if, like Saleh, you
find yourself challenged. With the support of the military, he insisted upon
his return to power, that he would not step down if his rivals remained in a

position to take over. If you sense your military is lacking resolve, impose kill quotas on them when they fire on protesters to ensure the right number of victims accrues. Syria's Bashar al Assad seems to have done this.[115]

Finally, while it's good to use your military to clear the streets of scum, it's better if someone else is paying them. Depending on your local circumstances, you might find that business interests with deep pockets might be willing to bankroll your crackdown. Entrepreneurs are notoriously impatient with unpredictability, so use the unrest caused by riots to squeeze cash from the business community, and then pay for your anti-riot campaign without raiding the treasury. Or else encourage individual army units to develop cash-for-crackdown contacts on a freelance basis. Far-fetched? Not so – this happened in Nigeria in the 1990s, when an oil company paid units of the Nigerian army to disperse protests that were threatening the smooth functioning of that country's oil industry and its profits.[477]

Cons Consider the negatives of using military force as well. The most important drawback is that your opposition will frequently benefit more than you will if your response is overly violent. In fact, they may often goad your military into a disproportionate response so they can "defend themselves" while blaming you. If your military is professional, competent, and well managed, they will resist the temptation of resorting to extreme violence (within reason), leaving the provocateurs looking amateurish and unimportant. Then, once the media has moved on to that weekend's big soccer match, you can arrest the protest leaders and have them jailed quietly.

If you do order your military to fire on protesters, the decision may come back to haunt you. Egypt's Hosni Mubarak, once deposed, was eventually wheeled into the courts in a hospital bed to answer for having given the order to kill demonstrators in the 2011 'Arab Spring' revolution. In the court proceedings, boxes of guns, ammunition casings, and grenades allegedly used in attacks on Egyptian protesters were presented to the court as evidence. Is that one decision the only reason Egyptians could demand justice? Potentially, despite a relatively long history as a repressive leader. That puts Mubarak in the same league as Chicago mobster Al Capone, who was finally jailed on charges of tax evasion despite a much more colorful criminal history.[153]

Another, less obvious danger, is that in pushing your military to punish demonstrators, you may cause some of them to turn against you in disgust (after all, you are presumably asking them to fire on their own people). An example of this includes the emergence of the "Free Syrian Army" in 2011 – a group of soldiers who defected over the role of the army in putting down the anti-government protests earlier that year.[279] Whether this group can grow to challenge the Assad regime remains to be seen, but it is clear that the brutality of the initial crackdown led to this first wave of defections from the army. In the worst case scenario, increasing army defections lead to civil war, so it's recommended that you consider subtler techniques before proceeding with an iron fist.

Committing to Total Engagement   If you do decide to send in the troops to quell an uprising, and particularly if it's a sustained intervention, you can expect a loud reaction from the international community, and scathing reports about you from the likes of Human Rights Watch International, citing individual responsibility for the atrocities.[482] But maybe you just don't care anymore and are going to deal with things your own way. In that case, here's a quick checklist for you, courtesy of Syria's Bashar al Assad:

1. Kill protesters

2. Arrest at random; torture and execute some prisoners. In particular, target young men older than 14.

3. Deny medical treatment to wounded protesters

4. Give your troops a kill quota; threaten punishment or death to those who defy your orders. Imprison military defectors, and subject them to the same detainment, torture, and interrogation as the others (but worse). Permit summary, on-the-spot execution of rebellious military or police by their (soon to be honored) colleagues

5. Institute checkpoints, and conduct sweeps through residential neighborhoods using heavy weaponry and armored vehicles

6. Mine the national borders to discourage would-be-refugees from escaping over the border and tattling [91]

Organized Violence: Countering with Your Supporters   You can counter some riots by unleashing supporters of your own, whose purpose is to escalate the tenor of existing, anti-government demonstrations. By emerging *en masse* in a show of strength, shouting pro-government slogans and demonstrating their loyalty, they show they can outnumber or can outperform the protesters, or even to do battle against them. You can also use such a confrontation to incite the protesters to violence, thus permitting your security forces to either swoop in violently in a wave of arrests and detentions, or even deaths.[284] It is, however, unwise to have your supporters violently attack the embassies of your diplomatic community, as it reveals your supporters for what they are – mobs – and undermines your relationship with nations you would probably prefer support you.[76]

Cowing protests via a display of strength worked well for Italy's Benito Mussolini. In the early years of his dictatorship, the assassination of socialist (oppositon) deputy Giacomo Matteotti was leading to simmering unrest. Matteotti had called for the annulment of recent, fraudulent elections, and Mussolini's connection to the assassin caused the opposition to coalesce against him. Rather than flinch, Mussolini strengthened the fearsome reputation of the *squadrisit* responsible for Matteotti's death, insinuating the *squadristri* were capable of much more violence if Mussolini ordered it. The opposition chose safety over confrontation and backed down, and Mussolini survived the crisis, emerging with a firmer grasp of power than before.[318]

8.7 Negotiation, Hedging Your Bets, and Denouement

Despite your best efforts, the protesters have backed you into a corner and even the military is urging you to be reasonable. This is usually a bad sign and may mean your grip on power is slipping. Fear not – even in the face of this kind of pressure there are still several useful tactics that can be employed to catch your enemies off guard, deflate the protests, and win back the support of the masses.

Insist Reform is Already Underway Give the people what they want – only point out that they'd had it all along. In insisting that reforms are already being studied, or even implemented, you can catch the opposition off guard and paint the protesters as misinformed, *agents provocateurs*, or simply traitorous malcontents. Note that, as Moroccans took to the streets in 2011, the Minister of Communication insisted that Morocco "has embarked a long time ago on an irreversible process of democracy and widening of public freedoms."[288] Those sounds you hear are the collective sighs of relief of on-the-fence Moroccans, the contented exhalations of many fence sitters, and relieved exclamations of the leadership.

The Art of the Half-Offer When pressed for electoral reforms, instead of opening the economy or dismantling your secret police apparatus, funnel some extra funds into "education" and allow local elections. In other words, offer table scraps when demonstrators call for a full-course meal. Offering something small and insignificant to appease the fomentors of public unrest is a time-worn tactic that works; most people are happy getting something for free, particularly if the price of what they've been agitating for is to be paid in blood.

There are many ways to propose the half-offer. Offer (but don't mention):

- Elections (The role your party will play in them, or the right of other parties to participate.)

- A Truth & Reconciliation Commission (How long it will take, whether the results will be published, or whether anything will result from the findings.)

- You'll step down (When you'll do so, who will rule after you, and what role you'll play henceforth.)

- Openness and Transparency (That the chair of the oversight committee is the former head of the secret police.)

All Talk: Using Negotiation to De-legitimize Protesters   Keep the street protests from expanding by offering to open talks with your political opposition. Let them think it's an overture toward a power sharing agreement; in reality it's just hotel conference rooms, free wi-fi, and coffee and cookies, and you can make "talks" last forever, if necessary (as in Yemen).[386] To encourage them to accept the invitation, extend the offer while pummeling the rebels in a particularly grueling way elsewhere.[77]

If you do consider this tactic, be sure to insist that, although you are willing to begin talks (whatever that means), you will not do so while people are in the streets. Be firm on this point: all protests, demonstrations, sit-ins, and equivalent stop immediately before the negotiations begin. This is a sound negotiating principle that recently has been on display during the unrest in the Middle East (Yemen).[386]

Cosmetic Changes: Staff Shuffling   It's not unreasonable to sacrifice a few lambs to the slaughter, particularly if cutting your losses in this manner can remove some un-trustworthy subordinates. Convince the protesters you are reacting to their demands by firing a few cabinet members and ministers, or shuffling them between posts. King Abdullah II of Jordan chose this route in 2011 as protests increased in force. Abdullah appointed a new Prime Minister whose objective, he said, would be to "[take] practical, swift and tangible steps to launch a real political reform process, in line with the king's version of comprehensive reform, modernization and development." The move indeed seemed to satisfy many protesters, who will nevertheless have to wait to see if that's the way it plays out.[269]

Appeasement through a Successor   You can potentially quell riots by offering to step down and hand power over to a successor. Your successor should be picked by you, and should be a person who will satisfy the rioters, continue your rule for you, and find a way to hand power back to you in the best tradition of *Continuismo* (see section 12.1). In the case of Hosni Mubarak, as the 2011 riots gathered strength, he nominated Omar Suleiman as his vice president, ensuring the support of the military and preparing the ground for a potential future military government.[443]

8.8 The Nuances of Violence and Confrontation

When you have no choice but to unleash the dogs of war, do so with style. Act fast and decisively, ensuring your security forces immediately – and probably violently – put down early protests wherever they start.[386] Don't delay, lest you be perceived as a weak prevaricator, but also take care not to proceed without thinking about how best you can apply physical pressure to break the protest and gain political advantage.

Fire on Protesters   This should be self-explanatory, and there's plenty of precedent for it. In some ways it's the easy way out and is often employed by the most unimaginative autocrats, but sometimes you just have to take the direct approach. Out-source this particular tactic to your foreign mercenaries, who will also kill your unruly subjects with few qualms, as they have no cultural or ethnic binds. Should you pursue protesters outside of the town squares in which they are staging their riots, claim you are pursuing bands of terrorists and criminals who have killed government troops, or worse.[77] Then shoot to kill so no one can counter your story.

The more thoughtful among you will think twice before rashly giving the order to fire on protesters, realizing that shooting indiscriminately carries many drawbacks. Just look at Uzbekistan's Islam Karimov, whose troops seem to have not only killed hundreds of probably unarmed protesters in an uprising-gone-wrong in 2005. Not only was the official government explanation ultimately cast into doubt, but blocking the massacred town from foreign journalists increased speculation.[140] It's hard to argue Karimov came out ahead, even if he did suppress the uprising.[4] Furthermore, while it will indeed contribute to the "Culture of Fear," it may also lead to increased resentment, resolve to undo your administration, and probably poison relations with foreign governments. Ultimately, more discreet methods are preferable.[71]

Then Fire on Dead Protesters' Mourners   If you have machine-gunned protests from your public squares, admit to yourself that you have gone all-in, and that you'd better not stop now. When mourners congregate to bury yesterday's victims, fire on them too (as in Libya).[386] Even if this brings you international condemnation, it's unlikely that the punishment will be terribly biting. For example, Suharto's military fired on mourners at an East Timorese funeral, killing 271. The "Dili Massacre" earned Suharto widespread international condemnation and required him to organize an investigative commission and punish those responsible, but in the end this amounted to a slap on the wrist for the perpetrators.[5][237]

---

[4]Well, hang on now. Six short years later he was given a hero's welcome and a barrage of photo opportunities during a tour of Western Europe. Time heals all wounds, perhaps?[132]

[5]The punishments for Suharto's military: three dismissals, eight court martials and a handful of jail sentences for junior officers, paled in comparison with the punishments normally meted

Or Prevent them from being Honored Perhaps a less bloodthirsty way
to punish those who survive dead protesters is to make sure the bodies are
never found. No one can 'wave the bloody shirt', to borrow a phrase from
American history, and roll out dead relatives to make a political point. Malawi protesters killed by the police, for example, were dumped in a mass
grave rather than being permitted transport back to their home villages. For
Africans, this is potentially just as offensive as the previous section.[69]

Offer a Period of National Mourning Perhaps the subtlest way to handle
those left behind after a violent confrontation is to suddenly announce a period of national reconciliation. Make sure to demand closure while choking
back (crocodile) tears. The clever aspect to inviting your people to participate in a period of national mourning is that they are probably gathering
to mourn things your own security forces did to them (as in Bahrain). But
it serves a practical purpose as well, if it truly happens: it gives everyone
a chance to calm down for a moment, and your security forces a chance to
reload and strategize the next step.[386]

Exploit Martyrdom If you find that the conflict is not going your way,
rather than covering up strategic and military losses, turn them into propaganda tools and get some use out of them. Casualties are symbolic and
important, and can be exploited to good effect. Even better, your personal
suffering – the death of one of your children, for example – will trouble the
less committed of your enemies and possibly weaken their coalition.[264]

Fire on Yourself There's also the classic ruse: stage an attack on the forces
of the State (a military outpost, a random police caravan, or similar) causing
limited death and destruction. Then respond with outrage and dismay, as you
are stunned by the audacity of the rebels, whom you now vow to crush with
"an iron fist." This allows you to escalate your involvement without waiting
for the other side to make the first move, and may permit you to attack them
"in response" before they are ready.[92]

8.9   The Aftermath: Political Benefits of Unrest

The riots are winding down, the protests dwindling, and every day fewer
bricks are launched through the windows of government offices. It's likely
that you won't mourn this lessening of public unrest, but don't let the mo-
mentary calm fool you. Unrest can foment at any time now that a pattern
has been established. But don't despair, because the aftermath of a period
of civil disobedience presents several opportunities to fine-tune your ruling
style and entrench or institutionalize checks on popular will.

out for the East Timorese separatist agitators.

Clamp down on civil liberties First of all, since you are the leader of an organized, God-fearing nation, you simply *can't have* the kind of embarrassing uprisings your detractors are wont to stage. They've already bloodied your nose once by staging a protest in the first place. Now that you know what they are capable of, and it has quieted down a bit, it's time to deal with your enemies. Do so harshly, and start by taking away the rights they thought were inalienable. Freedom of assembly? Not this week. Right to privacy? Well, you should have thought of that before you took to the streets.

The down time after a spent protest is the perfect occasion to clamp down on a movement's leaders and functionaries because you've seen what they can do, taken their measure, and presumably are prepared to deal with them (this means jail, harassment, and more violent means of persuasion). So deal with anyone who stirs unrest in the harshest possible way once the streets have been cleared – in other words, crush them and those that support them. Curbing civil liberties is a necessary first step in your secret plan to undermine additional protests.

It's not unreasonable to use violent protests as a pretext for further disenfranchising political rights rather than increasing them. It doesn't matter what the people are demanding, their violence calls into question your ability to peacefully carry out elections (or whatever) and forces your hand. In the aftermath of violent demonstrations in the Kazakh city of Zhanaozen, Kazakhstan's Constitutional Council decided it would be impossible to assure the safety of the people in Parliamentary Elections, and canceled them.[312]

Accuse your rivals Be aware of the classic reaction after a period of unrest: the desire to point fingers and assign blame. Why not use this natural human reaction to your advantage while tarring your enemies with spurious accusations? Once the riots die down, arrange for maximum time before the cameras deploring the unethical, uncivil behavior of your rivals in encouraging the protests, and it's likely that the timid middle classes (sometimes called the "Silent Majority") will support you. Question their patriotism, belittle their methods, deplore the danger they bring to the nation. And make sure to remind the respectable citizens who it was that started the recent trouble on their streets every chance you get. It will set the stage for the inevitable defeat you've engineered for them in the next election and inculcate you from accusations of election fraud.

Blame the Victim If riots lead to the victimization of a certain ethnic or economic group, make sure to blame them in the aftermath. Adolf Hitler, in the days following *Kristallnacht*, decided to blame the Jews for the violence that led to the destruction of so many of their businesses and synagogues, and vowed to ensure they were held both legally and financially responsible. Hitler decided to fine Jews for 'inciting' violence (on the grounds that it made no sense for a German insurance company to be held liable for the destruction of a Jewish warehouse) and used *Kristallnacht* as a reason enough to begin forcing the Jews out of Germany. The pogrom had begun, and the responsibility for the aftermath was attributed to the very victims of the same violence.[25] Hitler of course took this tactic to extremes, to the point where he may even have believed his own propaganda. In the end, in the bunker, he blamed international Jewry for launching a war that likely would not have happened – at least not the way it did – without him.

Consolidating Power: The Strategy of Tension   Straightforward tactics for cowing the populace in the aftermath of unrest may be effective, but in the glare of the media they may prove counterproductive in the long term. Learn, then, from parliamentary democracy. The Italian right is thought to have employed a "strategy of tension" during the 1960s and 70s, in response to growing civil unrest, street demonstrations, strikes, and revolutionary left-wing violence that was strengthening the Communist Party. It's thought that members of a secret anti-communist military and intelligence network engaged in a campaign of terrorist bombings and other violent acts that would permit a shift to a more authoritarian mode of government. And the violence was blamed on the opposition. Only partially successful – this strategy resulted in a failed and somewhat comical, aborted coup – the temptation to do a little damage and blame the opposition is too tempting not to mention.[97] [219]

A variation on this theme can be observed in Uganda in the 1970s. During the early 1970s the *Kondo phenomenon* – roving packs of thugs and thieves – presented a problem for Amin, as they had for his predecessor, Milton Obote. Unlike Obote, Amin saw Kondo-ism as a opportunity, and did not let the unrest generated by these groups go to waste. Ostensibly designed to squash the turmoil, the two decrees that Amin issued in March 1971 essentially gave his military *carte blanche* for repression, and this precipitated a wave of military thuggery, intimidation, and blatant theft. In effect, the decrees had transformed the rank and file soldiers into *Kondo* themselves. The result was a net increase in instability and violence, but since Amin was credited with "doing something" his popularity increased, at least temporarily. The blurring of Kondo-ism with military repression also allowed Amin to get away with the removal of several perceived enemies of the regime. But be careful in how you use this tactic, and remember, a little goes a long way. Amin pushed well beyond acceptable boundaries and after large-scale disappearances in October 1972 the populace was more or less aware that they had been duped.[334]

Chapter 9

The Press, Media, and Communication

> Government lies, and newspapers lie, but in a democracy they are different lies.

Anonymous

ONCE you've established and consolidated your power, you'll find that many of your day-to-day decisions will involve matters of the media. This is a very important aspect of the modern dictatorship, and crosses all channels and media formats, including print, television, audio, the Internet and electronic communication. Handle these decisions well and you will be able to access and control the flow of information over the airwaves and Internet, while using your media mastery to manage your public image. Do a poor job, though, and the media will be your undoing: it will permit your opposition a voice, enable your fiercest critics to attack you relentlessly, and draw the ire of the international community, who will skewer you day after day. Your goal is to ensure what people "think," and what they "know," is exactly what you want, while leveraging the tools of expression and communication to undermine or neutralize your opposition.

9.1   New Media, Old Tricks

A century ago all this was easy. Back then, managing the media meant monitoring local journalists, keeping foreign journalists on a short leash, and publishing written speeches and political pamphlets. Television reinforced those needs, and provided a new outlet for the clever tyrant intent on perpetuating an image of virility, omnipotence, and omnipresence. Then along came the Internet. Initially perceived as a great liberating force for democracy when it was first introduced, the Internet has also benefited anti-democratic forces in equal measure, facilitating both easier expression and easier monitoring. Here are three reasons not to fear the "new media":

1. You own the hardware. Internet access passes through the infrastructure of your state-owned telecommunications systems, or at least the infrastructure of private telecoms that depend on your goodwill for their existence and continued operations. As such, you have a high degree of control over what information enters and exits your national territory. The Chinese have proven you can safely filter out "harmful" information from the outside without stifling economic activity.[180]

2. You control the purse-strings. The Internet is run by corporations, and corporations are most influenced by economic, not political considerations. Google was forced out of China by economics, not human rights concerns; both Twitter and Facebook have refused to join the Global Network Initiative (an organization focused on the right to expression and privacy). Research in Motion (RIM) offered access to its otherwise encrypted and protected messaging servers as soon as Bahrain asked for them, prompting other nations to do the same.[1]

3. No better resource than the Internet has ever existed with which an individual's life and movements can be tracked via their cyber footprints by any curious autocrat. Imperial Russia's Okhrana, the East German Stasi, and the Soviet KGB: each was feared for its ability to track and monitor its prey. But they would be astonished with how much easier technology has made their work.

No wonder most autocracies have decided to clench access to the Internet in a tight fist – not necessarily out of fear, but because such a precious thing should be controlled exclusively by them. In 2011, a Freedom House survey revealed the nations who have most effectively ensured the government controls access to and information found on the Internet; the list reads like a who's who of anti-democratic practice. Congratulations Iran, Burma, Cuba, China, Tunisia, Vietnam, Saudi Arabia, Ethiopia, Belarus, Bahrain, and Thailand (in decreasing level of control).[276]

Prioritize your efforts as follows: Control radio and television first, then newspapers and magazines, and finally web sites and Internet. If your country is like most, you have a relatively high rate of illiteracy. Those who cannot read will depend on the radio or television for their information. Even in small African villages you find people clustered around somebody's battered B&W television listening to the evening news, *not* a newspaper. In fact, newspapers, which require daily purchasing and the ability to read, are the domain of your educated elite. Beyond that, the Internet is really only

---

[1]RIM's users were none too happy about it either. This may have been one factor that led to RIM's decline in market share.

accessible to the top of your political elite, who are wealthy, educated, and employed[2]. While the Internet increasingly poses a threat, it is not your first worry. But you can strike all these targets at once by simply controlling media via your government's oversight authority.

9.2 The Big Stick: Oversight Authority

Your most important line of defense is the institution that oversees, regulates, and licenses local media. This institution should be well funded, well trained, and ruthlessly aggressive. This is not the ministry where you want an incompetent bumbler in charge; make sure the head of your oversight entity is intelligent enough to move quickly when the danger signs appear. In a nutshell, your media commission should have teeth. Zimbabwe shows you how to make this work:

In Zimbabwe, the *Zimbabwe Media Commission (ZMC)* oversees all press and is responsible for the licensing of new outlets and sources of media. All broadcasters transmitting from within the nation are state-run and report only the government's news. The press is dominated by two pro-government daily newspapers, and private newspapers are extensively censored and controlled. A range of draconian laws and institutions ensure no "false news" is published, and any journalist that has not already registered with the ZMC risks imprisonment. [53]

Your own Media Commission will set the stage for the rest of your range of action. Its director should ideally report directly to you, as even an intermediary ministry could potentially exploit its control over the press to attack you – or let you be attacked – in the media. The Commission should allow you to completely and comprehensively shape political messages to meet your will and satisfy your needs. What to include in the authority? The right for media outlets to exist and have access to funding, your right to dictate what they do or do not report and the tone they use to do so, and your right to impose impressive punishments on violators.

Your oversight authority is doubly important where the Internet is concerned. Iran, always at the forefront of using the Internet to monitor, track, and spy on its population, finally took the bull by the horns in 2012 with the official creation of an *Internet Oversight Agency* charged with implementing and enforcing censorship rules, blocking websites deemed "unsuitable" or "immoral" and generally keeping its heel squarely on the heads of the Iranian people. The agency reports directly to the president, as should yours if you implement something similar.[309]

---

[2]hopefully, by you

9.2.1   Licensing and Content Controls

If you have legislation that prohibits certain kinds of opinion or discourse, you can use it to shut down forums used to disseminate radical, opposition opinions. Happily, this legislation can be crafted to ostensibly ensure reporting neutrality, prevent extremism, and clamp down on terrorism (however you define it). In China, such laws revolve around privacy concerns and protecting children from pornography.[490] Effective but trite – and you can do better.

Hungary passed a media law in 2011 that requires all media outlets to register with a "Media Council," that is authorized to levy fines totaling up to millions of dollars on journals charged with publishing articles that are offensive to the "majority," that are not properly sourced, or are deemed "unbalanced." The definitions of the two words in quotes are subjective, but these examples give an idea of what was intended: one paper deemed to have printed statements critical of the President was investigated, while another that printed offenses to the Jewish people ("anti-Semitic slurs of jaw-dropping offensiveness") was left alone.[146] Prime Minister Viktor Orban and his government went on to enact legislation in late 2010 that subjected all forms of broadcast, print, and online media to the authority of a new institution empowered to impose large fines for offenses vaguely defined as "breaching human dignity;" the new authority is composed entirely of supporters of the incumbent party.[175]

In Venezuela, the government ensures some programs are denied prime time airing, and private media are obliged to broadcast 70 minutes of government publicity per week at no charge to the government. And authorities threaten to deny the outlets access to hard currency via an exchange rate mechanism in which US dollars are limited, and threaten to curtail state spending in media outlets that don't toe the line.[256] Chávez' government passed legislation in 2010 to ensure messages critical of the government were effectively controlled: it makes the carrier or network responsible for the content of the messages, and imposes consequences for the distribution of any messages deemed by the government to promote disrespect for the government's institutions or for instigating popular "alarm." [168] Furthermore, a media law ostensibly ensuring "social responsibility" bans the dissemination of any messages contrary to "national security" at the government's definition, or disrespectful of elected officials.

Syria used its prohibition on extremism and outlaw of the radical Muslim Brotherhood to shut down the nation's last remaining discussion forum.[41] And in Italy, Silvio Berlusconi's administration passed legislation requiring any media talk shows devoted to politics to ensure that political discussion during the 4 week election season covered all thirty political parties "to ensure political neutrality;" programs that fail to do so were relegated to post-midnight time slots. Because the requirement was almost impossible to comply with, most programs were forced to do away with political content entirely.[275] Similar to Mussolini's 1925 "Press Law" outlawing all press not declared loyal to the government, Berlusconi has overseen the jailing of writers, firing of editors, and removal of television programs that have criticized him, and his government has raided newspaper offices and the homes of journalists (to "fight terrorism").[365]

Lastly, think about the companies that provide access to the Internet ("Internet service providers" or "ISPs"). Your media laws should require ISPs to be responsible for the actions of their users, with severe, criminal consequences for both violator and ISP whose services facilitated the transgression. That's the kind of move that keeps everybody looking over their shoulder.

9.3   The (Official) Facts

Embrace the media and enjoy its complement and amplification of your barrage of mis-information. Manage your news outlets and journalists with enough care and they will become propaganda machines for your government. Or imagine a journalistic ecosystem where all media are totally co-opted by the state. As the Russian comedian Yakov Smirnoff used to say, "In Russia we only had two TV channels. Channel One was propaganda. Channel Two consisted of a KGB officer telling you: Turn back at once to Channel One."

9.3.1   State Control

Shortly after taking power in 1994, Belarus' Alexander Lukashenko took control over the state printing house in Minsk, and required printing presses elsewhere in the nation to get authorization from the office of the president before entering into a contract with any non-state media.[479] The Venezuelan government under Hugo Chávez has simply bought out smaller, independent news sources en masse, ensuring few opposition voices are available to criticize or otherwise undermine government policies and decisions. In Venezuela in 2007, private station RCTV was denied an operating license, leaving only three private stations remaining, two of which offer little to no coverage of domestic politics.[256] And needless to say, in North Korea the only news you can get is the government's. Finally reporting your official drivel is not enough: they should be as thrilled about the latest crackdown as you are. Kudos then to Equatorial Guinea's Ministry of Information, who fired four journalists from one state-owned media outlet for "insufficient enthusiasm about the government's merits."[441] Show a little gum when you smile, over there.

Your government should ban or criminalize the publication of anything your administration deems unsuitable.[362] But consider a better and less heavy-handed way to achieve the same goal: limited, self-censorship. The

Chinese have employed this strategy expertly. In China, at face value, the private sector model rules, and both traditional and on-line media are permitted to operate commercially, collect revenue from advertising, and improve their production quality to attract audiences. But they are unequivocably required to carry out political directives from the state, such as the emphasis of certain news topics, the suppression of others, and other directives as required. News professionals who respect these boundaries succeed commercially and professionally; the rest do not and eventually disappear. Professionals furthermore recognize the system is underwritten by the "unfettered power of the state to harass, intimidate, imprison, and even execute those who fail to respond to its instructions."[256]

9.3.2   Your Own Show

If you don't trust your local news anchors to get the facts right on your behalf, forget karaoke night and take up the microphone yourself. Even American presidents have their Fireside Chats and equivalent. A regular, televised address is a good idea, especially if you are painting your administration as some sort of popular revolution, in which your speaking directly to the people is essential and urgent. If you are feeling generous, *buy* a time slot during prime time viewing hours. Otherwise, just take it. Since your Media Commission controls whether or not they'll get a license, you may find local television channels are quite generous if asked the right way. For bonus points, insist the other channels momentarily stop broadcasting during your slot, so yours is the only show available. Any television chain that refuses to comply will have "difficulty" renewing its broadcasting license.[3]

For time in front of the camera, Venezuela's Hugo Chávez is the undisputed king. Chávez made governing by television an art form: his "Alo Presidente" program lasts an average of 4 hours and 21 minutes per episode, but is known to stretch for as long as eight hours.[4] Government ministers tune in to find out whether they've been fired or changed, governors pay attention to see if they'll be publicly reprimanded for their missteps, and the show is a theatric tapestry, filmed on-set to showcase Chávez in hard hat inspecting industrial machinery that will "thwart the *Yanqui* (American) hegemony," flanked by Red-shirted flunkies. At intervals throughout the show a government reporter fires off emails to supporters summarizing the show's salient points and praising its stamina.[128][5] Hugo Chavez is also no stranger to the Internet or "social media"; he has used Twitter to promote his presidency, for example, by creating a Twitter feed that now has over a million

---

[3] You'll witness however a popular backlash like Nicaragua's, which saw the residents of the capital milling around outside during that time slot to emphasize the fact they were ignoring the presidential message. Time to ramp up police patrols in those neighborhoods, noting house numbers on a clipboard for "later."

[4] Watch it yourself on YouTube: [135]

[5] Karl Marx, you thought religion was the "opiate of the masses"? Welcome to the television age!

followers.[434]

Somalia's El Shabab movement provides a clumsy counter-example: in 2011, rather than taking control of the airwaves itself, it issued an edict prohibiting people from listening to the radio, on the grounds the radio had an anti-Muslim bias, aired misleading information about El Shabab, and that the reporters, who were Muslims turned heathen (*Murtadeen*), were not worth listening to anyway. El Shabab accomplished little while looking foolish – at least to the international world, but likely to Somalis as well.[280] The lesson here is to err on the side of strength, not diplomacy, and to not fight the media when you can instead exploit it.

There's a downside to rampant, consistent communication from your office. If for any reason you fall ill, speculation will immediately mount that you are unwell, and your opponents will capitalize on that uncertainty, as did Hugo Chávez's after surgery in Cuba in 2011, citing cancer, infection, surgical complications, and more.[191] The press in Eritrea assumed President Efawerki had died simply because he hadn't been seen on television in about a month! He was forced to make an appearance to state he was in good health: how embarrassing.[87] It is even more important that your state media keep the people well informed about your health and near-superhuman abilities if you have been unwell or particularly un-super. North Korea kept Kim Jong Il out of the media for months as he reportedly recovered from a debilitating stroke, and afterwards did things such as present photo exhibitions of the leader engaging in strenuous activities, to bolster the public opinion of their leader's otherwise failing health.[208]

9.3.3 Presenting "The Facts"

This is always useful, but more so during armed conflict, particularly in the case of an armed opposition against you. Trot out the victims, get ample video coverage of civilian funerals, invite the foreign media to tour the hospitals, where victims of the rebellion suffer in bloody rags. None of this has to be true, either. In Libya, to quote a reporter, "little happens in the vicinity of the foreign media that is not scripted." Bombing victims may have simply had a car crash, the funerals are frequently staged, the coffins empty. Video of bombing sites is repeatedly generated at the same sites. And journalists who dare suggest the facts can be sure they will be mercilessly harassed by security forces for doing so.[172]

9.4 Squelching Other Opinions

9.4.1 Shackling the Foreign Press

Face it, you need to validate your opinions and your strategic vision for the nation, and you need foreign media to do the hard work on your behalf

and report the greatness of your nation and your government. But otherwise, watch out for the foreign press: they can easily drag you into political
quagmires from which you will not easily escape. And you have every reason to mistrust that foreign journalists and their cameras are not actually
spies working for other nations. The government of Georgia discovered to
its displeasure that three photographers ostensibly employed by the foreign
press were actually working as spies for Moscow, and were routinely collecting confidential information on Georgia's pro-Western relations for use
by Putin's government.[197]

The tiny East African nation of Eritrea offers a good example of how
to handle foreign media. If the Western press hasn't paid much attention to
Eritrea after its independence from Ethiopia, it's because Eritrean authorities
had squashed all independent media in the lead-up to a program of intense
political repression, a situation that continues up until the present. Says Human Rights Watch, "Many journalists arrested at the start of the decade remain in prison. Foreign journalists of whom the government disapproves are
deported. State-run media broadcast a near-continuous diet of praise of the
president."[392] Syria enjoyed similar benefits during the riots of 2011: as
no foreign press was allowed in, statistics were hard to verify, and the government's account of the death tally on both sides was hard to dispute.[77]

The most extreme version of the strategy belongs certainly to North Korea, where extreme effort has gone into ensuring no outside information
reaches its people. Under Kim Jong Il, the only radios and television permitted for sale in country were hard-wired to receive only the official state
channels, access to the Internet was restricted only to the president and a
handful of top government officials, and everything else was drastically and
ruthlessly controlled.[474] Foreign reporters were infrequently invited to enter the country, and then could do so only under the constant guardianship of
a government chaperone whose sole purpose was to control the correspondent. Reporters were obliged to lodge in special hotels built only for that
purpose, and otherwise didn't see anything the Korean government didn't
want them to see. Those reporters were required to hand over their computers and cellphones upon arrival, and only received them back moments
before leaving the country.

No other country manages to control foreign media to such a degree, and
frankly, it's not a recommended method, as it requires an enormous amount
of work[6] and engenders too much ill will among countries that will otherwise help you fund projects. You are better off permitting foreign journalists
to do as they please, and attacking them and their conclusions, in other ways.
Brand them as enemies of the "revolution," for example, and see how much
influence they have, or how many peasants are willing to answer their ques-

---

[6]Think about it: do you really want to be in the business of building, managing, and running
hotels for the sole purpose of housing the occasional foreign journalist? Wouldn't it just be
better to let them get drunk on your dime once in while, and sit back while the hagiographies
roll in?

tions. It is rather your national press that you must oversee carefully and rigorously. Fortunately, you are well-equipped to do just that.

9.4.2 Shaking Down Journalists

Don't be afraid to shake down local journalists if they overstep their mandate. You can easily sue errant journalists for libel if they speak out against you, while simultaneously trumpeting and bemoaning the state of press freedom. In 2009, Silvio Berlusconi sued Italy's largest opposition newspapers for libel after they published articles linking him to a prostitute, saying "These days in Italy it's been demonstrated that there's freedom to mystify, slander and defame. This isn't a dictatorship." [425]

In Belarus, after an election independent observers reported as having been poorly run, the Belarusian secret police raided the homes and offices of independent journalists. Reporters without Borders claimed the purpose of the raids was to seize all documents and files related to reporting on the election.[57] In Nicaragua, journalist Louis Galeano began receiving death threats (often by SMS message: how concise) after publishing a pair of articles alleging gross corruption and mismanagement.[108]

Otherwise, you may opt for the violent route. Modern Russia in the age of Vladimir Putin is arguably one of the most dangerous countries for investigative journalism. In 2004, Paul Klebnikov, editor of *Forbes Russia* was shot nine times with a semi-automatic weapon outside his office. In 2006, Anna Politkovskaya, investigative journalist for *Novaya Gazeta* was killed in the elevator of her apartment building, and Ivan Safronov, defense correspondent for *Kommersant* newspaper plunged to his death from a balcony in circumstances that have never been clarified. Over two dozen journalists have died or been killed from 2004-2011.[479] In Kazakhstan, reporters investigating official corruption met untimely ends: Nuri Muftakh, following up on allegations that president Nursultan Nazer Nazarbaev had secretly moved public funds to an overseas account, was suddenly hit by a bus in what was officially described as an accident but popularly described as an assassination[7], and Sergei Duvanov was accused of rape and sentenced to several years' prison in 2003.[479]

9.4.3 Use Media to Harass the Opposition

Think of the Internet as a tool for empowering the thug lurking in the heart of every pimply loser or passive-aggressive intellectual who swears allegiance to your party. These types will likely be found in your party youth wing (they won't be out enjoying their lives in cafés or parks), so create a cadre of passionate supporters or state-organized hackers trained to attack where instructed. Your online army can make a sport out of attacking, harassing,

---

[7]Either way, it's a lousy way to go.

and threatening critics who dare publish or post their complaints. Venezuelan opposition bloggers have suffered greatly to such forces, and complain that despite claims the attackers have no connection to the Venezuelan government, they seem to go after only those who criticize Chávez .[372]

9.4.4   Limit, Disrupt, or Prevent Access

For starters, limit access to any websites, domestic or foreign, that annoy you, provide support to your opposition, or information to their supporters. Your legal framework should permit this explicitly, for example by declaring that all blogs qualify as "mass media" and are thus subject to government oversight and regulation.

Web Filtering   You can use key word filtering to eliminate access to web sites to which you don't want your populace to have access. A hardware and software filter developed within Iran by the Iranian government was provided to each ISP under mandated use provisions. Any access to a web site bearing a key word triggers its immediate blocking nationwide; up to 200 or 300 web sites are reportedly blocked per day.[276] This is also the case in Kazakhstan, who has gone on to block entire blogging web domains: wordpress.com, blogger.com, and livejournal.com.[301] Key word filtering is in widespread use in China, where an arms race has begun between bloggers using new "keys" and the government censoring posts that use them. So effective is the practice that most mainland Chinese remain somewhat unaware about issues – the status of some political activists, for example – that are the stuff of front page headlines elsewhere.[320]

For starters, you can simply block them at the border, since all Internet traffic passes through your government servers, or through private companies' service who operate under your authority. In Azerbaijan, the Azeri authorities first made it impossible to visit the tinsohbeti[8] website, which frequently criticized the Azeri government. As it was hosted abroad, it was simple to prevent browsers from reaching the site through the government-owned gateway.[9] Months later, susmayag[10] was blocked similarly, and the owner was jailed for 12 days.[479]

Just one month in advance of the 2006 Tajikistan elections, five opposition web-sites were shut down under orders from the Tajik Communications Ministry in order "to filter and block access to web-sites aimed at disrupting the state policy via information resources, and create all conditions for harmonious development of the republic's information infrastructure."[479] In

---

[8]www.tinsohbeti.com

[9]Aren't you glad you're in the modern age? In the era of radio, it was possible to broadcast radio transmissions over national boundaries, and a somewhat continuous effort to keep jamming the frequencies used. In the Internet age, you simply click a switch, and the website disappears.

[10]www.susmayag.biz

Syria, even before Bashar al-Assad's crackdown in 2011, the Internet was a somewhat limited resource with somewhat strict controls. Once Assad began cracking skulls, ratcheting up the severity of those controls was a simple affair. Over 240 websites were blocked (those discussing Kurdish affairs, those based in Israel, a forum promoting Israeli-Syrian dialog,[11] and anything the government considers "obscene." Once videos of Assad's brutal oppression of the 2011 uprising began showing up on on foreign sites, they were blocked too (as were Skype, several chat platforms, and Amazon.com, just for good measure).[107] If you have to go for the all-out disruption of blocking Internet access entirely, there are many filtering technologies that might allow you to do so, including devices from Western countries that can both block access to websites and record when people visit them. Once again, Syria is one of the leaders in using such devices to maintain an aggressive response to web-based opposition.[475]

If you don't want to block them – a tactic that's somewhat obvious to detect and that will be eventually traced to you – you can very publicly knock them off the Internet. It's a relatively easy affair to use software that attacks an unwanted website with so many simultaneous requests to "serve" a web page that the server is unable to respond to anyone else, or may even crash. These are called "Denial of Service" (DoS) attacks and they cost next to nothing. That makes them an obvious tool to reach for to ensure your opponents' or critics' web sites remain unavailable, as the Kazakh government found in 2011 when it (well, officially, when "unknown cyber attackers") hacked the website of opposition journalist Gulzhan Ergalieva, whose one month old web portal offered an opposition voice against the government of president Nursultan Nazarbaev.[302]

Of course, when your patience is spent, it is possible to cut off access to the Internet entirely. You won't be able to dissimulate this maneuver however, so own up to it. Egypt's Hosni Mubarak did so in January 2011 to disrupt his opponents' ability to organize protests in the aftermath of Tunisia's successful riots. This may make obvious your perceived self-weakness, as it did Mubarak's, so we recommend the more subtle methods demonstrated in this chapter.[434]

Disrupt your Opposition's Activities   There's no reason you can't deluge those same forums to disrupt protest organizers, or overwhelm their message queues with garbage to render them pointless. Pro-government forces, or perhaps the government itself in Syria defaced opposition Facebook pages, flooded Twitter opposition feeds with old sports scores and nature scenes, and developed web pages offering automated tools for cyber-attacking the opposition.[437] The Chinese government pays and trains staff – the salary has earned them the nickname "the 50 Cent party" – to post pro-government comments on the Web and ensure online discussion goes in the Party's fa-

---

[11]www.onemideast.org

vor. The Syrian counter-uprising however has been particularly instructive here. Think: how can your enemies use the Internet against you if their computers are infected with malware? This is the ultimate disruption, as many computer savvy protesters will be lost without the requisite hardware. During the uprisings in 2011-2012, many Syrian activists were enticed by fake video sites that planted malware on the computers of anyone leaving a comment.[23] For the more ironic and sly among dictators, setting up fake malware hosting sites with anti-government programming may be the perfect flypaper for anti-protest needs.

9.4.5 Limit Freedoms

Do Away with Anonymity   Or simply do away with anonymity entirely, and require your bloggers to register, using real names and addresses, with the authorities. The Internet becomes a dramatically less exciting medium when your every blog post, every email, every 140 character "tweet" is cataloged in the government database next to your name and address for convenient searching. China's Weibo users (the equivalent of Twitter) are subject to such a requirement.[12][85] Similarly, the Iranian Ministry of Telecommunications has required all Iranian banks, insurance firms, and telephone operators from using international webmail accounts, requiring them instead to use domain names registered under the Iranian government.[8]

Monitor Directly   More crudely, you can simply post your security personnel clandestinely in Internet cafés, to keep an eye on bloggers: who they are, what they're writing, and to whom they're writing. This is the practice in Myanmar[248]. Obviously this works best in countries with few Internet Cafés, and are best staffed with your non-doughnut eating cops.

Prohibit Encryption   If you clamp down on some Internet freedoms, make sure to ban virtual private network (VPN) and encryption technology as well, for if you can't read what messages your people are sending, you can't reasonably spy on them. Pakistan took this route in 2011.[13][454]

9.4.6 Free Downloads!

There is a counterargument to the approach that argues for banning access and curtailing freedoms associated with television, radio, and Internet use. To wit: let them have as much of it as they want (within reason). Although

---

[12]Don't kid yourself: users of those services will migrate to other services, which you'll have to control using other methods. But it will radically improve the quality of comments about you on the sites for which you require registration.

[13]Caveat: techies will almost certainly be able to circumvent this kind of ban. So it may well quiet down the bulk of the population, but your wiliest and most perspicacious opponents may well be able to thwart the legal ban with technical means.

your people will invariably use their freedom to rant about you on public forums, they will also depend on your leniency for entertainment, and the better they are entertained the less likely they are to demand your ouster. We've made the argument elsewhere, but a distracted population is likely to be a politically disengaged one, and that's to your advantage.

During the partition of Germany, giving East Germans access to West German television seems to have acted as a pacifier, reducing political discontent, much as access to entertainment, pornography, and illicitly downloaded movies keeps repressed populations happy today. And if they're well entertained they will likely stay away from politics and leave you alone.[180] Such was certainly the case in Ukraine, where a government decision to respect international copyright law led to the closure of popular download site EX.eu, and an uproar ensued.[363] So screw international copyright: let your people download pirated movies and be happy, and meanwhile you'll just go about your business running the nation.

9.4.7   Keeping The Arts in Line

A word about your singers, dancers, and other artists is necessary here. While culturally distasteful, it is often politically necessary: if your local musicians start releasing songs that deride you, call for revolution, or otherwise overstep the boundaries of banal entertainment, ban those songs. When Belarusian rocker Viktor Tsoi began singing "Our hearts demand change, our eyes demand change," the Belarusian government responded by outlawing the song.[14][402] Let your rock stars stick to love songs and sexual innuendo, and stay the heck out of politics.

Iranian actress Marzieh Vafamehr was imprisoned in 2011 for her leading role in the film "My Tehran for Sale," which examined the difficulties of young Iranians. Her arrest warrant was produced by the newly created Prosecutor's Office for Culture and Media, who replaced the already existing Culture and Islamic Guidance Ministry, for oversight of the arts. Two other arrests happened in mid-2011: actress Pegah Ahangarani, who had acted in the movie "Women's Prison" and documentary filmmaker Mahnaz Mohammadi, director of "Women Without Shadows."[404]

Win Them Over   Or, better yet, win your artists over and have them glorify you in their work. This strategy dovetails with the 'Free Downloads!' section above; wouldn't it be nice to have the Internet flooded with pop stars singing your praises, or streaming movies devoted to your early years? Fund his ridiculous art form and he becomes your employee. One of the best examples is Leni Riefenstahl, the talented German film-maker whose films were supported in part by Hitler and Nazi Party. In return, she crafted some

---

[14]That change enough for ya, buddy?

of the most enduring and technically brilliant propaganda films of all time, 'Triumph of the Will' and 'Olympia.'[163]

9.5   The Media as Political Leverage

If you are clever, the local media can be put to service to reinforce your government, undercut your enemies, and keep the public appropriately "informed" with whatever you need them to know. The entire range of media channels can be used to force your enemies to support you, denounce their political ambitions, put pressure on local embassies and foreign governments, and influence opinion. You can also multiply the utility of your very best insults (see section 2.5 for some good ones) by ensuring your jibes at the world's leaders and former leaders are broadcast as widely as possible.

For example, an expert media offensive can pave the way for your political ascension, as it did for Serbia's Slobodan Milosevic. Recently elevated to Communist Party Leader, in April 1987 Milosevic left a meeting and "wandered into a group of Serbian demonstrators in Kosovo Polje who were complaining that the police had used batons to push them back. Looking into the television cameras, Mr. Milosevic instantly vaulted into the Serbian consciousness by declaring, 'No one will dare to beat you again.' " [442] More than haphazard political luck, the beatings, the disaffected Serbs, and the careful media coverage had been all carefully orchestrated by Milosevic, who was president of a belligerent Serbian people whose violent nationalism had been awakened.

But more subtly, you can simply make use of the nation's newspapers and television to make sure current events go in your favor. Some examples:

Example 1: Outing an enemy   A political enemy, maybe a member of your government, like a current minister, is contemplating a run for the presidency in the upcoming election, and is trying to quietly and subtly build support. Have "your" journalist write a piece declaring that your enemy is contemplating being a candidate in the upcoming election, that he is increasingly critical of you and your government, and thinks he can do better. Repeat some of his recent public statements. Wait a day or two and let your enemy quickly respond to clarify his situation. If he is unable to do so, his potential candidacy has been confirmed and you can begin to destroy him and his reputation using other techniques.

Example 2: Insisting a subordinate remain loyal   One of your ministers is contemplating challenging your presidency, or is becoming vocally critical of you. A similar strategy is useful. Have "your" journalist write a piece declaring the minister's potential candidacy, pointing out his increasing vocal criticism and his recent public statements, particularly if they can be in any way represented as treasonous. Call the minister before you and the cameras to explain his position. If he wants to maintain his job he will deny everything, swear renewed loyalty, and vigorously sing your praises. Film everything, and make sure the local television and newspapers report his words verbatim.

Example 3: Leaning on local embassies A foreign government is criticizing your government and is perhaps contemplating revoking funding for an existing project, blocking funding for an upcoming project, or questioning your "eligibility" for economic assistance. Find out when the decision will be made, and several weeks before, have "your" journalist publish a piece stating a more extreme version of the above. The article should disparage you personally as well as your government, state the foreign government is considering rupturing all economic assistance for your impoverished, suffering people, and can no longer support you. Then, request a meeting with that ambassador to discuss. That embassy will either publish a response declaring its support for your people and denying any such desire to reduce funding for your important projects, or declare so during your meeting. Ask the ambassador questions that will lead to responses of the sort you need to be made public ("Does your government believe I am not eligible to run for presidency?" – "Of course not.") Then make sure that response is published broadly ("Ambassador reiterates his government is not opposed to candidacy of Richard M. Tater.") It will thus be extremely difficult for that government to reduce your funding having so energetically defended your "warm, cordial relations, long history of economic support, and desire to help your long-suffering people."

If you are careful – make sure you understand expertly the the personal character of the ambassador you're pressuring – you can strengthen this approach by ensuring this article appears on the front page of the paper, and that it includes either a composite photo that makes the foreign ambassador look angry or scolding while you look sheepish and childish, or a drawn caricature that evokes the same.

9.6   Your Education & Information Systems

Your goal is to disseminate your message, promote your vision, and indoctrinate your people. You do not have to limit yourself to speeches, televised appearances, and public proclamations to do that, when your existing educational systems and similar can be employed to the same effect.

9.6.1   Education

Your educational system should promote your ideas, including your national ideology (see section 2.2.4), and promote a view and understanding of history coherent with your administration's goals and your persona, including

your status as a demi-God. They should furthermore promote a nationalist or extremist ideology, and either suspicion or hostility of the "democracy" advocated by the West. For example, China has produced regime-
authorized textbooks that expound on expanded human rights as a political
instrument the West has invented for the purpose of continued repression of
China; they furthermore gloss over failed Communist experiments like the
Great Leap Forward, the Cultural Revolution, and Tiananmen Square massacre (1989). Russian textbooks evoke Stalin as one of the country's greatest
leaders and explain away his Great Terror as an unavoidable "product of the
times." Iran's textbooks promote the Muslim Clerics' theocratic ideology,
intolerance, and illiberal world view, and Pakistani school books teach the
demonization of all those who fail to follow an extreme interpretation of
Islam.[256]

9.6.2   Information and Propaganda

The Chinese government expertly renamed the Department of Propaganda
as the Department of Publicity (it's a nuance, really). The government ex-
ercises great control over the national media, develops educational materials
that gloss over unfortunate facts like the famines of Mao's Great Leap Forward, and similar. But furthermore, the government has taken great pains to
reinforce ideas convenient to the Communist Party (CCP) in an overt strategy
of group-think.[15] The CCP's propaganda strategy conforms to the idea of the
"Big Lie," which is to say anything, repeated frequently enough, becomes a
fact. And the CCPs facts reinforce the fear of foreign forces, the internal
threat of separatist movements (Tibet's Dalai Lama is regularly accused of
wanting to fracture the motherland). Political pressure on an individual is
called "help," violation of human rights characterized as "protection of human rights," and the unions are used to control the workers. Suppression of
Uyghur calls for autonomy is considered counter-terrorism, suppression of
local democratic movements is called counter-revolutionary action, and the
judicial system, who serves only to enforce the bidding of the Party elite,
is uplifted as the Rule of Law. Wherever possible, the CCP is hailed for
its great victories and achievements, and foreigners – especially the West –
are upbraided for the problems.[256] This is powerful language, and effective too, especially among politically-charged youth now known as *fengqing*
("angry youth").

The Chinese government has effectively created distractionary fears when
necessary to lessen the pressure of local calls for reform: incidents involving
Japan, Tibet, and the United States have strengthened the image of the CCP
and distracted the people from other concerns. In the case of Tibet, some of
the incidents seem to have been manufactured for that very purpose.

---

[15] See 1984 by George Orwell ([366]). This book sounded outlandish in 1950 but China is
increasingly showing that many of its tenets are not only entirely feasible, but even useful.

9.7 Gathering Intelligence in the Internet Age

The Internet, as we have suggested, is a boon to the tyrant wishing to collect actionable intelligence on his people. Feel free to use the Internet for your own purposes as well, instead of simply reducing your people's access to it. Check your dissidents' profiles to see to whom they are connected using Facebook and other social networks. Hugo Chávez uses Twitter for propaganda purposes, and you should also make use of available channels to get your message out.[180]

Email Webmail accounts – Gmail, Hotmail, Yahoo – are not hard to hack, and if you need to you can simply monitor the access of certain accounts to capture the passwords used. Reading the contents of those in-boxes will keep you adequately informed. Use this technique to track the activities of key journalists and potential political opposition. During crises you can monitor certain systems like Twitter and ensure all traffic with those services is cut. Or you can force those people to divulge their Twitter and Facebook login information, and use it to post misleading and incorrect information; have your professional *agents provocateurs* log in as an opposition rabble rouser and have some fun.[437]

The Iranian government was ground breaking in its use of so-called "social networking" media as an intelligence tool, as it followed opposition activists' digital trail across the net and expanded its dragnet to thousands on the basis of the information it learned this way. Similarly, the Iranian government used "crowd sourcing" techniques by posting photos of dissidents and inviting the public to identify them. In fact, the Twitter feeds, email, and networking habits of your opponent form a handy snapshot of his political views, his allies, colleagues who share his opinion, and his family.[434] Many Iranian activists report they were confronted with copies of their own email when interrogated, revealing Iran's ability to enter into email accounts and read the correspondence of its citizens. The fear of this ability is almost more useful than the ability itself.[276]

The Tunisian government prior to its fall in 2011 also reportedly used such a technique to monitor dissidents; targets of such hacks were surprised to see that Facebook groups they'd created had been deleted, and pictures they'd posted of recent protests had vanished.[473] The technique was simple and effective: a modified "log in" page was provided for users of Google, Facebook, and Hotmail, that siphoned off user names and passwords when Tunisians logged in. Once the government had that information it was easy to monitor those users' activities, delete posts, and be informed of impending anti-government activity.[221] Not surprisingly, the Syrian government took this to its logical conclusion, pushing malware to Syrian activists that infects their computers and installs "backdoors" that facilitate further surveillance by government officials.[445]

Cell Phones   Increasingly, rallies and protests are being organized by sending SMS messages over GSM cell phones. If properly managed, you can ensure those technologies are throttled, delayed, or kept off line, during and just before important moments. Furthermore, GSM technology is easily hacked, and it's not impossible to listen in on conversations of people you find necessary to follow. Iran's phone SMS services were shuttered in the days leading up to the 2010 elections, and did not resume until 40 days later.[276] Elsewhere, protesters planning their rallies find themselves stymied when their SMSes fail to be delivered just as your jack-booted thugs are pulling up in their armored vehicles. Cuba, infamous for having close to no telephone system whatsoever until recently (under Fidel Castro only foreigners and some senior officials were permitted to have a phone), installed a 3G phone system its locals are not permitted to access. But for safe measure, it ensured that telecom company Ericsson installed the system with every conceivable snooping feature set to 'on.'[188]

9.8   Exploiting Media in a Crisis

The day comes for every autocrat: unrest, political protests, bread riots, and opposition forces linking up with sympathetic foreign foes. Chapter 8 goes into great detail about how to handle uprisings and demonstrations, but it's worth looking into how your control of popular media plays into the equation. In an nutshell, use as many of the techniques noted above as you deem appropriate. Below is a useful checklist of suggestions that could turn the media to your side when the chips are down.

   1. Slow Internet service during periods of peak demand, like prior to an election (Iran, Libya)

2. Order blogging services to remove offensive posts (Iran)

3. Block access to offensive web sites. If your citizens can't see a web page, it no longer exists. (Iran)

4. Imprison, threaten, or kill offending bloggers (Iran)

5. Employ monitoring software on all public Internet access points (Cuba). Aggressively monitor online communications, including email, Facebook, Twitter, and blogs (Iran)

6. Aggressively pursue anyone who can be linked to the online-organization of protests or anti-government demonstrations (Iran)

7. Hack opposition news sites, forums, and web pages, possibly using them as distribution channels for tools that debilitate readers or divulge their personal credentials (Iran, Syria)

8. Hijack or crap-flood opposition Twitter feeds (Syria)

Chapter 10

The International Community

I̲N̲ a perfect world, you would run your nation in isolation, manage your local constituencies, extract and distribute resources, and live a happy life free from foreign scrutiny. In the real world, you have to cope with belligerent and untrustworthy neighbors, mixed ethnicities, and a bevy of self-appointed international observers, foreign intriguers, and interested third parties, all of whom may want to hurt, help, or exploit you. That's the best case; in the worst case (more likely), you will need to deal with these parties while running a cash-strapped nation (and you might have had something to do with that). Or, imagine a scenario where moneyed outside interests or reformers are pressing you to show "results" when your impoverished nation has a dearth of economic resources and no civil society. You may be able to rationalize many things away as supreme leader, but this is not one of them. Sooner or later you will need to deal with members of the foreign community, be it to discuss the upcoming election, convince them to fund your latest project, or simply show them the door if your position is strong enough. Since there is no escaping the international community, don't fight the current; channel its strengths to bolster your rule, and keep your finger on the pulse of international opinion so that you can manage this fickle thing and turn it to your advantage. This is an ambitious goal that requires some delicate handling, but it can be done.

10.1   Running Roughshod over Westphalia

The original Peace of Westphalia, a series of treaties that defined the international order in Europe after 1648, codified a kind of egalitarian approach
to the relations between neighboring states. Officially, you're all for the
principles espoused by Westphalia; in reality, ignore, bend, and break them
every time you find it convenient or useful. Making and breaking alliances,
meddling in the internal affairs of other countries, and vulgar saber-rattling:
these are the tools of the autocrat determined to use and abuse the tenets of
international order.

10.1.1   Alliances and Influence

No man is an island, as they say. At first, you may feel that your poorly-run
nation is too weak or isolated to benefit from collaboration with neighboring
countries, be they ideological soul-mates or regional powers. You may feel
particularly isolated if your nation is engaged in a "popular revolution" designed to spur nationalistic sentiment, or if you have decided to antagonize
or vilify a neighbor as part of your political platform. Regardless of your
internal situation, keep an eye on regional politics, as opportunities to extend your influence abroad may arise in the form of potential alliances or the
chance to push a tottering rival out of power. For example, if you are at odds
with the neighboring leader, you should scarcely be able to resist supporting
the rebel forces hoping to overthrow him. But that's just a starting point; for
more on these opportunities to extend international influence, see below.

Alliances   You ought to band together with like-minded nations, invest in
rebel movements that resemble the ones that brought you to power, and focus regional efforts for common causes. Several modern authoritarian nations have engaged in aggressive financial assistance programs with other
countries in a mostly-successful effort to build international alliances and
strengthen their collective cause. In other words, "Soft Power," or emphasizing prestige and economic influence rather than military might, is one way
to bind weaker nations to your will. China has long developed a policy of
lending based on a "win-win" ideology that easily appeals to poorer, developing nations. No-strings-attached loans have made China the number one
investor in much of Africa, while drawing attention to the stringent lending
policies of Western nations and the multilateral development banks. Russia,
Venezuela, and Iran have similarly used their oil wealth to build alliances
and support following nations. Nicaragua, for example, has benefitted richly
from Venezuela's largesse.[413]) [256]

Likewise, Iran's participation in various alliances has been an important element in President Ahmadinejad's political longevity. In the United
Nations, the Iranian delegation has diligently endeavored to create ad hoc
coalitions against the United States and Israel, and used the same coalitions

to pooh-pooh negative reports from the International Atomic Energy Agency (IAEA). It has furthermore capitalized on its relationships with China and Russia to block UN Security Council resolutions on the nuclear issue.[256] Iran has likewise forged political alliances with fledgling autocrats in Latin America with promises of financial support in exchange for political loyalty. Aligning Iran with Bolivia, Venezuela, Nicaragua, and Cuba, Iran's joint ventures tend to have greater political than economic benefits: witness the establishment of direct air travel between Venezuela and Iran, on mostly-empty aircraft.[256]

Support other Movements   Neighborly meddling is a timeless tactic, and if you can entrench or extend your power by stirring up trouble in the country next door (particularly if you can do so while not getting caught), then by all means, meddle away. The Iranian government has provided extensive support for movements in other nations in the Islamic world, from Hezbollah (Lebanon), a variety of Shiite forces in Iraq, Hamas (Palestine), and certain Afghan warlords. In Iraq, the two biggest recipients of Iranian aid have been radical cleric Moktada al-Sadr and the Islamic Supreme Council of Iraq; both have fielded militias. Hamas received over $300 million to cover public-sector salaries in the Gaza strip, and Iranian patronage of Hezbollah – financial, ideological, and military – is undisputed.[256] Iran has reached in to provide economic gifts for Muslims throughout the Middle East,[1] from $1B to help Lebanese Shiite Muslims rebuild their homes after the war with Israel, to offers of millions for Shiite Iraqis who lost electricity during the war. Iran has furthermore consistently manned the bully pulpit with regard to Israel, and as a result has taken a leading role in the Muslim world's attacks on that nation.[256]

Nicaragua's Sandinistas in the 1980s were so thrilled with their revolution they hoped to share it, and provided guns and money over the border to El Salvador in hopes the FMLN rebels would follow suit.[294] In a similar vein, Gambia's Yahya Jammeh caused a serious diplomatic row in 2010 when a shipment of Iranian arms destined potentially for the separatist movement in neighboring Senegal was interdicted in Lagos, Nigeria (the arms were stashed in 13 shipping containers labeled "construction materials"). Jammeh responded by breaking diplomatic relations with Iran, but Senegal broke them with Gambia as well.[321] Zaire's Mobutu couldn't resist helping his Angolan rebel friends in 1975. The Zairian army entered Angolan territory to back up the National Front for the Liberation of Angola, possibly with CIA assistance. But not only did Cuba back the incumbent regime, leading to a disastrous military loss for Mobutu, but his clear partisan role led Angola to subsequently return the favor by backing his opponents, and letting them stage their attacks of Zaire's Shaba province from Angolan territory. You reap what you sow, after all.[212]

---

[1]Despite criticism back home that valuable resources are being spent overseas rather than on often equally-needy Iranians back home.

Syria's Assad family has supported the Palestinian movement within Israel for decades.[72] And Libya's Mohammar Khadaffi created a particular niche for himself by supporting opposition factions worldwide, from the Irish Republican Army to the Palestine Liberation Front. Latin American tyrants from Venezuela's Hugo Chávez to Nicaragua's Daniel Ortega looked to him for inspiration and funding (and apparently got more of the former than the latter). He created dictatorship academies and trained some of the world's most brutal autocrats.[117] Likewise, the Cuban government under both Fidel and brother Raúl Castro has had such credentials as a Rogue State that its endorsement of other administrations is now nearly essential for their accreditation as a bad guy. Castro's approval of Hugo Chávez' government solidified Venezuela's reputation and permitted Chávez to "flaunt his anti-imperialism and score points among the most extreme elements of the left in Latin America."[256]

Exert Your Influence   Sometimes you may need to give events a shove to ensure a friend rather than a rival assumes power in a neighboring state. Under Vladimir Putin, Russia did not hesitate to influence the domestic politics of neighboring Central Asian nations, all former states of the U.S.S.R. The Kremlin supplied political consultants to support Ukrainian presidential candidate Viktor Yanukovich in 2004[2], and financially supported candidates in the Baltic states and Krygyzstan.[256] Putin also has not hesitated to use its petroleum as a strategic weapon, threatening neighboring Baltic or ex-Soviet states when they haven't toed the line, and even threatening to cut off oil to the West during a winter dispute.[408]

Sometimes, intervening is irresistible. In Africa, Darfur seems to be the conflict no neighboring nation can resist getting involved in "unofficially." Despite a UN Security Council arms embargo, a report published in December 2005 showed that Darfur militias had received arms, ammunition, and equipment from Chad, Eritrea, the Libyan Arab Jamahiriya, and non-governmental groups, and furthermore suggested that Eritrea had also provided military training and logistical support.[289]

Throw Around a little Assistance   Foreign aid is anything but philanthropic; this is true when wealthier countries try to help your citizens or when you try to reach out to other countries. Oil-rich Venezuela has had the cash resources to engage in a surprisingly broad program of international assistance, building alliances and exporting Chávez' Bolivarian Revolution to following countries. The assistance has bolstered Chávez' credentials as pro-poor, social justice advocate at the same time, consistent with section 2.2.4. It is estimated that Chávez has committed approximately $43 billion in overseas commitments since 1999, of which $17 billion could be classified as social investments or foreign aid. They assistance ranged from oil

---

[2]Yanukovich lost, and Russia did not repeat similarly overt operations elsewhere.

subsidies to Nicaragua and Cuba, and cash donations to Bolivia, to development assistance to Haiti for investments in health care, housing, education,
and other basic development needs. And for bonus points, it included an assistance program so the poor of the United States could purchase Venezuelan
heating oil. Nice touch! In sum, the commitments rival the American Mar-
shall Plan post World War II and puts Venezuela on par with donor countries
like Belgium, Norway, Denmark, and Switzerland.[256] See section 11.5 to
see how this plays out from the other perspective.

Paraguay's Alfredo Stroessner took this a step further, ensuring his nation became somewhat of a retirement haven for the wanted. Under his
watch, Paraguay became a haven for Nazis on the run and former dictators.
[424] It's no surprise that Nicaragua's former dictator Anastasio Somoza,
when ousted by the Sandinistas in 1979, wound up in Paraguay looking for
a place to stay.[282]

10.1.2   The Occasional, Neighborly Assassination

Having trouble with your neighbors, want to impress your supporters, or
worse? Send some armed men over the border to deal with your unruly presidential colleague, *the old fashioned way*. But be persistent. At least in 1968
and 1974, Kim Il Sung's administration tried to assassinate the president of
South Korea Park Chung Hee and senior government officials. On the second try, Hee's wife was killed. They tried again in 1983 with then-president
Chun Doo Hwan, killing 17 (but not Hwan). [235] Venezuela's Hugo Chávez
entered into a relationship with neighboring Colombia's FARC armed rebel
movement in order to secure the assassination of Colombian political figures
antagonistic to Venezuela. Though Chávez denied any knowledge of the
relationship, ostensibly between members of his security apparatus and the
Colombians, the facts, revealed in an archive of recovered documents dating
back to the 1980s, indicate otherwise.[414]

There are no shortage of inspirational examples, should you choose to
permanently eliminate a neighbor, but make sure you follow through – an
incompetent killer risks ridicule, contempt, or worse. In 1944, Dominican
president Rafael Trujillo was implicated in a plot to assassinate neighboring
Haitian president Elie Lescot. A sixteen page letter written by Trujillo, vili-
fying Lescot, was released to the press in 1945. Trujillo had scandalized the
nation. But fifteen years later on June 24, 1960, he made clear his earlier failure hadn't caused him to rethink his methods. He ordered the assassination
of Venezuelan president Rómulo Betancourt. The attempted assassination
failed, leaving Rómulo merely injured, but this time the incident earned Trujillo the disdain of most of the world. The Organization of American States
kicked the Dominican Republic out and member nations boycotted the Dominican Republic. The American CIA began backing opposition leaders,
and a year later Trujillo was assassinated in a roadside ambush outside the
capital.[239]

For reasons that aren't clear (and would probably not make sense any-way), Eritrea seems to have plotted to explode a bomb during a conference of African leaders in neighboring Ethiopia in 2011. Though the Eritrean government vigorously denied the UN's accusations, the UN posits Eritrean intelligence services plotted to explode a bomb during the African Union summit in Addis Ababa in January 2011, which would have potentially killed many civilians and perhaps some – or many – African heads of state. A clever plot to embarrass arch-rival Ethiopia or sheer madness destined to draw the wrath of every neighboring country on the continent?[81] The same could be said of an alleged plot by Iran to assassinate the Saudi Arabian ambassador to the US in October, 2011. It could have been retribution for Saudi Arabia's urging of the US to halt Iran's nuclear program via military strikes, could have simply been a strike in the endless Shi'ite – Sunni Muslim bitterness, or simple, blind hubris on the part of the Iranians. But there's no denying it was a bold move that defied easy explanation.[3][375]

Likewise, Paraguay's Alfredo Stroessner was widely believed to have co-ordinated the assassination of opposition leaders abroad, including a former Chilean ambassador, a staff associate, and a former Chilean defense minister plus his wife, and attempted as well the assassination of a Chilean senator traveling in Rome.[424]

10.1.3   Territorial Adjustment

Feeling hemmed in? Don't worry, the door hasn't shut on territorial acquisition. You are the leader of a nation whose national boundaries are the result of decisions made before your time and possibly by long-gone colonial powers; there is no reason they need to stay where they are. While the era of intense nation building and empire formation has mostly come to a close with the end of the Ottoman and Austro-Hungarian empires, there's no reason to think it will never be reopened. If you've got the finances and the troops, consider a land grab.

Nothing stated "Russia is back" more clearly than the five day Russian invasion of Georgia in August 2008, when Russian tanks came within inches of the Georgian capital before withdrawing to the separatist enclaves of South Ossetia and Abkhazia. While the invasion was not routine even for a resurgent Russia, it did send a clear signal that Russia had both the means and the willingness to deal aggressively with an opponent.[256] Taking advantage of neighboring Belarus' financial crisis, Vladimir Putin expressed his support for the idea that Belarus merge with Russia: the beginning of the reconstitution of the U.S.S.R.? At a minimum, it's a hefty price to pay for a Russian bail out.[405]

Even if it does nothing else, taking an aggressive stance with regard to some disputed territory will draw attention to you and your nation, cause

---

[3]It *did* however keep the conspiracy theorists blogging into the late hours of the night.

some discomfort for someone else and *his* nation, and reinforce your reputation as a bold leader: is it any surprise then, that a group of Philippino
politicians staked a claim on the Spratly Islands (for bonus points, they sang
the national anthem: jingoism at its best).[75]

Indonesia's Suharto, and his military, had a harder time of it when trying to make East Timor part of the Republic of Indonesia. Despite a thirty
year presence in that territory, East Timor eventually voted for independence under the auspices of the United Nations. An independent report from
the Commission for Reception, Truth and Reconciliation in East Timor, released in 2005, reported that the Indonesian government was responsible for
18,600 East Timorese citizens murdered or disappeared, and another 84,000
– 183,000 killed as a direct result of Indonesian policies intended to starve
the island and make it un-inhabitable. Rape, sexual slavery and sexual violence were an integral part of the campaign of intimidation, designed to
inflict a deep sense of terror, powerlessness, and hopelessness; torture and
violence were widespread. The report concluded that Indonesian security
forces intentionally employed starvation tactics to ensure the island could
not sustain its inhabitants.[237] And after all that, East Timor escaped Indonesia's control entirely. Think about that before you send in your generals:
you will eventually have to think about your legacy.

You don't necessarily have to invade your neighbors to cause them trouble. Every nation has trade restrictions, for a plethora of reasons. Yours
become an effective weapon against your neighbors' exports if they give
you trouble. This strategy quickly becomes a tit-for-tat however as they will
almost certainly respond in kind. A more enduring strategy is to reinforce
your neighboring administration's political opposition, arm their rebels, and
similar.[145]

10.1.4   Cultural Exportation

Mom always said, "You can catch more flies with honey than with vine-
gar," right? Though it goes against your brutal instincts, try calling your
assassins back home and instead concentrate on exporting the goodness of
your obviously and overwhelmingly superior culture. No one has seized
on this opportunity with more gusto than the Chinese. The Chinese governments' Confucius Institutes, carefully proscribed from espousing any but
the official party line, have been an effective form of soft power, encouraging the dissemination of Chinese values overseas, cultivating important
international relationships, and generating positive impressions of the nation
and the Communist Party. It has developed the China Association of Youth
Volunteers (not unlike the US Peace Corps) to work on agricultural and language projects overseas, and offered training programs for thought leaders,
which are now being extended to key media, police, and military contacts
in developing countries. Its economic largesse is almost unsurpassed. Already, the World Bank estimates that China is the largest investor in Africa,

and outstrips Western donors in Southeast Asia by an order of magnitude. These programs are clever: the police training in Central Asian countries has helped disseminate the idea that the Uyghur nationalists are radical separatists/ terrorists, and led to increased repatriation of Uyghurs, often with no reason.[438]

10.2   Working with the Foreign Diplomatic Community

Before we delve into your relationship with foreign diplomats take a moment to recognize the number of foreigners running small and medium-sized businesses in your nation. Besides propping up your economy, they may offer opportunities for extortion, particularly if they are ethnic minorities or simply expat entrepreneurs and retirees looking to have some fun on your soil. In general they are easy to handle, since they want essentially to be left alone to make profits and expand their business. And they will do just about anything to avoid the tangles of bureaucracy, limit the fines, licenses, taxes, permits and regulations your administration is capable of subjecting them to, and be left alone to make money. As for the money, they will be more than happy to provide some of it to you personally, if it seems to help them avoid the costs of all that other bureaucracy. Make sure they know that a healthy relationship with you personally will streamline their businesses, and an unhealthy relationship (the kind caused by not providing for your reelection fund, for example) will ensure the full force of the government will be used enforce every last tenet of your commercial code, with heavy fines for violators.

The diplomatic community – ambassadors, visiting technocrats, political advisors, and others – requires a much more delicate hand, as diplomats are accorded rights that limit your options. Furthermore, most arrive in your country with an arrogant sense of responsibility incommensurate with what you need from them.

10.2.1   Your Charm Offensive

First of all, everything, and we mean *everything*, goes better if foreign powers see you as a potential ally, a like-minded person whose values they share. They will happily imagine all sorts of things about you, much of which won't be true. Let them dream, but do make an effort to to be liked – at least at first – as it will help you gain some time later when your military starts pounding some rebel village.

The right look It was true about getting put into power and remains true while you are in power; it's true furthermore when it comes to getting funding: Westerners have a propensity for funding and supporting those leaders they feel are most like themselves. And they adore English-speaking technocrats with degrees from Western universities. If you have carefully groomed yourself on the way to power with the right accent (a British accent is well worth the trouble learning), the right look, and the right "persona," you may be richly rewarded.

The right talk Wax eloquent about democracy, transparency, decentralization, development, control of corruption, and accountability. This has worked astonishingly well for leaders who went on to practice none of those philosophies: Laurent Kabila (Congo), Yoweri Museveni (Uganda), Paul Kagame (Rwanda), Meles Zenawi (Ethiopia), and Isaias Afawerki (Eritrea).

Bill Clinton lauded these men as the "new generation of leaders" in the "African Renaissance" sweeping the nation.[26] They generally turned out to be nothing of the sort, and several of them figure prominently in this book.

It is also useful to present yourself as a reformer, blaming the country's ills on your predecessor or the "Old Guard" as a pretext for moving them on, and keeping the country's hopes pinned on you. This is the strategy practiced most ably by Syria's Bashar al Assad, who for many years also managed to convince the West just that.[4][60]

The right spouse   One point in Assad's favor was his charismatic and lovely wife Asma, raised in London and of course perfectly fluent in English. She became the "face" of what Westerners hoped was a more pro-West Syria. If you yourself are not the Western educated, fluent English speaker Western governments adore so much, it is a smart idea to marry one. She may have been the perfect spouse for other reasons as well, as she was mostly content to focus on shopping for luxury goods while her husband oversaw the extended slaughter of thousands of Syrians in 2011–2012.[102]

The right political philosophy   It's important to know your audience when you speak, as the right words can make the cash register go 'cha-ching!' During World War II, when the Allies were looking for support in Africa, several African leaders managed to persuade the West they were staunchly anti-Communist even as they erected neo-communist regimes at home. Likewise, when George W. Bush announced the American 'war on terror,' many African leaders otherwise well-skilled in the arts of terrorism where their own people were concerned – from Charles Taylor (Liberia) to Robert Mugabe (Zimbabwe) and Omar al Bashir (Sudan) – came forward with wars against terror of their own. And they were well-funded by the Americans for it. Charles Taylor, to his (ahem) credit, even established an "anti-terrorist" unit that went on to terrorize the Liberians, and the warlords of Mogadishu formed a "Coalition Against Terrorism" in 2006, which the CIA amazingly agreed to fund.[26] Well played, gentlemen.

An Emphasis on Cooperation   Diplomacy is vague, and frankly, other nations are providing diplomatic presence in your country because they want to remain in contact with you. If, in a huff, they withdraw their ambassador and sever relations, they have essentially ended the conversation, and neither they nor you want that. So keep them around. Couch all your relations with countries otherwise inclined to press you for reforms, in the language of "cooperation" and "dialogue." Both are politically neutral, infinite, and respectful. Neither commits you to do anything you don't want to do, and

---

[4]The ruse lasted around a decade, before the growing Jasmine Revolution forced his hand. As his military killed protesters, it became clear he was not planning reform of any sort, and was simply continuing his father's mandate, albeit probably more ham-fistedly.

neither insists on reform. Dialogue can go forever, lead to nothing, and keep the money flowing. And cooperation, of course, means money. Insist that your diplomatic relations remain at this level, and then get back to doing whatever you needed to do, like harassing your political opposition.[206]

Exploit the Circumstances   Even the worst case scenario may not mean permanent political isolation. What if you, a notorious dictator, were a friend of Hitler and Mussolini, and were aligned with the Axis powers in World War II? Surely this would render any political rehabilitation impossible? Not quite, particularly if you can exploit the changing political winds. In Spain, Francisco Franco bided his time, avoided actively fighting for Hitler's cause, and slowly used his anti-Communist credentials to refurbish his image once the Cold War spurred a geopolitical realignment. It helped that he was (as you should be) ideologically flexible, able to flatter the United States, reach out to the Conservative party in Britain, and consolidate his ties with the Vatican. The result was that he gave up official neutrality and received economic and military aid from the United States in 1953; not bad for a junior partner in the original Axis of Evil.[246]

10.2.2   Issues of Respect

Keep this in mind at all times: you are the head of a sovereign state and you are not obliged to put up with anything you wouldn't like to. Your state may have the GDP of a rent-a-car agency and the population of Chicago, but you are on the same political level as the President of the United States or any other head of state. In fact, you may be a step ahead of them for several reasons:

- They have to answer to their people and you mostly don't.

- You are popularly hailed as a demi-God, while they are meek, tethered public servants, and

- While their press excoriates them for their every move, your press is kept muzzled most of the time and flatters you whenever you want them to.

Use this sense of your potency to set the context for talks with Western governments and their ambassadors. For starters, demand the respect you deserve. Make ambassadors wait for you. Respond slowly to their requests (which annoyingly, are frequently "urgent," aren't they?) for meetings. Let them languish a bit in the waiting room. For bonus points, have your chief of protocol inform them after they've been in the waiting room for a bit, that you have been called away on urgent matters and will have to reschedule their appointment. Don't push this too far, but do make it clear who is the president and who is not.

If you absolutely have to, kick out a nosy ambassador. As far as you are concerned, their role is to ensure your demands are heard back home, not to get into the business of your country's sovereign affairs[5]. In 2010, when Venezuela's President Hugo Chávez rejected American ambassador nominee Larry Palmer, he said, "They will do what they want, but that man is not coming here as ambassador. Anyone who comes here as an ambassador has to show respect. This is a country that must be respected," and dared the United States to cut off diplomatic ties. Palmer's offense had been to comment that the Venezuelan army had low morale, and to accuse Venezuela of offering safe haven to FARC rebels coming from Colombia.[51] Similarly, Malawi's president Mutharika ejected the United Kingdom's envoy, Fergus Cochrane-Dyet, for the same reason, stating Malawi had no reason to accept insults just because Britain was Malawi's biggest donor (Cochrane-Dyet had described Mutharika as "becoming ever more autocratic and intolerant of criticism." – oops).[6][70]

But you don't need to – and actually, *shouldn't* – send ambassadors packing permanently, as by ejecting them you close the door on cooperation and financing. Rather, send them packing for a week or two before holding conciliatory talks. You've made your point that you must be respected and will not listen to just anything some foreign government wants to say. But reestablish diplomatic relations sooner rather than later, so foreign governments can try to "improve" relations with your country, hopefully by financing your projects.

So rather than expelling your critics, criticize them back. Lay into the groups they represent, while you're at it. Said Ethiopia's President Meles Zenawi Asres, when the European Union Election Observer Mission submitted a report disparaging the irregularities of the 2010 elections: "[The report is] useless trash that deserves to be thrown in the garbage" and "[it is] just the view of some Western neo-liberals who are not happy about the strength of the ruling party."[321]

Or give them the cold shoulder. Nicaragua's Daniel Ortega simply refused to respond to Amnesty International's request for meetings. You *are* a busy president, after all: if you don't want to see some pushy international group with an agenda that mismatches your own, don't pick up the phone.[124]

10.2.3   Encouraging Funding

No matter what kind of place you run, the world eventually comes to you. Just take the 1936 Berlin Olympics as an example that needs no explanation. So eventually the donors will show up to see how they can help you. Once your capital city is swarming with white SUVs with tinted windows

---

[5]They may feel otherwise about this subject

[6]Cochrane-Dyet may have been on to something though. It was several short months later that Mutharika finally just told the whole donor community to go to hell. [460]

and diplomatic (i.e. duty-free) plates, and the fancy restaurants are filled, evenings, with privileged individuals relaxing after a long day of hoping you'll "reform" by crying into their imported beer, the stage is set. Time to accept the good will of the international community.

Establishing the Emotional Framework   This is a delicate dance. But face it: the international diplomatic community has set up an office in your country because they want to "strengthen relations" with you, and that's an invitation for you to set the stage for "cooperation," i.e. their funding of your projects. At the same time, the international community is approaching you with a mind-set completely orthogonal to your own. They see you as a "project," and are here to "solve problems" or gain access to your nation's natural resources. They imagine you are desperate to make your nation look like theirs in terms of infrastructure and government, and imagine you are grateful for all the help they can or could provide. Nothing could be farther from the truth: you have things essentially where you'd like them, and now it's just a matter of ensuring you maximize the funding they provide, while minimizing the concessions or "institutional reform" they require of you. You must work hard to counter their psychological desperation to convince you you are a "recipient." You know better: they are desperate to fund your projects for reasons of their own, and your role is to channel their resources into projects that benefit you financially, politically, or both: after all, they are excited to report home they are "strengthening cooperation" and "engaging you" and you are excited to get those funds flowing. Start by reminding them why they need you more than you need them.

You Probably Have Something They Want   If your nation is blessed with natural resources coveted by the Western World – petroleum is a good one – you can rest easy. Western nations will press you for reform, complain about your government style, whine about your political prisoners, and then shut their mouths while they line up to purchase your fuel. Amazingly, as Libya erupted into riots in February 2011, journalists paused from criticizing Khadaffi long enough to criticize Britain's Tony Blair for having "legitimized" the Libyan leader in 2003.[7] Blair praised Khadaffi for having renounced his support for terrorism, leading to the dropping of economic sanctions, renewal of foreign contractors on Libyan oil fields, and the sale of lots and lots of weapons to Libya, some of which were surely used in 2010 to suppress the riots.[459] Likewise, Equatorial Guinea, a repressive, economically-morbid developing world country, still manages to garner lots of attention as a result of its steady production of petroleum: Equatorial Guinea is Africa's 4th largest oil exporter.[358] Sure, criticize all you like,

---

[7]Tony Blair may have an interesting post-diplomatic life playing a dictator's sad sidekick in a stand-up comedy routine. He certainly has made a habit of awkward public meetings with autocrats, as was the case during the famous upbraiding he received from Syria's Bashar al-Assad in 2001.[116]

but make sure to stop by the gift shop on your way out, so you can make your purchases.

Nor does it have to be minerals or raw materials. When the United States entered into protracted military action in Afghanistan in 2002, Uzbekistan's Islam Karimov found his nation's geostrategic usefulness as a base outweighed just about all other considerations. The political support, money, and dialog made Uzbekistan crucial to the war effort, and many believe it emboldened Karimov to further reject democracy and continue cracking down on the opposition. After all, it was the wrong time for the West to complain about his "methods," and for the most part, they didn't.[420]

Zaire's Mobutu Sese Seko found an immense source of power and influence simply by positioning Zaire as a bulwark against Communism in Africa at a time the Soviet Union was increasingly making incursions. It is widely believed the CIA provided resources to his administration over many years in order to continue buffering against Soviet encroachment.[212]

Using Diplomatic Competition to your Advantage   It's widely known a country's diplomatic relations are ultimately self-serving. Wealthy nations enter into diplomatic relationships with your nation because they want to further business opportunities either by selling you their goods or buying yours, because they want to exert regional or geopolitical influence (in which case they are using you as a proxy), because they want your geopolitical support (for example, voting in their favor in the United Nations or similar), or simply because by influencing ("helping") you they can better claim to be a super power. But whatever the reason, it's not an exaggeration to say wealthy nations are vying for your attention; understanding that will help you negotiate more efficiently.

At the same time, the world is changing: India and China are growing wealthier and more powerful, Brazil is exerting more geopolitical influence, and Iran is engaging the developing world. Use these newcomers to better your position. If a European country or the United States refuses to fund your pet project, or the multilateral development banks agree to do so only under onerous conditions, shop around. It's not unlikely one of these new powers will step in to fund it, and with fewer conditions. The Chinese government is extremely interested in Africa, in particular, and is funding large infrastructure projects throughout the continent, no questions asked.[26] Its diplomatic and strategic advantage *vis-a-vis* the Western world is an explicit policy of non-interference in the internal affairs of the states with which China does business: try getting a deal like that from the IMF![438]

You can achieve the same effect more subtly by playing the countries off each other. Let's say you want something from the West. Before asking them to fund your project, cuddle up to Iran, Russia, Pakistan, China, or Brazil. If you are lucky, Western governments will fall over themselves like jealous lovers to ensure they have the "right" to fund it and keep you "in their pocket." Mission accomplished!

No Funding Required Lastly, here's a little known trick: If what you're looking for is a political boost on the basis of your ongoing "projects," it's not strictly necessary for donors to fund anything new; the fact that you are speaking with them may already be enough to show your skeptical populace that you are working hard with the international community to improve their lot in life. Organize a round table, get ample video coverage of the donors sitting around tables, watching government-produced slide presentations, or respectfully listening to you. Then the next day report at length in the papers how the donor community is "studying," "considering," or "engaging in a plan including" funding of something spectacular. They may be doing nothing of the sort, and it may be disproven later, but you will have already benefitted in the short term from the positive press.

Demand Retribution Your country was likely once colonized by a foreign power. Not only should you 'never forget,' but also use history to your your advantage, and remind your interlocutor that many of your poor nation's problems are the direct result of colonial abuse, mismanagement, and intervention.[8] Never mind if your country received independence several generations ago: guilt is infinite.

You don't always have to dredge the well of history to tweak the Western guilt complex and demand compensation. Beginning around the time of World War II when developed nations started to fight for influence in the developing world, the West poured millions of dollars into developing countries, destroying the poor countries' economies and enrichening the corrupt, political elite. Western aid programs, developed in a labyrinth of conflicting justifications, methods, and objectives, did little to alleviate poverty and propped up tyrannical regimes that did little to help their own people.[9] In sum, the donor nations were selfish, ignorant, and grossly incompetent, and it's partially their fault your nation looks like it does. They should contribute to your development in order to set things right. Otherwise, they should at least cancel your external debt, as it was incurred by your predecessor and led to no real benefit for your people; furthermore paying it is crippling your ability to fund other things.[10][26]

Your position is stronger if your country ever experienced strife in which foreign powers intervened, even financially. When the U.S. withdrew aid funding to Nicaragua in 2008, president Ortega threatened to bill the U.S. for $17 billion in war reparations stemming from American military support for the Contras during the Nicaraguan civil war of the 1980s.[395]

---

[8]Sadly, it's more than likely totally true.

[9]Like yours, actually, but don't worry about it. The donor across the table from you probably won't make the connection and besides, what's past is past, right?

[10]... like your political campaign, your military, and your shopping trips to Europe.

10.3   Development Agencies, NGOs, and Banks

In theory, expertly managing the diplomatic community should allow you to influence their donor projects. But increasingly, that dynamic is changing as some donor projects have larger budgets and staff than many embassies themselves. Furthermore, the personnel of international aid organizations is not drawn from the same pool as the diplomats, and they work and respond differently. Manage your donors somewhat differently than you manage your diplomats.

The NGO community can be a large headache or, if approached correctly, a powerful tool. Understand where they are coming from. The donor community frequently focuses on two things only, as far as you can tell: to "help" someone (usually orphans, babies, women, minorities, gays, or your political rivals) and to keep their comfortable houses, expat lifestyle, household help, "living allowance" bonuses, tax-free lifestyle, and other perks of being overseas. The fact is, they're living a cushy, somewhat tax-free lifestyle and do *not* want to jeopardize it by going back home to their own countries. As their projects are permitted to operate in your country only because you have benevolently permitted them to be there, their demands for change are subject to your willingness to listen to them. You know it, they know it, and you both know if you shut down their project, they go back home to their crappy hometown to look for employment at the local gas station. They will be somewhat reluctant to criticize or contradict you if doing so puts their own lifestyle at risk.

10.3.1   Coordinating the Donors

Donors each have individual funding, reporting, and monitoring mechanisms, operate on different budget cycles, and respond to different political whims. This is an immense hassle for you and your ministries to manage, and while it should require your hiring additional government staff they'll prevent you from doing it. But all is not lost, for the burden is equally cumbersome for the donors themselves. In fact, it's hard for them to coordinate with each other. Furthermore, they tend to prefer different types of projects, and despite their rhetoric about coordination, don't very much like to work together, preferring to take credit individually for successful projects. Keep that in mind and you will find it's easy to keep donors working on separate projects, siloed and isolated. If they work in parallel, they each spend a bit more, are less able to demand complicated concessions from you, and have a harder time combining forces against you. So insist on a role for your government's appointed office in centrally coordinating, allocating, and distributing aid resources.

You'll be surprised to discover they love this idea! You are, after all a sovereign state, and this strategy is in perfect harmony with current donor thinking that beneficiary countries should be in charge of their own projects.

If you have a ministry of cooperation, economic development, or planning, it is a logical interlocutor for these donors. This ministry should be fully authorized to choose, distribute, request, and audit donor programs, and should ensure donors are neither fighting to work in the same sectors nor neglecting others. Naturally, that ministry should answer directly to you, so you can channel projects where you need them, and ensure areas held by your political opposition never seem to advance on the list for a new health center, school, or well.

It is possible to assign a representative from relevant ministries for individual projects. These individuals make convenient scapegoats when projects are not going as planned, or when donors grow anxious about one aspect or another of the work. It is also effective to change these points of contacts as necessary to keep the donors engaged and funding without making much progress. Remember, when the program ends, the funding does as well; it's clever to keep extending the goals, the reach, or the calendar of execution of the program to keep the money flowing, bearing in mind that too many failures in a row put you at risk that the donor will grow discouraged and give up.

10.3.2 NGO Crackdown

It's important – and not difficult – to proscribe the behavior of NGOs. You certainly don't want them nosing into your financial or extra-legal affairs. This takes some finesse, however, as you don't want to appear heavy handed unless it's required, as it will potentially limit their generosity to your nation. But neither do you want them to feel they are empowered to do as they please at times when dissenting voices would not be appreciated, such as the lead-up to elections.

Start with the licensing process, as every nation has a mechanism, probably through the Ministry of Foreign Relations or equivalent, in which NGOs are given permission to operate. If NGOs start hassling you, well it must be time to renew the licensing process, then, wouldn't you say? Make them line up one by one, file through your ministry, pay the "official" fees and fill out a lot of paperwork, which will be "examined" by your government. Impose a new requirement, like a special sticker required on all NGO vehicles driven outside the capital. Require a mandatory certification by your Ministry of Communication to ensure their public pronouncements are in line with official government policy: you get the idea. These NGOs are here on the basis of your having given them permission, and ostensibly they are here to help advance the goals of your administration. On that basis then, make sure it's clear they work for you, or they're out of there.

You can take it a step further, although you are effectively showing your poker hand in doing so: send in the thugs. In late 2011 Egyptian authorities raided the offices of 10 international NGOs focusing mostly on promotion of democracy, including the International Republic Institute, the National

Democratic Institute, and the Konrad Adenauer Foundation, to name a few.[11] The offices were shut, and the authorities carted away computers, files, documents, oh yeah, and all of their money.[348] Like Egypt, you may find that hassling foreign NGOs is entertaining and fun.

10.3.3   Channeling Humanitarian Assistance

Humanitarian groups are useful and important, and to the extent you can keep them around, you should do so. They provide things your government doesn't, like health care, mosquito nets and malaria medicine. They help the truly poor and bring resources for projects like building churches; they employ people, and they generally help out. All of these things allow you to use your own money, time, and resources, for other things of greater and more personal benefit to you and your family, like pumping up the military's hardware or paving the road to your beach house. Having them around similarly shows that you are a concerned leader working diligently with the international community to find solutions to real problems, like the reduction of poverty. Don't hesitate, however, to take measures to keep them in line, and under no circumstances should they be led to believe they can tell you what to do, rather than the other way around. Hugo Chávez neutered hostile NGOs by enacting legislation that prevented them from receiving funding from international sources, which will force many of them to disappear.[168] Or, prohibit human rights organizations from operating at all, as Eritrea's Isaias Afawerki did successfully.[392]

But watch out for "humanitarian funding," that is really something else in disguise. In 2011, for example, Germany loaned the Libyan rebels 100M Euros of funding for humanitarian reasons. How much of that funding was converted into Kalashnikovs and how much was converted into "medical care and food" remains unverified, but the fact that the humanitarian loan came in mid-civil war, and the fact that Germany paid up despite not having contributed to the NATO air strikes makes it seem this one-sided loan was anything but apolitical.[12][198]

Humanitarian aid is an astonishing business. Should your nation suffer some sort of catastrophe – a flood, a drought, an earthquake, a tsunami – you can expect a sudden and precipitous increase in contributions from the international community. These are frequently donations of food and clothing, medicine, and (re-)building supplies, the same things the international community might have otherwise refused you under more normal circumstances. There is easy money to be made here. Nicaragua's Anastasio Somoza turned the 1972 earthquake in Managua into a millionaire's personal funding mech-

---

[11]The authors would like to point out here that if the staff of those NGOs had only read *The Dictator's Handbook* they'd know democracy promotion is somewhat of a a fool's errand these days.

[12]Hey, what about Khadaffi? Do his supporters not also need medical care and food, since the rebels are shooting at them?

anism, by insisting on personally overseeing the relief effort.[282]

At a minimum, they are going to need you and your cronies to provide the better part of the distribution and logistics chain in-country, and if you negotiate well, you will benefit handsomely. You are in somewhat of a monopoly bargaining position, as the international community is totally unprepared to run the supply caravans into the countryside, and you can negotiate on the basis of safety, the need to assure the arrival of the goods, and local knowledge (including local language) to ensure your team does the delivery.

You will benefit again if you have enough control over the supply chain to ensure the relief supplies go to your supporters – or soon-to-be supporters – as part of the relief effort. Start by supporting those areas which have historically supported you the most vocally, and let the nay sayers and opposition-held territories languish a bit. They may come around. Next, condition their receipt of relief goods on pledges of political support for you, especially from the community leaders and religious leaders. If they are hungry enough, their ability to resist your deal will vanish.

10.3.4 Rejecting Assistance Outright

Sovereignty You should ensure your donors are managed the same way foreign embassies are, and for the same reason: they are guests, and probably need you more than you need them. Malawi, after passing laws that criminalized homosexuality and restricted the freedoms of the press, was surprised that the United States and Germany reduced their planned expenditures to Malawi by over $400M. The Minister of Justice and Constitutional Affairs, when commenting on the decision, railed against donors' insistence on protecting gays when a minority of nations worldwide do so, and insisted that Malawi, a sovereign nation, must make decisions on the basis of the interest of the Malawian people, not donors' preferences. "Malawi is a God-fearing nation," he said, "with its own cultural values and traditions; hence it can not embrace gay and lesbianism just for the sake of aid."[447] Several months later, and clearly fed up with the Washington consensus, he finally just exclaimed, "If any donor wants to withdraw from this country let them withdraw. Let me repeat, if any donor wants to abdicate from this county let them pack up and go. ... I'll not accept this nonsense any more; if donors say this is not democracy, to hell with you ... yes, I'm using that word: tell them to go to hell."[460]

Lack of Problem If you truly don't want any foreign governments poking around your business, you're better off not accepting their aid money, either. Deny there's a problem and refuse their "generosity" and carry on, hoping the press doesn't start to go against you. Somalia did this – despite a famine – in 2011.[74]

Foreign Incompetence   Likewise, you can expel a foreign mission or project on the grounds they are ineffective. Despite major governmental challenges and phenomenal food insecurity, Chad's Idriss Déby Itno refused to renew the United Nation MINURCAT mandate, claiming the project had failed to meet its goals. He proposed Chad's own security forces as a more competent alternative.[321]

10.4   Managing Development Projects

Development projects provide multiple mechanisms for benefitting from the international community's largesse, and the information here could just as equally be presented under chapter 11. But they require a steady hand on the tiller, too.

10.4.1   Sidestepping Requests for Change

The more aggressive embassies and generous donors (their word is "engaged," which means "in your face") – we're basically talking about the USA and Europe here – will badger you with demands that you change policies, treat your enemies more civilly, provide more rights to your political opposition, and so on. You probably don't have to do anything you don't want to until they link such changes to their ability to fund your projects, and there are many ways to deflect the demand. Read on:

1. Pass the buck: demand they see the relevant minister instead of bothering you with their requests. You are the head of state and have to be responsible for running your country; it's your minister who should be responsible for dealing with complaints. Then have your minister tell them he can't move until he is instructed to do so by you. Then have them see another minister, or sack the first one and have them start over with a new person. This can stretch out for a year at a time, during which time the political context will change or your interlocutors will be transferred, as most foreign diplomats rotate on a 2- or 3-year basis.

2. More study needed: "Your proposal is interesting," you'll say, "but we need time to analyze it to ensure it takes into consideration the needs of the people. I'll get my best people on it." Then, take your time. Set up a committee, as everyone loves committees. It should be provisionally headed of course by a second-rate intellectual who prefers obfuscation and empty sloganeering to actual work. Remove him after a while and have a vote on who should be the new committee chairman and let the ensuing dispute rage for a bit. Have the committee meet and produce a report (don't forget to ask for funding for the committee!), then dispute the report. If possible, prevent the committee from meeting by

keeping its members occupied with other tasks, or switch them out as necessary. Here is the enjoyable part: every single one of these steps can be the object of delay, dispute, reflection, and more delay. Setting up the committee alone requires input from various ministries, so your proposed committee chairman needs to write each a letter of invitation. Even nominating your committee chairman may require the consensus of your National Assembly or Prime Minister. Each step lengthens the process and saps the will of your foreign ambassador, who will eventually rotate on to his next foreign posting.

3. Revert with a request for resources: This one is easy and useful. Make it clear you accept the proposal whole-heartedly, and thank them for their support. But immediately request additional resources to ensure the program's success. Otherwise, how could your struggling nation possibly comply, no matter how willing? Let's say they request you reform the national procurement system to ensure competitive bidding. An interesting idea – but it won't happen until they fund a project, pay for consultants, analyze workshops, consult with the other donors in the community, pay for training for key ministry staff, pay for training for the new staff that replaces the suddenly-removed-after-training old staff, and so on. This strategy is useful for many reasons: it puts the burden of responsibility back on the donor, who will take ages to ramp up a program, secure funding, and bring on the staff necessary to run the project; secondly, it introduces a new revenue source you can potentially use for yourself, and it further consolidates your partner country's "engagement" with you, which is to say it makes it a heck of a lot harder for them to stop funding you, as they will soon have an army of program managers, technocrats, and local "interests" that will fight them (from the inside!) to insist the program continues. And of course, you can easily keep them hopping by rejecting the consultants' conclusions and myriad other strategies discussed in section 10.4.6.

4. Implement the minimum: when donors request reform, two things are important: to ensure the donor doesn't become accustomed to your trying to satisfy its every last request, and making sure the requested reforms don't upset your carefully-built status quo. As such, keep your reforms superficial and cosmetic. As George Ayittey describes, if the donor requests a smaller government, set up a committee (or even a ministry!) to work on the issue. If they require you better control corruption, establish an Anti-Corruption commission who happens to be powerless to do much of anything. If the Commission starts to bother your supporters and colleagues, sack the commissioner (as they did in Kenya in 2004), expatriate the Commissioner for further studies and training (kudos to Nigeria in 2007), or exonerate the corrupt ministers with a government decree (Ghana in 1996).[26] Naturally, when given the chance you should point out to your benefactors that their

requirements are too stringent, unrealistic, and ultimately defeat their intended purpose. Donors are generally staffed with good hearted people who might even take your advice to heart and lighten up a bit.

10.4.2   Insert Local Institution Roadblocks

First of all, make sure local government institutions are involved at every step of the way. If they aren't, insist on it, on the grounds that they play a fundamental role in representing the state, that they are essential to ensure knowledge transfer and capacity building, that their monopoly role in approving, accepting, or determining the validity of something can not be trusted to any other organization. This works especially well for your technical divisions, like customs, map making/land registry, and financial or resource regulators.

Once your institutions are properly inserted in a monopoly position they can delay, delay, delay. Encourage work slow downs and snail's pace decision-making. When the donor complains, start by reminding them of the importance of the work being completed to perfection or to exacting standards of quality. Then complain about that institution's challenges: lack of qualified personnel, good equipment, or adequate training (how can they possibly be expected to perform under such miserable, impoverished conditions?) It may open the funding spigot. In these instances, computers are fun to ask for as they're so quickly out of date, and permit your government staff to download MP3s they'll then probably sell on the black market.

Neither is it necessary to wait for the work to begin to demand resources. It's feasible to insist up front on a memorandum of understanding (MOU) or similar in which the roles and responsibilities of each side is laid out on paper. Make sure the MOU includes training, performance salary bonuses for the staff, and equipment, like new vehicles (get a fuel stipend while you're at it) and computers. Then allow the donor to chip in. After all, they're working for making your government more effective, and buying new equipment is an important part of doing that.

10.4.3   Insist on Local Contractors

It's reasonable and feasible to use development projects to strengthen the local labor market and employ some of your college educated population, especially if they've organized themselves as consulting firms. Keep the procurement plan focused on many small contractors, or insist all contractors speak the local language(s), giving your national firms either a competitive advantage or an all-out mandate. If all goes well, each consultant will need to begin work with a "needs analysis" or similar diagnostic to hone in on problems that had been diagnosed multiple previous times but never resolved (this is often the case when the solution requires institutional reform that would negatively impact your constituents).

10.4.4 Skim the Top

There are many ways to make this happen, but the overall goal is the same: make sure the donor provides something of market value at discount price or for free; then ensure that product is diverted from its intended channel and winds up being sold for full price or greater elsewhere. Follow this example involving malaria medicine:

First, impress upon the donor the urgent need for malaria medicine to combat the severe incidence of a deadly disease in your country and your nation's inability to combat it given your poverty. Take the donors out to the countryside to visit some of the sick and dying, who will easily advocate on your behalf (while giving you credit for being such a caring and thoughtful leader, too!). Hopefully, the donor will get the right idea and agree to provide to you a large quantity of the medicine necessary to combat the disease.

Upon retrieval of the medicine, make sure the appropriate government agents pick up the medicine, since such a valuable cargo couldn't possibly be entrusted to the private sector! Now, somewhere in the supply chain (and you can probably think of multiple ways to do this, as the opportunities vary from place to place) make sure the medicines get diverted.

Third, make sure that doctors, upon diagnosing a patient with malaria, inform the patient which local vendors can sell them the necessary medicine, since the free government clinic doesn't seem to have them in stock. Easy profit!

Of course, there are multiple variations of this scheme: either sell the medicines to the private clinics, making sure the clinics can't trace the origin of the medicine (at least, not back to you), or make sure only the clinics whose owners support you politically have access to the supply.

10.4.5 Stuff your Bureaucracy

At every opportunity possible, use existing or proposed donor programs as a pretext for building up a new bureaucracy, whose employees' salaries will be paid by the donor, whose office space will be furnished and maintained by the donor, whose vehicles will be bought by the donor. You can employ lots of people this way, while making sure the donors don't outnumber your people. Even in the case of natural disasters and similar you can propose an "Emergency Management Committee" whose role is to "report to the relevant government structures, include representatives from multiple ministries, provide updates on the situation, and work closely with international agencies to coordinate the aid."[13] Avoid questions about the following: your government's own plans, budgeted programs to respond to the tragedy, underlying structural deficiencies that caused the tragedy to happen in the first

---

[13]Unfortunately, the bureaucracy method will all but ensure the donor program fails to achieve much of anything at all. Weigh this disadvantage against the proposed goals of the program when deciding if you're more interested in funneling the donor funds through your inefficient bureaucracy "anchor" or in the results of the proposed program.

place, your government's lack of concrete data on precise needs, or why your government seems to have no vision for the role it will play other than as a recipient of your funding. Instead, keep the conversation focused on how much money the donors will provide, and when they'll provide it (after all, it's *urgent!*).

10.4.6   Projects: Fail While They Fund

Development projects are difficult anyway, but when they involve changing people or institutions, almost anything can happen. Development projects are most successful when you and your government want the results more than the donor does, and if that's not the case, you can cause the failure of just about anything by simply consigning it to benign neglect. Among your strongest arms are your ability to move people around, your right to approve, authorize, or declare valid the conclusions of different reports and projects, and your commitment to engage – or not – in different activities.

Let's say the donor has proposed a project that involves reforming your customs system, one of your primary sources of personal revenue and an institution you have effectively used as a prize for your supporters. It's not in your advantage to reject the project outright. But you can easily dampen its impact and the results it achieves. Accept the project gladly. But then: have previous studies been completed? Don't offer them outright, so the donor is forced to redo some of the work, or offers to fund something that has already been done. For each stage of the donor's work, insist on a validation of the results, to be attended by the customs system's employees and key stake holders. They should feel free to criticize missing elements, false conclusions, the methodology, the consultant's pre-existing cultural bias, or ignorance of "local working conditions." Repeat as necessary. Push the donor towards projects that involve the purchase and installation of expensive equipment, and the training of employees to use that equipment. If the equipment is put in place, commence blaming efficiency issues on the donor and its equipment; insist a new consultant come down to work on the problems, then repeat.

It's effective to question the methodology and/or scope of the work mid-project, when it's too late to reach the original goal but the donor is already too invested in terms of time and money to back out. Continuing the example of the customs system, insist the problem lies in the connection between customs and the ministry of finance (who does the accounting for the customs system), or the ministry of the interior (who polices your borders), or the port/airport. Insist the project be extended to encompass these aspects as well.

Donors will occasionally lose patience and threaten to withdraw funding. But seize the opportunity when this moment arises. Start with charm to reassure flustered bureaucrats, thanking them for support of your impoverished people, reminding them of their many years of support, your long and cordial relations, and your shared goals. This is the right moment to use the media to your advantage, publishing a negative commentary that will force the donor or foreign government to embrace you more strongly (see 9.5). Don't underestimate how easy it is to turn the diplomats against their own donors: you'd better believe the ambassador of some country is interested in keeping his agency's school-building program up and running (in the name of cooperation, and because he doesn't want to be the ambassador responsible for the failure of that important and high profile program), so when the development agency gives you trouble, call in the ambassador for some help. He will probably be able to make them jump.

To ensure the longevity of project funding, insist the monitoring indicators don't match the project activities, or keep them vague enough that multiple actors – state institutions, probably – will have to be involved, diluting the chance any one of them can be blamed for failure while ensuring their obligatory participation on committees and such.

10.4.7 Loss of Funding

Rarely, donors will finally exceed their emotional tolerance and actually withhold or even withdraw your funding, present or future. Handle this one carefully. For inspiration, follow the lead of Malawi's president Bingu Wa Mutharika in 2011. Having sent in the military to disperse a civilian protest, killing at least 18, and having threatened to "smoke out the opposition," Western donors balked and temporarily halted their funding. Mutharika's reaction:[123]

1. Express shock. It is unfathomable that a foreign government would so callously deny your long-suffering people the financial assistance they so desperately need and deeply deserve. Mutharika: "We are surprised they made such an announcement before hearing the facts on the ground."

2. Question the facts. These foreign scoundrels are misinformed, malintentioned, and incognizant of the real situation. Mutharika: "...before hearing the facts on the ground. There was no violent incident whatsoever. However in places far away, there were people looting, breaking into stores and banks. And this was not part of the demonstration. These are facts that can be verified ..."

3. Justify your responsibility for governing the nation despite difficult circumstances, and defend your democratic principles. Mutharika's spokesperson: "Mutharika is not autocratic. He follows laws enacted by Malawi's democratically elected parliament."

4. Embarrass the opposition. Mutharika's spokesperson: "The president and the government are aware of the demands that the civil society people are making. That's why on the 20th of July the president called

them all and said, 'Let's meet.' ... But so far the civil society has not presented their team for these negotiations."

Mutharika's reaction omitted only one final thing: reminding the cold-hearted Americans the impact their decision would have on Malawi's long-suffering poor. Ideally, film the press conference not in the capital but in some village where thin-looking peasants look up at you while you plead on their behalf.

10.5   International/Regional Organizations

There's no escaping the United Nations, the International Criminal Court, and Organization of American States, and others. In principle, the International "Rule-Based" organizations have been developed to strengthen democracy, provide neutral forums for peaceful arbitration of international disputes, and increase transparency of member nations. In practice, they are easily weakened or bypassed.

10.5.1   The Usual Suspects

God bless the United Nations. What other institution, after your decades of blatant abuse of human rights, mismanagement of the government, and boorish criticism of the Western World, would nonetheless campaign on your behalf to appeal for $500M of food aid? (Zimbabwe's Robert Mugabe says, "thanks, guys!")[360] Face it: find the UN office in any poor nation and you'll notice it's usually one of the nicest buildings in town, with a fleet of new 4x4s out front and an impressive staff of foreigners and locals inside. The UN isn't going anywhere, and the bureaucrats working there will be shipped home immediately if they run out of ways to help you. So that's what they do: find ways to help. The UN is equally suspect because of its democratic nature, allowing organized leaders to ensure votes go in their favor. Equatorial Guinea's Teodoro Obiang wanted a UNESCO award to be created in his name, and successfully organized the African nations to vote *en masse* in favor of it. The UN was forced to acquiesce, and the prize has become a reality, despite the outrage of Western nations offended by the prize's funding, provenance, and the way the UN was forced to accept it.[125].

The Organization for Security and Cooperation in Europe (OSCE)'s purview is Europe and the former Soviet states of Eastern Europe. But Russia and other members of the Commonwealth of Independent States (CIS, former USSR) have effectively pushed the OSCE away from election monitoring and the promotion of democratic processes, and encouraged it rather to focus on economic, environmental, and security issues. That keeps the shell in place, but ensures the OSCE is not involved in the things that matter most to you.

The International Criminal Court (ICC) was established in 2002 to try war criminals. However it has no police force and depends on member states to enforce its orders. As such, it is only as strong as its weakest member state. If the ICC attempts to impose its will on you, it's not hard to simply withdraw from the ICC, as Kenya threatened to do in 2011 when the ICC wanted to try riot leaders that had participated in the 2007–2008 election-related violence. Only the United Nations' Security Council is authorized to request the ICC defer a case it is currently trying.[323] But the International Criminal Court may put a crimp in your style, as it's possible to get convicted of war crimes and be imprisoned. Resist any proposed judgments by the International Criminal Court on the grounds that it will destabilize your already weak country, as did Kenya in 2011 when the ICC hoped to prosecute those who had led the post-electoral violence that killed dozens. Kenya cast doubt that the ICC would be any better able to produce justice than Kenya itself, and went so far as to even suggest it would withdraw altogether from the ICC.[323]

Latin American strongmen think the Organization of American States (OAS) is toothless, and though its member governments ascribe to an "Inter-American Democratic Charter" the OAS routinely looks the other way when a member state refuses to abide by it. Such was the case during the attempted power grab of Ecuador's Rafael Correa.[249] It has furthermore been an unfortunate sort of punching bag for Venezuela's Hugo Chávez, who has "obstructed almost any initiative that promotes democracy or human rights, and has apparently cowed other delegates with his threats to withdraw from the organization."[256] Chávez took particular umbrage with the OAS after its sternly-worded criticism of the Chávez administration after electoral irregularities in 2005. Chávez has publicly condemned the secretary general, resorting even to vulgarity[14].[256]

The African Union, ostensibly formed to provide a level of governance in Africa that transcended national borders, has never fully lived up to its potential. Modeled on the European Union – and still somewhat reliant on it for institutional development and financial support – the AU is composed of struggling states with governance and organization challenges of their own, and the AU suffers similar challenges at a higher level. Its lack of management systems and resources, and apparent inability to learn from its mistakes don't bode well for it, to say the least. Never mind the AU's right to intervene in African conflicts: a lack of trigger mechanisms, vague charter, and lackluster will of member nations to participate in missions mean if you are an African dictator you can probably do as you please.[289]

Take the 2011 famine in Somalia as a relevant example. Despite overwhelming international concern and obvious shenanigans on the part of el Shabab, who resisted food aid for months, the African Union remained silent. Finally, pressured to respond, it called for a "Summit of African lead-

---

[14]He called the secretary general a *pendejo* – "asshole" once

ers" to pledge support, at an unspecified – and therefore not likely anytime soon – date. Hardly the sort of body that will impose much of anything on you, or expect you to abide.[54]

A final word about your relations with international institutions is in order: should the World Bank, IMF, and friends intervene too regularly, or should national disputes be resolved only when an international institution puts you under duress, you will soon be painted as the lackey of the international community, which will immensely reduce your power nationally.[327]

10.5.2 Strategies for Wing-Clipping

Promote an Alternative If you're having trouble with existing international institutions, it is in your interest to provide a counter-balance in the form of an institution more conducive to your needs. The governments of Venezuela, Russia, and China have actively developed and promoted alternative institutions to counter-balance the effect of the others. China's Shanghai Cooperation Organization (SCO) is one example of these: present throughout Central Asia now, the SCO plays an important role in undermining the pro-democracy work of others.[256]

Autocrats like Hugo Chávez have found these organizations an effective forum for promoting alternate agendas and attempting to redress international, political imbalances. Since 2003, Chávez has attempted to "soft-balance" (i.e., through non-military means) the United States, either by eschewing cooperation on initiatives of American interest (like drug interdiction), building alliances with other enemies of the United States, generating diplomatic morasses (like promoting the deployment of Russian missiles in either Cuba or Venezuela), or instituting parallel forums like the anti-U.S. Summit of the Americas (2005).[256]

Send them Home Just like your foreign diplomats and development project technocrats, you are under no obligation to give them free reign of the country. If they start to cause too much trouble, send them home. In 2010, Algeria's Abdelaziz Bouteflika kicked out the International Federation of Human Rights, Human Rights Watch, and Amnesty International all at once. Buh-bye![321]

Take Advantage of your Victimhood Assume your nation is battling another and you are both committing atrocities against each other. Make sure to keep careful track of those committed against you when necessary. Hashim Thaci, Prime Minister of Kosovo, railed against a report citing his role as head of a mafia group in Kosovo, citing Kosovo's victimhood at the hands of the Serbs in the 1990s and inferring revisionist history for the purpose of undermining impending Kosovar statehood. "The world knows who was the aggressor and who were the victims in Kosovo," he said. "These tendencies to change history, to equate the aggressor and the victim will fail again."

It's a great defense because it has nothing to do with the charges leveled against him personally and deflects the conversation to a subject more easily defended than the charges actually leveled against the leader. Never hesitate to change the battle to suit your ability to win it.[382]

Chapter 11

Building your Financial Empire

> I laugh when I hear the amounts: '$400
> million, $800 million.' It's a lot of blah, blah,
> blah. ... There were the children to care for,
> school expenses, other bills. ... We were not
> perfect. Perhaps I was too tolerant."
>
> Jean Claude Duvalier [238]

RUNNING the nation is not cheap: the ministries need money, political campaigns cost a bundle, and the secret slush fund you may require for bribing turncoat judicial appointees always needs attention. And there are other expenses to consider as well, from your political supporters to your secret agents and more. Hey, the family's got expenses, too. So make sure you are funded, and that the funds keep coming. Says Blaine Harden about the typical African Big Man: [232]

> "He awards uncompetitive, overpriced contracts to foreign com-
> panies that grant him, his family, and his associates large kick-
> backs. He manipulates price and import controls to weaken
> profitable businesses and leave them vulnerable to takeover at
> bargain prices by his business associates. He affects a commit-
> ment to free-market reform to secure multi-million dollar loans
> and grants from the World Bank and International Monetary
> Fund. He espouses the political philosophy of whatever foreign
> government gives him the most money."

There are two aspects of finances to manage: making sure your government generates lots of revenue somehow, and then ensuring you benefit

personally from the revenue earned. Focus publicly on the former, and privately on the latter, but never forget that the two are linked, because the distinction between your nation's wealth and your personal fortune is artificial. In Nicaragua, the Somoza family maintained almost personal control over the economy of Nicaragua from the 1940s onward by manipulating government licensing requirements and importing duty-free goods with the complicity of the military. Over decades, they quickly took control of any industry that made money, from public utilities and the financial sector to cotton, beef, shrimp and lobster exports, food processing, sugar refining, cement production, cardboard, tobacco and recording industries, and sea and air transport. By the late 1970s, the Somoza family owned just about everything in Nicaragua worth owning.[494]

Ensure your government generates revenue by imposing the state on as many sectors of society as possible, by targeting those sectors, classes, and ethnicities most involved in the affairs of entrepreneurship, by shaking down the private sector and essentially by ensuring the political system and business framework require many, frequent, small payments for accomplishing the most mundane of tasks. Then get your piece of the pie. Ensure you or your family owns the key industries; ensure your ministers, in absolute fealty to you, will obligingly provide funding for your expenses, declared or undeclared, as you need; ensure your campaign needs are correctly understood as the financial imperative that conditions their personal economic well-being; and ensure any business deal of significant value is blocked until you yourself are at the center of it.[1]

To the extent your system of patronage has been established, these steps will fit naturally into place. And your own, personal fortunes will begin to grow. Here's a look at "the big boys," and where you too are headed, if you play your cards right:[252]

11.1   Your Predecessor's Economic Empire

Assuming you are recently arrived to power, an obvious first step is to assess your predecessor's economic empire, dismantle the parts that you don't need and keep the juicy bits for yourself. Carefully exploiting the former boss' economic web carries two advantages: First, he likely, through nepotism, influence trading, or simply by following the other advice in this book, has constructed a lucrative economic system centered on benefiting him and his family. Unraveling it and either privatizing or nationalizing those industries is an easy way to provide jobs, come across as a popular economic hero, and spread around a little wealth. You want the public to respect you, at least

---

[1] If the world were a better place you would focus on ensuring the *nation* generates revenue. You may wind up doing so anyway, in that a nation that produces lots of exports generates lots of revenue for the government. But in lots of poor nations we skip right to the second step, imposing the government on what little is there.

Head of Govt	Nation/Period	Amount (US$)
Suharto	Indonesia (67–98)	15 – 35 billion
Ferdinand Marcos	Philippines (72 – 86)	5 – 10 billion
Mobutu Sese Seko	Zaire (65 – 97)	5 billion
Sani Abacha	Nigeria (93 – 98)	2 – 5 billion
Slobodan Milosevic	Serbia (89 – 00)	1 billion
Jean Claude Duvalier	Haiti (71 – 86)	300 – 800 million
Alberto Fujimori	Peru (90 – 00)	600 million
Pavlo Lazarenko	Ukraine (96-97)	114 - 200 million
Arnoldo Alemán	Nicaragua (97 – 02)	100 million
Joseph Estrada	Philippines (98 – 01)	78 – 80 million

Table 11.1: Amount Allegedly Embezzled While In Office

at first, and if they have soured on the man or woman you've replaced then there's no better way to win the people's affection than showing them what an economic populist you are (even if, as is likely, you don't mean it for a second). Secondly, he almost certainly had slush funds and unsupervised spending accounts, and identifying and appropriating them is not only your right but your duty, as you will need and use them for the same purposes as he did.

Nonetheless, it's a good idea to start off your rule with a public audit of accounts. It will reveal the empty state coffers and the existence of dozens of secret accounts used for undisclosed purposes. That implicates your predecessor, takes the pressure off of you to provide immediate results, and may help earn you some sympathy, as the public will suddenly realize the difficulty your administration has, in the wake of your predecessor's avarice.

Tunisian former president Ben Ali offers a more complicated example. Investigations focused on 112 close acquaintances of the former president, 1.5B Euros, and a dependent workforce numbering about 15,000.[142] Such numbers give you an idea of the power of patronage available to you once the accounts are in your name, and the industries are owned by you and your family. Harnessing such an empire for the purposes of your administration – and eventually, your own, personal requirements – is a sound strategy for prosperity and power.

11.2 The Public Sector

This is important because sooner or later (sooner, probably) the difference between the nation's budget and your personal budget is going to blur irretrievably. In fact, most autocrats use the nation's resources as their own, as will you. Still, don't get too greedy, as too much conspicuous consumption may backfire and convince those who were formerly just content to daydream about your wealth to take up more robust forms of dream fulfillment.

11.2.1 The National Budget

It wasn't so long ago, in the days when multilateral institutions would loan your starving nation money without asking for much in return or insisting on pawing through your financial statements, that you could just use the national budget itself for your spending needs. From an autocrat's point of view, these were glorious days, largely gone now. In 1971 for example it was estimated that Haiti's François Duvalier had overseen the misappropriation of up to 64% of Haiti's government revenues; tens of millions of dollars went to "extra-budgetary expenses," including deposits to son Jean Claude's Swiss accounts.[2][238]

In nations where the populace is under-educated, where civil society is maintained on a tight leash, and journalists and the media have close to no rights, such *carte blanche* use of the national budget for an agenda of your own is still somewhat possible, but not if you expect help from the World Bank or the IMF. If that's a problem for you, you can easily go to non-traditional donors (China, for example) for economic project support. The Chinese don't ask many questions, and treat donor-financed projects in a much different way than the West. You may, however, have to sign some concessions or trade agreements. It's unlikely this bothers you, given the potential for short-term gain.

That doesn't mean the national budget doesn't provide you some opportunities, and in fact your existing legislation may already permit you a bite at the apple: have a close look. Venezuela's budget is somewhat volatile, as it is very impacted by swings in revenue occasioned by the volatility of oil prices, Venezuela's major export. To account for eventual discrepancies, the financial laws required any revenue above and beyond the budget to be deposited in a special "stabilization fund," ostensibly to ensure the money is accounted for. Sound financial prudence? Not in the hands of Hugo Chávez. Chávez benefitted by routinely submitting ridiculously low budgets year after year, which ensured national revenue would always be higher than budgeted, and that those funds would enter the stabilization fund. He then used the stabilization fund, for which little control had been designed, as a petty cash fund for his personal and political projects. For example, the 2008 budget was written on the basis of a "projected" oil price of $35 a barrel despite market prices at least double that figure. The "unexpected" budget surplus has been around 20% every year since 2002.[256]

When diverting funds from the budget, subtlety has its rewards, even if (as in the case of Chávez above) the jaw-droppingly obvious may pass muster with a citizenry that slavishly follows your television appearances. Blatant thievery is something that usually will be noticed, and if, like Slobodan Milosevic, you find yourself prosecuted after being removed from power, explaining what happened to the $390 million is not going to be easy – but then no one was going to let such gross larceny go unmentioned.[250]

---

[2]That's one heck of a college savings fund.

Angola's José Eduardo dos Santos may have chosen a similar mechanism in 2012 when suddenly a quarter of the nation's GDP was discovered to be missing. "Not to worry," his administration reassured the IMF, "[it's a matter of] oil revenue being inaccurately recorded, especially revenue of (state oil company) Sonangol ... which is not fully recorded in the accounts." Exactly – that's the way it works. For bonus points, dos Santos blamed the media attention over the matter on entities desperate to discredit his administration using any means possible.[478]

11.2.2 Public Procurement

If the national budget doesn't expressly provide a slush fund for your use, then consider using the mechanisms of government to create revenue streams, ostensibly for the needs of the government (and by extension, ostensibly for the good of the people). In reality, this common practice affords the opportunity to slice off large chunks of the budget for yourself under the cover of "good governance." One of these mechanisms is public procurement, and it is so rife with opportunities the multilateral donors and international "experts" have tied themselves in knots analyzing the subject. The fact is your government, like any government, has a long list of financial responsibilities and (to a lesser degree) the financial resources to provide for them. If the role of government is to provide public goods – anything from infrastructure (electricity grids, roads, dams and irrigation networks), public safety services (police and military), and a stable financial market (currency interventions, banking or financial regulations) – then the government use of public funds is mandated. Now considering that *you* are the government, for all intents and purposes, you can see how government action can be a lucrative endeavor. The trick is ensuring that you personally fit in somewhere between the need and the purchase.

Public procurement systems remain, in general, somewhat diverse (though they are gradually converging). Your own system may provide some nuances unique to your government. But in general, your opportunities fall into several distinct categories:

11.2.3 Government Contracting

The judicious use of government contracting can line your pockets with gold. It's not always an easy world to navigate, and often you will be dealing with former government ministers, potential rivals, pedantic state officials, and money-grubbing middlemen who, though nominally committed to helping you skim a contract are really out to rob you blind. No matter: follow some of the advice below and you can tap a nearly limitless stream of revenue. You can learn from some masters, such as Vladimir Putin, who have made an art out of concentrating wealth and power into the state's hands through government contracting. In Putin's case, he simply cut out pesky middlemen [3] and ensured his small circle of cronies were rewarded with long-term, exclusive contracts. The result of course was state coffers full of happy jingle.[245] His methods need not be yours however, and there are several ways you can go about collecting money from this lucrative enterprise. This is potentially how key members of the Ugandan government were charged with pocketing millions of Ugandan shillings while managing the growing Ugandan oil industry. On the list of those accused of corruption were the prime minister, foreign affairs minister, former energy minister (later minister for internal affairs), and the former security minister.[4][341]

The Ideal: Government Contracts with Companies You Own   Owning companies that provide the services your government needs is, if you are in the seat of power, the very definition of a "turn-key" operation. As you build your financial empire then, remember to focus on acquisition of companies and enterprises that maximize opportunities for government expenditure while positioning your family or front-men to bid on these contracts: engineering firms, construction firms, import-export ventures, office equipment suppliers (especially computers, since your government staff will be begging every donor that crosses their path for updated equipment), agricultural suppliers (fertilizer, especially), and concrete production (gypsum and clinker import, or concrete production itself) and any other industry where products and cash change hands rapidly. The more activity, the more money for your pocket.

Ideally, every time the government needs something, it hires *your* companies to provide those services. You benefit from the contract, at a minimum, assuming you charge a fair and market-based rate. But since you are unlikely to do that, you will benefit again by charging inflated, even astronomical prices for the services your companies render. Since the details of day-to-day government largely go unnoticed by the public, this isn't hard (the greatest risk is of an overly-inquisitive journalists, whom you will learn to keep under control in chapter 9).

Normally, the revenue should go to you personally. But if you want to share the wealth as part of your system of political patronage, this is the place to do it, for example by allowing your ministers to sign contracts and take percentages themselves: this is a job perk they will readily line up for, and their desire to remain in that role will make them your lackeys.

Or, have your government sign a contract with a business you own at a price your company determines unilaterally. As head of government, you have the means to ensure the government will have to accept the exorbitant price your company is charging. These 'sole source' contracts can be extremely lucrative, since only governments have the big bucks to spend. This

---

[3]We also call them, "honest businesses"

[4]Not bad – the Usual Suspects, probably, and all this long before the first drop of oil hits the Ugandan economy.

is an excellent way to set up a comfortable retirement, so plan on ordering your minister of the interior to purchase as many golden toilet seats as the budget will bear.

Open Bidding With Inside Information   Accept competitive bids for the provision of whatever it is your government needs. But make sure your family's company has a definite advantage in the bidding. You can do so by making sure they receive the bidding documents early and can thus submit a higher quality proposal, by ensuring they know aspects of the work the competition doesn't, or by ensuring they know the value of the procurement the government is able to spend, so their proposal is slightly higher while the competition is much higher. And of course you can simply instruct the evaluation panel which company to choose and to ensure the documents reflect that decision accurately and "fairly." Don't be afraid to cancel procurements and re-launch them as many times as necessary to ensure the "right" company wins the contract. Some members of the panel might need to be persuaded more thoroughly then others, and in these cases it's always helpful to remind them who signs their paycheck. After a session or two with the security services you can be sure that idealistic members of the contracts panel will have gotten their minds right.

Open Bidding, Winner Pays You Back   Lastly, and especially if the public is suspicious of contracts that go to your own companies, let some other company win the contract, and pay you anyway. The advantage to this method is that although losing the contract, your company avoids media attention and public scrutiny, but you benefit financially nonetheless. The company that wins the bid can be nudged to charge a higher-than-necessary price to cover the costs of your kickback, but it's the nation who pays that, not you. Using this mechanism you can even choose the contractor you want to win the bid, and ensure *they* have the information they need to come in with the lowest offer; alternatively, ensure the award panel does its work according to the choice you make. Either way, ensure the *right* contractor gets the contract, and remunerates you according to the deal you'd made with him prior to bidding.

Make the winning bidder understand that you expect to be compensated generously for allowing them the contract. The winner can inflate the price of his offer, and pay you that extra amount, or can fund your supporters and institutions that funnel the money to you. They can hire people you instruct them to, or simply pay you an honorarium for your benevolence. It's up to you.

Open, but Payment for Contract Signature   It's not impossible to make some money even if the bidding and award process are completely and legitimately transparent, as would be the case if you were under the scrutiny of a donor organization or multilateral financial institution. Just before those contracts are signed, take the relevant party aside, and *recommend* a little payment to ensure the contract truly does get signed, doesn't bear the brunt of an imposed audit, or similar. Contractors should be able to taste government money at that point and they will cough up every time. Should they not pay, your office will suddenly either de-authorize funding for the project given some other need (countries like yours will surely have regular catastrophes: teachers' strikes, terrorist attacks, or natural disasters that merit resources), backpedal contract signature for months and months (since it is not a priority), or simply cancel the procurement outright. The point is that by threatening to delay signature you can get nearly anything you want.

Similarly, since you probably have specific companies in mind when you solicit contractors for a task, make sure to publish your request for proposal on the open market "for free and open competition" but keep canceling and relaunching until you can be sure the "right" company has seen it and will be submitting the winning offer. If you suspect a stronger, non-preferential company is going to win it, cancel! And then relaunch when they're not suspecting. Repeat as necessary.

The power to sign – or not sign – contracts is a powerful and lucrative job perk and can play an important part of your system of patronage. If you institutionalize the right to sign contracts and demand a percentage, you are putting in place a revenue system that will benefit anyone who is permitted to participate. This is the approach taken in Equatorial Guinea, whose newfound oil wealth has led to some big contracts, and lots of opportunities for entrepreneurial-minded ministers, including the president's son, who has gone on to purchase mansions in Malibu, a private jet, and a fleet of fancy cars.[373].

The Role of the Review Panel   In an open bid, a panel of experts, probably working for your government contracting administration, is in charge of determining how to award the contracts. Having the right people here, beholden to you and your administration, is as good as awarding the contract yourself. You don't necessarily want to populate the review panel with mindless sycophants; rather, consider this a plum job for a former campaign manager, or defense lawyer who has proved his loyalty and skill. They'll be smart enough to realize that such a position places them perfectly for a little skimming, while also facilitating and covering up your own thievery.

If on the other hand a bank or donor agency insists on contracting on your behalf, you can still exert some control over the process using this mechanism. A panel of seven experts can be compromised by ensuring that the majority are government employees; as employees of your administration you can easily inform them of how you want the award to be granted, and punish those that don't comply. The members of the panel can also provide you inside information during the review process, that you can use to your advantage. For example, if the first two bids are extremely close in price, you can contact the second company – the one that would otherwise lose – and request an "additional" payment, off the books, for the privilege or your review panel finding additional fault with the first company. For a million dollar contract, this is worth many thousands of dollars as a service fee, and many companies will be more than willing to pay it.

11.2.4 Commercial Loans

There is no need to work exclusively with the international donor organizations, although their rates are often preferential (i.e., far lower). But the private sector is probably hungry for business opportunities in your nation, and you can just as easily enter into business with the private sector for funding, and an obvious funding loophole exists to make sure you benefit nonetheless.

For example, if you need to build a new bridge in your capital city, open negotiations with a private bank for a loan to finance the construction. When the banker offers you a percentage interest rate, offer to pay a higher interest rate on the basis of a cash payment he'll make you up front. That money is yours to play with, while your ministers go ahead and build the bridge. Note this scheme requires a high value project on the table, which is why it is so important to have a steady stream of public works projects ongoing (see 4.7.1), and ensure they don't all finish at the same time. You may also consider looking for bankers who've missed out on the last wave of commercial building, are thus are looking to get into the game and willing to cut corners in order to have a chance to support your new port or football stadium. Finding an eager and careless banker is like finding money in an old pair of jeans – serendipitous to say the least.

11.2.5 Customs System

In many countries reliant on importation of basic goods, the revenue from the customs administration is the biggest game in town, and the exclusive purview of the government. This can play out in several ways:

1. Your customs system is ruthless, well-organized, and efficient, generating lots of revenue for the government, that you then channel to your personal accounts using some other mechanism. Sadly, this is almost non-existent, but where it exists, it is because the customs system has been out-sourced to a private operator under contract.

2. Your customs system is rife with corruption, and the customs administration aggressively but obediently siphons off funding for your campaign and for off-the-books accounts that you and the party control exclusively. This is more like it, and these days it's probably the way the more un-enlightened and prosaic autocracies function.

3. Your customs system is rife with crooks, who each operate mini-fiefdoms, keep the money for themselves, and enjoy dipping their

snouts in the trough. You rotate your people through this patronage trough as often as you need to give someone the opportunity to make some money, as a favor, or because it's time to move someone else out. This scenario is more common than you'd think, and might even represent the status quo.

11.2.6   Key Industries and Public Utilities

Every nation has certain industries that, in terms of revenue generation and revenue potential, are essential. It might be your port, or the national airport, or export of a certain crop like tobacco or sugar cane. It goes to say that it's important (and inevitable) that you and your family take ownership of them. In Russia, where the government and the economic elite – an oligopoly – are essentially the same, many key government officials have management roles in the nation's key industries. They range from the First Deputy Prime Minister (aircraft) to the Deputy Head of the Presidential Administration (air transport), to the Deputy Prime Minister to the Special Envoy for International Energy Cooperation (petroleum), and dozens of others.[256]

But equally important is the existence of non-privatized state utilities that provide water, electricity, telecommunication, or transport services. Never mind the fact that governments typically run such things with massive inefficiencies and gross failure of customer service. You need large, amorphous, regionally-diffuse organizations with large numbers of bills and financial obligations to meet, large numbers of customers, a big staff, and a hard-to-understand budget. These structures become your cash cows, providing those little economic 'nudges' in times of need: a subsidy to the students, a perk for the village chiefs, a big-name band to back your election campaign kick-off, and similar.[5] They furthermore provide you with a broader array of cushy state jobs to offer people beyond simple government bureaucracy. Now instead of making someone clerk for the Ministry of Water, you can make him clerk for the national beverage bottling company (see 3.2.9 for more).

The telecommunication and electric services are good candidates for abuse, as their benefits are hard to quantify and track (electricity, especially) and they are easily billed using abstruse and difficult-to-understand metrics that most citizens will simply pay and move on. Your agencies can install meters, read them periodically, adjust them, assess small fees with national coverage (you'd be amazed at how fast a small fee paid by everybody monthly can add up), and fiddle in numerous and extraordinary ways.

---

[5]There's a downside, of course: if your leeching of the electrical company leads to power failures, you may engender more ill will than the perk you used the money for. Judiciousness is the name of the game here.

11.2.7 Public Works

The provision of public goods, and particularly infrastructure, is central to the role of government. And in doing so, your people will hail you as a provider of material goods, a modernizer, and a results-getter. Public works will give you many opportunities to stage ribbon cuttings (at which you'll recite a speech denigrating your political opposition), many happy announcements to make as new projects are designed, contracted, and begun, and many chances to provide updated information during the course of your presidency. Naturally, at the end of things, you'll have an opportunity to name things: memorial highways, bridges, monuments, traffic circles, airports, ports, concrete unloading facilities, and much more.

But public works are an opportunity to open the spigot of the national treasury as well. Any large project – highways, airports, ports, hospitals, and so on – will involve complicated contract management techniques, where government representatives and greedy entrepreneurs can strike deals not obvious to the general public. And beyond the opportunities that present themselves during the procurement and contracting phase, during the works themselves, your construction company, your government representative, or both will have myriad opportunities to profit.

Let's say you are building a road whose technical design requires 10 centimeters of grade 11 asphalt and 15 centimeters of crushed rock base. The entrepreneur can save money if your government supervisory engineer permits him to put down only 6 and 8 centimeters respectively. Calculate what the difference will mean in financial terms, and split the profit. You can, however, just as easily "insist" that the road be built using a technology that requires lots of concrete, and not just because you own the concrete plant!

The construction of state-owned villas in preparation for some sort of international conference lends itself as easily to rapid cash accumulation. To benefit, first offer to host some major event that will see visiting dignitaries – presidents, preferably – spending about a week in your country. Deplore the poor quality of existing accommodation, or insist the state provide "appropriate" housing for the visitors, and bingo: you have just justified a massive construction project that will get the cash flowing. Naturally, the project will require Herculean efforts on the part of your ministers, and maybe you yourself will have to get involved, to ensure the project is completed in time. The urgent nature of the work will lead to higher prices from scalping contractors, less oversight as the work progresses through the night, and fewer traces, all in the name of "hurrying." At the end of it all, you'll have your presidential villas, but more importantly you will have liberated large sums of currency you can use for other purposes. For bonus points, your ministers have now committed economic crimes for which you can later accuse them and have them arrested, ensuring none of those involved will ever become a political threat to you.

Be careful your public works don't undo your administration and legacy. Mobutu's ambitious – too ambitious – projects, in the context of falling prices for Zairian exports, led to bankruptcy and disaster. In particular, the Inga dam, intended to make Zaire self-sufficient in energy (and more: it was expected to produce fully one-third of the world's hydropower) led to a debt crisis and economic chaos. Similarly, the construction of a 1,100-mile high tension electric power connection to the copper producing region of Shaba, was a disaster. Economic mismanagement – not to mention rampant pilfering of state resources – strengthened his opposition and eventually led to his ouster.[212]

11.3   The Private Sector

You can make it necessary for wealthy corporations doing business in your country to enter into agreements with either local institutions or para-statals you can trust to funnel the money straight to you. Do you have a shipping company doing business at your port? Ensure that new legislation or some other creative strategy requires that shipping company to work with your para-statal freight-handling company (the fact they're incompetent isn't important here; the fact they can be trusted to take all the money from their new contract and give it to you, on the other hand, *is*). Is a foreign-owned concrete producer operating a factory within your borders? Insist that its operating permit be linked to their using your state-owned (or family-owned) shipping line for the transport of raw materials. If joint-ownership or contractual monopolies are too blunt a weapon for you, you can just as easily invent operating taxes that provide revenue at a lower and less offensive rate. Hungary's Fidesz party raised eyebrows with a series of crisis taxes that largely targeted foreign investors.[175]

Foreign Private Investment   Attracting foreign investors provides for economic growth and the creation of jobs, and lays the groundwork for a network of wealthy foreign companies you can milk from time to time for funding, license fees, and kickbacks. Foreign investors are also easily scapegoated, and in the meantime, they will provide services – telephone, health, products – your government is unable to. What to do if your country doesn't naturally inspire foreign investment? Hire a marketing consultant! Equatorial Guinea hired the Qorvis Communications group to produce documents that paint Equatorial Guinea as an economically well-off, responsibly-governed nation.[321] Now, that's thinking the modern way!

State Controls   The classic mechanism for coercing funds out of the private sector is 100% legitimate and is called *regulation*. Your legal framework should provide many stipulations for the requirements for companies to do business, and many of them will require a transfer of money. These transfers quickly add up and become a good funding source, particularly if the licenses your government grants require renewal on a periodic basis, say, yearly.

There's little nuance between this subject and the legal framework discussion in section 3.3.1. The name of the game is to impose state regulation on the private sector at key junctures that make payments a regular and necessary part of staying in business. This is a nuanced affair, though, and your neighboring countries are reducing their requirements to attract foreign investment. You need to charge where it's chargeable, without overstepping your mandate and driving away the investors whose purses you need to plunder. In Africa in the 1960s, state controls arose just after the end of the colonial period, as a mechanism to "eradicate the vestiges of colonialism and protect the new nations from foreign exploitation."[26] But it was fortunate that these controls put the means of production in the hands of the newly-baptized African economic elite, and it has stayed there ever since.

State controls generate artificial shortages and boundless opportunities for rent-seeking, as all economic activity suddenly requires intimate participation of the "right" people, and the blessing of those in charge, i.e. you. Import and exchange controls remain the easiest and most lucrative pressure points to maintain. Simply require a percentage commission on all profits related to import of something your economy requires and some entrepreneur has arranged to provide.[26]

One innovative example of using state controls to generate monies comes from Christian Democrat (DC)-led Italy in the 1960s. In the partially autonomous region of Sicily, state law decreed that taxes both direct and indirect were to be collected by the private sector and then turned over to the state; this lucrative tax concession was thus a very sought-after prize. In 1962 the brothers Nino and Ignazio Salvo (Sicilian businessmen famous for Corvo wines) won the contract with help from DC majordomo Salvo Lima, and accordingly began to funnel money to the Mafia – and to the Sicilian wing of the DC party, the ruling national party at the time.[154] Once again this shows that autocrats have a lot to learn from parliamentary democracies!

Tricky Business and Real Estate   Tricky real estate deals involving sells and buy-backs, multiple parties, and similar are nearly always a win-win situation. And you're in a good position to not only know what land is currently high value, but which land can be *made* high value with a few government decisions. Have a state agency purchase a prime piece of real estate at a price higher than it merits, and then sell part of it to a private developer. The state has gotten its money back, so you're off the hook, but the developer – who wouldn't have access to the land back when it belonged to the government – can now subdivide and sell properties at exorbitant prices. Naturally, for the privilege, he pays you a cut.

The leadership can happen on the side of the private sector, too. It's amazing how much more valuable an otherwise nondescript neighborhood can become when the state decides to invest the resources in an urban development project that brings in water, electricity, and sanitation. And since your team is the one making those decisions, sit back and let the developers come to you with their proposals. It's really as easy as that.

Of course, you can just get involved in deals all over the place, making government and business sort of the same thing. Look at the Philippines' Joseph Estrada, impeached in 2000 and accused of a battery of financial offenses: accepting millions of dollars in bribes to turn a blind eye to illegal lotteries, and of "extorting a share of tax revenues intended for tobacco-growing provinces; of interfering in an investigation into price manipulation at the Philippine Stock Exchange, in an attempt to ensure that a friend who had been implicated in the scandal was exonerated; and of possessing undeclared assets, mostly in the form of large houses where, it is rumoured, he has kept his various mistresses in the style to which they aspire."[158]

Special Target: Ethnic Minorities   If your country's business community is mostly composed of an ethnic minority, you have another easy funding source to target. This is the case for most of West Africa (the Lebanese), East Africa (Hindus), and Southeast Asia (Chinese). This minority community makes its profit thanks to your benevolence, and the day you stop protecting them they will, at a minimum, be slaughtered or run out of town. Election time is a good moment for them to thank you for your support in the way they're best suited: by coughing up some money.

11.4   Nationalization

Nationalization of the property of the wealthy – particularly if those wealthy are also your enemies – is extremely important, useful, and lucrative. Furthermore, if the wealthy happen to be an ethnic minority or a foreign corporation it's simple and will potentially have the backing of the bulk of your population. Here, Venezuela's Hugo Chávez is a star, and Bolivia's Evo Morales isn't far behind. But neither is the first to use political or social arguments to argue for the wholesale appropriation of foreign-owned businesses.

Use your existing laws to your advantage here: Chávez responded to the outcry over his nationalization of foreign businesses by insisting the industries seized had broken labor or environmental laws, or were monopolies whose strength was detrimental to the nation. But you can just as easily criticize the victim companies for being unproductive, for failing to ensure food sovereignty or security, or for failing to co-operate with national development. In summary:

When you nationalize	Justify it by citing
Banks	Failing to co-operate with national development, that is having the gall to tell you 'no.' Nationalize one bank and you can guarantee the rest will tell you 'yes!'
Dairies/Farms	Failing to ensure national autonomy in food production, or being beholden to foreign masters.
Industries	National or strategic importance, especially if it can be linked in any possible way to the military, such as production of steel or electronics.
Telecommunications	National security, of course. Claim the industry has been infiltrated by foreign spies.

Table 11.2: Justification for Nationalization

Uganda's Idi Amin declared an "economic war" in 1972, a year after his military dictatorship seized power. He accordingly expropriated land and businesses owned by foreigners such as Europeans and an Indian minority. He subsequently ordered those same foreigners deported – around 60,000 individuals, by some estimates. The expropriated businesses and industries were in fact the mainstay of Uganda's economy, and Amin gave them to his supporters.[6][95] Equally brazen – and several decades earlier! – was Nicaragua's Anastasio Somoza García, whose nation housed a small German, coffee-growing community. As World War II ramped up, Somoza nonchalantly seized the moment to declare war on Germany, as pretext and prelude to the expropriation of the property of most Germans living in Nicaragua.[282]

---

[6]... who ran them into the ground, causing a near-total economic collapse.

11.5   Sugar Daddies and Political Support

It's not impossible to find a benefactor nation that supports your programs in exchange for political recognition, comradeship, or shared vision. Nicaragua's Daniel Ortega found such a benefactor in Venezuela's Hugo Chávez, who kept the money flowing even as the traditional donors, notably the European Union and the United States withdrew their funding. Chávez provided loans and cheap oil worth up to $400m a year – about a third of the government's total income.[170] Ortega's Central Bank President Nelson Merentes finally reported in 2011 it amounted to 1.6 billion dollars over the period 2007-2011, well more than the similar amount of financial support withdrawn by the international donor community.[413] That money buys a lot of freedom, and a lot of supporters!

Mobutu Sese Seko's philosophy of "authenticity" left little room, either economically or philosophically, for foreign investment, and indeed led to a program of rapid nationalization of formerly Belgian assets. Mobutu's administration took these plantations, factories, and enterprises one by one, and distributed them to Mobutu's inner circle and economic elite. While it led to a happy and loyal *nouveau riche*, it also crashed the economy in less than two short years.[212]

11.6   Illicit Means

11.6.1   Facilitate the Baddies

The world is full of arms dealers, drug king pins, and the like, and all of them have more cash than they know what to do with. If you help them, they will pay you easily and pay you well, and they are almost certainly a cash business.

Panama's Manuel Noriega turned his tiny, Central American country into a lethal money-making machine specializing in gun-running, drug trafficking, and money laundering. Before he was forcibly captured in 1989 by the American Military in "Operation Just Cause," Noriega had made a bundle. He entered into agreements with Colombian cocaine cartels, conspired to push 4 tons of cocaine through Panama, and accepted millions of dollars in bribes. The Panamanian government became a highly efficient drug pushing organization, capitalizing on the railroad, airport, customs and passport offices, and the military to move illicit drugs from South to North America. As a result, he benefitted richly, eventually becoming worth nearly $600 million dollars and enjoying a dozen different houses and a fleet of luxury automobiles. Apparently a regular on the CIA payroll, Noriega's administration laundered up to $200 million on behalf of the CIA destined for the Nicaraguan Contra movement in the 1980s.[431] Like Noriega, you should target your efforts on narcotraffickers, the rebel movements in neighboring

countries, and governments or individuals engaged in producing and prolif-
erating nuclear weapons.

11.6.2   Get your Cut, Too

There are more ways than one to profit from the lucrative drug trade. Don't
feel limited to simply permitting others to do business on your soil. Consider
Augusto Pinochet as an example to follow: after he left power, a former commander of the Chilean secret police alleged that Augusto Pinochet had been
involved in the manufacture, distribution, and sale of cocaine throughout the
1980s.[234]

This is an easy way to keep your government funded as well: simply
turn a blind eye to the activities that benefit the baddies, making sure however they don't use their activities or cash to fund your overthrow or their
political campaign. Then ensure they reciprocate with money, support, and
information. But watch out your cozy relationship with drug smugglers and
worse doesn't trick you into letting your guard down: Witness South African
Minister of Intelligence Siyabonga Cwele, whose own wife was smuggling
cocaine.[73] You need to make your money at night, but look clean and
professional in the Presidential Palace the next morning, and so does your
family.

Hacim Thaci, Prime Minister of Kosovo, was eventually identified as
the leader of the Drenica crime ring, responsible for multiple atrocities in
Kosovo and Albania in the 1990s and the Naughts. Under Thaci's leadership, the Drenica mafia monopolized the heroin trade and managed six secret detention centers in Albania, in which the organs of Serbian prisoners
of war were harvested and sold. When it comes to atrocity, who says the
Middle Ages are dead?[130] There's money to be made in the unspeakable,
but watch out for the impact on your legacy if you are caught (see section
13).

11.6.3   Produce Your Own

Of course, neither should you content yourself with simply shipping other
peoples' products. Do like the North Koreans and get into production. Under Kim Jong Il North Korea's production of poppies for the production
of opium and heroin expanded immensely on the lands surrounding prison
camps, netting anywhere from $500M to $1B annually.[7] To beat customs
requirements, the drugs are often transported via North Korean diplomats,
leading to several diplomatic incidents.[29] Likewise, the Burmese military
is reputed to have cornered the market on Southeast Asia opium production
in the Shan highlands. Since they've got all the guns, it's an easy matter to

---

[7]The fact that the government was more willing to produce drugs than food because of the
massive black market in food may indicate North Korea has not gotten its policies exactly right.

permit their own trucks through checkpoints while stopping and "detaining" the drug shipments of competing producers.[185]

11.6.4 Blackmail

Blackmail is an ugly – but profitable – word. But North Korea has repeatedly threatened the rest of the world with continued development of a nuclear arsenal if its demands for economic aid and political favors are not met. And time and time again, it has received aid as a form of "political engagement" as a result. Some observers have cited the 1994 agreement between the US and North Korea as a classic case of blackmail begetting a windfall.[217] Although the North Koreans stopped their production of plutonium, the US was still faced with a lingering threat of a restart at any time in the future; for this, the North Koreans received nuclear power reactors with approximately $4 billion US dollars. Mahmoud Ahmadinejad's Iran may one day be in a similar position, particularly when wealthy, easily cowed targets like Saudi Arabia are obviously fearful of a nuclear neighbor.[229]

11.6.5 State Monopolies, Lucrative Industries, and Natural Disasters

Being president gives you the leverage and authority to ensure your family and close coterie benefit directly from lucrative financial opportunities. Money begets power, and power begets money, after all.

In Azerbaijan, President Ilham Aliyev and family control a company called SW Holding that has privatized many parts of the former national airline, AZAL. His three children are reported to own over $75M in Dubai real estate, and his wife and two daughters are believed to control several of Azerbaijan's largest banks. The nation's most powerful telecommunication company, Azerfon, is also probably controlled by Aliyev's daughters, through a classic mechanism: offshore shell companies (three in Panama, one in the Caribbean tax haven island nation of Nevis) whose existence makes it harder to identify the real owners (Panamanian tax records show the Panamanian companies are owned by Aliyev's daughters). Needless to say, daddy's girls did not have to comply with a 2001 law requiring any potential telecom companies to compete via tender, showing their company's technical qualifications for the market. Finally, Azerfon now has the monopoly on 3G telephony, since competitor Azercell, despite repeated applications for a permit, has yet to be granted a license to operate a 3G network.[8][254]

Slobodan Milosevic's children Marko and Marija benefitted richly from their father's presidency in Serbia. Given the choices they made while feeding at the paternal trough, it's clear they wouldn't have been business school material on their own. Marko, for example, owned the largest discotheque

---

[8]Thanks dad!

in the country, a radio station, and 'Bambipark,' Serbia's first recreational theme park that he characterized as proof of his concern for younger generations.[156] As usual, it was a partnership between Marko's privately owned import-export company and the state-owned biscuit-making company, Bambi.[127]

The Dominican Republic's Rafael Trujillo, once in power, built state monopolies in all important sectors, and ensured he and his family owned them. In the three decades he was in power the Trujillo family came to control production of milk, salt, beef, tobacco, and most of the nation's sugar industry, as well as the lottery, the media, and trade unions. Trujillo's personal wealth was approximately $500M only twenty years after taking power.[239]

Beyond state monopolies, it may pay to think about the country, and how good it will look in your hands. Again, Zimbabwe's Robert Mugabe is instructive. He was criticized for keeping 39 farms for himself as he reapportioned the land from white farmers to black.[400] But why stop at 39? And why limit yourself to farms? Mugabe certainly didn't. Rather, he used the powers of the state to also take over the infamous "blood diamond" industry and line his pockets (and those of his generals: a wise move) with millions of dollars.[324] As an added bonus, Mugabe created a partnership with Russian and Chinese officials, allowing them to benefit from the diamond trade while inoculating himself from the condemnation of the West. This is known colloquially as a win-win. The underlying message should be: keep on the lookout for lucrative semi-illegal industries that may draw protesters but otherwise very little in the way of punitive action.

The more ruthless autocrats know that, industry aside, the doe-eyed world of international aid and relief in the wake of acts of God is a ripe and luscious nipple primed for sucking. Donors will often line up quickly to pledge money when your country suffers a natural disaster, so be aware, act fast, and you can reap the rewards.[79]

One of the more infamous beneficiaries of a natural disaster was Nicaragua's Anastasio Somoza. After the 1972 earthquake that devastated the country, the already wealthy Somoza and his inner circle began to see an opportunity in the in-pouring of global relief aid. As reconstruction efforts began, Somoza and his partners illegally appropriated funds marked for earthquake relief; thereafter his personal wealth ballooned to $400 million US dollars (a nice payday in 1974).[336] Be careful that your rapaciousness is not too evident, however, or suffer the consequences. Somoza may have lived high on the hog in the aftermath of the '72 earthquake but soon after his corrupt ways alienated his former backers and led to his ignominious exile.

11.6.6 Denying the Obvious While Flaunting It

Remember to emphasize your poor upbringing, your impoverished family, your pauper's childhood, as you appeal to the people. Vigorously deny your wealth and mention your poor, schoolboy origins at every possible opportunity. It's not to induce envy, although there's a chance you will do that too. Rather, it's because of your daily political need for a straightforward connection with your people. You may also consider complaining that the press often confuses your wealth with the nation's wealth.

Remind everyone of your awful struggle, particularly if it was against a colonial oppressor, or can be so construed. Or, if there are no oppressors handy, milk your rags-to-riches narrative as long as you can: you started a poor but fun-loving crooner on a cruise ship and through your charisma and sweat improved yourself until you emerged at your present station in life. Although Berlusconi has never hidden his wealth, his political rise was characterized by appeals to middle-class bathos, which is a good definition of the glossy biography he mailed to every Italian during the elections of 1994. Titled *Una Storia Italiana*, its purpose was simply to convince Italians he was an ordinary man.[449]

Leader	Birth and Childhood
Nicolae Ceausescu	Son of a peasant laborer, worked as a shoemaker's apprentice at the age of eleven.
Adolf Hitler	Born into a lower-middle class family of peasant origins; his mother was a domestic servant and his father a customs official.[236]
François Duvalier	Father was a teacher and journalist, mother worked in a bakery
Slobodan Milosevic	The second son of a former orthodox priest and a schoolmistress. Both parents commit suicide, separately, before Slobodan is 35 years old.
Josef Stalin	The fourth and only surviving child of a poor and struggling family. His father is a violent alcoholic and his mother a seamstress.
Suharto	Only child of a peasant couple that divorced shortly after his birth. Shuffled among family members through childhood, while he worked as a laborer and military conscript.
Mamadou Tandja	Son of a shepherd
Mobutu Sese Seko	Born to a traditional chief of the Ngbaka ethnic group; Mobutu was adopted by a cook employed by Belgian missionaries.
Rafael Trujillo	Humble, mixed race background; engaged in petty theft and manual labor jobs

Table 11.3: Leaders and their Humble Origins

Best of all was Jean Claude Duvalier's categorical dismissal of claims he'd embezzled hundreds of millions of dollars from the Haitian treasury during his time as president: "I laugh when I hear the amounts '$400 million,

$800 million.' It's a lot of blah, blah, blah. ... There were the children to care for, school expenses, other bills. ... We were not perfect. Perhaps I was too tolerant."[238]

11.6.7 Your Banking Needs

Though during your daytime hours you may rail endlessly against Western capitalism, feel free to avail yourself of those same bankers and creditors to manage your money for you. Libya's Mohammar Khadaffi invested over $53B through Goldman Sachs, JP Morgan, HSBC Holdings, and the French Societé Générale.[261] These financial resources were ostensibly the funding of the Libyan Investment Authority, but since the Khadaffi family made no distinction between family wealth and national wealth, it's hard to know whose money was stashed overseas – that's exactly the point.

Think of it this way; when you start amassing your fortune, you'd better find a very private bank of the Swiss variety quickly. If great fortunes are the fruits of great crimes, the less the people know, the better (and more lucrative) for you.

Chapter 12

Elections

Adolf Hitler

DON'T turn your nose up at elections; they may not exactly match your principles, but it's possible that a fixed ballot somewhere will usher you into power, so keep an open mind. And when attempting to consolidate power under a nominally representative governmental system, knowing the ins and outs of the election process can be useful. After all, as the saying goes, there is a loophole to democracy: vast masses of stupid people.

Remember, nowhere does the concept of "democracy" stretch to the breaking point more often than during a popular election. The developed world believes an election in your country is an opportunity for the struggling proletariat to choose between honest candidates on the basis of their skills, wisdom, and ability to lead the nation towards prosperity and improved well-being. Well, let them. You and many of your people, to be honest, know better. The true leaders are, and always have been, those responsible for the distribution of wealth, and an election is a fight for which distributor – and network – gets a taste of that lucrative pie. And everyone struggles to ensure their own distributor gets into office, to ensure they will be the recipients of the ensuing largesse.

As such, elections don't necessarily mean the end of your administration, or your exile from the trough. Are you well loved? Have you used your power and connections to better the lives of your people, leading to economic growth, hope, and prosperity? If so, no problem – stand for re-election and let the people show you how much they adore you. Otherwise, keep reading. At a minimum you will be able to squeeze through; but if you're lucky you'll find your hold on power has been validated and entrenched by your pass through the polls.

12.1 Alternation in Power

Step down from office? If you're confident and have broad support within
the political elite, you can stage elections on a regular basis, cede control
graciously, and retain your position and control regardless of who is technically "elected." One of two things is necessary to make this possible: an
absolutely loyal party (a rarity these days) or a trusted second to whom you
can transfer authority while retaining full confidence in his subservience.

One variation of this strategy, 'continuismo,' involves allowing someone
else to become president, but in the context of a secret agreement that after
some time he will step down, fall ill, agree to 'spend time with his family,'
or lose the will to govern. He then returns power to you. To implement this
strategy, choose someone else to run for highest office on your party's ticket.
Don't overplay your hand and select a relative or close friend; rather consider a minor party functionary with few prior accomplishments, or else a
competent but bland administrator who can be justified because of his tech-
nocratic expertise. When that person wins, ensure he steps down for health
or personal reasons a year into his mandate. As the ensuing crisis of leadership mounts and the tension escalates, the party meets to discuss solutions
and you are finally, grudgingly, reluctantly, forced to step in and serve your
country. Repeat as often as necessary. Nicaragua's Somoza family used this
tactic expertly from the 1960s through the 1980s. Note table 12.1 showing
the Somoza family's use of proxies. Anastasio Somoza was assassinated in
September 1956; his son Luis Debayle took over until he was felled by a
heart attack. Luis Debayle's brother Anastasio Somoza Debayle took the
reins until his cruelty and avarice led the Sandinistas to overthrow him.[1]

Name	Dates of Presidency	In Office
Anastasio Somoza Garcia	**1 Jan 37 – 1 May 47**	**10 y, 4 m**
Léonardo Arguello-Barreto	1 May 47 – 27 May 47	1 m
Benjamin Lacayo Sacasa	27 May 47 – 15 Aug 47	2.5 m
Victor Roman y Reyes	15 Aug 47 – 21 May 50	2 y, 4 m
Anastasio Somoza Garcia	**21 May 50 – 29 Sept 56**	**6 y, 4 m**
Luis Debayle Somoza	**29 Sept 56 – 1 May 63**	**6 y, 6 m**
René Shick Gutierrez	1 May 63 – 4 Aug 66	3 y 3 m
Lorenzo Guerrero Gutierrez	4 Aug 66 – 1 May 67	9 m
Anastasio Somoza Debayle	**1 May 67 – 1 May 72**	**5 y**
Liberal-Conservative Junta	1 May 72 – 1 Dec 74	2 y, 7 m
Anastasio Somoza Debayle	**1 Dec 74 – 17 July 79**	**4 y, 7 m**

Table 12.1: *Continuismo:* Nicaraguan Presidents and their proxies

More recently, Russia's Vladimir Putin exercised this same strategy in
coordination with Dimitri Medvedev. The appointment of Dmitri Medvedev
in 2008 is now known to have been simply a constitutional dodge that per-

mitted Putin (president from 2000 – 2008) to side-step a rule limiting the president to two consecutive terms. Now that Medvedev has stepped in (and now out), Vladimir Putin is free to win another two terms. And since the constitution has been changed to lengthen a single term to six years, Putin is now welcome to another decade-plus in power, and everyone knows why: In late 2011 Medvedev spilled the beans on the gentlemen's deal that made it all possible. Well done, gentlemen.[367]

12.2 Overcoming Constitutional Barriers and Term Limits

Your lifelong rule may risk being thwarted by a constitution that stipulates you may only run a fixed number of terms (probably two, infrequently three, never one). Those kinds of barriers are short-sighted, written in by lawyers who hadn't counted on a leader like you, and respected by not-so-strong men who let themselves be governed by a piece of paper. More importantly, term limits will interrupt the flow of goodness from your leadership and wisdom, depriving your people of the very stuff they crave. If you find yourself blocked by a constitutional barrier, take comfort in the fact that you are not alone. Your predecessors have bequeathed you a rich menu of strategies for dealing with these pesky laws – constitutional reform.

A constitution is a sort of contract, a legal framework under which a populace agrees to be governed. Some are better contracts than others, but in any case, it is the will of the people that gives the document its weight. As a good autocrat, you know that the people's will can be molded, (mis)guided, or influenced by bad information. Don't accept the argument that your national constitution is some sort of sacred cow; it is very likely imperfect, and as such, you can and should modify it to your liking, particularly if it stands between you and your continued rule.[220] Remember, term limits are inherently artificial and there is no reason on earth to either *have* them or *heed* them. Take it from the experts:[290]

> "Relaxing presidential term limits is mostly justified," says Peter Kornbluh, an expert on dictators at the National Security Archive in Washington [DC]. " In those countries where leaders are 're-founding' nations to give the long-oppressed a voice, single terms have often been restrictive. 'The process of expanding term limits derives from pent-up demand for change,' he says. 'Four-year terms have not proven to be enough [to address] the intractable problems that Latin America faces."

And what's good for Latin America is good for you.

So use your legal experts to "reflect deeply" on the harm done by constitutional term limits, and make them history. Note we recommend you bring in *your* experts. Importantly, don't let *others* get involved, and cut down any demands by foreign observers or opposition leaders to liberalize and open the reform process. It's your process after all, and only changes that benefit you should be considered (remember, too much political openness could spark unrest – see chapter 8). For example, Equatorial Guinea's Teodoro Obiang, in mid-constitutional reform in 2011, eventually grew irritated by the persistent calls from the developed world to modify the constitution in ways that benefitted them more than him. Bristling, Obiang threatened he would defend the reform process vigorously against any "attempts by foreigners to influence ongoing constitutional reforms."[6] Smart move.

12.2.1 The 'Legal' Option

Lawyers can be your friend, under the right circumstances. In Nicaragua, Daniel Ortega used constitutional reform to permit a subsequent run for the president when faced with a constitutional ban on consecutive presidential re-elections. To skirt this bam, Ortega ensured that judges under his sway overturned the measure, a move justified in the name of protecting the people's "constitutional right" to vote for whomever they wanted. In doing so Ortega was merely following the lead of otherwise-respected Oscar Arias of Costa Rica, who appealed to the Constitutional court that the article that prohibited re-election of a president and vice-president was in violation of the Costa Rican Constitution, which insisted that all laws must apply equally to every citizen. Great ideas can come from anywhere, and not surprisingly, Ortega followed suit as soon as it was convenient (i.e., in time for Ortega's 2011 presidential candidacy).[343]

Here's how it played out: Ortega called for a last-minute, unannounced meeting of the Supreme Court's Constitutional Chamber. It happened to be on a Saturday, and when the telephone invitations went out, by luck only Ortega's Sandinista magistrates were available to meet. The magistrates representing the opposition parties were not called in time to participate, or were out of the country. Too bad for them! The Sandinista magistrates ruled that the constitutional term limits were not applicable and would be nullified. For good measure, the Deputy Chief Justice (also a Sandinista) added that the decision was unappealable.[471] Similarly, Niger's president Mamadou Tandja, who needed a referendum that would permit him to run for office a (constitutionally-prohibited) third time, got it by choosing the people who would make the decision on his behalf. After his constitutional court ruled three times that the referendum plan was illegal, he dismissed the entire court, and appointed a new one, composed of three hand-picked nominees, three magistrates chosen by (his) minister of justice, and a university professor. Not surprisingly, the new court had no problem with a third term at all.[48]

The direct approach not your style? You can appeal to the legal community in more subtle ways. If the constitutionality of your candidacy is in question, strengthen your case by bringing in the experts and their expensive law degrees. Nothing impresses masses like a bespectacled panel of frowning egg-heads, handsomely framed degrees on the wall behind them. Protest will melt away once your expert panel weighs in supporting your legitimacy. It should go without saying that any means necessary should be employed to ensure the experts see it your way. Treat them like VIPs: that means expensive cars (to keep if they wish after the right decision is made), elegant hotels, oceans of broiled lobster, and comely women to ease the mental and physical fatigue of legalistic parsing (what happens back at the hotel is not your business). Who knows, maybe they'll decide the constitution supports you after all!

12.2.2   Let the People Speak

If you can not trust the lawyers or judges, take your case to the people. This is what Venezuela's Hugo Chávez did in 2009, organizing a referendum that resulted in the elimination of term limits for all presidents, present and future[1] and all other elected officials. The referendum's conclusion was all but foregone because Chávez relied on extravagant state spending, intense use of public media to promote the official point of view, and intense efforts to mobilize the government workforce to vote for it. Two other elements of the referendum option are worth mentioning, both used by Chávez: 1) deny funding to those supporting the opposing viewpoint and 2) draft the referendum yourself (e.g. "Do you wish for the glorious and prosperous rule of your Leader to be cut short by misguided term limits? Yes or No?"). Do this and you suck oxygen from the opposition while framing the question on your terms and building mass enthusiasm for your supporters. In Chávez' case this is exactly what happened; the opposition didn't participate in drafting the referendum, which was drafted in a way that encouraged voters' support of Chávez' position. Collectively, these tactics won the day, and the voters decided in Chávez' favor.[256]

Once the constitutional barriers come down, the road to election-sanctioned power-grabbing is clear. Why not pile the powers on, if your people give you such a clear mandate? In 2010 in Madagascar, Andry Rajoelina won a national referendum with over 70% support that authorized more powers to Rajoelina (including the right to be president-for-life) and established a new, "Fourth Republic."[321]

Your bid to change the constitution via referendum will be immensely strengthened if you portray your administration as an enormous, world-changing project that remains incomplete. The people owe it to themselves to vote for you so the glorious heights can be scaled. Effectively, this strategy offers you the chance to have your megalomania sanctioned by the people while simultaneously removing constitutional roadblocks. Niger's Mamadou Tandja

---

[1] Since the referendum paved the way for Chávez to remain in office, however, it's safe to say there will *be* no other, future presidents.

took this approach, and advocated for constitutional reform after a two year term; he then organized a referendum to permit him to rule Niger for another three years, insisting he needed more time to complete several ongoing projects, including Niger's first oil refinery, a dam on the Niger River, and some uranium mines in the north. Tandja also noted that he was serving the people of Niger, not the International Community, an excellent use of the techniques discussed in section 6.2. [49] As Tandja might say, God had chosen him to lead his poor nation to greatness; it would be unreasonable to expect the project to be completed after an arbitrary two years.[2]

But a final cautionary note is essential here: if you go to the trouble of calling a referendum, ensure you will win it. In Chile, Augusto Pinochet's plebiscite of October 1988 confirmed to his astonishment that over half of Chile wanted him out. Announcing the results, Pinochet's rule came to an abrupt halt. The safeguards he had put in place to protect himself and his family crumbled over the next two decades, and by the early 21st century, Pinochet found himself under house arrest as judges opened investigations revealing his role in the secret security forces, the killings and disappearances of thousands, and exposing his finances. When he finally died of a heart attack, he had been sufficiently discredited to be denied a state funeral.[234] You can bet if he could go back in time and change one thing, it would have been the idea of calling for a referendum.

12.3   Avoiding Elections

Elections are messy things, unpredictable if you're not careful, and after winning one or two you'd be right to wonder what purpose they serve after you've achieved a solid mandate. Soon you might think it would be better to not have elections at all. The pros: your nation saves time and money, you get to invest your efforts in expanding the dictatorial project, and life under your all-knowing gaze goes on. Many of your people – certainly those who are benefitting from your leadership – would agree with you. But you might be surprised to learn many foreign companies and even some foreign nations might agree with you as well, despite their superficial commitments to transparent government and democracy. Yes, you have a temper, and journalists no longer have the freedom they'd like, but it will be clear to all that you are the one holding the nation together, rising magnanimously above the deep ethnic or socioeconomic divisions that threaten the peace, and for this most will be grateful, particularly the wealthy and the business class. Certainly they will prefer you to the unhinged opposition and if not, remind them that class warfare and political instability are almost sure to lead to lost business and talk of economic redistribution (see section 8.4). Study Mubarak's Egypt for a primer on the benefits of using class warfare to rally the support of your business class.[285]

---

[2]In fact, it might take your whole life, so prepare to settle in for the long haul.

The following strategies may help you do away with the charade of organizing elections, and let you focus on business:

12.3.1 Do Away with the Need to Vote

One Final Election

In 1964, Haitian president François Duvalier decided to put an end to the hassle of elections by having himself elected President-for-Life[3][238] Not bad: win that one, and you're there to stay (and the rest of this chapter will show you how to win). And clearly, Madagascar's Rajoelina is on the same track, given his successful referendum paving the way for a similar appointment.[321]

Better yet, make sure the election that brings you to power *is* the final election. One of the best historical examples to follow is the famous 1933 election in Germany that brought Hitler to power and, after the Reichstag Fire, allowed him to draft and pass the Enabling Act – which 'enabled' him to ensure there would be no more consequential elections in Germany for the remainder of his time in power.[199]

Let the Public Demand Your Continued Rule

Your people love you, presumably, so let them grant you your legitimacy without resorting to the ballot. Give the people stability and they may give you what you want – no elections. In 2010, a forum of 900 Kazakhs put forward a petition expressing its wish that president Nursultan Nazarbaev remain in power until 2020, suppressing the need for the upcoming 2012 election (this would make him one of the longest-serving presidents of an ex-Soviet state, having taken power in 1989). Despite some protest from the political opposition, Nazarbaev was popularly seen – both locally and abroad – as providing valuable stability to a nation whose neighbors are not stable. Says the Economist, "This is highly cherished in Central Asia's volatile neighbourhood, where last year's bloody overthrow of Kyrgyzstan's president, soon followed by ethnic violence and the introduction of a parliamentary republic, were seen as disasters. Although Mr Nazarbaev runs the country with an iron hand, he is not an outright dictator. Less of a control freak than Mr Karimov, he is a pragmatist who is credited with creating prosperity."[176] What better reason then to dispense with elections for a bit? Neighboring Uzbekistan's Islam Karimov took the same path, organizing a referendum in 1995 whose result was a resounding 99.8% popular support for canceling elections.[420]

---

[3]Given Duvalier's health trouble, that turned out to be just another seven years.

Abolish the Popular Vote

Angola's President José dos Santos had a new constitution passed in which the public no longer chose its president, handing the power instead to the winning party in Parliamentary elections. This presented no major challenge to dos Santos' authority, as his party had overwhelming control of Parliament and could be counted on to renew his mandate.[321]

Declare a State of Emergency

Chaos is a powerful justification for postponing elections, and you have at your disposal many ways to facilitate it. If you can create an incident that provokes a dangerous reaction, do it. The possibilities are limitless, but be creative and cunning and you'll provoke the requisite unrest. Have your goons 'detain' the opposition leader, firebomb the offices of a pesky newspaper, or provoke a border incident with the neighboring country, and before too long you'll have protests and armed conflict the people will have to deal with. Clearly, your people are going to rely on you to manage the emergency, and they'll therefore understand more easily if you postpone the election until matters are resolved. This gives you the time to better prepare the field for an electoral victory. Or, it may simply permit you to postpone elections indefinitely.

12.3.2   Facilitate Participatory Inertia

Chaos, which leads to problems in coordination, misinformation, confusion, and withdrawal, is your friend. Under pressure, ballot boxes go missing, instructions go unread, invoices go unchecked, funds go missing, and your opposition gets the shaft. The later in the process you introduce the changes, the greater impact they will have.

Bureaucratic Morass

So capitalize on your existing bureaucracy to delay or postpone any aspect of the lead-up to an election, to draw out the steps interminably, and to infuse the election with confusion and doubt. Interestingly, the tools you use to sow disorder will be the tools of order. Prior to an election it's reasonable to carry out a census to determine who and how many are eligible to vote, prepare voter registration procedures, carry out the registration process, agree on a ballot format, prepare, print, deliver, and store ballots, hire voter booth staff, and designate vehicles to carry staff and ballots around. And by "staff" it should be understood that we're not talking about Rhodes scholars or fellows with doctorates in PoliSci. Choose goons with thick necks and irascible tempers; illiteracy and alcoholism are a plus.

But, "Wait!" you might say. "It's not that simple." Indeed: you have international observers insisting on transparency, pressure from grass roots pro-democracy groups, and foreign diplomats making speeches on your soil about free and fair elections. Good! It offers you the opportunity to stir the pot some more. Now instead of simply delivering ballots, you can insist they are delivered at predetermined times in the presence of one representative from each party and at least one international election observer. If these criteria are not met, then no ballots.

Such a system also needs proper funding, which involves your Ministry of Finance, which has to modify the budget to permit the expense. For that matter, it might involve the multilateral banks and donors whose contributions to the budget require they ratify the changes. Then, instead of simply preparing ballots you can insist that regional committees must declare them reasonable, fair, and accurate. That process means setting up workshops in each region, agreeing on procedures for choosing who will participate, getting all the parties to agree to participate – and wait – agreeing on further procedures for the selection of which parties will be invited to participate. But hey, it's transparent! And that's what they want, right?

This approach is subtle and almost guaranteed to tie up opposition parties while enticing the donor community to step wholeheartedly into the tar-pit, since they want to "help." Once the bureaucratic machinery is spinning, step back to laud yourself for insisting on transparency and fairness, and then get back to running the nation while the machine churns. Finally, when commissions submit their summary reports, insist they be validated and approved by yet another committee, or reject them as biased, forcing the work to be repeated. Who will criticize you? Fairness takes work and money, after all! Do you want to get it right or not?

Throw a Spanner in the Works

For bonus points, stop the entire electoral process during mid-campaign, and watch the entire machine screech to a crashing halt. In the Ivory Coast, Laurent Gbagbo stopped the production of the electoral list midway through the process, due to violence that he capitalized on to suspend the government and abolish the independent electoral commission. Finalizing that database afterwards became a bureaucratic nightmare and took years.[350]

A similar maneuver guaranteed to sow some uncertainty into the electoral process is to change the person responsible for organizing the elections a short time before the elections themselves. You do so, obviously, out of your overwhelming concern that the election process be carried out professionally and in total transparence. Do so even at the demand of protesters who don't like the person previously chosen – and if you're particularly cunning you'll make sure they have a good reason to dislike him (you were 'shocked' to learn he was siphoning money from the Treasury or of his past human rights abuses). Fire him immediately, and smile when the new elections minister struggles with the learning curve of his new job.

The Early Elections Card

You can have the same effect by calling for early elections, ostensibly because your opposition has demanded them. You will benefit by appearing reasonable and magnanimous, and by ensuring the elections take place before the political opposition is ready and organized. If faced with a divided opposition, calling for early elections will oblige them to declare their candidates sooner than usual, and crucially before they've had the chance to work together against you. Those fledgling birds, thrust early from the nest, will find themselves immediately exposed to your coordinated attack before they have time to prepare a defense.

The resulting chaos in the lead-up to the elections always looks the same by the time you're done with the first part of this chapter: long, sad lines of bedraggled youth struggling – but failing – to acquire their voter registration cards, the Ministry struggling to finalize the official voter rolls, and urgent appeals for calm by harried government officials scrambling – but mostly failing – to deal with extensive logistics related to organizing the election.

Voting Laws and Election Chaos

Voting laws are also important weapons in your arsenal, and the right (or wrong) ones can do the opposite of what a good law is supposed to do: confuse, precipitate chaos, and grind progress to a halt. Consider mandating identity cards for voters, but make the process through which they are obtained a Byzantine affair. Or, require voter registration within 3 months of the election – but block access by limiting the days and hours one can be registered as a voter. In general, it's also a good idea to regulate voting as incompetently as possible, because in the wake of your mismanagement anarchy will flow (and that's what you desire). By the time you are through, no one will want to vote.

For example, Nicaragua's National Assembly did a royal job of botching the 1996 election, possibly unintentionally,[4] largely due to its management of national identity cards. The National Assembly delayed ratifying the law that made identity cards mandatory for voting until election year; this forced the Electoral Commission to scramble to prepare and distribute the cards in lieu of properly preparing for the election. The lack of preparation for the elections permitted relentless chaos and voting irregularities, including from mismanagement, inefficient handling, and even destruction of ballots and tally sheets. Not coincidentally, the greatest anomalies occurred in regions where the municipal government was the incumbent (Liberal), and the Electoral Commission steadfastly resisted demands for recounts. In one region, the president of the electoral council was discovered to have approximately thirty thousand unmarked ballots illegally in his possession after the

---

[4]The blunder cast serious doubt on an election that should have otherwise been the nation's first experience transferring power from one democratically-elected leader to another.

elections.[480]

The lesson here is to use the power of late planning, last minute decisions, and the ensuing chaos to permit elections to go awry. You can then either fudge them in your favor or use the irregularities to throw doubt on the election entirely and declare it null and void (you'll just stay in power until the problem is resolved, OK?)

12.4 The Correct Election Framework

You can count on the people to do the right thing if the right incentives are in place. This is in fact a preferable scenario, because at the close of "legitimate" elections in which the people have expressed their wishes, your hold on the government will be firmer than ever and no international party will be able to criticize you. If you feel confident about your electorate, you may even decide to minimize the skullduggery and actually hold the election for the sake of having people vote you back into office. Ideal!

12.4.1 Strawman: The Electoral Commission

Your government probably organizes elections through its Ministry of the Interior, the "Supreme Electoral Commission," or equivalent. This is a useful mask, because most Westerners will not see past it and count on this body for fairer and more transparent elections. Of course they will forget that *you* are the one calling the shots here, and can easily harness the Commission to strengthen your hand, all while remaining "democratic."

The Electoral Commission comes in handy throughout the entire electoral process: declaring which parties and which candidates are eligible to participate, establishing and/or abruptly changing the ground rules for the contest, managing the registration of voters, distributing and counting the ballots, staffing the voting booths, and announcing the victor. It will also be responsible for explaining any perceived anomalies in the process.

But as a government institution, its employees work for you, not the opposition. So for starters, make sure the Commission is staffed with your people. Remove the ones that sympathize with your enemies (see 5.4). Nicaragua's 1999 Pacto between Daniel Ortega and Arnoldo Alemán achieved this easily, ensuring the Commission was staffed by an equal number of judges from each of their parties and excluding other parties outright.[483] It was instrumental in propelling Ortega back into the presidency in 2006, and in 2008 when Ortega voted in the municipal elections his party eventually fraudulently won, the head of the Electoral Commission accompanied Ortega to the ballot box, in case there was any doubt at all for whom he worked.[165] Hungary's Viktor Orban passed a constitution in 2011 that did the same, ensuring the Electoral Commission had no representation from opposition parties.[286]

12.4.2   Parties, Candidates, and Managed Opposition

If you read chapter 6 you know that half the battle in winning in elections is determining against whom you must compete. Make sure those who run against you are credible as far as the outside world is concerned, but don't constitute a real challenge to your re-election. There are countless ways to do this. You can even go the route of Sani Abacha (Nigeria), who staged an election in which his was the only name on the ballot. [148] Djibouti's Ismail Omar Guelleh did the same in 2005, winning the election handily with 100% of the vote.[321]

The Electoral Commission or equivalent will set the rules for party participation in an election. Elections in which too many parties submit a candidate are unruly and unlikely to select a leader who commands a significant majority of popular support, so it's entirely legitimate to establish a bar to entry. Be subtle, but set a bar that excludes those you need excluded. Either require that any party wishing to propose a candidate acquire a minimum number of signatures on a petition (or better yet, a minimum number of signatures from each region in the nation), pay a fee you set high enough to exclude the riff-raff, or both. If they show up with the signatures, declare a proportion of them "invalid" and throw out the candidacy on that basis.

Alternatively, focus intensely on the rigorous, bureaucratic procedures necessary to register. Nicaragua's Daniel Ortega eliminated two opposition parties in the 2008 municipal elections through the Electoral Commission, which ruled that neither party had complied with the necessary paperwork, and were therefore not legitimate parties (Never mind that other parties that had committed the same error were not similarly excluded.)[164]. Such legal subterfuges are easy to engineer and difficult for your opposition to avoid.

These methods will require the opposition to exhaust their time, energy, and funds to demonstrate nationwide support. The financial bar is however easily attacked by meddlesome outsiders, who will prefer a lower fee so that minority candidates representing working voters have a chance to run. If faced with international consternation, you can argue, reasonably, that you want to exclude parties with so few resources they have no reasonable chance of diluting the vote, as well as the "vanity" candidates – pop music stars, wealthy egotistical brats, and ostentatious local businessmen unlikely to garner enough support.

Otherwise, if you can get away with it, simply invite only friendly, progovernment parties to participate. Uzbekistan's Islam Karimov used this tactic to his advantage in a 2009 parliamentary election in which the only four parties invited to participate in the election were all staunchly pro-Karimov.[132]

There's a flip-side to this issue. You *do* want competition, and as much of it as possible, because you're a staunch believer in democracy! No, we're kidding: you want competition because if you run against eight opposition candidates incapable of uniting forces[5] they will each earn a small percentage of the vote, allowing you to win with a much lower total percentage. Western nations seem not to understand this, and are easily manipulated into celebrating your democratic nature even as you encourage the opposition to multiply in number while dividing in power.

If you are feeling particularly crafty, you can establish shell organizations with no obvious link to your administration, that help fund opposition candidates in the 18 months before an election. At a minimum they will encourage the rallying and consolidation of many small candidates buoyed by pockets of local support, denying other candidates access to the larger pool of votes. Or take the leap and make the next logical move; use your skill at manipulating the opposition to ensure that only incompetent candidates challenge you. The odds of re-election rise when you are faced with a clown, a representative of an outdated ideology, or a dangerous, aggressive anti-Semitic nut. Such candidates will likely receive few votes, though they will succeed in reminding the electorate how fortunate they are to have you in power. At the very least they will depress voter turnout and enthusiasm and clear a path for your triumph at the ballot box (this is a tactic Vladimir Putin knows very well).[485]

12.4.3 What if the Opposition Abstains?

Forge ahead anyway! Abstaining from elections is frequently a last-gasp measure by parties that would lose anyway. They're hoping by abstaining they will throw the election into disrepute. They're not counting on the fact they are guaranteeing they will not be represented in any way, shape, or

---

[5]This is deliciously, surprisingly, common. Expect each of your opposition candidates to be so singularly self-important or ideologically at odds that they refuse to work together, each one devout in his unshakeable belief that only he can topple you from power.

form in your future government, and are shooting themselves squarely in the foot. If you have that luck, forge ahead in the elections anyway, as did Hugo Chávez in 2005. In the absence of opposition, Chávez claimed a new legislature in which the opposition had no representation at all.[6][256] Big success!

12.4.4   The Threshold for 1st-Round Victory

Assuming though, that you are facing a reasonably determined challenge from many opposition candidates, your next move should be to ensure that the final percentage required to declare victory in the first round is low enough to be within your reach. This is preferable because you'll be competing against many opponents, while if you go to a second round it will just be you and one other candidate behind whom all the opposition will rally. Don't take any chances at this stage – avoid going to a second round, and do your best to ensure you sweep the polls the first time around.

The threshold for getting elected is mutable: lots of aspiring tyrants have changed them before you, and the Electoral Commission will be able to change the threshold to suit your needs. Daniel Ortega of Nicaragua negotiated to have the election rules changed so that he could be elected with just 35% of the vote. Why that number? Simply, Ortega's team conducted research that had revealed with certainty Ortega would be unlikely to win much more than that amount. Lowering the threshold to 35% permitted him to win the 2006 election handily.

12.4.5   Voter Registration and Gerrymandering

One basic principle of voter registration is the fact that like-minded people tend to vote in blocks. It's prudent to study which way a particular group is leaning well before the election and encourage or discourage their registration.

The young are an extremely important group in your calculation. Was the last election many years ago? If so there are many new voters who were previously too young to participate. If your sources tell you the youth vote is leaning your way, make every effort to get them registered; offer free pens, T-shirts, electronic devices, beer, whatever it takes to sign them up. But if they're likely to push for "regime change" or its equivalent, make sure registration is a process fraught with difficulty to keep their opinions under-represented. Time to propose a voter registration tax? These simple steps can be applied to any voting block and should be considered, depending on your situation. Remember, no registration, no votes. Be judicious in your distribution of the voter cards that will allow your citizens to cast a ballot in the election. Distribute them efficiently among people who will support you, and screw it up among people who will not.

---

[6]Guess you should have shown up then, eh?

The public – and the young voters – may see through this and be furious, but here again you can use their anger to your advantage. Blame the youth movements that aggressively encouraged voter registration: had they done so earlier and less militantly your systems could have accommodated them in a more orderly fashion. All they've done is cause chaos, a rush of voter registrations at the last minute, and thus it's almost impossible to meet their demand.

Timing and delay tactics are also important. In general you should start the voter registration process as late in the game as you dare, and then channel the inefficiencies toward the regions where your opposition is strongest. We've noted above how you can effectively distribute voter cards to your advantage; also consider delaying their printing and distribution in areas where you have little support.

Not all cards should be played at the last minute. We looked at gerrymandering earlier, but here's where its benefits play out again, if you moved the district lines around in the year before the election. Since hardly anyone pays attention to their voting district until the week of the election, they may find out on election day they've gone to the wrong place, waited on line, and discovered their name is not in that register because they now live in a different district. Too bad for them! Better yet, by the time the media's glare falls on the redistricting mess at election time, it will be too late.

In the meantime, get your own supporters registered as efficiently as possible. Your people, when they flash their party card, should have few bureaucratic difficulties. Venezuela's Hugo Chávez expended a great deal of energy ensuring supporters (at least!) were registered before every initiative at the polls: elections, referendums, and so on. The result was a massive, 11.7% influx of voters registered to vote. Who cares if some of those registered turned out to be Colombian immigrants?[256] And while you are busy getting your own supporters registered, make sure someone – your Youth Wing, probably, using official funds – is buying the opposition voter's registration cards, meaning they won't vote. You'd be surprised at how little it costs to buy these cards back: often in the range of $5 each.

12.4.6 Managing Public Opinion

You, your ministers, and spokespeople, all have unequaled access to public media in the lead-up to elections. Traditionally, this bully pulpit has been used to deliver three important messages in support of your re-election:

- Sinister Threats. Gravely describe vague, unspecified threats that imperil the elections or even the nation. Suggest the elections are being manipulated[7] or subverted by foreign or cultural/religious/ethnic enemies and watch voter anxiety spike. Publicly express doubt that flawless, indisputable elections are logistically possible, and insinuate the

---

[7] Ha ha! They are: by you.

existence of an opposition plot to take advantage of this fact. Then, deepen the fear by stationing a somewhat intimidating military presence at voting booths ("to protect the peace"). The fear, uncertainty, and doubt of impending chaos will ultimately become self-fulfilling.

- Smear Your Rivals. Batter and belittle your opposition, who are clearly not up to the task of defeating you, are unqualified to lead the nation, and are not only stooges of foreign, neo-colonialist powers but might actually be mental cripples and moral or sexual deviants.

- Burnish Your Image. You are a semi-divine father of the nation, after all. Get on television and speak of your love for the nation and its peoples, its dogs and cats, and how your fondest wish is for everyone to be healthy and prosperous.

Follow through with visits to your foreign embassies, evoking the first threat at length (perhaps tone down the "foreign powers" bit here). Remind them of the strategic interests you share, and the real need for Western powers to supply funding to ensure your administration can ensure a transparent and fair election (They might just do so). You have, in the meantime, hopefully solidified their perception of you as a partner worth defending: American president Theodore Roosevelt allegedly once said about Nicaragua's Anastasio García Somoza, "He may be a son-of-a-bitch but he's *our* son-of-a-bitch." That's exactly the kind of friendship you're looking for.

If you sense you are ahead of the opposition in the lead up to elections, commission an independent poll – a truly independent one – whose findings will remind the public that betting on the opposition is a bet on the losing horse. If you are not sure, prevent any such poll from taking place. If you have laws on the books that prohibit the disturbance of the public peace, you may apply it here, on the grounds that such an incendiary report would certainly lead to violence and disruption.[380]

Don't limit your self-publicity to a few television appearances; keep working the public. Make an effort to appear un-harried, controlled, leader-like, invincible. Then, towards the end, place more emphasis on the amount of work you are doing. Wait until the day or two before the election, then bombard the media with clips of you losing your voice at a rally, or appearing in sweat-soaked shirt sleeves before raucous crowds, kissing babies and consoling widows. These last minute images should project strength and show your willingness to work but also demonstrate your tender side in an attempt to sway the widest possible spectrum of undecided voters. In the last precious hours before voters go to the polls, ensure the narrative focuses on you and your noble, compassionate, but firm and bold leadership, all set in national imagery like the flag, or iconic landscapes. Otherwise, pull a brazen publicity stunt. Adolf Hitler's 1932 barnstorming aerial tour of Germany ("Hitler over Germany") allowed him to dominate media coverage while speaking in as many as five different cities a day, all while demonstrating technical and military prowess, virility, and bravado.[247]

While you're monopolizing national media attention through paid advertising, dig up a scandal with which to ensnare the opposition. It's no matter if the allegations are false. Throwing your opposition a turd forces them to waste time and energy refuting it. Americans know this as the infamous "October surprise" in which, one month before the national election, some scandal surfaces and consumes one of the candidates.[8]

12.4.7 Managing the Voters

The period three to six months before the election is the time to ensure your civil servants are all on your side. Offer salary raises and improved benefit packages to your teachers, police, and municipal employees. You want them to think kindly on you as they vote, and worry about what would happen to them under other leadership.

Co-opt Traditional Leaders In traditional communities that generally accept the wisdom of the town elders, you should focus on these wise old men[148] (This is yet another reason to push for donor-loved "government decentralization" projects). Don't be afraid to let them know that recommending the "right" vote will pay big dividends for them; or try the direct approach and just put them on the payroll. Perhaps you offer the village chiefs a monthly stipend and simple benefits like a government-purchased cell phone, or a monthly invitation to participate in a meeting at the Presidential palace (requiring a travel allowance bigger than the real expenses would warrant). At face value, you are reinforcing their authority and supporting their ability to govern. But your failure to support local leaders who don't endorse you will ring crystal clear: they know what will happen to their benefits if your opposition – who has offered and is capable of offering them nothing – takes power. And as you visit village leaders, your assistant in the dark glasses holding the clipboard is taking careful notes of who has offered you their support, and how heartfelt it appears to be.

Throw Around the Pork Your administration probably doesn't have the money to do good work all year round, especially given your extensive personal financial requirements. But it is a good idea to get a little something done when elections approach. Pave the roads in a few pivotal neighborhoods, dedicate a school or two, cut the ribbons on a few projects that will directly affect specific groups of people. But mind the timing of these activities! If they happen too soon, it's likely the people will forget, and if they happen too late you won't be able to earn the full benefits of the work. Within 18 months of an election is a good target, and make sure that no matter what,

---

[8] Shout-out to John "Swift Boat" Kerry (American presidential election, 2004)![201]

the work is associated with you specifically. Put signs up on both sides of
the project that make crystal clear the fact that the work is courtesy of your
benevolence alone. These projects will require donor financing and support,
which takes time and determination: work on coaxing out the funding early,
so your projects are "shovel-ready" in the critical period before the elections
(See section 10.3).

Gifts   Paying for votes is a proven method for getting through elections.
Paul Collier cites a study by Pedro Vicente of Oxford University[476] in
which elections in São Tomé and Principe were observed on an experimen-
tal basis to see if bribery in an unrestrained environment led to more votes
for the candidate who paid out the bribes. The conclusion: big success![148]
But in lieu of cash you can as easily distribute T-shirts, baseball caps, and
similar. You are emphasizing that supporters receive perks, and your opposition does not, certainly a trend that will continue after the elections are
past. You are likewise emphasizing opposition parties' inability to match
your largesse. Make sure the gifts are distributed in the context of rallies
where non-supporters don't benefit, and make sure your slogan – promis-
ing prosperity and benefits for your supporters – is indelibly associated with
your administration in the minds of those who attend. There are lots of ways
to stage good rallies; see section 6.1.4.

Clear Consequences   Otherwise, ensure voters know exactly what will
happen to them if they don't vote "correctly." Make sure the civil servants
know that if you are elected out of office their salaries will probably be cut
or their jobs terminated (the fact that you are busy emptying the state coffers does in fact mean there will be little money left for their salaries). Or
use violence: Zimbabwe's Robert Mugabe made great use of street thugs,
whose efficient work made it clear the government would know exactly how
everyone has voted and would react accordingly when the time came. [148]
If push comes to shove, you can deny any association with or knowledge
of those thugs, who are just rambunctious supporters, as far as you know.
You may not convince your opposition to vote for you instead. But if you
convince them not to vote at all, your goal is equally achieved.[148]

Finally, follow through with the threat. Following the 2004 referendum,
the Venezuelan government under Hugo Chávez began to deny jobs and government contracts to Venezuelans who had signed a petition calling for a
recall vote earlier, and an additional 800 Venezuelans were investigated for
political treason for having participated in protests. The message was clear:
voting in Venezuela was *not* anonymous, and anyone found voting for the
wrong candidate would be identified and punished.[256]

Naturally, these techniques are not mutually exclusive. In fact, Paul Collier has observed that bribery, voter intimidation, and vote miscounting are
often employed together, as was demonstrated during the 2007 presidential

elections in Nigeria [149] and of course, elsewhere around the world since time eternal.

12.4.8 Balloting

You can use many of the techniques you employed during the voter registration process during the distribution of ballots to election centers. Ideally, the election should happen when ballots have been thoroughly distributed through zones of your support, and while they are still being distributed (or have gone missing) in districts likely to vote against you. Blame technicalities, last-minute planning, the subterfuge of your opposition, and lack of international support for your struggling country's struggling democratic process. If you are forced to delay the elections at the last minute, you will then find yourself well-placed to choose a new date for the elections. If history serves, it will be a date when your supporters are better equipped than your opponents'.

12.5 Pre-Election Calendar

You've got a lot of work to do in order to reap the benefits that winning an election will provide. No wonder leaders in even wealthy countries like the United States increasingly spend their time campaigning for the next election, in lieu of actually governing or getting any work done. This is your minimal checklist:

- Two Years Before

  - Question the mechanics of the election process
  - Gerrymander the voting districts
  - Change the threshold for victory
  - Change the criteria for parties to become eligible
  - Line up donor funding for projects you'll begin in a year or two

- One Year Before

  - Cut the ribbon on high profile construction projects
  - Begin the voter registration process, with all its inevitable trouble

- Six Months Before

  - Tighten your friendship with foreign embassies and evoke vague "threats to democracy" in the media
  - Sack the elections coordinator for incompetence; hire somebody worse

- Have your foreign minister refer to "nefarious outside elements" or talk up a recent border incident

- Raise salaries of public sector workers

- Put village leaders on a government stipend

- Three Months Before

  - Ensure ballot-printing process encounters some unforeseen snags

  - Accuse your political opponents of attempting to thwart free elections

  - Accuse foreign powers of intervening or pushing hidden agendas

- One Month Before

  - Mire your opponents in a last-minute "scandal"

  - Disqualify opposition candidates on the basis of electoral law – not enough signatures on the petition, or equivalent.

  - Engage in a High Profile Publicity Stunt

  - Instill fear in the civil service: they won't be paid, the factories will close, etc. if you don't win.

- One Week Before

  - Ensure the printed ballots have difficulty being distributed

  - Make sure the phone system has trouble and Internet access is sporadic

  - Move the voting centers to someplace unplanned

12.6   Managing Elections

Kick it Down a Notch   For starters, ensure your voting stations are chronically short of supplies and personnel. You can keep your opposition voters away by ensuring the voting line stretches around the corner in the hot sun. And of course, make sure to shut down the voting station at the designated hour, as the law stipulates. Don't put your sharpest people at the desks – assign the folks who don't read well, get their papers out of order, and have to methodically shuffle through the whole volume to find the voter before them. Aim for inefficiency and slowness.[184]

Call in your Voters You command the total attention of an army of civil servants, military personnel, and municipal officials drawing a government salary, all of whom can be counted on to cast a vote for you. Make sure every single one of them marches to their polling location to vote, and mandate early voting; the first exit polls will naturally reveal your swelling lead and discourage late risers who'd planned to vote for your rivals. Many of them will vote for you instead: no one likes to bet on the losing horse. Similarly, double your chances by making sure your people vote more than once: give party members multiple ballots they can use to support you.[243] Also give "carousel" voting a try: your voters can cast one "absentee" ballot in each of several different voting stations; provide them bus transportation if necessary so they can get around easily.[100]

About halfway through the day, get the press to declare an early victory regardless of how things are going. It may be that the exit polls support that statement, but the purpose here is simply to further deflate your detractors and push public opinion to accept your inevitable victory.

If you have legions of pro-you voters ready to go, have them overwhelm the polling stations and vote under other names and identities. More than one voter in Russia's 2012 election was surprised to get to the head of the line only to learn they had somehow already voted hours earlier! (voters who complained to the authorities got menacing calls on their cellphone as a consequence).[100]

Coach the Voting Public Many peasants have trouble knowing what to do when it comes time to fill out the ballot, and even those who think they understand might need a little extra coaching. Make sure that your staff running the voting centers show *exactly* how to do it, pantomiming the checking off of one of the boxes. They hold the ballot up for the voter, with the pen in their other hand. "Here's what you have to do: put an 'X' through the box." They check off your box as an example, and the peasant goes away having learned which box they should check off. As many will be illiterate, they will be glad to be saved the humiliation of not knowing how to perform their duty. "Now, any questions about what's expected of you, Mr. Gomez?" is a suitable way to end the repartee, just to remind the peasant that you do know who is standing in front of you, should he err.

Annulment and Chaos Consider this option when the race is too close to call, or when the early polls suggest the election is not going your way. Close some voting stations early; keep others open late. Make sure some stations have trouble with their paperwork, which can include missing voter rolls and duplicate names on the list, among other problems. Move some voting stations to places they were not expected: was it supposed to be at the town hall? Put it in the Catholic church, or vice-versa. Through your youth wing, invite your supporters to linger around polling stations *en masse*, making it somewhat difficult for common people to get through to the front of the line.

If you sense you are almost certain to lose the election, annulment becomes a tempting option. Nicaragua's Arnoldo Alemán allegedly threatened to do so in 2001, leading election observer Jimmy Carter to declare such a move absolutely unacceptable.[12] You can't just call off the elections: you need to push the nation towards chaos and violence by revealing or alluding to irregularities and inciting the people to riot (the trigger for riots is probably through your party's youth wing – see section 6.1.3 – who can be counted on to start burning voting booths, cars, and ballots). Once the violence "threatens to spiral out of control" you can magnanimously call for the election's annulment "for the peace of the country," conveniently remaining in power while the nation thinks about next steps.

Managing Observers   Election observers are increasingly a standard part of elections in countries like yours. But they are not necessarily a threat, as they arrive late in the game and are present only during the few days before and after the election. Then they deliver their report and leave. In the best case, you'll have years to lay the groundwork using all the other techniques in this book: dividing the opposition, eliminating your rivals, and buying votes through any number of clever mechanisms. Once you've done all that, and the election is down to you versus your hand-picked, utterly incompetent "opposition," who cares if the foreigners come to observe it? In fact, they will help bolster your claim to legitimacy by confirming the veracity of the election process. Who will dare contest you then?

But if you're late to the game, are facing a mobilized and motivated opposition, and resort to using your security forces, supporters, and bureaucracy to blatantly prevent and discourage voting, you need to take a different approach. Start by discrediting election observers outright, before the voting begins. Nicaragua's Daniel Ortega refused to provide accreditation to outside election observers in the 2008 contest, alleging foreign observers were all the henchmen of "foreign powers." Groups like the local Nicaraguan "Ethics and Transparency" were forced to remain outside polling stations.[9][165] Roberto Rivas Reyes, head of Nicaragua's Electoral Commission, when answering questions about why Voter Registration Receipts were not given to citizens upon registration, as they should have, explained "We didn't give the receipts to everyone because there are election observer groups that purchase them, in order to harass the electoral officials. We don't want to give out the receipts because there are election observer groups that do anything *but* observe elections; rather, they are a partisan mechanism that concentrates on purchasing the receipts so they can hassle the CSE authorities. And we don't want to give them any document they can use to torpedo the electoral process." These statements serve expertly to simultaneously

---

[9] You've got to appreciate the symbolism of leaving ethics and transparency at the door on election day. But Ortega may have been right: Ethics and Transparency was well known to be funded in part by the National Endowment for Democracy, which in turn is funded by the US government.[343]

defend the existing process and cast doubt upon the electoral observers, who find themselves suddenly in the position of accused, not accuser.[377]

Then, make sure your observers are sympathetic to the cause. The Kazakh embassy in Washington DC once tried to pack an OSCE election observation mission with staff sympathetic to the incumbent party's cause.[184] Or at least, invite in so many "competing" groups of observers that their discordant analyses tie them up in knots debating whose facts are more accurate. And it's not hard to find groups of election monitors that are lenient by reputation: Russia, Kenya, and Zimbabwe have all exploited the fact that observers tend to disagree about a third of the time.[184]

Secondly, control what they do and don't see. Require they have government escorts for safety reasons, and ensure they are taken to regions you count on winning and where the citizens are lining up to peacefully cast their ballots. Egypt's Hosni Mubarak used this technique expertly during his long reign.[137] Nicaragua's Ortega did too: the OAS envoy representing the election monitoring team estimated his observers were arbitrarily expelled from about 20% of voting stations.[134]

Otherwise, refuse, reject, or remove the observers outright. This was the strategy Belarus' Alexander Lukashenko took when the OSCE released a report about the December 2010 election critical of how the count was managed. A spokesperson for Lukashenko's Ministry of Foreign Relations said the decision to eject the OSCE had been made because no objective reason for retaining their mission could be found … and that an evaluation of the results achieved by the OSCE mission revealed the mandate had been fulfilled.[57]

Finally, here's a fun one: provide your own, fake election monitors. Then when the monitors arrive at their stations, have the military or police request they move on to avoid any conflict. There must be some mistake, but it's clear there are monitors are already in place, so sorry, old chap, but you'll have to depart.[100]

Webcam Transparency   And lastly, here's a new one, courtesy of Vladimir Putin: set up web cams at each polling station to ensure transparency. Then beam pre-recorded footage over the network to anyone interested in watching. Internet users in Magadan in 2012 reported video footage of sunlit voting booths long after the sun had set, and elsewhere the footage was too grainy to be of much use.[100]

12.7   Managing the Count

Election day over? Have all the ballots been cast? Then truck all those lovely slips of paper to your undisclosed location, to begin the counting process, remembering that all-important adage, "It's not the election that counts, it's the *count* that counts!" In fact, regardless of what happened in the polling stations, you still have one extremely good opportunity remaining to ensure the people request your continued leadership and eschew your competition: Miscounting the vote is perhaps the most reliable method of stealing elections in the modern age.

Stuffing ballots is old hat; you just need the time and the privacy to do so. For example, the head of the Ugandan electoral commission, Badru Kiggundu, is widely accused of having stuffed ballot boxes during the 2006 Ugandan election to ensure the victory of the incumbent and his boss, Yoweri Museveni.[396] But this is as tactic just about everybody knows, and it would be easier to cite the nations that have not succumbed to this practice than to list those that have.

One essential element of managing the vote count, however, is ensuring that the count happens *on site* rather than centrally, back in the capital. Insist that the ballots would be at risk of tampering if they were transported back to the capital, as they would be "unsupervised" en route. You are then free to count them out in the bushes, un-monitored, and call in the results you see fit. Should the opposition object, then take advantage of the long car ride back to the capital to sort, modify, and "improve" upon the contents of the ballot boxes. Hint: drive slowly.

The electoral commission itself can be put in charge of supplying the necessary votes for your victory as they count them. This takes time, which is why in elections where the opposition is stronger, it takes longer to count the votes (insist you are going more slowly for the purpose of accuracy, when in fact you are adjusting the results). Nicaragua's Arnoldo Alemán, having signed the Pact with Daniel Ortega, had agreed, in the case of a close vote, to shift votes to Ortega in order to deny reformist contender Enrique Bolaños an electoral victory.[10][15] But that's the story in a lot of elections, such as in Uganda, where the head of the Ugandan electoral commission, Badru Kiggundu, was widely accused of having stuffed ballot boxes during the 2006 Ugandan election to ensure the victory of the incumbent and his boss, Yoweri Museveni.[396]

Otherwise, assuming the electoral commission can't do it, ensure representatives of your party count the ballots alone. Only they have the proper incentives to get it "right." Nicaragua's dramatically flawed municipal elections of November 2008 provide a great example: Ortega's Sandinista party counted the ballots alone. Is it a surprise that the Sandinista party won with a 62% majority?[134]

If the actual count shows the electorate trounced you or your party, work it to your advantage: Adjust the votes, obviously, but when you announce the results, make the election seem like an unnaturally closer affair. Claim your victory by only a vote or two, a tactic that has the advantage of generally disparaging the electoral process, depressing the opposition and discouraging high voter turnout in future elections.[149]

---

[10]Bolaños went on to win anyway, denying Alemán the chance to do so.

Don't emerge from behind the curtain with the final verdict until your inevitable win has been assured, taking care to win by enough, but not so much that it calls into question the procedure. Be reasonable if you expect to pull off this farce with a straight face. Win by 68% or 72%. Don't win by 95% with a record that shows that even your political opponent voted for you, as did Nursultan Nazarbaev in Kazakhstan in 2011[182] or even 92% (Uzbekistan, Islam Karimov in 2000)[420]. Here the unabashed winner is François Duvalier (Haiti), who in 1961 won his reelection by a tally of 1,320,748 to zero.[465] Twenty years later, his son Jean Claude opted for a more "reasonable" approach, winning his 1984 election with only 99% of the votes.[238] He's a more modest man than Kim Jong Il then, who in 2011 was elected – as were 28,000 other members of the ruling party – with 99.97% of the vote.[11] And Belarus' Alexander Lukashenko came right out and admitted he'd been forced to tweak the numbers *downwards* to avoid the discomfort of such overwhelmingly total electoral support. Poor guy.

There are two final task to manage here before getting back to business. First, prevent recounts. Do as the Hungarian government has done, and destroy the ballots once you've finished counting.[286] No recounts will be possible. Second, as you announce your victory, aggressively and immediately clamp down on demonstrations, uprisings, and complaints of every kind. Your victory announcement is not an invitation to discuss. It is your final word on the matter, and it is irrevocable.[305]

12.8 Losing Elections

Lose the election and be obliged to concede defeat? Unthinkable! Inconceivable! But not impossible. That's why it's better to not call an election until you are absolutely convinced you can win it. But what if the counts show you have definitely, absolutely, lost?

Your first option – you weren't expecting to read this, but here goes – is to gracefully concede defeat, congratulate your opponent, and step down. Not only will you be lauded as a gentleman and a diplomat but your reputation – and thus your legacy – will soar! Soon people will forget about the two years you spent pounding the opposition into oblivion, emptying the government coffers to pay for your campaign, and sending the Secret Service out to dig up unspeakable scandals on your opposition. A decade from now you will be remembered fondly as the father of the nation, and nostalgic youth wingers from your party will lobby to have a bridge named after you.

Not what you were thinking? Well, then. Of course you can annul the election entirely on the basis of perceived fraud and vote rigging, harassment of the voters, and numerous other irregularities you yourself helped perpetuate. This is a bold move that will immediately draw the attention of the national and international press, and if the people begin to protest you

---

[11] Such unabashed support of the voters brings a tear to your eye, doesn't it?

will need to have already memorized the contents of chapter 8. So while it leaves you in power, it makes the next months and years almost intolerably more difficult until there's been another election; during this time you will spend more time and energy stamping out dissent and opposition and less distributing perks to your friends and enjoying the good life.

Secondly, you can accept the elections as valid, but dispute the results. Laurent Gbagbo (Ivory Coast), absolutely, positively refused to concede defeat even after losing an election in 2010.[357] Reject the advances of your peers and neighboring countries, including emissaries of any local international conferences you may belong to (in the case of Gbagbo, ECOWAS, the Economic Community of West African States). Gbagbo declared on public television the international community had declared war on the Ivory Coast, and that he was responsible for upholding the nation's constitution against intruders, including the United Nations. Accordingly, pro-Gbagbo thugs attacked a United Nations convoy the following week.[356] In fact, he defended the Ivory Coast's constitution even as the United Nations and the Organization of African States sent peace keepers to force his ouster.[12] This was not his most brilliant strategy, and it did not work. Read chapter 13 for his particular demise.

Thirdly, you can simply concede defeat but opt instead for some sort of power-sharing arrangement in which your opponent has won the power but you have not had to give it up. But we saw in section 6.1.5 these very infrequently work out for the best. That leaves you with, and you are on thin ice here: just let slip the dogs of war and say "to hell with subterfuge." They asked for it by trying to elect your opponent, did they not? In a way this extreme but clarifying option should come as a relief. Think of all the cleverness to which you were obliged to resort so you could swing election after election, all the glad-handing and bribery, the perks and publicity appearances. All for naught, as you have now been thrown out of office. Perhaps you feel relief the days of ruse and deceit are now over! The opposition should not celebrate yet – if you still have the military in your pocket (and they are there if they realize their livelihood depends on you maintaining power). Authorize the immediate use of force to sweep the opposition and their supporters out of office and launch a quick-strike campaign to proactively weed out your enemies in the general population. Then put down this book, because the nuances of calling your government a democracy and preserving your legacy are unlikely to be of much interest to you any longer.

---

[12]Never mind the constitution clearly defended his opponent's right to take the presidency, having won the election.

Chapter 13

Your End Game

> The paradoxical fact is that if you want to stay in office as a dictator, it is better to be a narcissistic totalitarian than a run-of-the-mill autocrat ... If you're going to be a tyrant, be a wacko. It's safer.
>
> David Brooks

13.1 Your Legacy

WHAT will they say about you when you're gone? This is a thorny question and not as simple as it might seem. You might part the world in a blaze of glory, having vanquished your enemies and secured your country's hegemony for a generation, only to be thought of as a tin-pot dictator who achieved nothing lasting, or worse – an embarrassment best not mentioned in polite company. Or, if you're fortunate, you might die or retire with a mixed legacy only to have history rehabilitate you. If it is your destiny to be judged by later generations, then time is your friend. But one thing is certain: some day you *will* shuffle off this mortal coil, your opposition will take possession of your palaces, and the international media will snicker over your collection of porno mags and your superman underpants. Your legacy is the one thing you absolutely *must* get right.

The historical debate on Napoleon's legacy is a useful example of the latter; some have described him as a kind of Prometheus in funny hats, a genius who battled insurmountable odds and failed after coming within a whisker of victory.[215] The many deaths and disasters attributable to his misjudgments are of course air-brushed from the conversation. Or consider Augustus Caesar, who founded a monarchy in all but name based on deception and mass killing, only to be memorialized as the near-divine (and later, completely divine) leader who established the Pax Romana. Many contemporaries saw

261

through this and realized what he was: a master politician exerting his domination. The difference between what they and posterity thought is striking, and it should be something you can learn from.[452] If you get the opportunity, always plan your end with a view toward the future.

Here are a range of adjectives posterity might use to describe you after you've passed on:

- Rafael Trujillo was "cynical, opportunistic, cunning, ruthless, conflicted."

- Benito Mussolini was "ambitious, a buffoon, intellectual, provincial, promiscuous, vain, and cruel."

- Adolf Hitler was often described as "evil, cold, anti-Semitic, genocidal, vegetarian, and (horrors), a teetotaler."

- Finally, Saddam Hussein was "brutal, egotistical, self-delusional, and germophobic."

- Alfredo Stroessner was "dour and crotchety, and amoral and in love with power." Surely you can do better than that.

- Mobutu Sese Seko was described as wily and savagely ambitious.

- Ferdinand Marcos was "as tough as he was debonair."[369] Not bad, but Tito wins:

- Josep Tito was, upon his death, remembered as being "a man of stubborn courage, ready to fight and intrigue, endure hardship and risk death for his beliefs."[18]

Consider this far from exhaustive list and then think how much better it might be with just a single epithet: "the Great." The most famous strongman to boast that name, Alexander, employed many of the habits and behaviors we're recommending in this book. He showed great interest in declaring himself divine, he possibly arranged for the unfortunate death of his father and predecessor, he dealt ruthlessly with any challenges to his authority, and he skillfully developed straw men to justify what we might today call an expansive foreign policy. Yet many remembered him as a horse-loving, semi-divine figure who wanted to bring East and West together through glorious imperialism. He is remembered as such most likely because he died young, just after completing his journey east, and long before his empire began to crumble.[224]

Although in recent years this view has fallen out of favor, the fact that it lasted so long should warm every tyrant's heart. The core lesson here can be summarized as: go out on top and let time take care of the rest. People will always forget the messy details.

13.2 End Game Scenarios

Even if you have been been telling folks you are a demi-god, your own mortality is imminent, and only your reputation, the odd bridge or highway with your name on it, and perhaps some rapidly-tarnishing statues will remain behind in the company of your offspring. Your acts towards the end of your reign will weigh more heavily on your legacy at first, but over time your entire career might be considered in any re-evaluation of your glorious deeds. None of this will matter, however, if you end badly. Getting your personal end game right is important; there are many different possible scenarios, some more or less the results of your decisions, so think through them carefully. Here are some of the more relevant, in declining order of preference:

- *Die in Power* ("Peacefully"): You are felled by a freak heart attack at the peak of your power, or at least so it is reported. The nation is overwhelmed with grief and remorse, and enters a frenzy of statue-building in your honor. You are buried with full honors, the nation takes a week holiday to recover from their irreparable loss, and your son assumes your throne to continue the family dynasty. One of his first acts is to declare you, posthumously, "President for Eternity." Congratulations Kim Il Sung.[235] Almost as good, your successor, who is not part of your family, turns out to be a woeful administrator or un-enlightened thug, immediately prompting a pleasing wave of nostalgia among the citizenry. Better yet: he involves the country in an unpopular war, prompting the citizenry to grumble "his father never did this." For a dictator, nothing is as sweet as a successor who drops the ball, raising the shine on your own legacy.

- *Install a son while alive*: You live out your days in quiet, regal obscurity, while your son steps up to continue your mandate. Your death is only preferable because it heightens your legend as a demigod and prevents the people from watching you slowly succumb to Alzheimers, incontinence, and senility. Elevating a son to the highest position is tricky and must be handled with care – and your timing needs to perfect. Don't anoint your son as an heir and then hold on to power, since this tactic encourages impatient youth to act, and you may find yourself retired (permanently) before your time. Something like this may have happened to Philip II of Macedon after he quarreled with his designated heir and son Alexander. Or, if junior is not willing to act, the people may; one of the factors that led to the uprisings against Hosni Mubarak in Egypt was the belief that he had chosen his son to succeed him as President, a prospect only Hosni himself found acceptable. In this case, it certainly did not help that Gamal Mubarak was perceived as a corrupt and arrogant cog in his father's autocratic machinery.[193]

Similiarly, Fidel Castro confounded the United States a final time in 2007. Despite decades of rumors that his health was failing, Castro lived long enough to peacefully install his brother Raúl in power and gracefully retire, managing minor affairs from behind the scenes. How disappointing this must have been to political scientists, politicians, and Cuba-watchers everywhere who were hoping Fidel's death would lead to massive revolt in Cuba and the overturning of Castro's revolution. They got neither.[451]

- *Comfortable Retirement*: This might be a preferred option, particularly if you are childless or your sons paid attention while you handled affairs of state. It is also an attractive way to spend your golden years if you have achieved all your goals or obtained some type of long-term political settlement. Georgia's Edward Shevardnadze was allowed to retire peacefully to his country villa: not bad, if you can get it. Indonesia's Suharto was permitted by his generals to die in peace on his own terms and in full liberty.[63] Baby Doc Duvalier (Haiti) spent most of his retirement in France's Côte d'Azur, Jean-Bedel Bokassa (Central African Republic) too wound up in France. Idi Amin (Uganda) cooled his heels in Libya and Saudi Arabia.[489] If, under strenuous circumstances, you are permitted to step down and keep your money, you are way ahead of your colleagues.

The Roman dictator Lucius Cornelius Sulla retired in 79 B.C. after showing his rivals how a tried and true dictator operates. Having won several wars, ruthlessly culled the ranks of those foolish enough to oppose him, and secured the power of the elites for another generation, he retired to a comfortable family life in Campania, where he wrote his life's story, hunted and fished in the lush countryside, and reportedly drank excessively.[429] After his death from liver failure he was given a lavish funeral at state expense.

Given the pressures of the modern world, 24-hour media coverage, and the ease with which opposition groups can procure arms, you may find retirement (early or otherwise) a more attractive option than some of the others listed here. But enjoy it in moderation or it's likely to be brief.

- *Exile*: You are guaranteed a retirement that will remain uneventful unless you do something stupid like return to your own country (Duvalier/ Haiti) or get hauled before an international court for war crimes (Charles Taylor/Liberia). You may be exiled someplace near home (Mengistu Haile Mariam/ Ethiopia: Zimbabwe), someplace lovely (Ferdinand Marcos/ Philippines: Hawaii, Jean-Bedel Bokassa/ Central African Republic and Jean-Claude Duvalier/Haiti: France), or someplace neutral that simply agrees to give you a home away from home (Idi Amin/Uganda and Zine al-Abidine Ben Ali/Tunisia: Saudi Arabia). Take up golf and enjoy the quiet life, but be careful not to ruffle your hosts' feathers: Nigeria sent ousted Liberian president Charles Taylor back to face 11 counts of war crimes and crimes against humanity, and his guilty verdict led to jail time: an inauspicious end. [461]

- *Overthrown by rebel force*: This is unpleasant because your dynasty comes to an abrupt end. It's worse if on the way out you are forced to commit atrocities against your people that ensure your ultimate legacy is inextricably linked to crimes against humanity. When other countries begin expelling your diplomatic staff and officially recognizing the insurgents, it does not bode well for you and your regime.[329] Another risk of this denouement is that the rebel leader may turn you into a historical footnote. This happened to Fulgencio Batista; his overthrow by Fidel Castro's guerrillas quickly removed him from the world stage, and now it is Castro who has become the face of Cuba.[1][352] Zaire's Mobutu Sese Seko found the same end, and worse. He had set the bar high for his successors from early on, vowing he would only ever be known as the "late" president, never the "ex-president." Imagine his disappointment then when he was essentially chased from power by a rebel group, and then succumbed while in exile to prostate cancer.[212]

- *Lose all your money in exile.* Jean Claude Duvalier, whose avarice while president of Haiti allegedly netted him between $300M – $800M,

---
[1]Give Batista credit at least for escaping with his life.

fled the country in 1986, and led an opulent lifestyle in a chateau out-side Paris. Six years later, his wife divorced him, taking much of the family assets with her, and about a decade later he found himself living in a modest, one bedroom apartment and begging for a chance to go back to Haiti, ostensibly for another bite at the apple.[238]

- *Killed by opposition forces.* You may or may be able to predict this, depending on your situation. Regardless, we recommend taking this possibility right off the list by ruthlessly eliminating your opposition: don't give them the chance to take you out! But if you find yourself overthrown, captured or arrested, then try to meet the end with a little dignity – you should certainly avoid being caught and killed while attempting to escape the utter ruin of your dictatorial project. It puts a bad light on things and history will not look on you kindly. Take Mussolini's example. By the time he tried to flee the collapsing republic of Salò with mistress in tow, he was no longer the strutting Duce of old but a humbled, broken figure disguised under an old army blanket. When executed by the partisans he reportedly was docile rather than defiant:[111] note, this is not the image you want to project. If you can arrange it beforehand, also make sure that your corpse does not fall into the hands of your enemies, because (as in Mussolini's case) the chances that it will be exposed to public anger and resentment are high.

  If ambushed, you won't see the end coming, and you might not have time to consult a priest or calm down your spouse/mistress before the firing squad takes aim. The Dominican dictator Rafael Trujillo, for example, was ambushed and assassinated by a group of disaffected elites,[353] possibly with the aid of the CIA.[488]

- *Killed by your own army.* If this happens, you likely deserve your sorry fate, since keeping the military happy should be one of the core tenets of any responsible dictator. Clearly, you did not read this book. Once you've lost the army there is little chance of anything going your way, but in most cases a military execution is slightly more dignified than public mockery of your corpse. There are however always exceptions, as Nicolae Ceausescu and his wife Elena found out in 1989. The former power couple was arrested and, after a quick ruling by a military court, swiftly executed. A low-fi video of the panicked couple after sentencing was circulated in Western countries and a little later within Romania.[281] The video also showed their bullet-riddled bodies covered by cheap army-issue blankets; this is the kind of image that you should do all in your power to avoid, because last impressions tend to linger. Trust us, if you go down in a hail of bullets the people won't remember that bridge you inaugurated in 1975, or your lavish spending on the national highway.

- *Forcibly "retired" by your ex-colonial masters*: Honestly, an embarrassing and all-around poor way to exit the world stage. Laurent Gbagbo's final days – cowering under the presidential palace in an underground bunker as his troops slowly abandoned him and the French military advanced – are about as bad as you can hope for. Worse still, rather than kill him they delivered him (reduced to an unprotected commoner) to his political opponent. Had he at least been killed in battle his supporters could have woven a tale in retrospect about neo-colonial oppression and Western intervention that could have portrayed him as somewhat of a hero. Zero points for style.[174]

- *Removed violently by your own people*, badly injured but alive and unable to govern. If this seems farfetched, think again. It happened very recently to Ali Abdullah Saleh in Yemen, who was wounded badly in a rocket attack on the presidential palace.[319] Once something like this occurs it's advisable to take the hint and begin thinking about all those lovely games of solitaire that await you during your comfortable retirement. Saleh eventually chose retirement, leaving the government to his vice president in 2011.

- *Brought before an international tribunal for war crimes*; appeal – but lose – on the grounds of senility and health problems; die overseas in mid-trial; be denied a state burial or honors of any kind. This was the short, unhappy downfall of Chile's Augusto Pinochet, but Guatemala's Efrain Rios Montt and Liberia's Charles Taylor both lived to face trial.[394] [418] Likewise, 'Baby Doc' Duvalier returned to Haiti after 25 years[2], where he was immediately sued for torture and other crimes against humanity.[56] Ethiopia's brutal Mengistu Haile Mariam, head of the Derg that terrorized Ethiopia for twenty years, was likewise convicted of war crimes, but in absentia, and by an Ethiopian tribunal.[2]

- *Prosecuted by your own nation*: This can be an embarrassing and potentially deadly way to spend your retirement, though experiences vary. After being tried by the Shiite majority he repressed for years, Saddam Hussein for example met his fate at the scaffold (and worse, had his execution filmed and distributed via the Internet; for more on this see below). The more savvy or lucky among you can have a more pleasant or at least more protracted time in court. Take Indonesia's Suharto, who in 2000 came under investigation for corruption during his presidency. A panel of court-appointed doctors found him physically unfit to stand trial, suffering from a brain disease that prevented him from speaking or remembering things.[3] Three years later

---

[2]His return was likely prompted by a new Swiss law that would permit the Haitian government to access the $6M in Duvalier assets frozen when he fled into exile [238]

[3]Ah yes, how convenient.

the Indonesian National Commission on Human Rights announced an inquiry into events dating back to Suharto's rise to power in 1965. Suharto appeared before neither commission before dying in January 2008.[237]

The sad final act of Hosni Mubarak is perhaps the best reason why you should do everything in your power to avoid the dock in your old age. Egyptians were shocked at the images of Mubarak during the initial stages of his trial, caged and prone on a gurney, and it is likely this is how they'll think of him from now on – as a broken and weak figure, not as the powerful leader they had previously held to be a modern-day Pharaoh.[331] Being tried by your former underlings makes it very likely that succeeding generations will judge you harshly, since the court record will almost certainly be a long record of your malfeasance, compiled to show you in your worst light. Although being considered a horrible dictator is a tad better than not being mentioned at all, if you are hauled before a judge or jury, don't be meek and humble. We recommend you make some noise.

It's clear that the prosecution of dictators is on the increase, and this fact is making some tyrants rethink a peaceful exit from the world stage. After all, if your enemies (or former subjects) are dead set on using legal proceedings to tarnish your legacy, why not give them something to really complain about? Barricade yourself in the presidential fortress and fight it out until the bitter end! Why not? One former strongman, Olusegun Obasanjo of Nigeria, expressed just such an opinion in 2011, shortly after witnessing the spectacle of Hosni Mubarak's trial in Egypt; he affirmed that authoritarian leaders would not be likely to transition peacefully from power if certain prosecution awaited.[13]

- *Tortured and/or killed by the survivors of your repressive regime*: Not only do you lose some of your panache, but in an ironic twist you die experiencing the same sort of pain you often inflicted on others. In fact, the more successfully you have employed physical persuasion, the more likely you are to be offered the same bloody cup to drink. Neither will your captors cut you any slack if your notoriety comes from the theft of millions of dollars in state funds. This was news to Liberia's Samuel Doe during his "interrogation" and death at the hands of rebels.[213] Iraq's Saddam Hussein wasn't tortured, per se, but he was hanged in the most unceremonious manner possible after a trial in 2006.[461] The hanging occurred with the executioners reportedly shouting "Moqtada" – the name of the Shiite leader that Hussein had ruthlessly expunged years earlier.[423] And of course the illustrious Mohammar Khadaffi was not only dragged out of the storm sewer in which he'd attempted to take cover, but he was mercilessly beaten by rebel forces overdosing on adrenalin. He was stabbed to death like a rat, but not before one of the rebels bent him over a car and sodomized him with a bowie knife.[436] Not the glorious finish he'd perhaps imagined for himself, to say the least.

- *Die in Western Captivity*: Above all, do your best to die of natural causes, a free man. Do *not* die alone in a cell in the Hague while await- ing trial, as did Slobodan Milosevic, at the age of 64. ("Death came as Mr. Milosevic's four-year trial for war crimes, crimes against human- ity, and genocide was drawing to a close. A verdict had been expected later [that] year.")[442] Panamanian strongman Manuel Noriega spent twenty years in a Miami prison before doing seven years in France before returning to Panama to face two more 20-year sentences there. Panamanian courts had tried him in absentia for the murder of two of his regime's opponents: an army major whose attempted coup d'etat failed to unseat Noriega, and a physician whose decapitated corpse turned up stuffed into a mail sack. But after suffering cancer and a stroke, Noriega returned a weakened and frail man, who walked with difficulty and was anything but the picture of power and authority he was in his heyday as 'strong man.' He must certainly have preferred to be shot in battle than suffer such an inglorious end.[260]

- *Corpse disinterred and burned by angry mob*: Just when you thought you were safely dead, something like this happens. It's not fun when your former subjects hate you enough even after your death to violate your corpse: a demeaning and putrid way to upset your eternal rest, as François Duvalier's corpse discovered fifteen years after first being buried (and immediately after his son was exiled from Haiti, unable to protect dad's grave).[238]

- *Crash and Burn, Tear it Down as you Go*: If you're going to go, you might as well take the whole country and half of the continent with you. Adolf Hitler, having fought the Allies mile after dogged mile during the last few years of the war, finally saw his end was near. But before his suicide and the death of his recent spouse, he gave an explicit order to Albert Speer to systematically destroy Germany. In his own words:"If the war is lost then the nation will be lost also. There is no need to show any consideration for the foundations which the German nation needs for its most primitive survival. On the contrary, it is better to destroy the thing ourselves."[230] This option is only recommended if you have the stomach for such defiant gestures. No one will remember you fondly, but they will, at least, remember.

13.3 Transferring Power

If you must go, keep it in the family: ideally your son or the cruel daughter who used to torment the family cat in grade school. But how to ensure that he or she takes the throne? Unless you are a royal monarch, and there are precious few of those left, you are going to have to be clever.

One direct way to ensure succession is to get your son into power elsewhere in the government and position him to take over. Be warned though; it's also an obvious maneuver and you will likely have to deal with slighted generals, impatient younger sons, and/or guerilla leaders who see an emerging power vacuum. In these cases it helps if your son has some ability; if he's the type to squander his talents on women, drink, or gambling, then in all probability your transfer of power won't last beyond the time it takes for your son to be out-flanked by a more capable rival. Deal with the presumed rival(s) yourself and send your son back to the whore houses, shaking your head at his lack of ambition.

However, if Junior is a chip off the old block, then by all means consider creating a new executive level position that would permit him to take the presidency automatically if you step down. Make sure the Constitution requires that, for example, the President of the Senate steps up to the presidency in case the president is ever incapacitated. Then make your son the head of the Senate. Finally, step down for health reasons. Easy! It was, at any rate, for Equatorial Guinea's Teodoro Obiang, who in May 2012 promoted *his* son to "Vice President in charge of National Defense and State Security," much to the surprise of the government press agency, who had just finished announcing his new role as "Deputy Prime Minister."[258] Oops.

If however your oldest son is unsuitable, then you will have to turn to your younger brother. Malawi's Mutharika, unable to run for election in the 2014 elections, was pleased when the Democratic Progressive Party (his own, of which he is the head) chose his younger brother Peter as the party's candidate for the upcoming election. "This decision has been arrived at by the whole [National Governing Council] after listening to calls from the party's regional and district committees, as well as other sectors including members of the clergy," related the spokesperson. Of course, the fact that all positions in the party were appointed by the president himself made the decision unsurprising: in fact, everyone in the party who opposed the selection was summarily fired by the president shortly thereafter.[139]

Finally, you might be in the position of a caretaker-ruler, remaking society in your and your party's image while you await the proper time for the restoration of the monarchy. If so, and you are able to hand power off to a Dauphin at the end of your reign, you might justifiably feel that your autocratic tenure has been a success. But trust the aristocracy at your peril; as many commentators have pointed out, Francisco Franco selected Prince Juan Carlos as his heir, only to have the monarch quickly dismantle the dictatorship after the Caudillo's death. Worse, from Franco's point of view, Spain would soon have a leftist, popularly elected government.[244] Don't be blinded by the prestige of royalty, and avoid damaging your legacy by picking the right man or woman as your successor.

13.4 Monuments, Museums, and Memorials

You or your successors, particularly if your successor is also your offspring, can effectively improve your nation's memory of you, posthumously, by building monuments, museums, and memorials in your honor. Nothing better says "Father of the nation" than a glorious, marble building thronged with school children and pensioners learning about your feats, your prowess, and your fatherly leadership. Look back to the Pharaohs of Egypt, whose immense pyramids – mausoleums, really – stand in testament to their greatness millennia later. If you can't build the pyramids, then perhaps a 500 foot high crucifix would do; if this interests you then visit Francisco Franco's memorial tomb complex, *Valle de los Caídos* ("Valley of the Fallen"), for pointers.[388]

But don't over do it: nothing says "loser" more clearly than the same museum, dead empty, slowly rotting into decrepitude. Late president of Azerbaijan Heydar Aliyev is now honored by 50 different museums throughout Azerbaijan, particularly in Baku, and the number is rising. The number of patrons however is not, and an international journalist visiting one museum in July 2011 found he was the only person there. Worse, Azerbaijanis asked why they didn't go to the museums reported they were unable to afford it. Continued poverty, and empty museums intended to honor your memory, both undermine your legacy in easily-mocked ways.[274]

13.5 Lovely Nostalgia

Some may consider a memorial at your gravesite a kind of backhanded testament to your legacy, particularly if you were toppled from power during a violent insurrection or if resistance fighters summarily executed you during a shameful flight from the ruin of your dictatorial project. Don't let these negative thoughts get you down. Though you won't live to see it, it's certainly possible that time will smile on your memory – your less perceptive followers and their descendants almost certainly will – and with luck your final resting place will become a rallying point for future generations. To this day Mussolini's tomb in Predappio draws thousands of pilgrims, from traditionalist Catholics to right wing enthusiasts and lovers of the color black. Despite his inglorious death and his role in precipitating the disastrous entry of Italy into World War II, many of these devotees continue to hail Il Duce for his unique ideas and contributions to the Italian nation. In the end, if your pathetic removal from power doesn't prevent people from flying flags on your grave in perpetuity ... well then, you *win!* [379]

Amazingly, time seems to truly heal old wounds, and Mussolini is not the only one whose image has remarkably improved with the passing of the decades. Remember that the former Soviet states increasingly look back on the Soviet Union with nostalgia and longing.[384] [271]. The same goes for the republics of the former Yugoslavia, who increasingly remember life under authoritarian Josip Broz Tito as being a bit better than life these days. Tito's image is used to sell lots of commercial products now, and Tito impersonators do great business at annual festivals and memorials.[101]

13.6   Bad Ideas

Genocide   It's safe to say that nothing will soil your legacy faster than genocide of any sort. Your goal should be to manipulate power, make money, crush your enemies while enriching your friends, conquer gloriously without risking too much, and die with the reputation of a demi-god. Mass exterminations of any sort will ensure your name is forever associated with evil, so don't do it. Just ask Adolf Hitler. Genocidal campaigns also have a way of boomeranging against you (for how this happened to Hitler, see below). Slobodan Milosevic succumbed to the temptation of "ethnic cleansing," but the slaughter of some estimated 8000 Muslims at Srebrenica in Bosnia finally pushed NATO to act; the resulting military onslaught led to Milosevic's ouster and incarceration.[267]

Easily Mocked Hypocrisy   Let's just say that if you once wrote a PhD thesis on "The Role of Civil Society in the Democratization of Global Governance Institutions" but then, under fire, resort to threatening to hunt your people down "house by house" to exterminate opposition forces, you have just nailed the coffin shut on your future career as benevolent dictator and will instead go down in history as a hypocrite. Nice work, Saif al-Islam Khadaffi.[17],[240]

Likewise, for all the effort Zaire's Mobutu Sese Seko put into developing "authenticity" and a pro-African, anti-Western stance, he unwittingly parodied much of what he professed to detest. His palace in Gbadolite was a knock off of the Belgium monarchy's Laekan Palace, and his penchant for the lush life led him straight to the shopping districts of the very nations he repudiated.[212]

Nigeria's General Sani Abacha, when he died of a heart attack in 1998, left behind a legacy easily characterized by one single word: hypocrisy. Upon entering office in 1993 he had committed himself to ridding Nigeria of corruption and promoting "transparency, accountability, and probity in public life." Instead, he proceeded to loot more from public resources than just about anyone in history, making off with more than a billion dollars. Nigerian security agents also prevented his widow Maryam from leaving Nigeria with 38 suitcases, many of them stuffed with cash. It doesn't matter what else he did or did not do during his five years in office: this is the image that will remain.[34]

Legacy Killers You hopefully kept your legacy in mind the entire time you ruled, avoiding white elephant projects bearing your family name, ensuring unflattering photographs of you were destroyed (and the photographer chastised), and so on. But you must also ensure your legacy is not overshadowed by the excesses of your family. Yes, the Philippines' Ferdinand Marcos ruled his nation for twenty years with an iron fist, and absconded into exile with millions or billions of dollars. But no one remembers that anymore: they remember his wife's extensive shoe collection. That's not right. What about all you've done?[226]

Poor Nickname Names matter. When all is said and done, you are probably better off being remembered as "the Genius of the Carpathians" (Nicolae Ceausescu) than "the Butcher of the Balkans." (Slobodan Milosevic). During your rule, try to make the most flattering nickname stick; if your subjects are used to calling you "The Punisher," then why not encourage them? Put up posters and pass out buttons with this name over your scowling face, and stamp out any movement that tries to brand you with the moniker "The Syphilitic Dandy." These examples give a sense of the range of available nicknames, but the point should be clear – pay attention to what people are calling you and always push a pen name, if you will, that leaves no doubt as to who carries the sword. No matter how lovingly used, a bad nickname usually means a weak or vulnerable dictator.

- *Excellent*: The Great (numerous examples), Il Duce (Mussolini, Italy), Der Führer (Hitler, Germany), Genius of the Carpathians (Ceausescu, Romania), El Caudillo (Franco, Spain), The Reasoning Terminator (Putin, Russia), Great Leader (Kim Il Sung, North Korea), Dear Leader (Kim Jong Il, North Korea)

- *Good*: El Jefe (numerous), El Comandante (Castro, Cuba), Papa Doc (Duvalier, Haiti), The Grey Cardinal (Putin, Russia)

- *Middling*: El Generalissimo (Franco, Spain), The Delayer (F. Cunctator, Rome), El Hombre (Batista, Cuba), Cowboy (Pervez Musharraf, Pakistan), Hardman (Putin, Russia)

- *Poor*: The Goat (Trujillo, Dominican Republic), Butcher of the Balkans (Milosevic, Serbia), Pineapple Face (Noriega, Panama), Baby Doc (Duvalier Jr., Haiti), Hitler-in-Africa (Idi Amin, Uganda)

Underestimate Your Successor This can damage your image and ruin your plans for canonization by the Catholic Church after your death. Don't trust the sycophants who agree with everything you say while you are alive to respect your memory; these yes-men will be the first to abandon you, sell the sordid stories of your regime to the tabloids, and confess that you were personally responsible for countless atrocities. Stick with family if you can, but if not keep a watchful eye on your designated successor. Nikita Khrushchev's famous "Secret Speech" to the 20th Party Congress in 1956 criticized the purges of Stalin's Great Terror, marked the (small-scale) opening of Soviet society, and in part contributed to the blackening of Stalin's image in the years after his death.[223]

13.7   Your Legacy Undone

There is a tipping point in the career of every dictator, a time when everything you want to achieve is there for the taking. If you get to this point and choose wisely, you might be remembered as a glorious conqueror (Napoleon, Alexander the Great), even if the usual dissenters will object. But go too far, indulge your worst tendencies, and use the power you've accumulated to alienate your subjects and you risk destroying the empire you worked so hard to build. As we've detailed elsewhere, Hosni Mubarak arguably went too far in Egypt, particularly by arranging for his son to succeed him; similarly, Manuel Noriega mistakenly assumed he could count on US support after a rigged election, and for this act of hubris he was removed from power by the US military, and his regime dismantled.

The dictator who goes too far and destroys his own legacy is best illustrated by the example of Adolf Hitler. In 1940, before the invasion of the Soviet Union, it's likely that Hitler could have, if not for Winston Churchill, won some kind of limited European war and established a continental hegemony that would have lasted decades. Turning on Stalin and declaring war on the United States in 1941 were not prudent decisions, to say the least, and engaging in a genocidal campaign against the Jews did much to ensure that no one was going to reach an accommodation with Germany. In addition to blackening his name forever, these acts achieved the exact opposite of Hitler's goals in many cases. Consider:[230]

1. Hitler intended to exterminate the Jews; after the war the widespread knowledge of the Holocaust in part facilitated the creation of the state of Israel

2. Hitler did not want to wage war against Britain or deprive her of her overseas empire; Britain proved to be Germany's nemesis and as a result of the war lost much of her empire, including India

3. Hitler wanted to establish a thousand-year Reich in Germany; he left Germany in ruins, a country soon to be divided for nearly 50 years

In sum, be ruthless and terrible, but not too much.

13.8   A Final Word

Lastly, never assume the end is the end. History shows it is anything but. In 1979, Nicaragua's Somoza family was discredited, and a popular revolution had seen the Somoza regime's overthrow. Hated president Anastasio "Tacho" Somoza had been blown to bits by an unknown assailant's rocket launcher in Paraguay. The end? No way. Fast-forward thirty years or so to the 21st century, where "liberated" Nicaragua was now such a mess that Tacho's nephew, Alvaro decided to return to Nicaragua and begin a career in politics. And a career with lots of potential, too: the past thirty years of war, revolution, and a panoply of weak, inept, corrupt, and increasingly autocratic (but democratically elected) leaders put Nicaraguans in the mood to think back favorably on the "good old years" under the Somoza family.[368] Turns out, time does heal all wounds: in the context of growing fondness and nostalgia for the good old days, the last name "Somoza" is no longer a liability. Rather, it actually inspires support among people who wish Nicaragua were making any sort of economic progress at all. Guess which family is back in the running? Game on, gentlemen.

Bibliography

[1] Les presidents du Nicaragua. Internet. http://www.abc-latina.com/nicaragua/div/presidents_nicaragua.htm Accessed 6 June 2011.

[2] Lorraine Adams. Battle scars. *New York Times*, 29 December 2009. http://www.nytimes.com/2010/01/03/books/review/Adams-t.html.

[3] Federal Aviation Administration. International travel. Internet. http://www.faa.gov/passengers/international_travel/ Accessed 20 May 2011.

[4] Heba Afify and Rick Gladstone. Egyptian forces roust Tahrir square sit-in. *New York Times*, 1 August 2011. XXX.

[5] AFP. Coup d'État manqué de 2009: un ancien chef d'état-major Togolais arrêté. *Jeune Afrique*, 23 July 2011. http://www.jeuneafrique.com/Article/DEPAFP20110723170512/.

[6] AFP. E. Guinea veteran leader to mark 32 years in power. *Africa Review*, 3 August 2011. http://www.africareview.com/News/E+Guinea+leader+to+mark+32+years+in+power/-/979180/1212716/-/14ftvy7/-/index.html.

[7] AFP. Presidente Morales teme viajar por EE.UU por supuesto complot en su contra. *La Prensa*, 25 July 2011. http://www.laprensa.com.ni/2011/07/25/internacionales/67827.

[8] AFP. Iran crubs foreign-sourced email providers. *AFP*, 12 May 2012. http://www.google.com/hostednews/afp/article/ALeqM5jzh5OHjE_YOFj7PeAz8thcxLDXHg?docId=CNG.9db1cb87109712fd31475e3f2399e01e.251.

[9] Jeune Afrique. Guineé: la résidence d'Alpha Condé attaquée, le général Nouhou Thiam arrêté. *Jeune Afrique*, 19 July 2011. http://www.jeuneafrique.com/Article/ARTJAWEB20110719094831/.

[10] Jeune Afrique. Niger: des militaire arrêtés suite á une tentative de putsch. *Jeune Afrique*, 26 July 2011. http://www.jeuneafrique.com/Article/ARTJAWEB20110726131749/.

[11] Catholic News Agency. Stasi: Persecution against the church in Nicaragua was "serious error" of sandinistas. *Catholic News Agency*, June 2008. http://www.catholicnewsagency.com/news/stasi_persecution_against_the_church_in_nicaragua_was_serious_error_of_sandinistas/.

[12] Eloy O. Aguilar. Tight race as former leader Daniel Ortega seeks comeback. *Associated Press*, 4 November 2001.

[13] Mark Agutu. Obasanju dismayed at Mubarak court images. *Africa Review*, 5 August 2011. http://www.africareview.com/News/Obasanjo+dismayed+at+Mubarak+court+show/-/979180/1213878/-/in9k3/-/index.html.

[14] Issam Ahmed. Why Musharraf is risking a return to Pakistan. *Christian Science Monitor*, 9 January 2012. http://www.csmonitor.com/World/Asia-South-Central/2012/0109/Why-Musharraf-is-risking-a-return-to-Pakistan.

[15] Filadelfo Aleman. Election monitor says Nicaraguan president told him of plan to steal election. *Associated Press*, 2 November 2003.

[16] Karen Allen. Has Kenya's power-sharing worked? *BBC*, 3 March 2009. http://news.bbc.co.uk/2/hi/africa/7921007.stm.

[17] Saif Al-Islam Alqadhafi. *The Role of Society in the Democratisation of Global Governance Institutions: from 'Soft Power' to Collective Decision-Making?* PhD thesis, London School of Economics, September 2007.

[18] Raymond H. Anderson. Giant among Communists governed like a Monarch. *New York Times*, page A1, 5 May 1980.

[19] Edmund L. Andrews. New U.S. allies, the Uzbeks: mired in the past. *New York Times*, 31 May 2002. http://www.nytimes.com/2002/05/31/world/new-us-allies-the-uzbeks-mired-in-the-past.html?ref=islamkarimov.

[20] Yovshan Annagurban. The short distance between sanity and madness in Turkmenistan. *Radio Free Europe/Radio Liberty*, http://www.rferl.org/content/commentary_short_distance_sanity_madness_turkmenistan/24280051.html 2011.

[21] Rabah Arezki and Markus Brückner. Food prices, conflict, and democratic change. Research Paper 2011-04, University of Adelaide, School of Economics, January 2011. http://www.economics.adelaide.edu.au/research/papers/doc/wp2011-04.pdf.

[22] Sophie Arle. Revival for Mussolini rock tribute. *The Guardian*, 1 February 2004. http://www.guardian.co.uk/world/2004/feb/02/italy.sophiearie.

[23] Charles Arthur. Syrian activists targeted by fake Youtube. *The Guardian*, 20 March 2012. http://www.guardian.co.uk/technology/2012/mar/20/syrian-activists-fake-youtube.

[24] Martin Asser. Abu Ghraib: dark stain on Iraq's past. *BBC*, 25 May 2004. http://news.bbc.co.uk/2/hi/americas/3747005.stm.

[25] Ben S. Austin. Kristallnacht. Internet. http://frank.mtsu.edu/~baustin/knacht.html Accessed 21 February 2011.

[26] George Ayittey. Misleading Africa. *The American Interest*, Spring, March/April 2009.

[27] Nada Bakri. Syrians rally in support of Assad. *New York Times*, 12 October 2011. http://www.nytimes.com/2011/10/13/world/middleeast/syrians-rally-in-support-of-assad.html.

[28] Tom Balmforth. Putin cast as heartthrob in raunchy video urging girls to strip for him. *Radio Free Europe/Radio Liberty*, 19 July 2011. http://www.rferl.org/content/putin_cast_heartthrob_raunchy_video_calling_for_girls_to_strip_for_him/24270436.html.

[29] Ed Barnes. Flourishing poppy fields outside prison camps are heroin cash crop for North Korea. *Fox News*, 10 May 2011. http://www.foxnews.com/world/2011/05/10/north-korea-growing-heroin-outside-prison-camps-satellite-photos/.

[30] Robert H. Bates. *When Things Fell Apart*, chapter 4: Policy Choices, pages 55–74. Cambridge University Press, New York, NY, 2008.

[31] Robert H. Bates. *When Things Fell Apart*, chapter 3: Political Legacies, pages 33–53. Cambridge University Press, New York, NY, 2008.

[32] Mohamad Bazzi. What did Qaddafi's Green Book really say? *New York Times,* 29 May 2011. http://www.nytimes.com/2011/05/29/books/review/ what-did-qaddafis-green-book-really-say.html.

[33] BBC. On this day: 22 April 1971: Haitian dictator dies. Internet. http://news.bbc.co.uk/onthisday/hi/dates/stories/april/ 22/newsid_2525000/2525501.stm Accessed 28 June 2011.

[34] BBC. Nigeria recovers Abacha's cash. *BBC,* 10 November 1998. http://news. bbc.co.uk/2/hi/africa/211324.stm.

[35] BBC. Obituary: Abacha: leader with an iron grip. *BBC,* 18 February 1999. http: //news.bbc.co.uk/2/hi/109297.stm.

[36] BBC. Flashback: Caravan of Death. *BBC,* 25 July 2000. http://news.bbc.co. uk/2/hi/americas/850932.stm.

[37] BBC. Fujimori's controversial career. *BBC,* 18 September 2000. http://news. bbc.co.uk/2/hi/americas/705482.stm.

[38] BBC. Obituary: Ne Win. *BBC,* 5 December 2002. http://news.bbc.co.uk/2/ hi/asia-pacific/1581413.stm.

[39] BBC. Berlusconi admits plastic surgery. *BBC,* 28 January 2004. http://news.bbc. co.uk/2/hi/europe/3439801.stm.

[40] BBC. Ukraine candidate 'was poisoned'. *BBC,* 11 December 2004. http://news. bbc.co.uk/2/hi/europe/4088345.stm.

[41] BBC. Syria quashes last dialogue forum. *BBC,* 24 May 2005. http://news.bbc. co.uk/2/hi/middle_east/4575987.stm.

[42] BBC. Chavez tells UN Bush is 'devil'. *BBC,* 20 September 2006. http://news. bbc.co.uk/2/hi/5365142.stm.

[43] BBC. Nicaragua brings in abortion ban. *BBC,* 18 November 2006. http://news. bbc.co.uk/2/hi/6161396.stm.

[44] BBC. Ortega wins Nicaragua election. *BBC,* 8 November 2006. http://news.bbc. co.uk/2/hi/americas/6117704.stm.

[45] BBC. Profile: Chad's hissene habre. *BBC,* 3 July 2006. http://news.bbc.co.uk/2/hi/africa/5140818.stm.

[46] BBC. Shut up, Spain's king tells Chavez. *BBC,* 10 November 2007. http://news. bbc.co.uk/2/hi/7089131.stm.

[47] BBC. Africa's top 10 'big men'. *BBC,* 12 June 2009. http://news.bbc.co.uk/ 2/hi/africa/8094012.stm Accessed 22 February 2011.

[48] BBC. Niger anger at court appointment. *BBC News,* July 2009. http://news.bbc. co.uk/2/hi/africa/8132581.stm.

[49] BBC. Profile: Mamadou Tandja. Internet, August 2009. http://news.bbc.co. uk/2/hi/africa/8181537.stm.

[50] BBC. Khodorkovsky gets six more years in Russia jail. *BBC,* December 2010. http: //www.bbc.co.uk/news/world-europe-12093922.

[51] BBC. US revokes Venezuela ambassador's visa amid Chavez row. Internet, December 2010. http://www.bbc.co.uk/news/world-latin-america- 12091689.

[52] BBC. Venezuela parliament gives Hugo Chavez more powers. *BBC,* 2010. http: //www.bbc.co.uk/news/world-latin-america-12024935.

[53] BBC. Zimbabwe country profile, February 2010. http://news.bbc.co.uk/2/ hi/africa/country_profiles/1064589.stm.

[54] BBC. African Union to hold Somalia famine summit. *Africa Review*, 2 August 2011. http://www.africareview.com/News/-/979180/1212020/-/h82i3kz/-/index.html.

[55] BBC. Amnesty: Saudi terror law 'would strangle protest'. *BBC*, 22 July 2011. http://www.bbc.co.uk/news/world-middle-east-14239259.

[56] BBC. 'Baby Doc' Duvalier sued for torture in Haiti. *BBC*, 19 January 2011. http://www.bbc.co.uk/news/world-latin-america-12233343.

[57] BBC. Belarus closes down OSCE office after poll criticism. *BBC*, 1 January 2011.

[58] BBC. Egypt court stops virginity tests in military prisons. *BBC*, 27 December 2011. http://www.bbc.co.uk/news/world-middle-east-16339398.

[59] BBC. Egypt unrest: Cairo clashes reveal deep divisions. *BBC*, 19 December 2011. http://www.bbc.co.uk/news/world-middle-east-1625829.

[60] BBC. Family dynamics drive Syrian president Assad. *BBC*, 30 April 2011. http://www.nytimes.com/2011/03/12/world/asia/12china.html.

[61] BBC. Gaddafi threatens to attack Europe. *BBC*, 2 July 2011. http://www.bbc.co.uk/news/world-africa-14000956.

[62] BBC. History's lessons: Dismantling Egypt's security agency. *BBC*, 9 March 2011. http://www.bbc.co.uk/news/world-middle-east-12679632.

[63] BBC. How revolutions happen: patterns from Iran to Egypt. *BBC*, 2011. http://www.bbc.co.uk/news/world-middle-east-12674714.

[64] BBC. Is Algeria immune from the Arab spring? *BBC*, 27 July 2011. http://www.bbc.co.uk/news/world-africa-14167481.

[65] BBC. Kim Jong-Il death: 'nature mourns' N Korea leader. *BBC*, 22 December 2011. http://www.bbc.co.uk/news/world-asia-16297811.

[66] BBC. Kim Jong Il, the cinephile despot. *BBC*, 19 December 2011. http://www.bbc.co.uk/news/entertainment-arts-16245174.

[67] BBC. Libya crisis: Gaddafi vows to fight to the death. *BBC*, 7 June 2011. http://www.bbc.co.uk/news/world-africa-13688003.

[68] BBC. Libya protests: Gaddafi's son warns of civil war. *BBC*, 21 February 2011. http://www.bbc.co.uk/news/world-middle-east-12520586.

[69] BBC. Malawi anti-Mutharika protesters buried in Mzuzu. *BBC*, 22 July 2011. http://www.bbc.co.uk/news/world-africa-14246739.

[70] BBC. Malawi president says UK's expelled envoy insulted him. *BBC*, 8 May 2011. http://bbc.co.uk/news/world-africa-13327013.

[71] BBC. Nigerian military accused of killings in Maiduguri. *BBC*, 26 July 2011. http://www.bbc.co.uk/news/world-africa-14292427.

[72] BBC. Profile: Syria's Bashar al-Assad. *BBC*, page 25 March, 2011. http://www.bbc.co.uk/news/10338256.

[73] BBC. Sheryl Cwele: SA minister's wife gets 12-year jail term. *BBC*, 6 May 2011. http://www.bbc.co.uk/news/world-africa-13310034.

[74] BBC. Somali militants maintain aid ban. *BBC*, 22 July 2011. http://www.bbc.co.uk/news/world-africa-14246764.

[75] BBC. South China Sea dispute: Philippine MPs visit Spratlys. *BBC*, 20 July 2011.

[76] BBC. Syria: Assad supporters attack US and French embassies. *BBC*, 11 July 2011. http://www.bbc.co.uk/news/world-middle-east-14111198.

[77] BBC. Syria unrest: 'new violence' near Homs amid talks call. *BBC*, 14 May 2011. http://www.bbc.co.uk/news/world-middle-east-13398608.

[78] BBC. Syrian army 'surrounds Damascus suburb'. *BBC*, 9 May 2011. http://www.bbc.co.uk/news/world-middle-east-13330069.

[79] BBC. Timeline: Haiti. *BBC*, 19 April 2011. http://news.bbc.co.uk/2/hi/americas/country_profiles/1202857.stm.

[80] BBC. Trio 'abducted and abused' for Belarus topless protest. *BBC*, 20 December 2011. http://www.bbc.co.uk/news/world-europe-16275566.

[81] BBC. UN report accuses Eritrea of plotting to bomb AU summit. *BBC*, 28 July 2011. http://www.bbc.co.uk/news/world-africa-14335752.

[82] BBC. Venezuela honours Simon Bolivar with new coffin. *BBC*, 18 December 2011. http://www.bbc.co.uk/news/world-latin-america-16236105.

[83] BBC. Yemen: security forces fire on protesters in Sanaa. *BBC News*, 17 April 2011. www.bbc.co.uk/news/world-middle-east-13111439.

[84] BBC. Zimbabwe egypt uprising activists in treason trial. *BBC*, 18 July 2011. http://www.bbc.co.uk/news/world-africa-14181176.

[85] BBC. Beijing orders new controls on 'Weibo' microblogs. *BBC*, 16 December 2012. http://www.bbc.co.uk/news/world-asia-china-16212578.

[86] BBC. El Salvador head apologies for 1981 El Mozote massacre. *BBC*, 12 January 2012. http://www.bbc.co.uk/news/world-latin-america-16589757.

[87] BBC. Eritrea president Isaias Afewerki goes on tv to dispel health rumours. *BBC*, 28 April 2012. http://www.bbc.co.uk/news/world-africa-17883320.

[88] BBC. Libya: semi-autonomy declared by leaders in east. *BBC*, 6 March 2012. http://www.bbc.co.uk/news/world-africa-17271431.

[89] BBC. Mali soldiers loot presidential palace after coup. *BBC*, 23 March 2012. http://www.bbc.co.uk/news/world-africa-17474946.

[90] BBC. Syria crisis: Assad issues 'terrorism' vow to Annan. *BBC*, 10 March 2012. http://www.bbc.co.uk/news/world-middle-east-17323093.

[91] BBC. Syria laying landmines along border: Human Rights Watch. *BBC*, 13 March 2012. http://www.bbc.co.uk/news/world-middle-east-17349593.

[92] BBC. Syria pledges 'iron fist' in response to Damascus bombing. *BBC*, 12 January 2012. http://www.bbc.co.uk/news/world-middle-east-16452984.

[93] BBC. Thousands of Hungarians rally to back embattled PM Orban. *BBC*, 21 January 2012. http://www.bbc.co.uk/news/world-europe-16669498.

[94] BBC. Turkmenistan leader wins his country's first car race. *BBC*, 7 April 2012. http://www.bbc.co.uk/news/world-asia-17646368.

[95] Peter Beaumont. Idi Amin Dada, VC, CBE .. RIP. *The Guardian*, 17 August 2003. http://www.guardian.co.uk/world/2003/aug/17/peterbeaumont.theobserver.

[96] Gioconda Belli. Desperate acts of faith. *The Guardian*, 30 October 2006. http://www.guardian.co.uk/commentisfree/2006/oct/30/nicaragua.

[97] Giovanni Maria Bellu. Strage di Piazza Fontana spunta un agente Usa. *La Repubblica*, 11 February 1998.

[98] Cristopher Bennett. *Yugoslavia's Bloody Collapse*, chapter 2: "The South Slavs: Language, Culture, Lands", pages 16–18. New York University Press, January 1997.

[99] Cristopher Bennett. *Yugoslavia's Bloody Collapse*, chapter 6: "Disintegration", pages 93–94. New York University Press, January 1997.

[100] Claire Bigg. Russian election-fraud tactics: something old, something new. *Radio Free Europe/Radio Liberty*, 5 March 2012. http://www.rferl.org/content/russia_election_fraud_tactics_putin/24505805.html.

[101] Dan Bilefsky. Oh Yugoslavia! How they long for your firm embrace. *New York Times*, 30 January 2008. http://www.nytimes.com/2008/01/30/world/europe/30yugo.html?ref=josipbroztito.

[102] Peter Biles. 'assad emails' shed light on Syrian leader's private life. *BBC*, 15 March 2012. http://www.bbc.co.uk/news/world-middle-east-17387754.

[103] Giorgio Boatti. *Caro duce, Lettere di donne italiane a Mussolini, 1922-1944*. Rizzoli, 1989.

[104] Alistair Boddy-Evans. Biography: Antonio Agostinho Neto. Internet. http://africanhistory.about.com/od/angola/p/BioAgostinoNeto.htm Accessed 22 February 2011.

[105] Theresa Bond. The crackdown in Cuba. *Foreign Affairs*, 82(5):118, September/October 2003. http://www.foreignaffairs.com/articles/59191/theresa-bond/the-crackdown-in-cuba.

[106] Ib Bondebjerg and Peter Madsen, editors. *Media, Democracy, and European Culture*, chapter 4: The Berlusconi Case: Mass Media and Politics in Italy, page 111. University of Chicago Press, 2006.

[107] Reporters Without Borders. Enemies of the internet: Syria. Technical report, Reporters Without Borders, 11 March 2011. http://en.rsf.org/syria-syria-11-03-2011,39779.html.

[108] Reporters Without Borders. Nicaragua. *Reporters Without Borders*, 22 February 2011. http://en.rsf.org/nicaragua-newspaper-threatened-and-harassed-22-02-2011,39599.html.

[109] Reporters Without Borders. Syria. *Reporters Without Borders*, 12 March 2012. http://en.rsf.org/syria-syria-12-03-2012,42053.html.

[110] James Bosworth. Guatemala's military to tackle internal threats. *Christian Science Monitor*, 19 January 2012. http://www.csmonitor.com/World/Americas/Latin-America-Monitor/2012/0119/Guatemala-s-military-to-tackle-internal-threats.

[111] R. J. B. Bosworth. *Mussolini*. Arnold/Oxford University Press, 2002.

[112] Mark Bowden. Tales of the tyrant. *Atlantic Monthly*, 289(5;35), May 2002.

[113] Keith Bradsher. China bars prominent writer from overseas travel. *New York Times*, 9 May 2011. http://www.nytimes.com/2011/05/10/world/asia/10writer.html.

[114] Arthur Bright. Iranian government may be behind hack of Dutch security firm. *Christian Science Monitor*, 6 September 2011. http://www.csmonitor.com/World/terrorism-security/2011/0906/Iranian-government-may-be-behind-hack-of-Dutch-security-firm.

[115] Arthur Bright. Syrian Army defector: We were given killing quotas by Assad regime. *Christian Science Monitor*, 16 December 2011. http://www.csmonitor.com/World/terrorism-security/2011/1216/Syrian-Army-defector-We-were-given-killing-quotas-by-Assad-regime.

[116] Benedict Brogan. Assad hits at Blair over war deaths. *The Telegraph*, 1 November 2001. http://www.telegraph.co.uk/news/worldnews/middleeast/syria/1361190/Assad-hits-at-Blair-over-war-deaths.html.

[117] David Brooks. Op-ed: The Ego advantage. *New York Times*, 24 March 2011. http://www.nytimes.com/2011/03/25/opinion/25brooks.html?hp.

[118] Chris Brummitt. Pakistan's civil government and Army in war of words. *Christian Science Monitor*, 11 January 2012. http://www.csmonitor.com/World/Asia-South-Central/2012/0111/Pakistan-s-civilian-government-and-Army-in-war-of-words.

[119] Alan Bullock. *Hitler: a Study in Tyranny*, chapter 5: Revolution after Power, page 141. Harper Perennial, 1991.

[120] Alan Bullock. *Hitler and Stalin: Parallel Lives*, pages 109–120. Vintage, New York, 1993.

[121] Alan Bullock. *Hitler and Stalin: Parallel Lives*, chapter 13, pages 500–501. Vintage, New York, 1993.

[122] Alan Bullock. *Hitler and Stalin: Parallel Lives*, pages 177–179. Vintage, New York, 1993.

[123] James Butty. Malawi government shocked by MCC aid withholding decision. *Voice of America*, 28 July 2011. http://www.voanews.com/english/ news/africa/Butty-Malawi-MCC-Aid-Withholding-React-Ntaba-28july11-126306108.html.

[124] Lucydalia Baca C. FSLN rehuye compromiso con Amnestía. *La Prensa*, 27 July 2011. http://www.laprensa.com.ni/2011/07/27/politica/67995.

[125] Rukmini Callimachi. Tainted African ruler may get UN prize in his name. *Associated Press*, 29 September 2011. http://www.google.com/hostednews/ ap/article/ALeqM5h7ig4hwCTcFVothVjr80SAQ8wz1w?docId=3d579cf61c1a49d4849ca6ce7d0554f0.

[126] Ernesto Cardenal. *La revolución perdida*. Ediciones Centroamericanas Anama, October 2003.

[127] Rory Carrol. Milosevic's son unveils Bambipark. *The Guardian*, 5 July 1999. http://www.guardian.co.uk/world/1999/jul/05/balkans.

[128] Rory Carroll. Government by TV: Chávez sets 8-hour record. *The Guardian*, 24 September 2007. http://www.guardian.co.uk/media/2007/sep/25/ venezuela.television.

[129] Rory Carroll and Andrew Osborn. Exhumations dig up old controversies, perhaps to cover new ones. *The Age*, 23 July 2010. http://www.theage.com.au/world/ exhumations-dig-up-old-controversies-perhaps-to-cover-new-ones-20100722-10mwq.html Accessed 22 February 2011.

[130] Doreen Carvajal and Marlise Simons. Report names Kosovo leader as crime boss. *New York Times*, 15 December 2010. http://www.nytimes.com/2010/12/16/ world/europe/16kosovo.html?ref=hashimthaci.

[131] Dio Cassius. *Roman History*, volume Books 74. 76, 77, chapter 15. Loeb Classical Library, 1924.

[132] Stephen Castle. Question on European welcome of Uzbek leader. *New York Times*, 24 January 2011. http://www.nytimes.com/2011/01/25/world/europe/ 25uzbek.html.

[133] Damien Cave. Desperate Guatemalans embrace an 'Iron Fist'. *New York Times*, 9 September 2011. http://www.nytimes.com/2011/09/10/world/ americas/10guatemala.html.

[134] Carlos F. Chamorro. Daniel Ortega's new kind of coup. *Tico Times*, 15 December 2011. http://www.ticotimes.net/Opinion/Previous-perspectives/Daniel-Ortega-s-New-Kind-of-Coup.

[135] Hugo Chávez. Alo Presidente. Youtube (Internet). http://www.youtube.com/ watch?v=Mwka2ytMjLY&feature=related.

[136] Kristen Chick. Coptic Christians in Egypt battle state's version of deadly protest. *Christian Science Monitor*, 11 October 2011. http://www.csmonitor.com/ World/Middle-East/2011/1011/Coptic-Christians-in-Egypt-battle-state-s-version-of-deadly-protest.

[137] Kristen Chick. Egypt's military rulers ban foreign election observers. *Christian Science Monitor*, 21 July 2011. http://www.csmonitor.com/World/Middle-East/2011/0721/Egypt-s-military-rulers-ban-foreign-election-observers.

[138] Kristen Chick. Why did Egypt's army violently suppress Christian protestors? *Christian Science Monitor*, 10 October 2011. http://www.csmonitor.com/World/Middle-East/2011/1010/Why-did-Egypt-s-Army-violently-suppress-Christian-protesters-VIDEO.

[139] Rex Chikoko. Malawi's Mutharika chooses brother for 2014 presidency. *Africa Review*, http://www.africareview.com/News/Malawi+Mutharika+plans+to+pass+baton+to+brother/-/979180/1212046/-/9nucgz/-/index.html 2011.

[140] C. J. Chivers. Toe tags offer clue to Uzbek's uprising. *New York Times*, 23 May 2005.

[141] Amy Chua. *World on Fire*. Anchor, 2nd edition, 2004.

[142] Julien Clemençot. Biens mal acquis: un empire a demanteler. *Jeune Afrique*, 27 July 2011. http://www.jeuneafrique.com/Articles/Dossier/ARTJAJA2636p074-075.xml0/justice-belhassen-trabelsi-entreprise-sakhr-el-materibiens-mal-acquis-un-empire-a-demanteler.html.

[143] Robert Coalson. Belarussian president says Western leaders 'have no balls'. *Radio Free Europe/Radio Liberty*, 15 December 2011. http://www.rferl.org/content/belarus_president_says_western_leaders_have_no_balls/24422959.html.

[144] Robert Coalson. Taking action against inaction in Belarus. *Radio Free Europe/Radio Liberty*, 2 August 2011. http://www.rferl.org/content/taking_action_against_inaction_in_belarus/24284214.html.

[145] Robert Coalson. As WTO member, will Russia be able to continue using health concerns to block trade? *Radio Free Europe/Radio Liberty*, 18 January 2012. http://www.rferl.org/content/as_wto_member_will_russia_be_able_to_continue_using_health_concerns_to_block_trade/24455826.html.

[146] Ben Cohen. Hungary's anti-semitic double standard. *Radio Free Europe/Radio Liberty*, 25 July 2011. http://www.rferl.org/content/commentary_hungary_anti-semitic_double_standard/24276165.html.

[147] Rachelle G. Cohen. Next Cuban revolution on hold. *Boston Herald*, 12 March 2012. http://bostonherald.com/news/opinion/op_ed/view/20220312next_cuban_revolution_on_hold_democracy_movement_lacking_necessities.

[148] Paul Collier. The dictator's handbook. *Foreign Policy*, April 2009. www.foreignpolicy.com/articles/2009/04/15/the_dictator_s_handbook.

[149] Paul Collier. *Guns, Wars, and Votes: Democracy in Dangerous Places*. Harper Collins, 2009.

[150] Robert Conquest. *Stalin: Breaker of Nations*. Viking, New York, 1991.

[151] Jenny Cuffe. Call to stop Rwandan aid over death threats to exiles. *BBC*, 2 August 2011. http://www.bbc.co.uk/news/uk-14217337.

[152] Andrew Curry. Piecing together the dark legacy of East Germany's Secret Police. *Wired*, 18 January 2008. http://www.wired.com/politics/security/magazine/16-02/ff_stasi?currentPage=all.

[153] DBC. Egypt al-Adly trial: gun evidence shown in court. *BBC*, 4 August 2011. http://www.bbc.co.uk/news/world-middle-east-14407595.

[154] John Dickey. *Cosa Nostra*, chapter 9 "The Origins of the Second Mafia War", page 283. Palgrave Macmillan, New York, 2004.

[155] Dusko Doder and Louise Branson. *Milosevic: Portrait of a Tyrant*, chapter 1: "Cold Narcissus", pages 18–19. The Free Press, New York, 1999.

[156] Dusko Doder and Louise Branson. *Milosevic: Portrait of a Tyrant*, chapter 8: "A Question of Loyalty", page 194. The Free Press, New York, 1999.

[157] Economist. Curious chance. *Economist*, 1 June 2000. http://www.economist.com/node/313855.

[158] Economist. Impeached, but not yet impaled. *Economist*, 16 November 2000. http://www.economist.com/node/423439.

[159] Economist. Latinobarometer poll: An alarm call for Latin America's Democrats. *Economist*, 26 July 2001.

[160] Economist. Luck of the devil. *Economist*, 2 August 2001. http://www.economist.com/node/718820.

[161] Economist. Don't mess with Russia. *Economist*, 13 December 2006. http://www.economist.com/node/8413048.

[162] Economist. Murder most opaque. *Economist*, 13 December 2006. http://www.economist.com/node/8407464.

[163] Economist. Leni Riefenstahl: Hitler's friend. *Economist*, 8 March 2007. http://www.economist.com/node/8810664.

[164] Economist. Daniel Ortega bans his foes. *Economist*, 14 August 2008. http://www.economist.com/node/11920797.

[165] Economist. How to steal an election. *Economist*, 13 November 2008. http://www.economist.com/node/12607338?story_id=12607338.

[166] Economist. Myanmar's sad anniversary. *Economist*, 13 August 2008. http://www.economist.com/node/11916590.

[167] Economist. Dredging up votes. *Economist*, November 11 2010. http://www.economist.com/node/17463483?story_id=17463483.

[168] Economist. Hugo Chavez's Venezuela: a coup against the constitution. *Economist*, December 28 2010. http://www.economist.com/node/17796581.

[169] Economist. Politics of hate. *Economist*, November 18th 2010. http://www.economist.com/node/17525830?story_ID=17525830&fsrc=nlw|wwp|11-18-2010|politics_this_week.

[170] Economist. The show goes on. *Economist*, April 29 2010.

[171] Economist. The Castro cult: Fidel's fanclub. *Economist*, 26 August 2011. http://www.economist.com/blogs/americasview/2011/04/castro_cult.

[172] Economist. Close your window: reporting from Libya. *Economist*, 1 July 2011. http://www.economist.com/blogs/newsbook/2011/07/reporting-libya.

[173] Economist. Demonstrations in Iran: bouncing back? *Economist*, 17 February 2011. http://www.economist.com/node/18187128.

[174] Economist. From potentate to prisoner. *Economist*, 14 April 2011. http://www.economist.com/node/18561015.

[175] Economist. Hungary's other deficit. *Economist*, January 6 2011. http://www.economist.com/node/17851275.

[176] Economist. Kazakhstan's benevolent father: Long live the khan. *Economist*, January 11 2011. http://www.economist.com/node/17858817.

[177] Economist. Mubarak Toppled. *Economist*, 11 February 2011. http://www.economist.com/blogs/newsbook/2011/02/egypts_revolution.

[178] Economist. Nemtsov in prison: frozen out. *Economist*, 6 January 2011. http://www. economist.com/node/17851285?story_id=17851285dic.

[179] Economist. The perils of extreme democracy. *Economist*, 20 April 2011.

[180] Economist. Politics and the Internet: Caught in the net. *Economist*, 6 January 2011. http://www.economist.com/node/17848401?story_id=17848401.

[181] Economist. Russia's Presidency: Guess who! *Economist*, 1 October 2011. http://www.economist.com/node/21530997.

[182] Economist. Sensational: Kazakhstan's thumping election. *Economist*, 7 April 2011. http://www.economist.com/node/18530591.

[183] Economist. Taken to the cleaners: political affray in Malaysia. *Economist*, 14 July 2011. http://www.economist.com/node/18959359.

[184] Economist. How to steal an election. *Economist*, 3 March 2012. http://www. economist.com/node/21548933.

[185] Economist. Myanmar's army and the economy: the road up from Mandalay. *Economist*, 21 April 2012. http://www.economist.com/node/21553091.

[186] Economist. Never again? North Korea's gulag. *Economist*, 21 April 2012. http://www.economist.com/node/21553029.

[187] Economist. Presidential motorcades: you got a fast car. *Economist*, 6 April 2012. http://www.economist.com/blogs/baobab/2012/04/presidential-motorcades.

[188] Economist. Telecoms in Cuba: talk is cheap. *Economist*, 24 January 2012. http://www.economist.com/blogs/americasview/2012/01/telecoms-cuba.

[189] El Economista. Nicaragua estrena línea aérea. *El Economista . Net*, 21 March 2011. http://www.eleconomista.net/empresas/124172-nicaragua-estrena-linea-aerea.html.

[190] Editorial. Editorial: Ethics reform, Albany style. *New York Times*, 6 June 2011. http://www.nytimes.com/2011/06/07/opinion/07tue1.html.

[191] Washington Post Editorial. Hugo Chavez's long silence after surgury in Cuba stirs speculation back home about his health. *Washington Post*, 24 June 2011. http://www.washingtonpost.com/world/americas/hugo-chavezs-long-silence-after-surgery-in-cuba-stirs-speculation-back-home-about-his-health/2011/06/24/AG2yamiH_story.html.

[192] Juliet Eilperin. The gerrymander that ate America. *Slate*, 17 April 2006. http://www.slate.com/id/2140054/.

[193] Gamal Essam El-Din. How Gamal brought the whole Mubarak house down. *Ahram*, 15 April 2011. http://english.ahram.org.eg/NewsContentPrint/1/0/9988/Egypt/0/How-Gamal-brought-the-whole-Mubarak-house-down.aspx.

[194] Steven Emerson. Where have all his spies gone? *New York Times Magazine*, 12 August 1990. http://www.nytimes.com/1990/08/12/magazine/where-have-all-his-spies-gone.html.

[195] Steven Erlanger. Kim Philby, double agent, dies. *New York Times*, 12 May 1988. http://www.nytimes.com/1988/05/12/obituaries/kim-philby-double-agent-dies.html.

[196] Golnaz Esfandiari. Iranian 'Mothers' ask, 'who really endangers national security?'. *Radio Free Europe/Radio Liberty*, 7 January 2012. http://www.rferl.org/content/iran_persian_letters_mothers_of_laleh_park/24443427.html.

[197] Radio Free Europe. Georgia photojournalist admits working for Russia. *Radio Free Europe*, 18 July 2011. http://www.rferl.org/content/georgia_photojournalist_admits_working_for_russia/24269287.html.

[198] Radio Free Europe. Germany to loan Libyan rebels 100 Million Euros. *Radio Free Europe/Radio Liberty*, 24 July 2011. http://www.rferl.org/content/germany_loans_libya_rebels_100_million_euros/24275253.html.

[199] Richard J. Evans. *The Coming of the Third Reich*, chapter 5: 'Creating the Third Reich', pages 349–353. Penguin Press, 2003.

[200] Think Exist. Saparmurat Niyazov quotes. Internet. http://thinkexist.com/quotes/saparmurat_niyazov/.

[201] Factcheck.org. Republican-funded group attacks Kerry's war record. *Factcheck.Org*, 6 August 2004. http://www.factcheck.org/republican-funded_group_attacks_kerrys_war_record.html.

[202] Hassan M. Fatah. Hezbollah leads huge pro-Syrian protest in central Beirut. *New York Times*, 8 March 2005. http://www.nytimes.com/2005/03/08/international/middleeast/08cnd-beirut.html.

[203] Ferloo. Accusation de coup d'etat: la société civile monte au créneau et invite les accusés à porter plainte contre le gouvernement pour laver leur honneur. *Seneweb*, 24 March 2011. http://www.seneweb.com/news/Politique/accusation-de-coup-d-rsquo-etat-la-societe-civile-monte-au-creneau-et-invite-les-accuses-a-porter-plainte-contre-le-gouvernement-pour-laver-leur-honneur_n_42864.html.

[204] Joachim Fest. *Hitler*, volume 5, chapter 2, pages 465–466. Harcourt, 2002.

[205] Filadelfo. Unlikely duo in National Assembly. *Associated Press*, 6 November 2001.

[206] William Fisher. Diplomacy, a fig leaf for inaction. *Oped News*, 2011. http://www.opednews.com/articles/Diplomacy-Fig-Leaf-for-In-by-WILLIAM-FISHER-110+125-194.html.

[207] Gary Forsythe. *A Critical History of Early Rome: From Prehistory to the First Punic War*, chapter 9: Rome's Rise to Dominance, page 309. University of California Press, Berkeley, 2006.

[208] Peter Foster. Kim Jong-il celebrates 69th birthday. *Telegraph*, 16 February 2011. http://www.telegraph.co.uk/news/worldnews/asia/northkorea/8327989/Kim-Jong-il-celebrates-69th-birthday.html.

[209] The Heritage Foundation. Inside Communist Nicaragua: The Miguel Bolanos transcripts. Backgrounder 294, The Heritage Foundation, September 30 1983. http://www.heritage.org/research/reports/1983/09/inside-communist-nicaragua-the-miguel-bolanos-transcripts.

[210] Francisco EnriquezCabistán. El Pacto Soy Yo. *El Nuevo Diario*, 24 January 2000.

[211] William H. Frederick and Robert L. Worden, editors. *Indonesia: A Country Study*, chapter 1: History. GPO for the Library of Congress, 1993. http://countrystudies.us/indonesia/86.htm.

[212] Howard W. French. Mobutu Sese Seko, 66, longtime dictator of Zaire. *New York Times*, 8 September 1997. http://partners.nytimes.com/library/world/090897obit-mobutu.html.

[213] Guy D. Garcia. Liberia: Death of a president. *Time Magazine*, 24 September 1990. http://www.time.com/time/magazine/article/0,9171,971217,00.html.

[214] Zayda Garméndez. Acusan a Pedro Solórzano por supuesta corrupción. *La Jornada*, 1 April 2009 http://www.lajornadanet.com/diario/archivo/2009/abril/1/7.html.

[215] Peter Geyl. *Napolean: For and Against*. Yale University Press, New Haven and London, 1963.

[216] Edward Gibbon. *The Decline and Fall of the Roman Empire*, volume 2. Heritage Press, New York, 1946.

[217] Victor Gilinsky. Nuclear Blackmail: The 1994 U.S.–Democratic People's Republic of Korea Agreed Framework on North Korea's Nuclear Program. Monograph, The Hoover Institute at Stanford University, Stanford University, Palo Alto, California, 1 April 1997.

[218] David Gilmour. *The Pursuit of Italy*, chapter 13: Modern Italy, pages 380–381. Farrar, Straus, and Giroux, New York, 2011.

[219] Paul Ginsborg. *A History of Contemporary Italy: Society and Politics, 1943-1988*, chapter 9: "The Era of Collective Action", pages 333–335. Penguin Books, London, England, 1990.

[220] Michael Goldfarb. Written or unwritten – is there a perfect constitution? *BBC News*, 17 February 2011. http://www.bbc.co.uk/news/world-us-canada-12482351 Accessed 19 February 2011.

[221] Dan Goodin. Tunisia plants country-wide keystroke logger on Facebook. *The Register*, 25 January 2011. http://www.theregister.co.uk/2011/01/25/tunisia_facebook_password_slurping/.

[222] Mikhael Gorbachev. Gorbachev on 1989. *The Nation*, 16 November 2009. http://www.thenation.com/article/gorbachev-1989.

[223] Mikhail Gorbachev. First steps toward a new era (foreward). In *Great Speeches of the 20th Century*. The Guardian, 26 April 2007. http://www.guardian.co.uk/theguardian/2007/apr/26/greatspeeches4.

[224] Peter Green. *Alexander of Macedon, 356-323 B.C.: A Historical Bibliography*, chapter 10: "How Many Miles to Babylon?", pages 482–483. University of California Press, Berkeley, 1991.

[225] Joseph R. Gregory. Hassan II of Morocco dies at 70; a Monarch oriented to the West. *New York Times*, 24 July 1999. http://www.nytimes.com/learning/general/onthisday/bday/0709.html.

[226] Jane Gross. Ferdinand Marcos, ousted leader of Philippines, dies at 72 in exile. *New York Times*, 29 September 1989. http://www.nytimes.com/1989/09/29/obituaries/ferdinand-marcos-ousted-leader-of-philippines-dies-at-72-in-exile.html.

[227] Crisis Group. The Myanmar elections. Asia Briefing 105, The Crisis Group, May 27 2010. http://www.crisisgroup.org/en/regions/asia/south-east-asia/burma-myanmar/B105-the-myanmar-elections.aspx.

[228] Osvaldo Hurtado Gustavo Jalkh et al. Is Ecuador on the brink of a Perfect Dictatorship? *Latin American Advisor*, 25 May 2011. http://www.thedialogue.org/page.cfm?pageID=32&pubID=2667.

[229] Yoel Guzansky. Arab Gulf States and the Iranian Nuclear Challenge. *Global Politician*, 22 February 2011. http://www.globalpolitician.com/26750-iran-arabs-nuclear-weapons.

[230] Sebastian Haffner. *The Meaning of Hitler*. Harvard University Press, 1979.

[231] Hussain Haqqani. *Pakistan: Between Mosque and Military*, chapter 4: "From Islamic Republic to Islamic State", pages 131–139. Carnegie Endowment for International Peace, July 2005.

[232] Blaine Harden. *Africa: Dispatches from a Fragile Continent*. Houghton Mifflin, 1990.

[233] Luke Harding. Anna Politkovskaya trial: the unanswered questions. *The Guardian*, 19 February 2009. http://www.guardian.co.uk/media/2009/feb/19/politkovskaya-trial-background-kremlin.

[234] Bruce Harris. Augusto Pinochet killer file. *More or Less*, February 2001. http://www.moreorless.au.com/killers/pinochet.html.

[235] Bruce Harris. Kim Il Sung and Kim Jong Il killer file. *More or Less*, February 2001. http://www.moreorless.au.com/killers/kim-il-sung.html.

[236] Bruce Harris. Nicolae Ceausescu killer file. *More or Less*, Feb 2001. http://www.moreorless.au.com/killers/ceausescu.html.

[237] Bruce Harris. Suharto killer file. *More or Less*, 26 May 2009. http://www.moreorless.au.com/killers/suharto.html Accessed 1 July 2011.

[238] Bruce Harris. The Duvaliers killer file. *More or Less*, February 2011. http://www.moreorless.au.com/killers/duvalier.html Accessed 30 June 2011.

[239] Bruce Harris. Rafael Trujillo killer file. *More or Less*, 24 June 2011. http://www.moreorless.au.com/killers/trujillo.html Accessed 27 June 2011.

[240] Kieran Healy. The Political Theory of Saif al-Islam Gaddafi. *Crooked Timber*, 22 February 2011. http://crookedtimber.org/2011/02/22/the-political-theory-of-saif-al-islam-gaddafi/.

[241] Tom Hennigan. After the Revolution. *Irish Times*, 7 May 2011. http://www.irishtimes.com/newspaper/magazine/2011/0507/1224295952855.html.

[242] Timothy Heritage and Steve Gutterman. Vladimir Putin mocks Moscow protesters, says they were paid. *Radio Free Europe/Radio Liberty*, 15 December 2011. http://www.csmonitor.com/World/Latest-News-Wires/2011/1215/Vladimir-Putin-mocks-Moscow-protesters-says-they-were-paid.

[243] Javier C. Hernandez. Nicaragua poised to re-elect Ortega. *New York Times*, 6 November 2011. http://www.nytimes.com/2011/11/07/world/americas/president-daniel-ortega-poised-to-win-third-term-in-nicaragua.html.

[244] Christopher Hitchens. To die in Madrid. *Slate Magazine*, 15 March 2004. http://www.slate.com/id/2097138/.

[245] Jim Hoagland. The Post-Putin Russia. *Washington Post*, 17 September 2006. http://www.washingtonpost.com/wp-dyn/content/article/2006/09/15/AR2006091501063.htm.

[246] Gabrielle Ashford Hodges. *Franco: A Concise Biography*, chapter 6-8, pages 149–150,186. Saint Martin's Press, New York, 2000.

[247] Heinrich Hoffmann and Josef Berchtold. *Hitler über Deutschland*. Frz. Eher Nachf, 1932. http://www.calvin.edu/academic/cas/gpa/hitler3.htm.

[248] Freedom House. Worst of the worst 2010: The world's most repressive societies. Technical report, Freedom House, Washington, DC, May 2010.

[249] Osvaldo Hurtado. Democracy's demise in Latin America: Ecuador on brink of a 'perfect dictatorship'. *Christian Science Monitor*, 4 May 2011. http://www.csmonitor.com/Commentary/Opinion/2011/0504/Democracy-s-demise-in-Latin-America-Ecuador-on-brink-of-a-perfect-dictatorship.

[250] The Independent. Defiant Milosevic denounces his arrest. *The Independent*, 2 April 2011. http://www.independent.co.uk/news/world/europe/defiant-milosevic-denounces-his-arrest-753112.html.

[251] Freedom House International. Transfer to military control moves Kazakhstan penal system in wrong direction. Press Release, Internet, 1 August 2011. http://www.freedomhouse.org/template.cfm?page=70&release=1474.

[252] Transparency International. Introduction to political corruption. Technical report, Transparency International, 25 March 2004. http://www.transparency. org/content/download/4459/26786/file/Introduction_to_ political_corruption.pdf.

[253] We Love the Iraqi Information Minister. Internet. http:// welovetheiraqiinformationminister.com Accessed 21 February 2011.

[254] Khadija Ismayilova. Azerbaijani President's daughters tied to rast-rising telecoms firm. Radio Free Europe, 27 June 2011. http://www.rferl.org/content/ azerbaijan_president_aliyev_daughters_tied_to_telecoms_ firm/24248340.html.

[255] Jr. James C. McKinley. Ethiopia tries former rulers in '70s deaths. New York Times, 23 April 1996. http://www.nytimes.com/1996/04/23/world/ethiopia- tries-former-rulers-in-70-s-deaths.html?

[256] Daniel Kimmage Javier Corrales et al. Undermining Democracy: 21st Century Authoritarians. Technical report, Freedom House, Washington, DC, June 2009. http: //freedomhouse.org/uploads/special_report/83.pdf.

[257] Tamba Jean-Matthew. Burkinabe president shuffles army leadership. Africa Review, 2 November 2011. http://www.africareview.com/News/Burkinabe+ President+reshuffles+army+leadership/-/979180/1266282/- /10ivjebz/-/index.html.

[258] Mark John and Richard Valdmanis. Equatorial Guinea leader promotes son in reshuffle. Reuters, 22 May 2012. http://www.reuters.com/article/2012/05/22/ us-guinea-equatorial-idUSBRE84L0ZC20120522.

[259] Scott Johnson. Bring me my Machine Gun. The Daily Beast, 17 April 2009. http://www.thedailybeast.com/newsweek/2009/04/17/ bring-me-my-machine-gun.html.

[260] Tim Johnson. Noriega, 'old and tired,' heads back to Panama cell. Miami Herald, 8 December 2011. http://news.bbc.co.uk/2/hi/109297.stm.

[261] David Jolly. Qaddafi reportedly stashes billions in Western institutions. New York Times, 26 May 2011. http://www.nytimes.com/2011/05/27/world/africa/ 27qaddafi.html.

[262] Arnold H. M. Jones. Sparta, chapter 9: The Discipline, pages 34–39. Barnes and Noble, 1994.

[263] Shashank Joshi. Arab Spring: nature of armies decisive in revolutions. BBC, 28 June 2011. http://www.bbc.co.uk/news/world-middle-east-13941523.

[264] Shashank Joshi. Death of Saif Al-Arab gaddafi may backfire for NATO. BBC, 1 May 2011. http://www.bbc.co.uk/news/world-africa-13252192.

[265] Global Journalist. Pedro Joaquin Chamorro. Internet, July 2000. http: //www.globaljournalist.org/stories/2000/07/01/pedro- joaquin-chamorro-nicaragua/.

[266] James C. McKinley Jr. Nicaraguan councils stir fear of dictatorship. New York Times, 4 May 2008. http://www.nytimes.com/2008/05/04/world/americas/ 04nicaragua.html?_r=1.

[267] Tim Judah. From Balkan tyranny to a lonely cell. The Observer, 12 March 2006. http://www.guardian.co.uk/world/2006/mar/12/warcrimes. theobserver1.

[268] Juvenal. Juvenal, satire 10. Internet. http://www.tertullian.org/fathers/ juvenal_satires_10.htm Accessed 29 September 2011.

[269] Ranya Kadri and Ethan Bronner. King of Jordan dismisses his cabinet. New York Times, 1 February 2011. http://www.nytimes.com/2011/02/02/world/ middleeast/02jordan.html.

[270] Robert D. Kaplan. Was democracy just a moment? *The Atlantic*, December 1997. http://www.theatlantic.com/magazine/archive/1997/12/was-democracy-just-a-moment/6022/.

[271] Lisa Karpova. Sixty percent of Russians nostalgic for the Soviet Union. *Pravda*, 29 December 2009. http://english.pravda.ru/society/22-12-2009/111328-sovietnostalgia-0/.

[272] Joseph Kayira. Amid riots, Malawi's president issues harsh warning to opposition. *Christian Science Monitor*, 22 July 2011. http://www.csmonitor.com/World/Africa/2011/0722/Amid-riots-Malawi-s-president-issues-harsh-warning-to-opposition.

[273] Joseph Kayira. Malawi riots spread as president blames Britain, IMF for economic woes. *Christian Science Monitor*, 21 July 2011. http://www.csmonitor.com/World/Africa/2011/0721/Malawi-riots-spread-as-president-blames-Britain-IMF-for-economic-woes.

[274] Arife Kazimova. Underwhelming response to museums for late Azerbaijani president. *Radio Free Europe/Radio Liberty*, 19 July 2011. http://www.rferl.org/content/no_people_and_not_many_personal_exhibits_at_musums_dedicated_to_azerbaijani_president/24270039.html.

[275] Joshua Keating. Berlusconi's latest assault on free speech. *Foreign Policy Blogs*, February 11 2010. http://blog.foreignpolicy.com/posts/2010/02/11/berlusconis_latest_assault_on_free_speech.

[276] Sanja Kelly and Sarah Cook. Freedom on the net 2011. Technical report, Freedom House, 18 April 2011. http://www.freedomhouse.org/images/File/FotN/FOTN2011.pdf.

[277] Ian Kershaw. *Hitler, 1889 – 1936: Hubris*, chapter XXX, pages 137–143. Penguin Books, 1998.

[278] Ian Kershaw. *Kitler, 1936 –1945: Nemesis*. W.W. Norton & Company, New York, 2000.

[279] Wadi Khaled. In Syria, defectors from dissident army is sign uprising may be entering new phase. *Washington Post*, 25 September 2011. http://www.washingtonpost.com/world/middle-east/in-syria-defectors-form-dissident-army-in-sign-uprising-may-be-entering-new-phase/2011/09/24/gIQAKef8wK_story.html.

[280] Abdulkhadir Khalif. Al Shabaab warns against listening to radio. *Africa Review*, 11 September 2011. http://www.africareview.com/News/Al+Shabaab+warns+against+listening+to+radio+/-/979180/1234338/-/d9ik7nz/-/index.html.

[281] John Kifner. Upheaval in the East; Army executes Ceaucescu and wife for 'genocide' role, Bucharest says. *New York Times*, 26 December 1989. http://www.nytimes.com/1989/12/26/world/upheaval-east-army-executes-ceaucescu-wife-for-genocide-role-bucharest-says.html.

[282] Stephen Kinzer. *Blood of Brothers: Life and War in Nicaragua*. Harvard University David Rockefeller Center for Latin American Studies, Cambridge, Massachusetts, 1st edition, 1991.

[283] David Kirkpatrick. Mubarak's grip on power is shaken. *New York Times*, 1 February 2011. http://www.nytimes.com/2011/02/01/world/middleeast/01egypt.html.

[284] David Kirkpatrick and Kareem Fahim. Mubarak's allies and foes clash in Egypt. *New York Times*, 2 February 2011. http://www.nytimes.com/2011/02/03/world/middleeast/03egypt.html.

[285] David D. Kirkpatrick and Mona El-Naggar. Rich, poor and a rift exposed by unrest. *New York Times*, 31 January 2011. http://www.nytimes.com/2011/01/31/world/africa/31classwar.html.

[286] Laurence Knight. Hungarians despair of political class. *BBC*, 12 January 2012. http://www.bbc.co.uk/news/business-16446682.

[287] Marc Lacey. Sandinista fervor turns sour for former comrades of Nicaragua's president. *New York Times*, 23 November 2008. http://www.nytimes.com/2008/11/24/world/americas/24nicaragua.html.

[288] Laila Lalami. Arab Uprisings: what the February 20 protests tell us about Morocco. *The Nation*, 17 February 2011. http://www.thenation.com/blog/158670/arab-uprisings-what-february-20-protests-tell-us-about-morocco.

[289] Guy Lamb and Dominique Dye. African solutions to an International Problem. *Journal of International Affairs*, 62(2), Spring/Summer 2009.

[290] Sara Miller Lana and Tim Rogers. Nicaragua is latest in Latin America to reject term limits. *Christian Science Monitor*, 2010. http://www.csmonitor.com/World/Americas/2009/1119/p10s01-woam.html.

[291] M. Larmer. "a Little Bit Like a Volcano": The United Progressive Party and Resistance to One-Party Rule in Zambia, 1964-1980. Typescript, 2006. referenced by Robert H. Bates.

[292] Alastair Leithead. Egyptians demand secret police give up torture secrets. *BBC*, 8 March 2011. http://www.bbc.co.uk/news/world-middle-east-12674714.

[293] Charles Levinson. Libya rebels tap army defectors. *Wall Street Journal*, 4 April 2011. http://online.wsj.com/article/SB10001424052748704587004576241170124440808.html.

[294] Neil A. Lewis. Election in Nicaragua; Bush says climate will warm if fair vote is seen. *New York Times*, 26 February 1990. http://www.nytimes.com/1990/02/26/world/election-in-nicaragua-bush-says-climate-will-warm-if-fair-vote-is-seen.html.

[295] Radio Free Europe/Radio Liberty. Armenian opposition leader: 'Serzh, please open the toilets.'. *Radio Free Europe/Radio Liberty*, 5 October 2011. http://www.rferl.org/content/armenia_opposition_to_step_up_protests_after_government_snub_toilets/24349392.html.

[296] Radio Free Europe/Radio Liberty. Chavez questions if U.S. behind cancer in Latin American leaders. *Radio Free Europe/Radio Liberty*, 12 December 2011. http://www.rferl.org/content/chavez_questions_if_us_behind_cancer_in_latin_american_leaders/24437207.html.

[297] Radio Free Europe/Radio Liberty. China executes two Uyghur suspects from weekend's violence. *Radio Free Europe/Radio Liberty*, 2 August 2011. http://www.rferl.org/content/china_executes_two_uyghur_suspects/24284059.html.

[298] Radio Free Europe/Radio Liberty. Georgian court rules against billionaire with political ambitions. *Radio Free Europe/Radio Liberty*, 27 December 2011. http://www.rferl.org/content/georgia_court_rules_against_ivanishvili/24435146.html.

[299] Radio Free Europe/Radio Liberty. Jailed Belarusian activist's fiancee also jailed. *Radio Free Europe/Radio Liberty*, 4 August 2011. http://www.rferl.org/content/jailed_belarus_activists_fiancee_jailed/24286883.html.

[300] Radio Free Europe/Radio Liberty. Jailed Belarusian activit's lawyer not allowed to see him. *Radio Free Europe/Radio Liberty*, 28 July 2011. http://www.rferl.org/content/lawyer_denied_access_to_jailed_belarusian_client/24280179.html.

[301] Radio Free Europe/Radio Liberty. Kazakh blog ban demonstrates complexity of digital free speech. *Radio Free Europe/Radio Liberty*, 25 July 2011. http://www.rferl.org/content/prominent_kazakh_journalist_ website_attacked_blocked/24273734.html.

[302] Radio Free Europe/Radio Liberty. Prominent Kazakh journalist's website attacked, blocked. *Radio Free Europe/Radio Liberty*, 22 July 2011. http://www.rferl.org/content/prominent_kazakh_journalist_ website_attacked_blocked/24273734.html.

[303] Radio Free Europe/Radio Liberty. Authorities shut down Tymoshenko protest site 'for repairs'. *Radio Free Europe/Radio Liberty*, 12 January 2012. http://www.rferl.org/content/authorities_ukraine_shut_ down_tymoshenko_protest_site_for_repairs/24449354.html.

[304] Radio Free Europe/Radio Liberty. Belarusian presidential candidate gets three years in 'closed regime'. *Radio Free Europe/Radio Liberty*, 12 January 2012. http://www.rferl.org/content/belarus_statkevich_closed_ regime_prison/24449782.html.

[305] Radio Free Europe/Radio Liberty. Dozen arrested as Moscow protesters call for new elections. *Radio Free Europe/Radio Liberty*, 27 March 2012. http://www.rferl. org/content/moscow_opposition_rally/24510968.html.

[306] Radio Free Europe/Radio Liberty. Ex-Belarusian presidential candidate 'abducted'. *Radio Free Europe/Radio Liberty*, 19 December 2012. http://www.rferl. org/content/exbelarusian_presidential_candidate_abducted/ 24427204.html.

[307] Radio Free Europe/Radio Liberty. First statue appears of Turkmenistan's (latest) autocratic president. *Radio Free Europe/Radio Liberty*, 8 March 2012. http://www.rferl.org/content/first_statue_appears_ turkmenistan_autocratic_president/24509096.html.

[308] Radio Free Europe/Radio Liberty. A flood of unwanted attention for Georgian president. *Radio Free Europe/Radio Liberty*, 17 May 2012. http://www.rferl.org/ content/saakashvili_milan_shopping-georgia/24584209.html.

[309] Radio Free Europe/Radio Liberty. Iran's supreme leader sets up Internet-control group. *Radio Free Europe/Radio Liberty*, 7 March 2012. http://www.bbc.co.uk/ news/in-pictures-17371468.

[310] Radio Free Europe/Radio Liberty. Jailed Belarus presidential candidate not allowed to see lawyer. *Radio Free Europe/Radio Liberty*, 24 January 2012. http://www.rferl.org/content/jailed_belarus_presidential_ candidate_not_allowed_to_see_lawyer/24422931.html.

[311] Radio Free Europe/Radio Liberty. Kazakh opposition leaders fined for 'unsanctioned gathering'. *Radio Free Europe/Radio Liberty*, 19 January 2012. http://www.rferl.org/content/kazakh_opposition_leaders_ fined_for_unsanctioned_gathering/24457207.html.

[312] Radio Free Europe/Radio Liberty. Parliamentary elections cancelled in restive Kazakh city. *Radio Free Europe/Radio Liberty*, 6 January 2012. http://www.rferl.org/content/parliamentary_elections_ canceled_in_restive_kazakh_city/24443761.html.

[313] Radio Free Europe/Radio Liberty. Turkmen one-party rule may end soon. *Radio Free Europe/Radio Liberty*, 4 April 2012. http://www.rferl.org/content/ turkmen_one_party_rule_may_end_soon/24528529.html.

[314] Radio Free Europe/Radio Liberty. Tymoshenko supporters' tents downed in Eastern Ukraine. *Radio Free Europe/Radio Liberty*, 10 January 2012. http://www.rferl.org/content/tymoshenko_supporters_tents_ dismantled_in_eastern_ukraine/24447796.html.

[315] Radio Free Europe/Radio Liberty. Ukraine's jaile Tymoshenko under 24-hour spotlight. *Radio Free Europe/Radio Liberty*, 3 January 2012. http://www.rferl.org/content/ukraines_jailed_tymoshenko_under_24-hour_sporlight/24441399.html.

[316] Mark Lowen. Libya's ex-rebels reluctant to down arms. *BBC*, 7 January 2012. http://www.bbc.co.uk/news/world-africa-16443441.

[317] Annie Lowrey. Protesting on an empty stomach: how the Egyptian economy is fueling unrest in Egypt. *Slate*, 31 January 2011. http://www.slate.com/id/2283217/.

[318] Adrian Lyttelton. *The seizure of power: fascism in Italy*, chapter 10: "The Matteotti Crisis", pages 199–200. Routledge, New York, 2009.

[319] Neil MacFarquhar. Yemeni leader badly burned, raising doubts about his rule. *New York Times*, 7 June 2011. http://www.nytimes.com/2011/06/08/world/middleeast/08saleh.html?_r=1&hp.

[320] Rebecca Mackinnon. The Shawshank prevention. *Foreign Policy*, 2 May 2012. http://www.foreignpolicy.com/articles/2012/05/02shawshank_prevention.

[321] East African Magazine. The African presidents index. *The East African Magazine*, 27 December 2010.

[322] Life Magazine. The world's worst dictators. *Life Magazine*, Accessed 2010. http://www.life.com/image/first/in-gallery/22899/the-worlds-worst-dictators.

[323] Tom Maliti. Kenya tries to delay ICC post-vote violence cases. *Washington Post*, 19 January 2011. http://www.washingtonpost.com/wp-dyn/content/article/2011/01/19/AR2011011902552.html.

[324] Andrew Malone. Mugabe's darkest secret: an £800bn blood diamond mine he's running with China's Red Army. *The Daily Mail*, 18 September 2010.

[325] Robert Marquand. Hungary turns away from democracy. *Christian Science Monitor*, 10 January 2012. http://www.csmonitor.com/World/Europe/2012/0110/Hungary-turns-away-from-democracy.

[326] Mark Mazzetti and Emily B. Hager. Secret desert force set up by Blackwater's founder. *New York Times*, 14 May 2011. http://www.nytimes.com/2011/05/15/world/middleeast/15prince.html.

[327] Shelley A. McConnell. *Nicaragua Without Illusions*, chapter Institutional Development. Scholarly Resources, Inc., Wilmington, Delaware, 1997.

[328] Robert McCrum. Watching the dictators: Interview with Mario Vargas Llosa. *The Guardian*, 7 April 2002. http://www.guardian.co.uk/books/2002/apr/07/fiction.features.

[329] Damien McElroy and Barney Henderson. Britain expels all staff from Libyan embassy in London. *The Telegraph*, 27 July 2011. http://www.telegraph.co.uk/news/worldnews/africaandindianocean/libya/8665101/Britain-expels-all-staff-from-Libyan-embassy-in-London.html.

[330] Patrick McGreevy. New redistricting panel takes aim at bizarre political boundaries. *Los Angeles Times*, 19 December 2010. http://articles.latimes.com/2010/dec/19/local/la-me-gerrymander-20101220 Accessed 20 February 2011.

[331] Jenna McGregor. Hosni Mubarak, the caged leader. *Washington Post*, 3 August 2011. http://www.washingtonpost.com/blogs/post-leadership/post/hosni-mubarak-the-caged-leader/2011/04/01/gIQADm24rI_blog.html.

[332] Susan Meiselas. *Nicaragua, June 1978 – July 1979*. 1st Aperture, 547 W 27th St., NY, NY 10001, 2008.

[333] Thomas P. Melady and Margaret Melady. *Idi Amin Dada: Hitler in Africa*, pages 18–19. Sheed, Andrews, and McMeel, 2: "The Brutal Tyrant Emerges" 1977.

[334] Thomas P. Melady and Margaret Melady. *Idi Amin Dada: Hitler in Africa*, pages 37–39. Sheed, Andrews, and McMeel, 3: "The Brutal Tyrant in Action 1977.

[335] Thomas P. Melady and Margaret Melady. *Idi Amin Dada: Hitler in Africa*, pages 37–39. Sheed, Andrews, and McMeel, 5: "The Expulsion of the Asians" 1977.

[336] Tim Merrill. *Nicaragua: A Country Study*, chapter "The Somoza Era, 1936-1974". GPO for the Library of Congress, 1993. http://countrystudies.us/nicaragua/11.htm.

[337] James A.R. Miles. *The Legacy of Tiananmen: China in Disarray*, chapter 2, pages 22–23. University of Michigan Press, 1997.

[338] Chris Mitchell. Ortega defends Qaddafi abroad, blocks democratic activists at home. *Prime Policy Group*, 11 April 2011. http://www.prime-policy.com/practitioners-corner/ortega-defends-qaddafi-abroad-blocks-democratic-activists-home.

[339] Charles Mkula. Bingu Wa Mutharika names his new cabinet and appoints his wife as minister in Malawi. *Newstime Africa*, 7 September 2011. http://www.newstimeafrica.com/archives/22435.

[340] Le Monde. La légende vestimentaire de Mouammar Kadhafi. *Le Monde.Fr*, 25 February 2011. http://www.lemonde.fr/week-end/infographe/2011/02/25/la-legende-vestimentaire-de-mouammar-kadhafi_1485021_1477893.html.

[341] Daily Monitor. Key Uganda ministers fingered over oil kickbacks claims. *Africa Review*, 11 October 2011. http://www.africareview.com/News/Key+Uganda+ministers+fingered+over+oil+kickbacks+/-/979180/1253510/-/dqmo7m/-/index.html.

[342] Roger Moorehouse. Germania: Hitler's Dream Capital. *History Today*, 62(3), March 2012. http://www.historytoday.com/roger-moorhouse/germania-hitlers-dream-capital.

[343] Fred Morris. Nicaragua: the other side. *Council on Hemispheric Affairs*, 22 December 2011. http://www.coha.org/nicaragua-the-other-side/.

[344] Kenneth E. Morris. *Unfinished Revolution: Daniel Ortega and Nicaragua's Struggle for Liberation*, chapter 5: Governing from Below, page 197. Lawrence Hill Books, 2011.

[345] Annie Mosher. Central Asia – Saparmurat Niyazov (Turkmenbashi). Internet. http://fccorn.people.wm.edu/russiasperiphery/d6cfddade34044b4b10b5e1fb707cd57.html Accessed 29 July 2011.

[346] Mark Moyer. The kings we crown. *New York Times*, 1 May 2011. http://www.nytimes.com/2011/05/02/opinion/02Moyar.html?hpw.

[347] Dan Murphy. With US gone, Iraq's Maliki is setting the board for a power grab. *Christian Science Monitor*, 21 December 2011. http://www.csmonitor.com/World/Backchannels/2011/1221/With-US-gone-Iraq-s-Maliki-is-setting-the-board-for-a-power-grab.

[348] Dan Murphy. US democracy NGOs in Egypt still shuttered. *Christian Science Monitor*, 6 January 2012. http://www.csmonitor.com/World/Backchannels/2012/0106/US-democracy-NGOs-in-Egypt-still-shuttered.

[349] Farangis Najibullah. My personality cult is better than yours. *Radio Free Europe/Radio Liberty*, 13 February 2012. http://www.rferl.org/content/turkmenistan_berdymukhammedov_cult_of_personality/24482468.html.

[350] United Nations. Final electoral list immediate priority for Côte d'Ivoire, says UN envoy. *UN News Centre*, June 10 2010. http://www.un.org/apps/news/story.asp?NewsID=34983&Cr=&Cr1=.

[351] Anna Nemtsova. Life under Europe's last dictator. *Foreign Policy*, December 16 2010. http://www.foreignpolicy.com/articles/2010/12/16/life_under_europes_last_dictator.

[352] BBC News. Castro: Profile of the great survivor. *BBC*, 19 February 2008. http://news.bbc.co.uk/go/pr/fr/-/2/hi/americas/244974.stm.

[353] BBC News. I shot the cruellest dictator in the Americas. *BBC*, 27 May 2011. http://www.bbc.co.uk/news/world-latin-america-13560512.

[354] BBC News. Iran police fire tear gas at opposition rally in Tehran. *BBC News*, 14 February 2011. http://www.bbc.co.uk/news/world-middle-east-12447225.

[355] Marcus Noland. *The Political Economy of North Korea*, chapter 2, page 17. Korea Economic Institute, 2004.

[356] Adam Nossiter. African unity faces a test in Ivory Coast. *New York Times*, 29 December 2010.

[357] Adam Nossiter. Ensconced in the presidency, with no budging in Ivory Coast. *New York Times*, December 2010. http://www.nytimes.com/2010/12/26/world/africa/26ivory.html?ref=laurentgbagbo.

[358] Adam Nossiter. US engages with an iron leader in Equatorial Guinea. *New York Times*, 30 May 2011. http://www.nytimes.com/2011/05/31/world/africa/31guinea.html?partner=rss&emc=rss.

[359] Kitsepile Nyathi. MP arrested for saying Mugabe is gay. *Africa Review*, 20 December 2011. http://www.africareview.com/News/MP+arrested+for+saying+Mugabe+is+gay/-/979180/1292750/-/919x51z/-/index.html.

[360] Kitsepile Nyathi. UN appeals for $500m aid for Zimbabwe. *Africa Review*, 3 August 2011. http://www.africareview.com/News/-/979180/1212670/-/h82d9ez/-/index.html.

[361] Norimitsu Onishi. Glimpse of new president as Joseph Kabila takes oath in Congo. *New York Times*, 27 January 2001. http://www.nytimes.com/2001/01/27/world/glimpse-of-new-president-as-joseph-kabila-takes-oath-in-congo.html.

[362] Nation Online. Toward salvaging lost donor trust. *Nation Online*, 16 February 2011. http://www.nationmw.net/index.php?option=com_content&view=article&id=1449+4:towards-salvaging-lost-donor-trust&catid=32:feature&Itemid=27 Accessed 22 February 2011.

[363] Yuriy Onyshkiv. Closing of EX.eu sparks intense cyberwarfare. *Kyiv Post*, 2 February 2012. http://www.kyivpost.com/news/business/bus_general/detail/121754/.

[364] Davin O'Regan. Cocaine and Instability in Africa: Lessons from Latin America and the Caribbean. Africa Security Brief 5, Africa Center for Strategic Studies, National Defense University, Fort Lesley McNair, Washington DC, www.africacenter.org, July 2010.

[365] The Organizer. Five surprising similarities between Berlusconi and Mussolini. *NewsFlavor*, April 16 2008. http://newsflavor.com/politics/world-politics/five-surprising-similarities-between-berlusconi-and-mussolini/.

[366] George Orwell. *1984*. Signet Classics, 1950.

[367] Arkady Ostrovsky. Vladimir II. *Economist*, 17 November 2011. http://www.economist.com/node/21537032.

[368] John Otis. Another Somoza eyes the presidency in Nicaragua. *Global Post*, 3 January 2012. http://www.globalpost.com/dispatch/news/regions/americas/111221/another-somoza-eyes-the-presidency-nicaragua.

[369] Eric Pace. Autocrat with a regal manner, Marcos ruled for 2 decades. *New York Times*, 29 September 1989. http://www.nytimes.com/1989/09/29/obituaries/autocrat-with-a-regal-manner-marcos-ruled-for-2-decades.html.

[370] Pa.Di. Hugo Chavez liberates Simon Bolivar from the grave. *Panama Digest*, 17 July 2010. http://www.thepanamadigest.com/2010/07/hugo-chavez-liberates-simon-bolivar-from-grave/.

[371] Jennifer Pak. Anwar Ibrahim acquitted of sodomy charges in Malaysia: Analysis. *BBC*, 12 January 2012. http://www.bbc.co.uk/news/world-asia-16463989.

[372] Naky Soto Parra. Ante las amenazas de un delincuente informático. *El Zaperoco de Naky*, 7 January 2012. http://zaperoqueando.blogspot.com/2012/01/ante-las-amenazas-de-un-delincuente.html.

[373] William JF Paul. Whatever floats your boat: African dictator's son fancies a luxury yacht. *Faster*, 1 March 2011. http://thefastertimes.com/news/2011/03/01/whatever-floats-your-boat-african-dictators-son-fancies-a-luxury-yacht/.

[374] Eugenia Peretz. La dolce Viagra. *Vanity Fair*, July 2011. http://www.vanityfair.com/politics/features/2011/07/silvio-berlusconi-201107.

[375] Scott Peterson. Assassination plot? why Iran and Saudi Arabia are such bitter rivals. *Christian Science Monitor*, 11 October 2011. http://www.csmonitor.com/World/Middle-East/2011/1011/Assassination-plot-Why-Iran-and-Saudi-Arabia-are-such-bitter-rivals.

[376] John-Peter Pham. *Liberia: Portrait of a Failed State*. Reed Press, Park Avenue South, New York, New York, 2004.

[377] Gloria Picón et al. Rivas se saca justificación de la manga. *La Prensa*, 26 July 2011. http://www.laprensa.com.ni/2011/07/26/politica/67896.

[378] Henry Porter and Annabel Davidson. Colonel Qaddafi – a life in fashion. *Vanity Fair*, 12 August 2009. http://www.vanityfair.com/politics/features/2009/08/qaddafi-slideshow200908.

[379] Elisabetta Povoledo. A dead dictator who draws tens of thousands in Italy. *New York Times*, 2 November 2011. http://www.nytimes.com/2011/11/03/world/europe/tourists-still-drawn-to-tomb-of-mussolini-il-duce-in-italy.html.

[380] La Prensa. La encuesta y la oposición. *La Prensa*, 27 July 2011. http://www.laprensa.com.ni/2011/07/27/opinion/68003.

[381] Associated Press. Chronology of Milosevic's career. *Boston.com*, 12 March 2006. http://articles.boston.com/2006-03-12/news/29247308_1_milosevic-allies-pozarevac-in-central-serbia-broad-interim-autonomy.

[382] Associated Press. Kosovo: Premier denies organ dealing. *New York Times*, 16 December 2010. http://www.nytimes.com/2010/12/17/world/europe/17briefs-Kosovo.html?ref=hashimthaci.

[383] Associated Press. True love, Berlusconi style: former Italian premier releases new album. *The Guardian*, 22 November 2011. http://www.guardian.co.uk/world/2011/nov/22/silvio-berlusconi-love-songs-cd.

[384] Agence France Presse. Nostalgia for Communism on the rise. *Sydney Morning Herald*, 4 November 2009. http://www.smh.com.au/world/nostalgia-for-communism-on-rise-20091103-hv9t.html.

[385] Arch Puddington et al. Freedom of association under threat: the new authoritarians' offensive against civil society. Special Report 74, Freedom House, Washington, DC, 13 November 2008. http://www.freedomhouse.org/template.cfm?page=383&report=74.

[386] Sudarsan Raghavan. Arab leaders use varying tactics to try to calm anger in the streets. *Washington Post*, 21 February 2011.

[387] Sudarsan Raghavan. Saleh says he won't step down until rivals are out. *Washington Post*, 29 September 2011. http://www.washingtonpost.com/world/middle-east/saleh-says-he-wont-step-down-until-rivals-are-out/2011/09/29/gIQAPu9u7K_story.html.

[388] Sarah Rainsford. Fate of Franco's Valley of Fallen reopens spain's wounds. *BBC*, 18 July 2011. http://www.bbc.co.uk/news/world-europe-14189534.

[389] B. Raman. Pakistani Madrasas: Questions & answers. Paper 1487, South Asia Analysis Group, 5 August 2005. http://www.southasiaanalysis.org/papers15/paper1487.html.

[390] Adam Raney. Venezuelans split over Bolivar monument. *Al Jazeera*, 14 May 2012. http://www.aljazeera.com/video/americas/2012/05/20125145448438999.html.

[391] Marcus J. Ranum. Anarchy. Internet, Accessed 4 May 2011. http://www.ranum.com.

[392] Ben Rawlence. Eritrea: slender land, giant prison. *Human Rights Watch*, May 8 2009. http://www.hrw.org/en/news/2009/05/06/eritrea-slender-land-giant-prison.

[393] Rivonala Razafison. Toppled Malagasy president forced to return to exile. *Africa Review*, 23 January 2012. http://www.africareview.com/News/Toppled+Malagasy+President+forced+to+return+to+exile/-/979180/1311486/-/.

[394] Monte Reel and J.Y. Smith. A Chilean dictator's dark legacy. *Washington Post*, 11 September 2006. http://www.washingtonpost.com/wp-dyn/content/article/2006/12/10/AR2006121000302.html.

[395] Reuters. Nicaragua asks U.S. for war reparations in aid row. Internet, December 2 2008. http://www.reuters.com/article/idUSTRE4B115920081202.

[396] Reuters. Ugandan vote boss says won't resign despite pressure. *Reuters*, 10 June 2010. www.foreignpolicy.com/articles/2010/06/21/postcards_from_hell.

[397] Reuters. Burkina Faso: President appoints himself as Defense Minister. *New York Times*, 23 April 2011. http://www.nytimes.com/2011/04/23/world/africa/23briefs-Burkinafaso.html.

[398] Reuters. Malian ex-minister indicted over misuse of aid. *Reuters*, 3 June 2011. http://af.reuters.com/article/maliNews/idAFLDE7520V420110603.

[399] Reuters. Opposition seeks to block Zambia's Banda from vote. *Reuters Africa*, 4 August 2011. http://af.reuters.com/article/zambiaNews/idAFL6E7J40MH20110804.

[400] Africa Review. Zimbabwe land reform cost $12bn: farmers. *Africa Review*, 4 August 2011. http://www.africareview.com/News/Zimbabwe+land+reform+cost++12bn/-/979180/1213308/-/1pq7rf/-/index.html.

[401] RFE/RL. Belarusian protesters detained after latest weekly protest. *Radio Free Europe/Radio Liberty*, 21 July 2011. http://www.rferl.org/content/belarus_protesters_detained/24271799.html.

[402] RFE/RL. Belarusian State Radio reportedly bans politically sensitive song. *Radio Free Europe/Radio Liberty*, 19 July 2011.

[403] RFE/RL. Former Ukrainian Prime Minister Tymoshenko arrested. *Radio Free Europe/Radio Liberty*, 5 August 2011. http://www.rferl.org/content/ukraine_tymoshenko_detention_arrest_court_trial_kyiv/24288010.html.

[404] RFE/RL. Iranian film actress in custody. *Radio Free Europe/Radio Liberty*, 21 July 2011. http://www.rferl.org/content/iran_film_actress_in_custody/24272987.html.

[405] RFE/RL. Putin backs unification of Russia with Belarus. *Radio Free Europe/Radio Liberty*, 4 August 2011. http://www.rferl.org/content/russia_putin_supports_unification_with_belarus/24283808.html.

[406] Jeffrey T. Richelson and Michael L. Evans. Tiananmen Square 1989, the Declassified History. National Security Archive Electronic Briefing Book 12, George Washington University, 1 June 1999. http://www.gwu.edu/~nsarchiv/NSAEBB/NSAEBB16/documents/#d12.

[407] Chris Rickleton. Tajikistan: where size matters. *Global Voices*, 11 April 2012. http://globalvoicesonline.org/2012/04/11/tajikistan-where-size-matters/.

[408] David Rogers. Putin threatens gas crisis as Faymann visits Moscow. *Austrian Times*, 11 November 2009. http://www.austriantimes.at/news/Business/2009-11-11/18002/Putin_threatens_gas_crisis_as_Faymann_visits_Moscow.

[409] Tim Rogers. Have yourself a Sandinista Christmas .... *Time Magazine*, 21 December 2009. http://www.time.com/time/world/article/0,8599,1948835,00.html#ixzz0aKyWZWRu.

[410] Tim Rogers. Could Honduras crisis prompt a power grab in Nicaragua? *Christian Science Monitor*, February 2010. http://www.csmonitor.com/World/Americas/2010/0209/Could-Honduras-crisis-prompt-a-power-grab-in-Nicaragua.

[411] Tim Rogers. Mystery shrouds shooting death of Ortega enemy 'Comandante Jahob' in Nicaragua. *Christian Science Monitor*, 15 February 2011. http://www.csmonitor.com/World/Global-News/2011/0215/Mystery-shrouds-shooting-death-of-Ortega-enemy-Comandante-Jahob-in-Nicaragua.

[412] Tim Rogers. Nicaragua to vote on bills tightening Daniel Ortega's grip on security, media. *Christian Science Monitor*, 13 December 2011. http://www.csmonitor.com/layout/set/print/content/view/print/349407.

[413] Tim Rogers. Venezuela's Chavez bankrolled Nicaragua with 1.6 billion since 2007. *Christian Science Monitor*, 7 April 2011. http://www.csmonitor.com/World/Americas/2011/0407/Venezuela-s-Chavez-bankrolled-Nicaragua-with-1.6-billion-since-2007.

[414] Simon Romero. Venezuela asked Colombian rebels to kill opposition figures, analysis shows. *New York Times*, 10 May 2011. http://www.nytimes.com/2011/05/10/world/americas/10venezuela.html.

[415] Ron Rosenbaum. *Explaining Hitler*, chapter 9, pages 166–167. Random House, 1998.

[416] Will Ross. Would Uganda's Museveni recognise his former self? *BBC*, 7 May 2011. http://news.bbc.co.uk/2/hi/programmes/from_our_own_correspondent/9477930.stm.

[417] RT. Vladimir putin demuestra sus habilidades para el hockey en un partido amistoso. *RT*, 7 May 2012. http://www.youtube.com/watch?v=ilXg_DtnLyo.

[418] Romina Ruiz-Goiriena. Efrain Rios Montt, Guatemala's ex-dictator, gets second genocide charge. *Huffington Post*, 21 May 2012. http://www.huffingtonpost.com/2012/05/22/efrain-rios-montt-genocide_n_1535216.html.

[419] Julian Ryall. 30 North Korean officials involved in South talks die in 'traffic accidents'. *Telegraph*, 25 May 2012. http://www.telegraph.co.uk/news/worldnews/asia/northkorea/9289608/30-North-Korean-officials-involved-in-South-talks-die-in-traffic-accidents.html.

[420] Muhammad Salih. America's shady ally against terror (op-ed). *New York Times*, 11 March 2002. http://www.nytimes.com/2002/03/11/opinion/america-s-shady-ally-against-terror.html.

[421] Isabel Sanchez. Cuba's neighborhood watches: 50 years of eyes, ears. *AFP*, 27 September 2010. http://www.google.com/hostednews/afp/article/ALeqM5gq3GU2QzFyRWT84_YNvI3mgOy7tg?docId=CNG.cd0ab416a2c7901c0abb23f392c5057d.ad1.

[422] David E. Sanger. Kim Il Sung dead at 82; led North Korea 5 decades; was near talks with South. *New York Times*, 9 July 1994. http://www.nytimes.com/1994/07/09/world/kim-il-sung-dead-at-age-82-led-north-korea-5-decades-was-near-talks-with-south.html.

[423] Mark Santora. On the gallows, curses for U.S. and 'traitors'. *New York Times*, 31 December 2006. www.nytimes.com/2006/12/31/world/middleeast/31gallows.html.

[424] Diana Jean Schemo. Stoessner, Paraguay's enduring dictator, dies. *New York Times*, 16 August 2006. http://www.nytimes.com/2006/08/16/world/americas/16cnd-stroessner.html.

[425] Steve Scherer. Berlusconi says not a 'dictator;' papers haven't been shut down. *Bloomberg*, September 8 2009. http://www.bloomberg.com/apps/news?pid=newsarchive&sid=aPP4ea3Vo5j0.

[426] Blake Schmidt. Ortega firms up family ties to Sandino for Nicaragua vote. *New York Times*, 16 February 2011. http://www.nytimes.com/2011/02/16/world/americas/16nicaragua.html.

[427] Barbet Schroeder. General Idi Amin Dada. Film, 1974. 1 hr, 30 mins.

[428] Michael Schwirtz. Charges for opposition protest in Georgia. *New York Times*, 30 May 2011. http://www.nytimes.com/2011/06/07/opinion/07tue1.html.

[429] H. H. Scullard. *A History of the Roman World: 133 B.C. to A.D. 68*, chapter 4, "The Rise and Fall of Sulla", page 83. Methuen, 5th edition, 1982.

[430] H.H. Scullard. *A History of the Roman World: 75 to 146 BC.*, chapter XXXXX, pages 208–210, 219–224. Routledge, 4th edition, 1980.

[431] Michael S. Serrill. Panama Noriega's money machine. *Time Magazine*, 24 June 2001. http://www.time.com/time/magazine/article/0,9171,1101880222-148712,00.html.

[432] Haaretz Service. Ahmadinejad at Holocaust conference: Israel will 'soon be wiped out.'. *Haaretz Service and Agencies*, December 2006. http://www.haaretz.com/news/ahmadinejad-at-holocaust-conference-israel-will-soon-be-wiped-out-1.206977.

[433] Taimoor Shah and Jack Healy. Taliban blamed in death of Afghan officer's 8 year old son. *New York Times*, 25 July 2011. http://www.nytimes.com/2011/07/25/world/asia/25afghan.html.

[434] Scott Shane. Spotlight again falls on web tools and change. *Washington Post*, 29 January 2011. http://www.nytimes.com/2011/01/30/weekinreview/30shane.html.

[435] Gene Sharp. *From Dictatorship to Democracy*. Albert Einstein Institution, P.O. Box 455, East Boston, MA 02128, www.aeinstein.org, 4th edition, May 2010. http://www.aeinstein.org/organizations/org/FDTD.pdf.

[436] Tracey Shelton. Gaddafi sodomized: video shows abuse frame by frame. *Global Post*, 24 October 2011. http://www.globalpost.com/dispatch/news/regions/middle-east/111024/gaddafi-sodomized-video-gaddafi-sodomy.

[437] Mary Beth Sheridan. Autocratic regimes fight web-savvy opponents with their own tools. *Washington Post*, 23 May 2011. http://www.washingtonpost.com/world/autocratic-regimes-fight-web-savvy-opponents-with-their-own-tools/2011/04/19/AFTfEN9G_story.html.

[438] David H. Shinn. The United States and China Court the Continent. *Journal of International Affairs*, 62(2), Spring/Summer 2009.

[439] ShortList. Hilary Swank wishes happy birthday to a war criminal. *Shortlist.com*, 12 October 2011. http://www.shortlist.com/home/hilary-swank-wishes-happy-birthday-to-a-war-criminal Accessed 14 December 2011.

[440] Laura Silber. Milosevic family values. *The New Republic*, 30 August 1999. http://www.tnr.com/article/politics/milosevic-family-values.

[441] Ken Silverstein. Le monde selon Obiang fils. *PressAfrik*, 1 May 2011. http://www.pressafrik.com/Le-monde-selon-Obiang-fils_a56644.html.

[442] Marlise Simons and Alison Smale. Slobodan Milosevic, 64, former Yugoslav leader accused of war crimes, dies. *New York Times*, 12 March 2006. http://www.nytimes.com/2006/03/12/international/europe/12milosevic.html.

[443] Michael Slackman. Choice of Suleiman likely to please the military, not the crowds. *New York Times*, 30 Janauary 2011. http://www.nytimes.com/2011/01/30/world/middleeast/30suleiman.html.

[444] Roger M. Smith. *Southeast Asia: documents of political development and change*. Cornell University Press, 1974.

[445] Max Smolaks. Syrian government pushing malware to activists via Skype. *TechWeek Europ*, 4 May 2012. http://www.techweekeurope.co.uk/news/syrian-government-malware-skype-76480.

[446] Aleksandr I. Solzhenitsyn. *The Gulag Archipelago*. Harper and Row, 1973.

[447] Bright Sonani. Malawi tells donors off. *The Nation*, 10 February 2011.

[448] Der Spiegel. Interview with Andrei Illarionov. 'A Climate of Fear'. *Der Spiegel*, 23 April 2007. http://www.spiegel.de/international/world/0,1518,478817,00.html.

[449] Alexander Stille. *The Sack of Rome*, chapter 1: "The Miracle Worker", page 22. Penguin Press, New York, 2006.

[450] Rachel L. Swarns and Norimitsu Onishi. Africa creeps along path to democracy. *New York Times*, 2 June 2002. http://www.nytimes.com/2002/06/02/world/africa-creeps-along-path-to-democracy.html.

[451] Julia E. Sweig. Fidel's final victory. *Foreign Affairs*, January/February 2007. http://www.foreignaffairs.com/articles/62269/julia-e-sweig/fidels-final-victory.

[452] Ronald Syme. *The Roman Revolution*. Oxford University Press, New York, 1939.

[453] Tacitus. *Tacitus – The Annals*. Random House, 1942.

[454] Reports claim that Pakistan is trying to ban encryption under telco law. Internet, 29 July
       2011. http://www.techdirt.com/articles/20110729/03142715310/
       reports-claim-that-pakistan-is-trying-to-ban-encryption-
       under-telco-law.shtml.

[455] Telegraph. Pol Pot. Telegraph, 17 April 1998. http://www.telegraph.co.uk/
       news/obituaries/politics-obituaries/5131454/Pol-Pot.html.

[456] Telegraph. Swaziland minister caught hiding in the queen's bed. Telegraph, 24
       September 2010.   http://www.telegraph.co.uk/news/worldnews/
       africaandindianocean/swaziland/8021962/Swaziland-minister-
       caught-hiding-in-the-queens-bed.html.

[457] Telegraph. North Korea: Kim Jong-Il and his 19 private train stations. The Telegraph,
       3 October 2011. http://www.telegraph.co.uk/news/worldnews/asia/
       northkorea/6530134/North-Korea-Kim-Jong-il-and-his-19-
       private-train-stations.html.

[458] The Telegraph. General Manuel Noriega: a profile. The Telegraph, 27 April 2010.
       http://www.telegraph.co.uk/news/worldnews/northamerica/
       usa/7637790/General-Manuel-Noriega-a-profile.html.

[459] The Telegraph.   A deal struck with tyranny.   The Telegraph, 21 Febru-
       ary 2011. http://www.telegraph.co.uk/comment/8337433/A-deal-
       struck-with-tyranny.html.

[460] Raphael Tenthani. Mutharika: donors 'can pack up and go', DPP cadets must protect
       regime. Maravi Post, 4 March 2012. http://www.maravipost.com/malawi-
       national-news/malawi-political-news/587-mutharika-donors-
       %E2%80%98can-pack-up-go%E2%80%99,-dpp-cadets-must-
       protect-regime.html.

[461] Tom Teoghegan. What happens to deposed leaders? BBC News Magazine, 14 April
       2011. http://www.bbc.co.uk/news/magazine-13052996.

[462] Ian D. Thatcher, editor. Late Imperial Russia: problems and prospects, chapter 4: The
       Okrana: security policing in late imperial Russia, pages 45–49. Manchester University
       Press, 2005.

[463] Paul Theroux. Ghost Train to the Eastern Star. McClelland and Stewart, September
       2008.

[464] Alex Thurston. Niger's new leader faced coup attempt for pursuing corruption investi-
       gation. Christian Science Monitor, 27 July 2011. http://www.csmonitor.com/
       World/Africa/Africa-Monitor/2011/0727/Niger-s-new-leader-
       faced-coup-attempt-for-pursuing-corruption-investigation.

[465] New York Times. 1,320,748 Haitians voted for Duvalier. New York Times, page 8, 10
       May 1961.

[466] New York Times.   Spain's dictator.   New York Times, 23 November
       1966.   http://select.nytimes.com/gst/abstract.html?res=
       F3091EFA3B54117B93C1AB178AD95F428685F9.

[467] New York Times. Mobutu's Xanadu. New York Times Magazine, 26 September 1999.
       http://www.nytimes.com/1999/09/26/magazine/mobutu-s-xanadu.html.

[468] New York Times.   Pol Pot.   New York Times, 17 February 2009.   http:
       //topics.nytimes.com/top/reference/timestopics/people/p/
       pol_pot/index.html.

[469] Liberty Tree.ca. Benito Mussolini quotes/quotations. Liberty Tree, accessed 2010.
       http://quotes.liberty-tree.ca/quotes_by/benito+mussolini.

[470] Liberty Tree.ca. Despotism quotes/quotations. Liberty Tree, accessed 2010. http:
       //quotes.liberty-tree.ca/quotes_about/despotism.

[471] Latin America Herald Tribune. Nicaragua's chief justice denounces pro-Ortega ruling. *Latin America Herald Tribune*, 20 October 2009. http://www.laht.com/article.asp?ArticleId=345896&CategoryId=23558.

[472] Mao Tse Tung. *On Guerilla Warfare*, chapter III: "Strategy, Tactics, and Logistics in Revolutionary War", page 21. University of Illinois Press, 1961. Samuel B. Griffith, translator.

[473] Neal Ungerleider. Tunisian government allegedly hacking Facebook, Gmail accounts of dissidents and journalists. *Fast Company*, 10 January 2011. http://www.fastcompany.com/1715575/tunisian-government-hacking-facebook-gmail-anonymous.

[474] UNHCR. Predators of press freedom: North korea – kim jong il. Technical report, UNHCR, 3 March 2011. http://www.unhcr.org/refworld/country,,,,PRK,,4dc2b52b8,0.html.

[475] Jennifer Valentino-Devries. U.s. firm acknowledges Syria uses its gear to block web. *Wall Street Journal*, 29 October 2011. http://online.wsj.com/article/SB10001424052970203687504577001911398596328.html.

[476] Pedro Vicente. Evidence from a field experiment in west africa. Working paper, University of Oxford, 2007. http://ipl.econ.duke.edu/bread/papers/working/161.pdf.

[477] John Vidal. Shell oil paid Nigerian military to put down protests, court documents show. *The Guardian*, 2 October 2011. http://www.guardian.co.uk/world/2011/oct/03/shell-oil-paid-nigerian-military?INTCMP=SRCH.

[478] Arnaldo Vieira. Africa review. *Africa Review*, 18 January 2012. http://www.africareview.com/News/Angola+ends+silence+on+missing+public+funds/-/979180/1309606/-/mcsyxmz/-/index.html.

[479] Christopher Walker. Muzzling the media: the return of censorship in the commonwealth of independent states. Special report, Freedom House, Washington, DC, 2007. http://www.freedomhouse.org/template.cfm?page=383&report=54.

[480] Thomas W. Walker. *Nicaragua Without Illusions: Regime Transition and Structural Adjustment in the 1990s*, chapter 6, pages 305–311. Scholarly Resources, Inc., Wilmington, Delaware, 1997.

[481] James Walston. Why Silvio Berlusconi is still standing. *Daily Telegraph*, 6 November 2010. http://www.telegraph.co.uk/news/worldnews/europe/italy/8114902/Why-Silvio-Berlusconi-is-still-standing.html.

[482] Human Rights Watch. By any means necessary: Individual and command responsibility for crimes against humanity in syria. Technical report, Human Rights Watch, December 2011. http://www.hrw.org/reports/2011/12/15/all-means-necessary.

[483] Lauren Watts. The Upcoming Nicaraguan Elections. *Council on Hemispheric Affairs*, 10 August 2006. http://www.coha.org/the-upcoming-nicaraguan-elections/.

[484] Tim Weiner. *Legacy of Ashes: the History of the CIA*. Doubleday, New York, 2007.

[485] Martha Wexler. As election nears, Russians express frustrations. *NPR*, 1 March 2012. http://www.npr.org/2012/03/01/147637798/as-election-nears-russians-express-frustrations.

[486] Brian Whitmore. Russia's indispensable man. *Radio Free Europe/Radio Liberty*, 16 August 2011. http://www.rferl.org/content/putin_is_russias_indispensable_man/24298918.html.

[487] Mark Whittington. Hugo Chavez digs up Simon Bolivar's body. *Associated Content*, 17 July 2010. http://www.associatedcontent.com/article/5594798/hugo_chavez_digs_up_simon_bolivars.html.

[488] James A. Wilderotter. CIA matter. US government memorandum, Central Intelligence Agency (CIA), 3 January 1975. Paragraph 11. http://www.gwu.edu/
~nsarchiv/NSAEBB/NSAEBB222/family_jewels_wilderotter.pdf.

[489] Michael Wines. The world; if you're thinking of living in exile. *New York Times*, 7 March 2004. http://www.nytimes.com/2004/03/07/weekinreview/
the-world-if-you-re-thinking-of-living-in-exile.html.

[490] Michael Wines. China establishes new internet regulator. *New York Times*, 5 May 2011. www.nytimes.com/2011/05/05/world/asia/05china.html.

[491] Natalie Wolchover. People aren't smart enough for democracy to flourish, scientists say. *LiveScience*, 28 February 2012. http://news.yahoo.com/people-arent-
smart-enough-democracy-flourish-scientists-185601411.html.

[492] Edward Wong. Human rights advocates vanish as China intensifies crackdown. *New York Times*, 11 March 2011. http://www.nytimes.com/2011/03/12/world/
asia/12china.html.

[493] Graeme Wood. A literal disaster. *Foreign Policy*, June 21 2010. http://www.
foreignpolicy.com/articles/2010/06/21/a_literal_disaster.

[494] Randall Wood and Joshua Berman. *Moon Handbook Nicaragua*, chapter Background. Avalon Travel Publishing, 4th edition, 2010.

[495] Ian Worthington. *Philip II of Macedonia*. Yale University Press, October 2008.

[496] Peter York. Dictators of taste. *Financial Times*, 27 January 2012.
http://www.ft.com/intl/cms/s/2/bef52c36-4291-11e1-97b1-
00144feab49a.html#axzz113mzOV3Z.

[497] Fareed Zakaria. The rise of Illiberal Democracy. *Foreign Affairs*, November/December 1997. http://www.foreignaffairs.com/articles/53577/fareed-
zakaria/the-rise-of-illiberal-democracy.

[498] Claudine Zap. Man's name in sand visible from space. *The Upshot*, 20 July 2011. http://news.yahoo.com/blogs/upshot/man-name-sand-
visible-space-190516989.html.

[499] Ariel Zirulnick. Is Syria's uprising taking a sectarian turn? *Christian Science Monitor*, 19 July 2011. http://www.csmonitor.com/World/
terrorism-security/2011/0719/Is-Syria-s-uprising-taking-
a-sectarian-turn-VIDEO.

[500] Ariel Zirulnick. Syria detains hundreds, hindering protesters' efforts to organize. *Christian Science Monitor*, 7 May 2011.

[501] Ariel Zirulnick. Syria threatens to expel US ambassador. *Christian Science Monitor*, 21 July 2011. http://www.csmonitor.com/World/terrorism-security/
2011/0721/Syria-threatens-to-expel-US-ambassador.

[502] Zombie. The top ten gerrymandered Congressional districts in the United States. *Pajamas Media*, 11 November 2010. http://pajamasmedia.com/zombie/
2010/11/11/the-top-ten-most-gerrymandered-congressional-
districts-in-the-united-states/ Accessed 22 February 2011.

Index

Abacha, Sani, 11, 102, 246, 272
Abdallah II, 158
Abramovich, Roman, 36
Abu Graib, 136
Achebe, Chinua, 101
Adelaide, University of, 71
Afawerki, Isaias, 130, 200
Afawerki, Isais, 4
Agents provocateurs, 157
Ahidjo, Ahmadou, 9
Ahmedinejad, Mahmoud, 16, 108, 134, 146, 230
AIDS, curing of, 30
Airports, 78
al Ahyan, Hamad, 23
al Assad, Asma, 192
al Assad, Bashar, 2, 9, 105, 122, 123, 147, 155
al Assad, Basil, 9
al Assad, Hafez, 2
al Bashir, Omar, 192
al Hashemi, Tareq, 112
al Islam, Said, 4
al Maliki, Nouri, 84
al Sahaf, Saeed, 153
al-Maliki, Nouri, 112
Albania, 229
Aleksandrovna, Lyudmila, 32
Alemán, Arnoldo, 35, 73, 107, 112, 246, 256, 258
Alexander the Great, 69, 262, 274
Aliyev, Heydar, 271
Aliyev, Ilham, 230
Amin, Idi, 5, 15, 17, 18, 27, 30, 86, 111, 162, 227
Angola, 217
Annan, Koffi, 147
Appeasement, 158
Arab Spring, 122
Archives of Terror, 100
Arias, Oscar, 238
Armenian National Congress, 144
Augustus Caesar, 262
Authenticity, 22
Axis of Evil, 108
Azerfon, 230

Aznar, José María, 37

Ba'ath party, 7
Bahrain, 160
Bambipark, 231
Banking, Offshore, 233
Batista, Fulgencio, 63, 265
Belarus, 171
Belisarius, 125
Belli, Gioconda, 117
Ben Ali, Zine Al-Abidine, 10, 63, 143, 215
Berdymukhammedov, Gurbanguly, 15, 17, 23
Berlusconi, Silvio, 25, 28, 29, 31, 67, 167, 171, 232
Biao, Teng, 117
Bin Laden, Osama, 109
Biya, Paul, 9, 35, 63
Blackmail, 230
Blame, 161
Bokassa, Jean-Bedel, 37, 264, 265
Bolívar, Simón, 22, 23
Bolaños, Enrique, 258
Bongo, Ali, 2, 35, 63, 119
Bongo, Omar, 2, 63
Bourguiba, Habib, 10
Bouteflika, Abdelaziz, 143, 210
Bowden, Mark, 24, 29, 85
Bozizé, François, 5
Bread and Circuses, 67
Burkina Faso, 122
Bush, George W., 81, 108, 147

Caesar, Augustus, 33, 69
Caesar, Julius, 22
Campania, 265
Capone, Al, 155
Caravan of Death, 90
Carballo, Father, 96
Carlos, Juan, 37, 270
Carter, Jimmy, 256
Castro, Fidel, 24, 63, 91, 102, 186, 264, 265
Castro, Raúl, 52
Casualties, 160
Ceasar, Augustus, 2, 22
Ceasar, Julius, 2

305

Printed in Great Britain
by Amazon

33335712R00178